NEOREALISM AND NEOLIBERALISM: THE CONTEMPORARY DEBATE

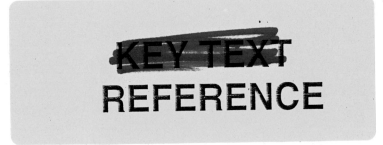

NEW DIRECTIONS IN WORLD POLITICS,
Helen Milner and John G. Ruggie, General Editors

NEW DIRECTIONS IN WORLD POLITICS
Helen Milner and John Gerard Ruggie, General Editors

NEOREALISM AND NEOLIBERALISM:

The Contemporary Debate

David A. Baldwin, *editor*

COLUMBIA UNIVERSITY PRESS
NEW YORK

Columbia University Press
New York   Chichester, West Sussex
Copyright © 1993 Columbia University Press
All rights reserved

Library of Congress Cataloging-in-Publication Data

Neorealism and neoliberalism : the contemporary debate
      David A. Baldwin, editor.
            p.   cm. — (New directions in world politics)
      Includes bibliographical references and index.
      ISBN 978-0-231-08441-3 (pbk.)
         1. International relations—Philosophy.
   2. International relations—Political aspects.
   3. Liberalism.   4. Realism.
   I. Baldwin, David A. (David Allen), 1936–   .   II. Series.
   JX1395.N385   1993
   327—dc20   93–17701
   ⊛   CIP

Casebound editions of Columbia University Press books
are printed on permanent and durable acid-free paper.
Printed in the United States of America

p 10

CONTENTS

INSTITUTE OF WAR
AND PEACE STUDIES

Neorealism and Neoliberalism: The Contemporary Debate is one of a series of publications sponsored by the Institute of War and Peace Studies of Columbia University. More than eighty books have been sponsored by the Institute since its founding in 1951. Other books of related interest sponsored by the Institute are:

Kenneth N. Waltz, *Man, the State, and War.* (1959)

William T. R. Fox, ed., *Theoretical Aspects of International Relations.* (1959)

Samuel P. Huntington, *The Common Defense.* (1961)

W. T. R. Fox, *The American Study of International Relations.* (1968)

Louis Henkin, *How Nations Behave.* (1968)

Leland M. Goodrich, *The United Nations in a Changing World.* (1974)

John G. Ruggie, ed., *The Antinomies of Interdependence.* (1983)

David A. Baldwin, *Economic Statecraft.* (1985)

David A. Baldwin, *Paradoxes of Power.* (1989)

Robert Jervis, *The Illogic of American Nuclear Strategy.* (1984)

Robert Jervis, *The Meaning of the Nuclear Revolution.* (1989)

Jack Snyder, *Myths of Empire.* (1991)

Robert Jervis and Jack Snyder, eds., *Dominoes and Bandwagons.* (1991)

W. Howard Wriggins, ed., *Dynamics of Regional Politics.* (1992)

CONTRIBUTORS

Robert Axelrod is Professor of Political Science at the University of Michigan.

David A. Baldwin is Ira D. Wallach Professor of World Order Studies at Columbia University.

Joseph M. Grieco is Professor of Political Science at Duke University.

Robert O. Keohane is Stanfield Professor of International Peace at Harvard University.

Stephen D. Krasner is Graham H. Stuart Professor of International Relations at Stanford University.

Charles Lipson is Associate Professor of Political Science at the University of Chicago.

Michael Mastanduno is Associate Professor of Government at Dartmouth College.

Helen Milner is Associate Professor of Political Science at Columbia University.

Robert Powell is Associate Professor of Political Science at the University of California, Berkeley.

Duncan Snidal is Associate Professor of Political Science at the University of Chicago.

Arthur Stein is Professor of Political Science at the University of California, Los Angeles.

ACKNOWLEDGMENTS

This volume would never have appeared without the encouragement and support of Helen Milner, John Ruggie, and Kate Wittenberg. The authors owe them an unusual amount of thanks. Joseph DePiro, Administrative Assistant of the Institute of War and Peace Studies, deserves credit for organizing efforts to create a unified bibliography, standardizing references, and proofreading the manuscript. We are also grateful to Miriam Fendius for preparing the index and checking citations. Previously published articles have been slightly edited to eliminate confusing references to material not included here. In addition, the articles by Stephen Krasner and Michael Mastanduno were shortened by elimination of case studies.

The editor and publisher are grateful for permission to reprint the following previously published materials:

Arthur Stein, "Coordination and Collaboration: Regimes in an Anarchic World," *International Organization* 36 (Spring 1982): 294–324, by permission of MIT Press.

Charles Lipson, "International Cooperation in Security and Economic Affairs," *World Politics* 37 (October 1984): 1–23, by permission of Johns Hopkins University Press.

Robert Axelrod and Robert Keohane, "Achieving Cooperation Under Anarchy: Strategies and Institutions," *World Politics* 38 (October 1985): 226–54, by permission of Johns Hopkins University Press.

Joseph M. Grieco, "Anarchy and the Limits of Cooperation: A Realist Critique of the Newest Liberal Institutionalism," *International Organization* 42 (August 1988): 485–507, by permission of MIT Press.

Helen Milner, "The Assumption of Anarchy in International Relations Theory: A Critique," *Review of International Studies* 17 (January 1991): 67–85, by permission of Cambridge University Press.

Duncan Snidal, "Relative Gains and the Pattern of International Cooperation," *American Political Science Review* 85 (September 1991):

701–26, by permission of the American Political Science Association.

Robert Powell, "Absolute and Relative Gains in International Relations Theory," *American Political Science Review* 85 (December 1991): 1303–20, by permission of the American Political Science Association.

Stephen D. Krasner, "Global Communications and National Power: Life on the Pareto Frontier," *World Politics* 43 (April 1991): 336–66, by permission of Johns Hopkins University Press.

Michael Mastanduno, "Do Relative Gains Matter? America's Response to Japanese Industrial Policy," *International Security* 16 (Summer 1991): 73–113, by permission of MIT Press.

David A. Baldwin
New York City
February 1993

I INTRODUCTION

1

NEOLIBERALISM, NEOREALISM, AND WORLD POLITICS

David A. Baldwin

In 1986 Robert O. Keohane edited a volume entitled *Neorealism and Its Critics*, which focused on the reformulation of traditional realist thinking about international politics by Kenneth Waltz (1979) and reactions from a variety of scholars. Waltz had recast the tenets of classical realism in order to delineate more clearly the effects of the structure of the international system on the behavior of nation-states. In addition, Waltz viewed his work as different from that of earlier realists in its treatment of power and of states as units of the system (Waltz 1979; 1990). The critics, according to Keohane (1986a:24), sought to move beyond the nation-state by "devising new international institutions or regimes," by reinterpreting the principles of sovereignty, or by challenging the "validity of the 'state as actor' model on which neorealism relies." Whereas some critics called for more attention to economic and environmental interdependence as well as changes in governmental functions, information, and international regimes, others attacked the epistemology on which Waltz based his argument.

In a sense, this volume picks up where *Neorealism and Its Critics* ended. Unlike that volume, however, the contributors to this one share many fundamental assumptions about the nature and purpose of social scientific inquiry. This allows them to engage one another's arguments directly and results in a more focused and productive debate.

In recent years the most powerful challenge to neorealism, some-times labeled *structural realism*, has been mounted by neoliberal insti-tutionalists. The term distinguishes these scholars from earlier vari-eties of liberalism, such as commercial liberalism, republican liberal-ism, and sociological liberalism (Nye 1988; Grieco 1988a:488n; Keohane 1990a). *Commercial liberalism* refers to theories linking free trade and peace; *republican liberalism* refers to theories linking democracy with peace; and *sociological liberalism* refers to theories linking transnational interactions with international integration. The immediate intellec-tual precursors of liberal institutionalism are theories of international regimes (Krasner 1983a).

NEOLIBERALISM AND NEOREALISM: TERMS OF THE CONTEMPORARY DEBATE

Six focal points, described below, characterize the current de-bate between neoliberalism and neorealism.

The Nature and Consequences of Anarchy

Although no one denies that the international system is anarch-ical in some sense, there is disagreement as to what this means and why it matters. Arthur Stein (1982a:324) distinguishes between the "independent decision making" that characterizes anarchy and the "joint decision making" in international regimes and then suggests that it is the self interests of autonomous states in a state of anarchy that leads them to create international regimes. Charles Lipson (1984:22) notes that the idea of anarchy is the "Rosetta stone of international relations" but suggests that its importance has been exaggerated by the neorealists at the expense of recognizing the importance of inter-national interdependence. Robert Axelrod and Robert O. Keohane (1985) emphasize the importance of anarchy defined as the absence of government but argue that this constant feature of world politics permits a variety of patterns of interaction among states. Joseph M. Grieco (1988a:497–98) contends that neoliberals and neorealists fun-damentally diverge with respect to the nature and consequences of anarchy. He asserts that the neoliberal institutionalists underestimate the importance of worries about survival as motivations for state behavior, which he sees as a necessary consequence of anarchy.

Helen Milner (1991:70, 81–82) identifies the "discovery of orderly features of world politics amidst its seeming chaos" as "perhaps the central achievement of neorealists," but she agrees with Lipson that the idea of anarchy has been overemphasized while interdependence has been neglected. Duncan Snidal (1991b) views Prisoner's Dilemma (PD) situations as examples of the realist conception of anarchy, while Grieco (1988a) associates PD with neoliberalism. In general, neorealists see anarchy as placing more severe constraints on state behavior than do neoliberals.

International Cooperation

Although both sides agree that international cooperation is possible, they differ as to the ease and likelihood of its occurrence. According to Grieco (this volume), neorealists view international cooperation as "harder to achieve, more difficult to maintain, and more dependent on state power" than do the neoliberals. None of the neoliberals represented in this book disagrees with this assessment. Both Keohane and Grieco agree that the future of the European Community will be an important test of their theories. If the trend toward European integration weakens or suffers reversals, the neorealists will claim vindication. If progress toward integration continues, the neoliberals will presumably view this as support for their views.

Relative Versus Absolute Gains

Although it would be misleading to characterize one side as concerned only with relative gains and the other as concerned only with absolute gains, the neoliberals have stressed the absolute gains from international cooperation, while the neorealists have emphasized relative gains. The basic reference point for many of the authors in this volume is the following passage by a leading neorealist:

> When faced with the possibility of cooperating for mutual gain, states that feel insecure must ask how the gain will be divided. They are compelled to ask not "Will both of us gain?" but "Who will gain more?" If an expected gain is to be divided, say, in the ratio of two to one, one state may use its disproportionate gain to implement a policy intended to damage or destroy the other. Even the prospect of large

absolute gains for both parties does not elicit their cooperation so long as each fears how the other will use its increased capabilities (Waltz 1979:105).

Stein (1982a:318) depicts the liberal view of self interest as one in which actors with common interests try to maximize their absolute gains. Actors trying to maximize relative gains, he asserts, have no common interests. Lipson (1984:15–18) suggests that relative gains considerations are likely to be more important in security matters than in economic affairs. Grieco (1988a:487) contends that neoliberal institutionalism has been preoccupied with actual or potential absolute gains from international cooperation and has overlooked the importance of relative gains. He suggests that *"the fundamental goal of states in any relationship is to prevent others from achieving advances in their relative capabilities"* (Grieco 1988a:498; italics in original). Snidal (1991b) disputes the neorealist contention that concerns about relative gains inhibit cooperation except in the special case of bipolar relationships between states preoccupied with relative gains. He also suggests that the distinction between relative and absolute gains is not so clear-cut as it might seem. The relative gains problem can be stated in terms of trade-offs between long- and short-term absolute gains. Powell (1991b) uses deductive models to argue that concerns about relative gains will inhibit cooperation when the utility of military force is high but not when the utility of force is low.[1] Mastanduno (1991) uses empirical case studies to address the questions of whether and how relative gains matter. His conclusions provide some support for both sides of the debate. While he finds concerns about relative gains present in the policy-making process in all of his three cases, such concerns were not reflected in the policy outcomes for all the cases. In his essay for this volume Keohane acknowledges that neoliberal institutionalists have underestimated the importance of relative gains in world politics under certain conditions. The important thing, according to Keohane, is to specify those conditions. He notes that this may be difficult since the behavior of states pursuing relative gains may be very similar to the behavior of states pursuing absolute gains.

Priority of State Goals

Neoliberals and neorealists agree that both national security and economic welfare are important, but they differ in relative emphasis on these goals. Lipson (1984) argues that international cooperation is more likely in economic issue areas than in those concerning military security. Since neorealists tend to study security issues and neoliberals tend to study political economy, their differing estimates of the ease of cooperation may be related to the issues they study. Grieco (1988a) contends that anarchy requires states to be preoccupied with relative power, security, and survival. Powell (1991b) constructs a model intended to bridge the gap between neoliberal emphasis on economic welfare and neorealist emphasis of security. In his model, states are assumed to be trying to maximize their economic welfare in a world where military force is a possibility. For the most part, neorealists or neoliberals treat state goals by assumption. As Keohane (this volume) points out, neither approach is good at predicting interests.

Intentions Versus Capabilities

The classical realist Hans J. Morgenthau depicted concern about the motives of statesmen as a fallacious way to understand foreign policy. Instead he advocated assuming that statesmen "think and act in terms of interest defined as power" (1967:5–6), which, he believed, would enable analysts to understand the actions and thoughts of statesmen better than they themselves do. Although contemporary neorealists are unlikely to take such an extreme position, they are likely to emphasize capabilities more than intentions. Grieco (1988a:498, 500) points out that uncertainties about the future intentions and interests of other states lead statesmen to pay close attention to capabilities, "the ultimate basis for their security and independence." In a similar vein, Krasner (1991) criticizes the neoliberals for overemphasizing intentions, interests, and information and underemphasizing the distribution of capabilities. Keohane (this volume) argues that the sensitivity of states to the relative gains of other states is significantly influenced by perceptions of the intentions of such states. Thus states worry more about relative gains of enemies than of allies. Stein (1982a) explains international regimes in terms of the pattern of preferences of member states. In Stein's analysis, capabilities count only insofar as they affect the preferences and intentions of states. Differing views of the relative importance of capabilities and intentions thus provide another focal point of the debate.

Institutions and Regimes

Both neorealists and neoliberals recognize the plethora of international regimes and institutions that have emerged since 1945. They differ, however, with respect to the significance of such arrangements. "Much of the contemporary debate," according to Keohane (this volume), "centers on the validity of the institutionalist claim that international regimes, and institutions more broadly, have become significant in world politics." The neorealists agree that this is an important point of contention. They believe that neoliberals exaggerate the extent to which institutions are able to "mitigate anarchy's constraining effects on inter-state cooperation" (Grieco 1988a:485).

These six focal points are not the only points of contention in the debate, but they should help orient the reader to the main arguments. Not every contributor to this volume addresses all six points, and the careful reader will notice that individual scholars contributing to the debate may introduce qualifications that make the six focal points seem overly simplified. And rightfully so. Any attempt to characterize the carefully wrought arguments of eleven scholars inevitably oversimplifies.

Important as it is to clarify the terms of the debate, it is also important to clarify what the debate is *not* about. Although the following four issues have figured prominently in earlier debates between realism and its critics, none is central to the current debate between neorealism and neoliberal institutionalism. First, the current debate does not revolve around techniques of statecraft. In 1977 Keohane and Nye listed the assumption that military force is a "usable and effective instrument of policy" (pp. 23–29) as one of the fundamental tenets of realism, one that they proceeded to call into question. Yet in 1988, Grieco's description of the five central propositions of realism mentions only a concern for power and security and says nothing about the utility of military force. Despite fleeting references to this issue by some of the authors (e.g., Grieco 1988a:491n; Milner 1991:76, 78; Krasner 1991:342), only Robert Powell (1991b) devotes much attention to the question of the utility of military techniques of statecraft. It is not clear why this issue receives so little attention since it does not seem to have been resolved. One should not be surprised if it resurfaces as the debate evolves.

Second, earlier critics of realism, especially in the 1930s, 1940s, and 1950s, often cast the debate as one between altruistic moralists and egoistic power calculators. In the current debate, however, both sides argue from assumptions that states behave like egoistic value maximizers. Moral considerations are hardly mentioned. Third, the question of whether to treat states as the essential actors in international politics has been pushed into the background. Although neorealists and neoliberals disagree on the relative importance of nonstate actors, both treat states as the primary actors. And fourth, this is not a debate between conflict theorists and cooperation theorists. The twin ideas that conflict and cooperation are intrinsic elements of international politics and that both can be studied at the same time are accepted by both sides. The books by neorealist Joseph M. Grieco (1990) and neoliberal Robert O. Keohane (1984) are contributions to theories of conflict *and* cooperation. Although neorealists are more likely to emphasize conflict and neoliberals are more likely to emphasize cooperation, both sides have moved beyond the simple dichotomy between cooperation and conflict that characterized earlier discussions.[2]

The quality of scholarly debate in this volume is extraordinarily high. That is to say, the authors genuinely try to understand and address one another's arguments. The overall tone of the essays in this volume signals a desire to advance knowledge rather than to score debating points in defense of entrenched positions.

There is, however, one unsatisfactory aspect of the debate. This might be called the terminological dimension. Loaded terms and semantic sleight of hand are anathema to scholarly debate. In this volume each school of thought carries an unfortunate label. Research programs, as Stephen Krasner (1991) points out, have connotations as well as denotations. And the connotation of "realism" (or "neorealism") is one of looking at the world as it really is. This was not only the connotation but the denotation as well for two of the intellectual forefathers of neorealism. For E. H. Carr, realism focused on "what was and what is" in contrast to utopianism, which focused on what could and should be (Carr 1946:11). For Hans J. Morgenthau, realism earned its name by concentrating on "human nature as it actually is" and on "historic processes as they actually take place" (Morgenthau 1967:4). Inis L. Claude's characterization of the usage of the phrase "balance of power" by an earlier generation of realists reminds us that scholarly debate can be impaired by loaded terminology:

> [There is a] widespread tendency to make balance of power a symbol of realism, and hence of responsibility, for the scholar or statesman. In this usage, it has no substantive meaning as a concept. It is a test of intellectual virility, of he-manliness in the field of international relations. The man who "accepts" the balance of power, who dots his writing with approving references to it, thereby asserts his claim to being a hard-headed realist, who can look at the grim reality of power without flinching. The man who rejects the balance of power convicts himself of softness, of cowardly incapacity to look power in the eye and acknowledge its role in the affairs of states. (Claude 1962:39).

It is unfortunate that the current debate still uses the misleading terms *realism* and *neorealism*. The debate in this volume is not between those who study the world as it is and those who study the world as it should be; it is between two groups of scholars with reasonable disagreements as to how to describe and interpret the real world.

The term *liberalism* is objectionable less because of value loading than because it is likely to confuse and mislead. Neither realism nor liberalism has traditionally been considered the opposite of the other. The usual opposite of liberalism is conservatism. The term liberalism has figured more prominently in discussions of domestic politics than in discussions of international politics. Except for the relatively recent debate with respect to the propensity of liberal democracies to make war, the term liberalism has been largely confined to the discussion of economic aspects of international relations.[3]

Despite such objections, the terms *neorealism* (or *structural realism*) and *neoliberalism* (or *neoliberal institutionalism*) are so deeply embedded in the literature that little can be done. Perhaps as the debate progresses, we can develop more satisfactory labels for various schools of thought. Keohane (this volume) is also uncomfortable with the labels. He suggests that liberal institutionalism "borrows as much from realism as from liberalism."

This section has sketched the main outlines of the debate. The remainder of this essay will discuss the historical roots of the contemporary debate and the related topics of anarchy, social order, and power. After that, some possible directions for future research will be reviewed.

HISTORICAL ROOTS OF THE DEBATE

The previous section suggested that the current debate between neorealism and neoliberalism has moved beyond a mere rehashing of old arguments between realists and their critics. This does not mean, however, that there are no historical antecedents for various strains of the current debate.

There have been many thinkers over the centuries who have emphasized international anarchy, reliance on self help, the utility of military force, and the importance of balance-of-power calculations. Thucydides, Machiavelli, and Thomas Hobbes are frequently cited as intellectual ancestors of realism.

Likewise, various thinkers have emphasized international economic interdependence, international law and institutions, international communication, and societal norms. The ancient Stoics' conception of themselves as citizens of the world could be viewed as a challenge to a state-centric view of world politics. Early Christian philosophers believed that "God had endowed different regions with limited but varied products in order to give mankind an incentive to trade, so that through a world economy they would become united in a world society, and as children of one God they would learn to love each other" (Viner 1937:100).

The mercantilists, who dominated international thought in the seventeenth and eighteenth centuries, viewed both wealth and power in zero-sum terms. That is, one country's gain was another's loss. In their emphasis on preparation for war and relative gains, the mercantilists can be viewed as foreshadowing some of the concerns of later realists.[4]

Perhaps the closest counterpart of the modern debate between realism and neoliberalism is found in the works of the *philosophes* at the end of the eighteenth century. They attacked almost all the ideas embraced by realists. They espoused the idea of a world civilization and world citizenship, promoted the idea of the primacy of domestic affairs over foreign affairs, denounced military alliances, and disputed the idea that the balance of power could ensure peace. They emphasized the mutual interests of states and advocated free trade, which they argued would help prevent war (Russell 1936; Gilbert 1951, 1961; Hinsley 1963).

In the twentieth century Woodrow Wilson joined the idea that free trade promotes peace with the idea of a universal international organization to promote the same goal. According to Felix Gilbert, "intellectually, a straight line leads from the enlightenment to Wilson's concept. His ideas about a 'new diplomacy' were definitely dependent on and influenced by the ideas which the eighteenth century had developed on this subject" (Gilbert 1951:37).

During the period between the two world wars, international relations began to emerge as an academic field, especially in the United States. William T. R. Fox describes this period as characterized by the assumption of an underlying harmony of international interests coupled with a belief that improved understanding and international institutions could rid the world of the scourge of war (Fox 1949). He points to the "failing of events in the 1930s to accord with the expectations generated by the academic study of international relations in the 1920s" (Fox 1949:67). The invasion of Manchuria, the signing of the Molotov-Ribbentrop agreement, and the failure of League of Nations sanctions against Italy disillusioned international relations scholars and planted the seeds from which modern realism grew.

After World War II realism emerged as the dominant paradigm among international relations scholars. Although a debate between realism and idealism occurred in the 1945–55 period, among political scientists "authentic self-proclaimed idealists were hard to find" (Fox 1989:239; *see also* Wolfers 1949; Herz 1950; Morgenthau 1952; Wright 1952; Cook and Moos 1953; and Schilling 1956). Despite the dominance of realism, David Mitrany's treatise on functionalism as an approach to peace appeared in the 1940s (Mitrany 1943; Claude 1956), and Ernst Haas's *The Uniting of Europe* appeared in 1958. Haas's neofunctionalism spawned numerous studies of regional integration in the 1960s.

During the 1970s and 1980s the debate between neorealism and liberal institutionalism began to take more definite shape. Three especially important works on the liberal side were the special issue of *International Organization* on "Transnational Relations and World Politics" in 1971 (Keohane and Nye 1972); Keohane and Nye's *Power and Interdependence* in 1977; and the special issue of *International Organization* on "International Regimes" in 1982 (Krasner 1983a). The first raised questions about the state-centric focus of realism and discussed such nonstate actors as the Roman Catholic Church, the Ford Foundation, and multinational business enterprises. In the second, Keohane and Nye, in their introduction and conclusion to the published book, explicitly challenged realism with respect to the state-as-actor assumption, the relative importance of military security on foreign policy agendas, the role of military force in international politics, and the fungibility of power resources among issue areas. The third, edited by Stephen D. Krasner, set forth both realist and liberal (labeled Grotian) views on international cooperation and institutions.

Three especially important works of neorealists during the 1970s and 1980s included Kenneth Waltz's "Theory of International Relations" in 1975, his *Theory of International Politics* in 1979, and Joseph Grieco's "Anarchy and the Limits of Cooperation: A Realist Critique of the Newest Liberal Institutionalism" in 1988. The first was a preliminary version of the second, which has become the touchstone for neorealists, much as Morgenthau's text (1948) served as a touchstone for realists in the 1950s. The third explicitly challenged neoliberal institutionalism from a neorealist perspective and is included in this volume.

Although the realist vision has dominated thinking about world politics much of the time since Thucydides wrote his treatise on the Peloponnesian War, alternative visions have always existed. The contemporary debate between neorealism and neoliberalism is different from, yet rooted in, a debate that has been going on for centuries.

In order to lay the intellectual groundwork for the debate, the next three sections address conceptual and theoretical problems raised by the contributors. Two fundamental concepts used by both neoliberals and neorealists are anarchy and power. The next two sections are intended to alert the reader to some of the difficulties associated with these concepts.

ANARCHY AND SOCIAL ORDER

Although the concept of anarchy has always been important to realist theories of international politics, it has been less prominent in liberal theories. In this volume, however, the assumption of anarchy plays an important role for most of the neoliberal authors as well. The reader, however, should not be lulled into thinking that neorealists and neoliberals necessarily agree on the meaning of anarchy or its consequences.

The term *anarchy* is one of the most slippery terms in political discourse. Often it is used to denote chaos and disorder—a Hobbesian war of all against all. Neorealists and neoliberals, however, agree that world politics exhibits some order—even though they may disagree on the nature, extent, and causes of that order. Thus, many theorists define anarchy in terms of the absence of government. This definition, however, begs the question of what is meant by "government." Many of the activities carried on by governments have counterparts at the international level. Providing welfare support, management of economic affairs, interpreting laws, regulating commerce, regulating mail delivery, regulating air travel, promoting public health, and ensuring public safety are all governmental activities with counterparts at the international level. This suggests that conceptions of anarchy as the absence of government are based on some distinctively governmental characteristic that is missing at the international level. As Helen Milner's contribution to this volume demonstrates, agreement is lacking as to precisely which governmental characteristic defines anarchy.

Readers should carefully scrutinize not only the definitions of anarchy used by various authors but also the consequences they attribute to it. In particular, readers should ask whether such consequences can logically be deduced from an assumption of anarchy or whether they should be treated as empirical hypotheses to be tested. There is confusion among both neoliberals and neorealists on such matters (Milner 1992).

Social scientists try to develop generalizations about social phenomena. When asked to explain a social phenomenon, social scientists are supposed to ask: "Of what is this an instance?" Perhaps the debate about the nature and consequences of international anarchy would benefit from asking this question. The problem of explaining international order can be thought of as a subtype of the general problem of explaining social order. Social science theories developed outside the field of international relations may provide helpful insights. Kenneth Boulding, for example, suggests that the same three social mechanisms that produce order in families are also responsible for order at the level of the nation-state and the international political system (Boulding 1963; 1978; 1989). He identifies them as exchange relations, threat systems, and image integration. The first emphasizes rewards, the second punishments, and the third harmonization of perceptions and interests. Boulding postulates that all social systems rely on some combination of these processes to achieve and maintain social order.

It is easy to see examples of each process at the international level. Exchange processes are closely associated with trade, economic interdependence, and other kinds of problems studied by neoliberals. Threat systems relate to deterrence and similar phenomena of particular interest to neorealists. Image integration processes are the domain of those who study preference formation, learning, and misperception. Boulding's theory is but one example of the kind of general social science model that might be helpful in illuminating the problem of social order in world politics. It illustrates how a single model can incorporate the neoliberal emphasis on economic interdependence, the neorealist emphasis on military deterrence, and the psychologists' emphasis on preference formation.

CAPABILITIES AND COOPERATION

"Although power is a key concept in realist theory," Waltz observes, "its proper definition remains a matter of controversy" (Waltz 1986:333). Another leading neorealist, Robert Gilpin, describes the "concept of power as one of the most troublesome in the field of international relations" (1981:13) and suggests that the "number and variety of definitions should be an embarrassment to political scientists" (1975:24). Although power plays a less crucial role in neoliberal theory, it has also proved to be a troublesome concept for them (Baldwin 1989). In preparing the reader for the essays that follow, therefore, it might be helpful to identify some of the problems of power analysis (or capability analysis). These include the specification of scope and domain, the zero-sum problem, and the fungibility question.[5]

Scope and Domain[6]

When neorealists and neoliberals debate the significance of relative gains in international politics, they sometimes neglect to specify precisely what kinds of gains they have in mind. Usually the answer is gains in capabilities. This answer, however, begs yet another question, namely: "Capabilities to get whom to do what?"

The most common conception of power in social science treats power relations as a type of causal relationship in which the power wielder affects the behavior, attitudes, beliefs, or propensity to act of another actor. As Nagel points out, "Anyone who employs a causal concept of power *must* specify domain and scope" (1975:14). This is easier to see if one restates the phrase "country A has power" as "country A causes." The latter phrase prompts one to ask what effects country A causes with respect to whom. Indeed, the phrase makes little sense without answers to such questions. It should be noted that the requirement that scope and domain be specified or clearly implied says nothing about the level of specificity. Thus the requirement is satisfied by either of the following two statements: "The United States has the power to get Iraq to destroy its nuclear weapons." "The United States has the power to get lots of nations to do lots of things." Although the phrase "lots of things" may be rather vague, it does satisfy the minimum requirements for a meaningful statement of a causal power relationship.

Waltz rejects the causal notion of power and proposes "the old and simple notion that an agent is powerful to the extent that he affects others more than they affect him" (Waltz 1979:192). Waltz's proposed alternative, however, does not eliminate the need to specify scope and domain. In terms of scope, one is entitled to ask which effects matter. In terms of domain, one is entitled to ask which "others" can be affected.[7] Some neorealist and neoliberal scholars have sought to avoid the need to specify scope and domain by using the term *capabilities* (or *power resources*) in their theories. This merely shifts the analytical focus from actual causes to potential causes. Any statement about a state's capabilities is based on a prediction about which other actors can be affected in which ways. The observation that a state has a great deal of capability to win a war against many other countries is meaningful. The observation that a state has a great deal of capability begs two vital questions—"capability to get whom to do what?" Without some sort of answers to these two questions, the attribution of capability makes little sense.

Waltz (1979:131) suggests that the capabilities of states can be ranked according to "how they score on *all* of the following items: size of population and territory, resource endowment, economic capability, military strength, political stability, and competence." It is not clear, however, what criteria are to be used for the scoring. Perhaps his reference to the need for states to use their capabilities to "serve their interests" (1979:131) provides a clue as to the appropriate criteria, but this is a little vague.

Lists of the determinants of national capabilities, such as that by Waltz, resemble Morgenthau's famous "elements of national power" (1967:106–44). A careful reading of Morgenthau, however, provides clues as to the scope and domain that underlie his elements of national power. Why is the geography of Italy important? "For, under all conditions of warfare of which we know, this geographical situation has made it extremely difficult to invade Central Europe from Italy" (107). Why is self-sufficiency in food production important? Because "countries enjoying self-sufficiency, such as the United States and Russia, need not divert their national energies and foreign policies from their primary objectives in order to make sure that populations will not starve in war" (109). Why are raw materials important? Because "what holds true of food is of course also true of those natural resources which are important for industrial production and, more particularly, for the waging of war" (110). Why is industrial capacity an important element of national power? Because "the technology of modern warfare and communications has made the overall development of heavy industries an indispensable element of national power. Since victory in modern war depends upon the number and quality of highways, railroads, trucks, ships, airplanes, tanks, and equipment and weapons of all kinds, from mosquito nets and automatic rifles to oxygen masks and guided missiles, the competition among nations for power transforms itself largely into the production of bigger, better, and more implements of war" (113). And in discussing military preparedness as an element of national power, Morgenthau removes all doubt about the policy-contingency assumptions underlying his analysis: "What gives the factors of geography, natural resources, and industrial capacity their actual importance for the power of a nation is military preparedness" (114). Regardless of Morgenthau's denials elsewhere of a military notion of power, his analysis of the elements of national power leaves little doubt as to what he has in mind.

Scholars who incorporate the concept of capability in their theories need to come to terms with the works of Harold and Margaret Sprout (1945; 1965; 1971). As realists during the 1930s and 1940s, the Sprouts subscribed to the idea that national power could be reduced to basic elements or foundations. Their *Foundations of National Power* (1945) foreshadowed Morgenthau's treatment of the elements of national power. During the 1950s and 1960s, however, they came to believe that the capabilities of nation-states could not be estimated outside the context of a set of assumptions about who was trying (or might try) to get whom to do what. As they put it:

> Without some set of given undertakings (strategies, policies), actual or postulated, with reference to some frame of operational contingencies, actual or postulated, there can be no estimation of political capabilities. . . . Failure to keep discussions of capabilities . . . within some such policy-contingency frame of reference is all too common. Such failure tends to reduce statements about the "elements" or "foundations" of a given state's power and influence to various irrelevancies. The data of physical geography, or of demography, or of economic production, or of any other field have no intrinsic political relevance whatever. Such data acquire political relevance and significance only when related to some frame of assumptions as to what is to be undertaken or attempted in what operational contingencies (Sprout and Sprout 1965:215–16).[8]

The Zero-Sum Problem

The idea that power is zero-sum, in the sense that more for one actor means less for another, is common in the literature of international relations. Discussions of relative capability gains are especially prone to employment of this notion. In its extreme form (i.e., insistence that more power for one actor *always* means less for another), it is easy to refute. Logically, a single actual or hypothetical example should do the job. I have discussed three examples elsewhere and will only briefly mention them here:

1. Before Friday comes to live on Robinson Crusoe's island, neither has any power. After Friday's arrival, Crusoe may acquire power with respect to Friday; but this power gain cannot be offset by a loss in power by Friday, since Friday had no power to begin with.

2. If Crusoe handcuffs himself to Friday, he may increase his ability to affect Friday's movements; but he simultaneously increases Friday's ability to affect his (Crusoe's) movements.

3. The United States' military involvement in Vietnam increased not only American ability to affect Vietnamese policy but also Vietnamese ability to affect American policy. (Baldwin 1971; 1989).

Those who espouse the view that power is necessarily zero-sum are unlikely to be persuaded by such examples. They seem to be using a unidimensional conception of power along the following lines: If battleships (or whatever) are the measure of power, it is impossible for two countries to improve their power position vis-à-vis one another at the same time. The question, of course, is whether this sort of monolithic measure of power is useful. A multidimensional concept of power, which allows for variations in scope, weight, and/or domain, makes such monolithic measures problematic. Once scope and domain are introduced, it is both possible and plausible to describe an increase in battleships by both actors as an increase in the ability of each to destroy (scope) the other (domain).

It is, of course, true that politics is sometimes a zero-sum game. In presidential elections, for example, a win for Republicans is a defeat for Democrats. In international politics, however, such situations are rare. Thomas Schelling pointed out long ago that such a situation "would arise in a war of complete extermination, [but] otherwise not even in war" (Schelling 1960:4–5). "Winning" in a conflict, he observed, means gaining relative to one's own value system, not relative to one's adversary. Except for the rare situation of pure conflict, Schelling's approach enables one to envision conflict situations in which everyone may be a winner or a loser. It is worth noting that Schelling's view of winning relative to one's own value system captures the essence of Clausewitz's conception of victory in war. The important thing, according to Clausewitz, is to accomplish one's political goals, not necessarily to destroy the enemy (Clausewitz

1976). Several essays in this volume by authors on both sides of the debate seem to employ a zero-sum conception of power. The reader will have to decide whether such usage is appropriate in the context of a particular essay.

Fungibility

"Fungibility" refers to the ease with which capabilities in one issue-area can be used in other issue-areas. Although the assumption that power resources are highly fungible is often associated with neorealism, it is also found in some neoliberal works. Robert Axelrod's (1984) discussion of the strategy of TIT-for-TAT, for example, implies an underlying standard in terms of which a TIT is equivalent to a TAT (Baldwin 1990:112–15). In reading the contributors to this volume, the reader should ask what level of power fungibility the author is assuming and what the implications are for the essay in which it is found.

The question of what assumption about the fungibility of power resources (capabilities) is most useful for international theorizing has more than one good answer. It is instructive to note that one of the most successful efforts based on an assumption of high fungibility is the Correlates of War Project, which has a narrow focus in terms of scope (i.e., winning wars), and a broad focus in terms of time (i.e., several centuries).

This is not surprising. If one studies only one issue-area, then variations in the utility of power resources from one issue-area to another do not matter. And the longer the time frame of one's analysis, the more useful a high-fungibility assumption is likely to be. In politics, as in economics, more things are fungible in the long run than in the short.

Debates about whether the fungibility of power resources is high or low often seem rootless in the sense that the criteria for judgment are unspecified. Many would agree that Japan has much more influence on economic issues than on military ones, that "the power to knock down a person does not give us the power to teach that person to play the piano," and that the power "to bomb and burn a village cannot be completely or easily transformed into the power to win the sympathies of the inhabitants" (Deutsch 1988:30); but such examples do not *prove* that power resources *in general* are low in fungibility.

When addressing the question of whether to judge political power resources high or low in fungibility, it is useful to ask, "Compared to what?" The answer sometimes given is money.

But why use money as a standard of comparison? In the first place, it is the best example we have of fungible resources actually operating in social processes. In the second place, there is a large scholarly literature describing and analyzing what money is and how it works. In the third place, on the principle that it is useful to start from what we know and move to what we understand less well, it may be useful to compare money's role in economic exchange with the role of power resources in political exchange. In the fourth place, it is not clear what other standard is available. Although one might use the other end of the liquidity continuum as a standard of comparison (i.e., a situation in which each resource has only one use), most people would probably find it more useful to compare political power resources with the real-world phenomenon of money than with a hypothetical case that has never been found in the real world. And fifth, it has often been suggested that power is like money (Parsons 1963; Baldwin 1971; 1989; Deutsch 1988). It is important to understand both the advantages and disadvantages of such an analogy (Baldwin 1971).

Discussions of concerns about relative gains as motivators of state behavior often assume that states calculate and compare the value of capability gains more or less the way consumers calculate and compare the value of goods in a market. Although states do attempt such calculations, they face difficulties that consumers do not. In a monetized market, money serves not only as a medium of exchange but also as a standardized measure of economic value. In politics, however, there is no generally recognized measuring rod of political value to facilitate comparisons. It is sometimes suggested that money facilitates theorizing about economic behavior and that the absence of a political counterpart to money impedes theorizing about politics. Waltz (1990) has disputed this view, dismissing it as a mere measurement problem. He concedes that political capability "cannot be expressed in units, such as dollars, that would have clear meaning and be applicable to different instruments and ends" (1990:27–28); but he cites the absence of numbers in Adam Smith's theory in support of his contention that the lack of a political counterpart to money has nothing to do with theory construction.

From the standpoint of theory construction, however, the clarity of key concepts is essential. Although it is true that numbers do not play an important part in Adam Smith's analysis, he devotes considerable attention to clarification of the concept of money as both a measure of value and as a medium of exchange. When Adam Smith talks about the combined wealth of a country, it is clear what this means. When Waltz refers to the "combined capabilities" of a country, however, there is no comparably clear meaning. What makes the absence of a political counterpart to money an impediment to theory construction is not so much the difficulty of measurement; rather it is the clarity of the concept of political value. We have a much better idea of what it means to attribute economic value to something than we have of what it means to attribute political value to something.[9]

FUTURE DIRECTIONS

Anatol Rapoport (1960) once distinguished among "fights" (in which opponents try to harm one another), "games" (in which opponents try to outwit one another), and "debates" (in which opponents try to convince each other). The essays in this volume clearly deserve to be classified as debates. Although neither side is likely to convince the other completely, each can learn from the other and thereby advance our understanding of international politics. Relative gains may be important in politics, but in scholarship absolute gains are what matter.

The debate between neorealism and neoliberalism continues to evolve. Each of the essays in this volume constitutes an important contribution to this debate. There are, however, several dimensions of the debate that need further elaboration and research.

The most important research need is better understanding of the conditions that promote or inhibit international cooperation. The debate between neorealism and neoliberalism has generated at least six hypotheses worthy of more research and testing.[10] The first concerns the strategy of reciprocity. Both the theoretical and practical conditions under which such strategies promote cooperation deserve attention. The second hypothesis suggests that the number of actors affects the likelihood of cooperation. Although cooperation might seem easier with fewer actors, Milner (1992) has recently suggested that the relationship may be more complicated than that. The third hypothesis relates actor's expectations about future interaction with one another in their willingness to cooperate. Although this topic has been studied deductively, relatively little empirical work has focused on it. Fourth, international regimes have been hypothesized as promotive of cooperation. The question of how much difference regimes make, however, remains a matter of dispute. In 1992 the journal *International Organization* devoted a special issue to a fifth hypothesis focusing on "epistemic communities" in fostering cooperation. Although the contributors to that volume test the hypothesis in several issue-areas, many opportunities for further research remain. The sixth hypothesis concerns the extent to which international cooperation is affected by the distribution of power among actors. Although hegemonic stability theory constitutes one variation of this hypothesis, others deserve to be explored. These six hypotheses provide a rich research agenda for both neoliberal and neorealist scholars.

The question of whether and how to take account of domestic politics is another avenue of research. As the essays in this volume demonstrate, one cannot blithely assume that neoliberals acknowledge the importance of domestic politics while neorealists ignore it. In these essays for this volume, both Grieco and Keohane urge greater efforts to forge theoretical links between domestic politics and international relations. Milner (1992) argues that consideration of domestic politics is relevant to understanding how states define their interests, why they choose some strategies and reject others, and the conditions under which states are likely to abide by international agreements. And Mastanduno's contribution to this volume provides an impressive conclusion that domestic factors are vital to understanding the way in which relative gains concerns are translated into policy.

One traditional point of contention between liberals and realists has been disagreement with respect to the utility of military force. Has this disagreement disappeared in the debate between neoliberalism and neorealism? The answer is unclear. Although some of the authors in this volume raise the issue, only Robert Powell gives it a prominent place in his analysis. Without further clarification of each school's position, it is difficult to determine whether this issue has been resolved or merely put on the back burner.

In any case the relative utility of various techniques of statecraft in promoting international cooperation is a potentially rewarding avenue of research. Military statecraft, economic statecraft, propaganda, and diplomacy can be—and have been—used to promote cooperation. Both neorealists and neoliberals need to move beyond a priori assumptions about the utility of these techniques. More empirical research is desirable.

Looking back on the post–World War II debate between realism and idealism, Inis L. Claude (1981:198, 200) challenged the "notion of the essential opposition of realism and idealism" and suggested that they "are more properly regarded as complementary rather than competitive approaches to international affairs." John Herz (1981:202) agreed with Claude and described his own position as "realist liberalism." Joseph Nye (1988:238, 251) has echoed the view that the two approaches are complementary and expressed the hope that "the 1990s will be able to synthesize rather than repeat the dialectic 1970s and 1980s." The essays in this volume are a step toward such a synthesis.

The debate between those who emphasize the constraints on international cooperation and those who stress the opportunities for such cooperation, however, will not—and should not—disappear. Humankind needs a healthy tension between what Reinhold Niebuhr has labeled the "children of light" and the "children of darkness":

> Pure idealists [children of light] underestimate the perennial power of particular and parochial loyalties, operating as a counter force against the achievement of a wider community. But the realists [children of darkness] are usually so impressed by the power of these perennial forces that they fail to recognize the novel and unique elements in a revolutionary world situation. The idealists erroneously imagine that a new situation automatically generates the resources for the solution of its problem. The realists erroneously discount the destructive, as well as the creative, power of a revolutionary situation. (Niebuhr 1944:176)

NOTES

1. Powell refers to situations in which "the use of force is at issue." I interpret this to refer to situations in which force is feasible or high in utility. For a discussion of how the utility of a technique of statecraft is determined, see Baldwin (1985).
2. For a poignant example of both the importance and difficulty of combining studies of conflict and cooperation, see the preface added in 1980 to Thomas C. Schelling's classic *The Strategy of Conflict* (1960).

3. For discussion of liberalism in the international context, see Doyle (1983; 1986); and Zacher and Matthew (1992).
4. On mercantilist thought, see Viner (1948); and Heckscher (1955).
5. Each of these topics is discussed in more detail by Baldwin (1989).
6. *Domain* refers to the actor or actors with respect to which power is exercised, and *scope* refers to the dimension of their behavior that is affected.
7. Waltz's conception of power in terms of ability to affect others seems to be just as much a causal notion of power as Robert Dahl's (1968). Causal notions of power can be stated in a variety of ways. Waltz's definition of power in terms of who affects whom more strongly is similar to the views of Harry Eckstein (1973) and Peter Blau (1964). For a critique of such notions, see Baldwin (1978; 1989:114–18).
8. The Sprouts (1965:217*n*) cite their own earlier work (1945) as an example of failure to set the discussion of power in such a context. They cite S. B. Jones (1954) as an example of an early essay on capabilities, "in which the essentiality of such assumptions is quite explicit." Cf. Sprout and Sprout (1971:176–78).
9. The concept of political value unconnected with a specific set of activities is analogous to the concept of athletic prowess unconnected with a specified set of athletic activities. It is not just difficult to *measure* athletic prowess in the abstract, it is difficult to conceive what it *means*. The question of whether Babe Ruth was a better athlete than Jack Dempsey not only raises measurement problems, it raises conceptual problems as well.
10. The discussion of the six hypotheses is based on Milner (1992). See this work for further elaboration.

II THE NEOLIBERAL CHALLENGE
AND NEOREALIST RESPONSE

2

COORDINATION AND COLLABORATION: REGIMES IN AN ANARCHIC WORLD

Arthur Stein

Grappling with the problem of trying to describe and explain patterns of order in the anarchic world of international politics, scholars have fallen into using the term *regime* so disparately and with such little precision that it ranges from an umbrella for all international relations to little more than a synonym for international organizations. This essay develops a conceptualization of regimes as serving to circumscribe national behavior and thus to shape international interactions. Because it is theoretically rooted, the formulation can be used to delineate the nature and workings of regimes and to explain why and under what conditions they arise, how they are maintained and transformed, and when they may be expected to break down or dissolve. Further, it helps us understand why there are many different regimes rather than a single overarching one.

At one extreme, regimes are defined so broadly as to constitute either all international relations or all international interactions within a given issue-area. In this sense, an international monetary regime is nothing more than all international relations involving money. Such use of the term *regime* does no more than signify a disaggregated issue-area approach to the study of international relations and, so defined, "regimes" have no conceptual status; they do not circumscribe normal patterns of international behavior. They do no more than delimit the issue domain under discussion. Similarly, a conceptual definition of regimes as, for example, "the rules of the game," in no way limits the range of international interactions to which it refers. We can, after all, describe even the most anarchic behavior in the international system as guided by the rules of self-interest or self-help.[1] To specify the rules of the international political game is to say that anything and everything goes. If this is all that we mean by regimes, then we have made no conceptual advance by using the term.

At the other extreme, regimes are defined as international institutions. In this sense, they equal the formal rules of behavior specified by the characters or constitutions of such institutions, and the study of regimes becomes the study of international organizations. This formulation reduces the new international political economy to the old study of international organizations and represents nothing more than an attempt to redress a tired and moribund field.

ANARCHY AND REGIMES

The conceptualization of regimes developed here is rooted in the classic characterization of international politics as relations between sovereign entities dedicated to their own self-preservation, ultimately able to depend only on themselves, and prepared to resort to force. Scholars often use anarchy as a metaphor to describe this state of affairs, providing an image of nation-states that consider every option available to them and make their choices independently in order to maximize their own returns. In this view, states are autonomous sovereign entities that "develop their own strategies, chart their own courses, make their own decisions" (Waltz 1979:96).

The outcomes that emerge from the interaction of states making independent decisions are a function of their interests and preferences. Depending on these interests, the outcome can range from pure conflict to no conflict at all and, depending on the actors' preference orderings, may or may not provide a stable equilibrium. Such independent behavior and the outcomes that result from it constitute the workings of normal international politics—not of regimes. An arms race, for example, is not a regime, even though each actor's decision is contingent on the other actor's immediately previous decision. As long as international state behavior results from unconstrained and independent decision making, there is no international regime.

A regime exists when the interaction between the parties is not unconstrained or is not based on independent decision making. Domestic society constitutes the most common regime. Even the freest and most open societies do not allow individualism and market forces full play; people are not free to choose from among every conceivable option—their choice set is constrained. The workings of a free market require a developed set of property rights, and economic competition is constrained to exclude predatory behavior.[2] Domestic society, characterized by the agreement of individuals to eschew the use of force in settling disputes, constitutes a regime precisely because it constrains the behavior of its citizens.

Some argue that the advent of complex interdependence in the international arena means that state actions are no longer unconstrained, that the use of force no longer remains a possible option. If the range of choice were indeed this circumscribed, we could, in fact, talk about the existence of an international regime similar to the domestic one. But if the international arena is one in which anything still goes, regimes will arise not because the actors' choices are circumscribed but because the actors eschew independent decision making.[3] International regimes exist when patterned state behavior results from joint rather than independent decision making.

International politics is typically characterized by independent self-interested decision making, and states often have no reason to eschew such individualistic behavior. There is no need for a regime when each state obtains its most preferred outcome by making independent decisions, for there is simply no conflict. Examples include barter and some forms of foreign aid (e.g., disaster relief aid). Figure 2.1 illustrates one such situation, a case in which actors A and B both agree on a most preferred outcome, A_1B_1. In addition, both actors have a dominant strategy—a course of action that maximizes an actor's returns no matter what the other chooses. A prefers A_1 whether B chooses B_1 or B_2, and B prefers B_1 regardless of A's decision. The result of their independent choices, A_1B_1, is an equilibrium outcome, one from which neither actor can shift unilaterally to better its own position.[4] The equilibrium outcome leaves both actors satisfied. Because their interests are naturally harmonious and coincident, there is no conflict. The actors reach what is for both the optimal result from their independent choices.[5] No regime is needed.

There is also no need for a regime when the actors share a most preferred outcome but neither has a dominant strategy. In figure 2.2, A prefers A_1 only if B chooses B_1, and B prefers B_1 only if A chooses A1. The equilibrium outcome that emerges, A_1B_1, leaves both satisfied. There is, however, a second equilibrium outcome possible in this case, one that emerges from each actor's desire to maximize its minimum gain. Such a minimax decision rule would lead A to choose A_2 and B to choose B_2, the courses of action that would assure that, at the very least, they avoid their worst outcomes. Yet the A_2B_2 outcome, although an equilibrium one, is mutually undesirable.[6]

FIGURE 2.1
A No-Conflict Situation

ACTOR B

	B_1*	B_2
A_1*	4, 4 **	3, 2 **
A_2	1, 3	2, 1

ACTOR A

In this and all following figures in this essay, cell numerals refer to ordinally ranked preferences: 4 = best, 1 = worst. The first number in each cell refers to A's preference and the second number in each cell refers to B's preference.
*Actors's dominant strategy
**Equilibrium outcome

Thus, as long as both actors are aware of the other's preferences, they will converge on the A_1B_1 outcome that both most prefer. No regime is needed since both actors agree on a most preferred outcome, one that they can reach by acting autonomously.[7]

The international extradition of criminals is an example of such an "assurance game." States began in the early nineteenth century unilaterally to adopt statutes stipulating extraditable offenses. Some states, such as the Federal Republic of Germany, are satisfied with assurances of reciprocity before they agree to extradite criminal fugitives. Other states, however, are unsatisfied with such informal arrangements because of the potential limitations that other nations may place on extradition. They require treaties to provide them with assurances that the other state will behave in a predictable fashion when questions of extradition arise.[8] It is important to understand, however, that these treaties only provide assurances and no more.

FIGURE 2.2
The Assurance Game

ACTOR B

	B_1	B_2
A_1	4, 4 **	1, 3
A_2	3, 1	2, 2 **

ACTOR A

** Equilibrium outcome

Nor will a regime arise when some actors obtain their most preferred outcome while others are left aggrieved. Figure 2.3 illustrates
a situation in which both actors have dominant strategies leading to
an equilibrium that is actor A's most preferred outcome but actor B's
second-worst one. In such situations, the satisfied actors have no
reason to eschew independent decision making, and the aggrieved
actors would only succeed in making themselves still worse off by
being the only ones to forgo rational self-interested calculation. Voluntary export restraint is an example in which one actor gets its most
preferred outcome while the other is left aggrieved by that equilibrium result.

In the foregoing examples, behavior and outcome result from the
independent decisions of actors interacting in a context, prototypical
of international relations, characterized by anarchy. There are situa-

FIGURE 2.3
An Equilibrium Outcome That Leaves One Actor Aggrieved

ACTOR B

	$B_1{}^*$	B_2
$A_1{}^*$	4, 2 **	3, 1 **
A_2	2, 4	1, 3

ACTOR A

*Actor's dominant strategy
**Equilibrium outcome

tions, however, in which all the actors have an incentive to eschew independent decision making: situations, that is, in which individualistic self-interested calculation leads them to prefer joint decision making because independent self-interested behavior can result in undesirable or sub optimal outcomes. I refer to these situations as dilemmas of common interests and dilemmas of common aversions.[9]

DILEMMAS OF COMMON INTEREST

The dilemma of common interests arises when independent decision making leads to equilibrium outcomes that are Pareto-deficient—outcomes in which all actors prefer another given outcome to the equilibrium outcome. The classic example is, of course, the Prisoner's Dilemma (PD), in which the actors' dominant strategies lead them to an equilibrium outcome that is Pareto-deficient. There is an alternative outcome that both actors prefer to the equilibrium one. Figure 2.4 illustrates the two-actor PD in which both actors prefer the A_1B_1 outcome to the A_2B_2 equilibrium. But the preferred A_1B_1 outcome is neither individually accessible nor stable. To arrive at the Pareto-optimal outcome requires that all actors eschew their dominant strategy. In addition, they must not greedily attempt to obtain their most preferred outcome once they have settled at the unstable outcome they prefer to the stable equilibrium.[10]

The Prisoner's Dilemma is used as an allegory for a variety of situations. It is, for instance, the classic illustration of the failure of market forces always to result in optimal solutions—that is, of market rationality leading to suboptimal outcomes. Oligopolists, for example, prefer collusion to the deficient equilibrium that results from their competition.[11] Ironically, government intervenes in order to prevent collusion and to enforce the outcome that is suboptimal for the oligopolists. There are other situations of suboptimality, such as problems of collective goods and externalities, that also require government intervention to insure collusion and collaboration and thus to insure avoidance of the suboptimal equilibrium outcome.[12]

Political theorists use the Prisoner's Dilemma to explain the contractarian-coercion conjunction at the root of the modern state, arguing that the state of nature is a PD in which individuals have a dominant strategy of defecting from common action, but in which the result of this mutual defection is deficient for all. Yet the outcome that results from mutual cooperation is not an equilibrium one since each actor can make itself immediately better off by cheating. It is for this reason, political theorists argue, that individuals came together to form the state by agreeing to coerce one another and thus insure the optimal outcome of mutual cooperation. In other words, they agreed to coerce one another in order to guarantee that no individual would take advantage of another's cooperation by defecting from the pact and refusing to cooperate. States are thus coercive institutions that allow individuals to eschew their dominant strategies—an individual actor's rational course—as a matter of self-interest in order to insure an optimal rather than a Pareto-deficient equilibrium outcome.[13]

Put more simply, the argument is that individuals come together to form the state in order to solve the dilemma of common interests.

FIGURE 2.4
Prisoner's Dilemma

ACTOR B

	B_1	$B_2{}^*$
A_1	3, 3	1, 4
$A_2{}^*$	4, 1	2, 2 **

ACTOR A

*Actor's dominant strategy
**Equilibrium outcome

The existence of a PD preference ordering creates the likelihood that individual rationality will lead to suboptimal outcomes, a classic case of market failure. Individuals have a common interest in constraining the free rein of their individuality and independent rationality and form domestic political regimes to deal with the problem.

This view of the state is reinforced by the literature on collective goods, in which scholars argue that the suboptimal provision of collective goods stems from the individual's incentive to be a free rider, to enjoy the benefits of goods characterized by nonexcludability. Under certain conditions, the problem of collective goods is a classic PD in which each individual is better off not contributing to the provision of a collective good, but in which the equilibrium outcome of everyone's deciding to be a free rider is a world in which all are worse off than if they had contributed equally to the provision of the good.[14] Some in fact argue that the state is formed to assure the provision of collective goods; the state coerces contributions from all individuals, each of whom would rather be a free rider but goes along because of the guarantee that all others will be similarly coerced. They form the state because the alternative outcome is a Pareto-deficient world in which collective goods are not provided. The most basic collective good provided by the state is, of course, security from outside attack. Thus we have an explanation for the rise of states that also illuminates the anarchic character of relations between these states. The anarchy that engenders state formation is tamed only within domestic society. Individuals sacrifice a certain degree of autonomy—but the newly established nations do not do so. A world of vying individuals is replaced by a world of vying nations.

Regimes in the international arena are also created to deal with the collective suboptimality that can emerge from individual behavior.[15] There are, for example, international collective goods whose optimal provision can only be assured if states eschew the independent decision making that would otherwise lead them to be free riders and would ultimately result in either the suboptimal provision or the nonprovision of the collective good. One such problem of international politics, that of collective security, was in fact the focus of some of the earliest studies of collective goods.[16]

Collective goods issues are not the only problems characterized by PD preferences for which international regimes can provide a solution. The attempt to create an international trade regime after World

War II was, for example, a reaction to the results of the beggar-thy-neighbor policies of the depression years. All nations would be wealthier in a world that allows goods to moved unfettered across national borders. Yet any single nation, or group of nations, could improve its position by cheating—erecting trade barriers and restricting imports.[17] The state's position remains improved only as long as the other nations do not respond in kind. Such a response is, however, the natural course for those other nations. When all nations pursue their dominant strategies and erect trade barriers, however, they can engender the collapse of international trade and depress all national incomes. That is what happened in the 1930s, and what nations wanted to avoid after World War II.[18]

DILEMMAS OF COMMON AVERSIONS

Regimes also provide solutions to dilemmas of common aversions. Unlike dilemmas of common interests, in which the actors have a common interest in insuring a particular outcome, the actors caught in the dilemmas of common aversions have a common interest in *avoiding* a particular outcome. These situations occur when actors with contingent strategies do not most prefer the same outcome but do agree that there is at least one outcome that all want to avoid. These criteria define a set of situations with multiple equilibria (two equilibria if there are only two actors each with two choices) in which coordination is required if the actors are to avoid the least preferred outcome.[19] Thus these dilemmas can also lead to the formation of regimes by providing the incentive for nations to eschew independent decision making.

Figure 2.5 provides one example of a dilemma of common aversions. Neither actor in this situation has a dominant strategy; nor does either most prefer a single given outcome. Rather there exist two outcomes that both value equally and two outcomes that both wish to avoid. Thus, the situation has two equilibria, A_1B_1 and A_2B_2, but since the actors have contingent strategies, they cannot be certain that they will arrive at one of these outcomes if they act independently and simultaneously. Without coordination they may well end up with one of the outcomes that neither wants.[20]

This example of common aversions is relatively easy to deal with because the actors do not have divergent interests; neither cares which of the two equilibria emerges. Any procedure that allows for a convergence of their expectations makes coordination possible by allowing the actors to arrive at one of the equilibria. It is in such situations that conventions play an important role. In the United States, for example, driving on the right is a simple coordination mechanism that allows for the smooth movement of traffic in opposite directions without collisions and bottlenecks. It is an arbitrary convention that allows actors' expectations to converge on one of the equilibrium outcomes. The alternative convention of driving on the left permits coordination by convergence on the other equilibrium. The actors are indifferent between the two equilibria.

There are times, however, when, although both still agree on the least preferable outcome or outcomes, each prefers a different one of the possible equilibria. In figure 2.6, for example, there are two

FIGURE 2.5
Dilemma of Common Aversions and Common Indifference

ACTOR B

	B_1	B_2
A_1	1, 1 **	0, 0
A_2	0, 0	1, 1 **

ACTOR A

In this example, 1 = most preferred, 0 = least preferred.
** Equilibrium outcome

equilibria (A_2B_1 and A_1B_2), both of which the actors prefer to either of the other possible outcomes. Each does, however, most prefer one of the two equilibria—although they do not most prefer the same one. Actor A prefers A_1B_2, whereas B favors A_2B_1.[21]

When actors confront mutual aversions but diverge in their assessments of the equilibria, coordination can be accomplished in two different ways. In either case, the coordination regime establishes rules of behavior that allow actor expectations to converge whenever the dilemma arises. One means of insuring coordination is to specify behavior according to actor characteristics. Alternatively, the prearrangement can specify behavior by context. One example of this dilemma is provided by the simultaneous arrival of a north- or southbound and an east- or westbound car at an intersection. In this case, both drivers most want to avoid a collision. They would also prefer not to sit at their corners staring at one another. There are two ways

FIGURE 2.6
Dilemma of Common Aversions and Divergent Interests

ACTOR B

		B_1	B_2
ACTOR A	A_1	2, 2	3, 4 **
	A_2	4, 3 **	1, 1

** Equilibrium outcome

for them to move through the intersection safely: either A goes first, or B does. The problem is that neither wants to be the one to wait. A coordination rule based on actor characteristics would specify, for example, that Cadillacs drive on while Volkswagens sit and wait. Under such a regime, more likely than not "coordination for the powerful," the same actor always gets the equilibrium that it prefers. Alternatively, the actors could adopt a contextual rule; one example is the specification that the actor on the right always gets the right of way. In this case, the context determines whether any actor gets its more preferred equilibrium; sometimes it does, and sometimes not. Ideally, this "fairness doctrine" would insure that all actors get their most preferred equilibrium half the time.

COLLABORATION AND COORDINATION

Regimes arise because actors forgo independent decision making in order to deal with the dilemmas of common interests and common aversions. They do so in their own self-interest, for, in both cases, jointly accessible outcomes are preferable to those that are or might be reached independently. It is in their interest mutually to establish arrangements to shape their subsequent behavior and allow expectations to converge, thus solving the dilemmas of independent decision making.[22] Yet, the need to solve the dilemmas of common interests and aversions provides two different bases for international regimes, which helps to explain the differences between regimes that have often confused analysts. Regimes established to deal with the dilemma of common interests differ from those created to solve the dilemma of common aversions. The former require *collaboration*, the latter *coordination*.

The dilemma of common interests occurs when there is only one equilibrium outcome that is deficient for the involved actors. In other words, this dilemma arises when the Pareto-optimal outcome that the actors mutually desire is not an equilibrium outcome. In order to solve such dilemmas and assure the Pareto-optimal outcome, the parties must collaborate, and all regimes intended to deal with dilemmas of common interests must specify strict patterns of behavior and insure that no one cheats.[23] Because each actor requires assurances that the other will also eschew its rational choice, such collaboration requires a degree of formalization. The regime must specify what constitutes cooperation and what constitutes cheating, and each actor must be assured of its own ability to spot others' cheating immediately.

The various SALT agreements provide examples of the institutionalized collaboration required in a regime intended to deal with the dilemma of common interests, for the security dilemma is an example of a PD situation in which all actors arm themselves even though they prefer mutual disarmament to mutual armament. Yet international disarmament agreements are notoriously problematic. Indeed the decision to comply with or cheat on an arms control agreement is also a PD situation in which each actor's dominant strategy is to cheat. Thus it is not surprising that arms control agreements are highly institutionalized, for these regimes are continually concerned with compliance and policing. They must define cheating quite explicitly, insure that it is observable, and specify verification and monitoring procedures.

Oligopolists also confront the dilemma of common interests, and their collusion represents the collaboration necessary for them to move from the suboptimal equilibrium that would otherwise result. Such collusive arrangements require policing and monitoring because of the individual's incentive to cheat. International market-sharing arrangements exemplify this collusive form of collaboration and require the same sort of monitoring provisions. Not surprisingly, such successful market-sharing regimes as the International Coffee Agreement have extensive enforcement provisions and elaborate institutional structures for monitoring compliance.[24]

"The tragedy of the commons" exemplifies the dilemma of common interests. The commons were pasture and grazing grounds open to all, and the tragedy was the overgrazing that resulted from unrestrained individual use. This is not, as it may seem at first, a dilemma of common aversions in which the actors' least preferred outcome is the depletion of a valuable common resource. Rather each actor most prefers to be the only user of a common resource, next prefers joint restraint in the mutual use of the good, then prefers joint unrestrained use even if it leads to depletion, and least prefers a situation in which its own restraint is met by the other actors' lack of restraint. Each actor would rather share in such use of the resource that leads to depletion than to see its own restraint allow either the continued existence of the resource for others' use or the disappearance of the resource because the others show no restraint. The actors have a common interest in moving from their suboptimal (but not least preferred) outcome to one in which they exercise mutual restraint by collaboratively managing the resource. The commons thus represent a class of dilemmas of common interests in which individually rational behavior leads to a collectively suboptimal outcome.[25] Current international commons problems, such as the overfishing of a common sea, are all international manifestations of this dilemma of common interests.

By contrast, regimes intended to deal with the dilemma of common aversions need only facilitate coordination. Such situations have multiple equilibria, and these regimes must assure neither a particular outcome nor compliance with any particular course of action, for they are created only to insure that particular outcomes be avoided.[26] Nevertheless, such coordination is difficult to achieve when, although both actors least prefer the same outcome, they disagree in the choice of preferred equilibrium. The greater this conflict of interest, the harder it is for them to coordinate their actions. Yet once established, the regime that makes expectations converge and allows the actors to coordinate their actions is self-enforcing; any actor that departs from it hurts only itself.[27] Thus there is no problem here of policing and compliance. Defections do not represent cheating for immediate self-aggrandizement, but are expressions of relative dissatisfaction with the coordination outcome. An actor will *threaten* to defect before actually doing so; it may choose to go through with its threat only if the other actor does not accede to its demands. Again, such defection is never surreptitious cheating; it is a public attempt, made at some cost, to force the other actor into a different equilibrium outcome. Departures from regime-specified behavior thus represent a fundamentally different problem in coordination regimes than in collaboration ones.

There are many international regimes that serve to facilitate coordination and thus solve the dilemma of common aversions. These solutions provide mechanisms that allow actor expectations to converge on one of the possible equilibria. Conventions alone are adequate in these situations; institutions are not required. Not surprisingly, many involve standardization. The adoption of a common gauge of railroad tracks throughout western Europe is one example.[28] Traffic conventions are also examples of international regimes.[29]

Under the rules of the International Civil Aviation Organization, for example, every flight control center must always have enough English-speakers on duty to direct all those pilots who do not happen to speak the native language of the country whose airspace they happen to be crossing.[30] Communication between ground and aircraft may be in any mutually convenient language, but there must be a guarantee that communication is indeed possible; finding a language matchup cannot be left to chance. Thus English is recognized as the international language of air traffic control, and all pilots who fly between nations must speak enough English to talk to the ground. The pilot who never leaves French airspace is perfectly safe knowing only French; and should a Mexicana Airlines pilot wish to speak Spanish to the ground in Madrid, that is also acceptable. But if no one on the ground speaks the pilot's language, the parties can always converse in English. The mutual aversion, an air disaster, is avoided and a safe equilibrium is assured.[31]

Preemption provides still another solution to dilemmas of common aversions. In these situations with multiple equilibria and a mutually least preferred outcome, an actor's incentive is often to preempt the other because it knows that the other must then go along. If it is wrong, of course—assuming, for example, that an oncoming car will swerve if it keeps going—the attempted preemption leads directly to the common aversion. Often, however, preemption is based on firm knowledge or safe assumptions and is therefore successful. In these cases, preemption forms the basis of coordination, and it works well when it involves the exercise of squatters' rights in an area where they are traditionally respected or are likely to be so. One striking example has been the preemption of radio frequencies within accepted constraints. International meetings have allocated various portions of the radio spectrum for specific uses, and countries have then been free to broadcast appropriately along whatever frequency is available. They are required to register the frequencies they have claimed with the International Frequency Registration Board, but even then, other nations sometimes broadcast on the same wavelength when it is available. This practice is not permitted, but it is accepted. It has been without challenge that the Soviet Union prowled the shortwave band for unused frequencies on which it then broadcast its own propaganda. The result is a system of allocation that allows all nations the use of an adequate number of frequencies for broadcast with minimal international interference.

As the number of nations in the world has increased, however, the radio band has become more crowded, and Third World nations have demanded greater access to radio frequencies.[32] To some, the allocation of frequencies has now become a dilemma of common interests, for their worst outcome is to fail to get on the radio at all. In other words, they actually prefer the radio traffic jam that previously constituted the dilemma of common aversions in the hope that the other broadcaster will eventually give up and leave them an unimpeded signal. No longer willing to accept what has become in practice a form of coordination for the powerful, they are calling for "planning" (i.e., collaboration) to replace the current system. Broadcasting has long been a traffic problem requiring only coordination in order to facilitate access to the airwaves. With greater congestion, however, it is rapidly becoming a dilemma of the commons, which requires a *collaborative* allocation of a scarce resource.

REGIMES AND INTERESTS

This conceptualization of regimes is interest-based. It suggests that the same forces of autonomously calculated self-interest that lie at the root of the anarchic international system also lay the foundation for international regimes as a form of international order. The same forces that lead individuals to bind themselves together to escape the state of nature also lead states to coordinate their actions, even to collaborate with one another. Quite simply, there are times when rational self-interested calculation leads actors to abandon independent decision making in favor of joint decision making.

This formulation presumes the existence of interdependence— that an actor's returns are a function of others' choices as well as its own. If actors were independent in the sense that their choices affected only their own returns and not others', then there would be no basis for international regimes.[33] Interdependence in the international arena, especially given the relatively small size of the system, makes mutual expectations (and therefore perceptions) very important.[34] An analogy from economics is often used to make this point. There are so many firms in a perfectly competitive market that each firm is assumed to have a dominant strategy and to make decisions without taking into account expectations of others' potential behavior by responses. Oligopolistic or imperfect competition is distinguished precisely by the small number of actors, which makes necessary and possible the incorporation of expectations in the context of interdependence.

This conceptualization also explains why the same behavior that sometimes results from independent decision making can also occur under regimes. Arms buildups provide one example. On one hand, an arms race is not a regime, despite the existence of interaction and although each actor's decisions are contingent on the other's. An arms race is not a regime because the behavior, although patterned, is the result of independent decision making. On the other hand, arms increases can result from an arms control agreement that *is* a regime because the arms buildup results from mutual arrangements that shape subsequent decisions. Indeed, most arms control agreements have not been arms reduction agreements, but agreements of controlled escalation. By arriving at such an agreement, both actors thus participate in shaping their subsequent actions.[35]

This conceptualization of regimes also clarifies the role of international institutions, which many equate with regimes. Even those who recognize that regimes need not be institutionalized still suggest that institutionalization is one of their major dimensions. Indeed one scholar refers to noninstitutionalized regimes as quasi-regimes (Alker 1977:37–38). But the conceptualization I have presented here suggests that international organizations and regimes are independent of one another; each can exist without the other. Regimes can be noninstitutionalized as well as institutionalized, and international organizations need not be regimes, although they certainly can be.[36] The United Nations is an example of an international organization that is not a regime, for mere membership in no way constrains independent decision making. The UN provides a forum for formal and informal interaction and discussion, but it is not a regime because membership generates no convergent expectations that constrain and shape subsequent actions.

The presumption of the existence of dilemmas of common interests and common aversions that give rise to regimes assumes that self-interested actors do indeed have things in common. This is very much a liberal, not mercantilist, view of self-interest. It suggests that actors focus on their own returns and compare different outcomes with an eye to maximizing their own gains.

An alternative conception of competitive self-interest is that actors seek to maximize the difference between their own returns and those of others. This decision rule, that of difference maximization, is competitive, whereas a decision-criterion of self-maximization is individualistic. When applied by any actor, it transforms a situation into one of pure conflict in which the actors have no mutual interests or common aversion; it implies a constant-sum world in which an improvement in one actor's returns can only come at the expense of another's.[37]

Actors who are competitors rather than individualists do not confront dilemmas of common interests or common aversions. Out for relative gain, they have nothing in "common." The Prisoner's Dilemma is an interesting illustration of this point. When both actors apply a difference-maximization decision rule to the preference ordering that defines a Prisoner's Dilemma, the situation that results is one in which the actors' dominant strategies are the same. They no longer find the equilibrium outcome deficient and do not prefer an alternative one. The situation no longer provides them with a rational incentive to eschew independent decision making in order to create and maintain a regime. Thus, to see the existence of international regimes composed of sovereign entities who voluntarily eschew independent decision making in certain cases is to see the world in nonconstant-sum terms, a world in which actors can have common interests and common aversions.[38] It is self-interested actors who find a common interest in eschewing individuality to form international regimes.

This conceptualization of regimes also explains why there are many regimes and why they vary in character, why they exist in some issue-areas and not in others, and why states will form regimes with one another in one domain while they are in conflict in another. The existence or nonexistence of regimes to deal with given issues—indeed the very need to distinguish them by issue—can be attributed to the existence of different constellations of interest in different contexts.

STRUCTURAL BASES OF REGIME FORMATION

In this formalization, the factors that others argue to be the bases of regime formation, whatever they may be, should be understood instead as constituting the determinants of those different patterns of interests that underlie the regimes themselves. More specifically, I argue here that behavior is best explained by constellations of preferences that are in turn rooted in other factors. Many of these foundations are structural. The view most widely held among international relations theorists, for example, is that the global distribution of power is the structural characteristic that determines the nature of global order. One currently popular proposition links global predominance to stability; more specifically, it links a hegemonic distribution of power to open international economic regimes.[39] Most blithely tie the distribution of power to the nature of the economic order, but few make the explicit causal argument that depends on deducing a set of interests from a particular distribution of power and then ascertaining what order will emerge given power and interests.[40] The argument here is that interests determine regimes, and that the distribution of power should be viewed as one determinant of interests. In other words, a state's degree of power in the international system is one of the things that explains its preferences, and the distribution of power between states determines the context of interaction and the preference orderings of the interacting states and thus determines the incentives and prospects for international regimes. Structural arguments should be recognized as constituting the determinants of those different patterns of interest that underlie the regimes themselves.

A similar structural argument can be used to explain subsystemic regimes, for the extraregional context or structure can determine the constellation of preferences among intraregional actors. Great powers can often structure the choices and preferences of minor powers and thus shape regional outcomes. Many of the cooperative arrangements between Western European states immediately following the Second World War can be said to reflect the way in which, through carrot and stick, the United States structured the choices and preferences of those states. The Prisoner's Dilemma also illustrates this, for the dilemma can be seen as a parable of domination in which the district attorney structures the situation to be a dilemma for the prisoners (Burns and Buckley 1974). Divide-and-conquer is one strategy by which the powerful can structure the interactions between others by determining for them their preferences among a given set of choices.

There are other structural factors, such as the nature of knowledge and the nature of technology, that also determine actor preferences and thus the prospects for regimes. The nature of technology, for example, is critically important to a state's decision whether or not to procure weapons. Typically, scholars have argued that states confront a security dilemma in which they have PD preferences. All states have a dominant strategy of arming themselves, yet all find the armed world that results less preferable than a totally disarmed one. Yet the security dilemma presumes either that offensive weapons exist and are superior to defensive ones, or that weapons systems are not easily distinguishable (Jervis 1978). If only defensive weapons existed, however, then no security dilemma could arise. The actors would no longer have dominant strategies of arming themselves, for the arms could not be used to exploit those who had not armed, and procurement would not be a required defense against exploitation at the hands of others' defensive weapons. The interaction between states would no longer lead to a Pareto-deficient equilibrium outcome, therefore, and there would be no need for an arms regime. Thus the different constellations of preferences that exist in different areas and create different incentives and prospects for international regimes are in part a function of the nature of technology.

Changes in the nature of human understanding about how the world works, knowledge, can also transform state interest and therefore the prospects for international cooperation and regime formation. As late as the middle of the last century there was enormous variation in national quarantine regulations, for example. As long as there was no agreed body of validated knowledge about the causes of communicable disease and the nature of its transmission and cure, then state policy could and did reflect political concerns. Regulations to exclude or isolate goods and individuals, ostensibly for health reasons, were used as instruments of international competition and became the basis of conflict. But new scientific discoveries transformed this situation. There were medical discoveries about the microbes that caused cholera and leprosy, among other diseases; discoveries of the transmission of yellow fever by mosquitoes and plague by rat fleas; and discoveries of preventive vaccines such as the one for cholera. "The numerous international sanitary conferences, from 1851 up to the Constitution of the World Health Organization in 1946, clearly expressed the various milestones of medical insight." [41] International agreements on quarantine rules grew on this foundation. New knowledge thus changed state preferences and provided the basis for international cooperation and the depoliticization of health care policy. [42]

Just as structural factors underpin actor preferences, so do internal national characteristics. The interest of domestic economic sectors, for example, can be the basis for national interest (Gourevitch 1977; Kurth 1980). Even if a state's interests do not reflect those for any specific sector or class, they may emerge from a state's attributes. Large populations and high technology generate demands that will require that a state go abroad for resources if domestic access to resources is inadequate (North 1977). Yet needed resources can be obtained by exchange as well as by plunder. One cannot, therefore, move from a delineation of internal characteristics to state behavior without incorporating some aspect of a state's relations and interactions with others. Internal characteristics may determine a single actor's preferences but, in order to ascertain outcomes, it is also necessary to know the interests of other actors and to have a sense of the likely pattern of strategic interaction. [43]

REGIME CHANGE

The same factors that explain regime formation also explain regime maintenance, change, and dissolution. Regimes are maintained as long as the patterns of interest that gave rise to them remain. When these shift, the character of a regime may change; a regime may even dissolve entirely. Incorporating the determinants of interest leads one to argue that regimes are maintained only as long as the distribution of power (or the nature of technology, or knowledge, and so on) that determines a given constellation of interests remains. When the international distribution of power shifts, affecting, in turn, the preferences of actors, then the regime will change. Those who make a direct link between structure and regimes necessarily conclude that changes in the distribution of power lead to regime change. The argument here is more subtle. If interests intervene between structure and regimes, then only those structural changes that affect patterns of interest will affect regimes. Further, since other factors also affect interest, it may be that the impact of changing power distributions on actor preferences can be negated by other structural changes, such as those in technology. Or, changes in the other factors, such as knowledge, can lead to regime change without a change in the distribution of power. This describes the history of quarantine regulations, for example. Together, these might explain why some changes in the distribution of power have clearly been linked with regime changes whereas others have not.[44]

Regimes may be maintained even after shifts in the interest that gave rise to them, however. There are a number of reasons why. First, nations do not continually calculate their interactions and transactions. That is, nations only periodically reassess interests and power or the institutional arrangements that have been created to deal with a particular configuration of them. Once in place, the institutions serve to guide patterned behavior, and the costs of continual recalculation are avoided. Decision costs are high, and once paid in the context of creating institutions, they are not continually borne.[45]

An alternative argument is that the legitimacy of international institutions does not emerge from any waiving of national interest, but from an interest developed in the institutions themselves. Any shift in interest does not automatically lead to changes in the regime or to its destruction, because there may well be uncertainty about the permanence of the observed changes. The institutions may be required again in the future, and their destruction for short-term changes may be very costly in the long run. Institutional maintenance is not, then, a function of a waiving of calculation; it becomes a factor in the decision calculus that keeps short-term calculations from becoming decisive. There are sunk costs involved in international institutions, and thus they are not likely to be changed or destroyed. The costs of reconstruction are likely to be much higher once regimes are consciously destroyed. Their very existence changes actors' incentives and opportunities.[46]

There is, however, an alternative to the explanation that regime maintenance is merely a perpetuation of the exogenous factors that occasioned their rise. It may be that neither sunk costs nor delays in recalculation or reassessment are responsible for the maintenance of regimes. Max Weber argues that tradition provides legitimacy and is one basis for the maintenance of a political order, and this argument can be extended to international relations. International regimes can be maintained and sustained by tradition and legitimacy. Even those international institutions that exist in an anarchic environment can attain a legitimacy that maintains patterned international behavior long after the original basis for those institutions has disappeared. Thus, even though the constellations of interest that give rise to regimes may change, the regimes themselves may remain. This can be explained by means of interests by arguing that actors attach some value to reputation and that they damage their reputations by breaking with customary behavior (Akerlof 1980). An actor that no longer prefers the regime to independent decision making may nevertheless choose not to defect from it because it values an undiminished reputation more than whatever it believes it would gain by departing from the established order.

Finally, there is a possibility that the creation of international regimes leads not to the abandonment of national calculation but to a shift in the criteria by which decisions are made. Institutions created to assure international coordination or collaboration can themselves serve to shift decision criteria and thus lead nations to consider others' interests in addition to their own when they make decisions. Once nations begin to coordinate their behavior and, even more so, once they have collaborated, they may become joint-maximizers rather than self-maximizers. The institutionalization of coordination and collaboration can become a restraint on individualism and lead actors to recognize the importance of joint maximization. Those who previously agreed to bind themselves out of self-interest may come to accept joint interests as an imperative. This may be especially true of collaboration regimes, which require that actors trust one another not to cheat since they all have an incentive to do so. In these situations, one nation's leaders may come to have an interest in maintaining another nation's leaders in power, for they have worked together to achieve the optimal nonequilibrium outcome and they trust one another not to cheat. Recognition of the importance of maintaining the position of others may become the basis for the emergence of joint maximization as a decision criterion for actors.

The problems of analyzing regime formation, maintenance, and dissolution demonstrate the clear necessity for a strategic interaction approach to international politics. State behavior does not derive solely from structural factors like the distribution of power; neither can state behavior be explained solely by reference to domestic sectors and interests. Structure and sectors play a role in determining the constellation of actor preferences, but structural and sectoral approaches are both incomplete and must be supplemented by an emphasis on strategic interaction between states. It is the combination of actor preferences and the interactions that result from them that determine outcome, and only by understanding both is it possible to analyze and understand the nature of regimes in an anarchic world.

We have long understood that anarchy in the international arena does not entail continual chaos; cooperative international arrangements do exist. This essay differentiates the independent decision making that characterizes "anarchic" international politics from the joint decision-making that constitutes regimes. In doing so, it distinguishes the natural cooperation that results from harmonious interests from those particular forms of collective decision making that define regimes. Sovereign nations have a rational incentive to develop processes for making joint decisions when confronting dilemmas of common interests or common aversions. In these contexts, self-interested actors rationally forgo independent decision making and construct regimes.

The existence of regimes is fully consistent with a realist view of international politics, in which states are seen as sovereign and self-reliant. Yet it is the very autonomy of states and their self-interests that lead them to create regimes when confronting dilemmas.

NOTES

1. This is the basis of my disagreement with several other authors. Donald J. Puchala and Raymond F. Hopkins, for example, treat international regimes as coextensive with international politics. Similarly, although Oran Young does not formally equate international politics with regimes, his definitions, both of regimes and of international relations, suggest such an equivalence (see, e.g., Young 1979; 1980). My concern is to develop a conceptualization of regimes that delineates a subset of international politics.
2. On the importance of property rights, see Thomas M. Carroll, David H. Ciscil, and Roger K. Chisholm (1979). On the constrained sense of economic competition, see J. Hirshleifer (1977; 1978).
3. The term *complex interdependence* is most fully presented in Robert O.

Keohane and Joseph S. Nye (1977); yet it remains unclear, for example, if the use of force remains an option in the relations between advanced industrial societies but is dominated by other choices. Alternatively, it may be that nations sometimes prefer to threaten the use of force on a contingent basis, but recognize that the outcome resulting from the mutual *use* of force is the least preferred outcome for all actors.

4. The A1B1 outcome is also a coordination equilibrium, which David K. Lewis defines as an outcome from which neither actor can shift and make *anyone* better off (see Lewis 1969:14).

5. Individual accessibility is discussed by Jon Elster (1979:21).

6. Only A1B1, however, is a coordination equilibrium. The other equilibrium outcome, A2B2, is not a coordination equilibrium because each actor can shift from it and make the other better off by doing so. For Lewis this does not pose a coordination problem, which requires the existence of two or more coordination equilibria (1969:24).

7. For Elster, this case is individually inaccessible. Nonetheless, he expects convergence because the outcome is individually stable. I consider this case to be individually accessible precisely because there are convergent expectations. Note that if regimes are understood to include any devices that help actor expectations to converge, then regimes might arise even in this case, although solely to provide information. The proffered information would provide each actor with assurance about the other's preferences, as would be necessary for expectations to converge on the one of the two equilibria that all prefer.

   I find a problem with Robert O. Keohane's treatment of the role of information (1982). He argues that, given a demand for international agreements, the more costly the information the greater the actual demand for international regimes (one of whose functions is to improve the information available to actors). It is unclear whether he means to suggest that all mechanisms that provide information are examples of regimes even when the actors' interests are harmonious, or that they are not regimes because there is no demand for agreements in such cases. Since he presents the demand for agreements as a given in his formulation, we do not know if the demand for information can be a basis for a demand for agreements or simply a basis for a demand for regimes which assumes a demand for agreements. His formulation is too imprecise to adduce the standing of assurance mechanisms and whether they do or do not constitute regimes.

8. In some cases, actors may require mechanisms for assurance, which extradition treaties exemplify. These treaties might thus be seen as "assurance regimes," regimes that arise when each actor's knowledge of others' preferences is enough to allow the actors' autonomous decisions to bring them to the outcome they all most prefer.

9. The conceptualization of regimes presented here, that they arise to deal with the dilemmas of common interests and common aversions, is not,

therefore, based on any inherent notion of "principles." Indeed it is easy to conceive of unprincipled regimes, such as OPEC. Regimes may, but need not, have some principle underlying them.

10. The Prisoner's Dilemma is the only two-actor example of a Pareto-deficient equilibrium that occurs when both actors have dominant strategies. It is for this reason that it has received so much scholarly attention.

11. The role of game models in analyzing oligopolistic relations is described by Jesse W. Markham (1968:283–88). F. M. Scherer (1970) discusses the Prisoner's Dilemma as a model for oligopolistic interaction. The same observation is made by Lester G. Telser, who redubs the PD as it applies to oligopolies the "cartel's dilemma" (1972:143).

12. For a general discussion of suboptimality, see Jon Elster, (1978:122–34).

13. In one formulation, Jon Elster defines politics as "the study of ways of transcending the Prisoner's Dilemma" (see Elster 1976:248–49). Laurence S. Moss (1980) provides an assessment of modern and somewhat formal equivalents to the Hobbesian and Lockean views of state formation. See also Michael Taylor (1976). Elster criticizes Taylor's alternative (1978:156–57) and (1979:64, 143, 146).

14. Russell Hardin (1971). Note Elster's distinction between counterfinality and suboptimality in explaining the behavior of free riders (1978:122–23).

15. The dilemmas discussed in this essay refer to specific actors and not necessarily to the system as a whole. In the Prisoner's Dilemma, for example, only the prisoners themselves face a Pareto-deficient outcome. The rest of society finds the outcome of their dilemma to be optimal. This is precisely analogous to the situation of oligopolists, who prefer collusion to competition. The rest of society, however, would prefer that they compete rather than collude. The collective suboptimality need not necessarily exist for all actors in the system.

16. This literature was spawned by Mancur Olson, Jr. and Richard Zeckhauser (1966). Other essays linking collective goods and international cooperation include Bruce M. Russett and John D. Sullivan (1971); John Gerard Ruggie (1972); and Todd Sandler and Jon Cauley (1977). More recent work stresses different institutional arrangements for international collective goods. See Todd M. Sandler, William Loehr, and Jon T. Cauley (1978), and Duncan Snidal (1979).

17. Indeed international trade regimes have historically exemplified the subsystemic character of many regimes. Scholars often characterize the mid-nineteenth century, for example, as the era of free trade. Yet several major states, including the United States and Russia, did not take part. Similarly, the post-1945 era is now commonly referred to as the period of American economic hegemony. Ironically, this characterization is of a postwar economic system established by and within the sphere of only one pole of a bipolar international system—a bipolarity that has typically been offered as the most important characterization of the age. In other words, we should continually be reminded that references to "the"

postwar economic system are, in fact, to a subsystem that excludes the Soviet bloc. See Arthur A. Stein (1981).

18. A similar argument can sometimes be made about the decision to devalue a currency or maintain par value in a fixed exchange-rate system when devaluation, although every nation's dominant strategy, results in the suboptimal outcome of mutual devaluation. Richard N. Cooper (1975) uses simple games in his discussion of the choice of an international monetary regime.

19. In the dilemma of common interests, actors are averse to the suboptimal equilibrium outcome, and resolution involves their arriving at the outcome they prefer to the equilibrium one. The dilemma is their inability individually to arrive at the outcome they prefer to the equilibrium one. In the dilemma of common aversions, on the other hand, the actors do have a common interest in avoiding a particular outcome, but their dilemma is the possibility that they might arrive at a mutual aversion without some coordination. Beyond their desire to avoid that aversion, however, they disagree about which of the multiple equilibria they prefer.

20. Both equilibria are also coordination equilibria. In this case, there is no minimax solution.

21. If each of the actors chooses its minimax option, the A1B1 outcome results. This outcome is not their mutual aversion, but it is a Pareto-deficient nonequilibrium outcome because both prefer it less than either equilibrium.

22. Precommitment has been variously described as the power to bind, as imperfect rationality, and as egonomics; see Thomas C. Schelling (1960:22–28; 1978a) and Elster (1979:36–111). Such a formulation of prior agreement on principles does not require John Rawls's veil of ignorance; see Rawls (1971). Thinking ahead without agreement in strategic interaction, however, is no solution; see Frederic Schick (1977).

23. The Prisoner's Dilemma is the only situation with a Pareto-deficient equilibrium in which all the actors have dominant strategies. There are other cases of Pareto-deficient equilibria in which some have dominant strategies and some contingent strategies. These too are dilemmas of common interests and require regimes for solution; in these cases, however, only those actors with dominant strategies must eschew independent decision making. Thus, the regime formed to insure collaboration in this case is likely to have stipulations and requirements that apply asymmetrically to those who must eschew independent decision making to achieve optimality and to those who must be assured that the others have actually done so and will continue to do so.

Some argue that the cooperative nonequilibrium outcome of the PD can emerge spontaneously—without collaborative agreement. Social psychologists have done extensive experiments on the emergence of cooperation in repeated plays of the PD game; the most recent review is by Dean G. Pruitt and Melvin J. Kimmel (1977). See also Anatol Rapoport, Melvin J. Guyer, and David G. Gordon (1976). For a mathematician's deductive assessment of the prospects of the emergence of such cooperation, see Steve Smale (1980). See also Robert Axelrod (1981).

The conditions for this are rarely met in international politics, however. The first such requirement is that play be repeated indefinitely. Because states can disappear, and because they are therefore concerned with their own survival, international politics must be seen as a finite game by the actors. Moreover, the stakes in international politics are typically so high that fear of exploitation will *insure* that states follow their dominant strategy, to defect, in the absence of a collaborative agreement.

24. Bart S. Fisher (1972) and Richard B. Bilder (1963). The latter appeared in a special issue of the journal *Law and Contemporary Problems* devoted to "International Commodity Agreements."

25. Garrett Hardin (1968); Thomas C. Schelling (1978c:110–15) characterizes the commons as a PD.

26. The following authors all discuss coordination, although they do not agree fully on a definition: Schelling (1960); David K. Lewis (1969): Philip B. Heymann (1973); and Robert E. Goodin (1976:26–46). The distinction between collaboration and coordination made here can be compared to distinctions between negative and positive *coordination* and between negative and positive *cooperation* made by the following: Marina Whitman (1977:321); and Jacques Pelkmans (1979:97–123).

27. This notion of self-enforcement differs from that developed by Telser (1980). For Telser, an arrangement is self-enforcing if the actor calculates that defection may bring future costs. Thus even if cheating brings immediate rewards, an actor will not cheat if others' responses cause it to bear a net loss. For me, regimes are self-enforcing only if the cost that an actor bears for defecting is immediate rather than potential and is brought about by its own defection rather than by the response of others to that defection.

28. Standardization may reflect harmonious interests rather than coordination solutions to dilemmas of common aversions. This may, for example, explain the adoption of a common calendar.

29. Schelling (1978c:119–21) provides an interesting discussion of the traffic light as a self-enforcing convention.

30. The organization is the governing body for almost all international civil air traffic.

31. There does exist a dilemma of common aversions that can be solved by coordination *or* by collaboration. Like other situations characterized as dilemmas of common aversions, the actors in the game of Chicken have contingent strategies, do not agree on a most-preferred outcome, but do share a mutual aversion. In this case, the actors diverge in their assessment of the two equilibria. Unlike those of other dilemmas of common aversions, the two equilibria in Chicken are not coordination equilibria. In Chicken, the nonequilibrium minimax outcome is the second choice

of both actors and is not Pareto-deficient. Thus the situation is not merely one of deadlock avoidance, but one that can be solved either by coordination to arrive at one of the two equilibria or by collaboration to accept second-best. Here, too, the collaboration is not self-enforcing and requires mutual assurances about defection from a particular outcome. No-fault insurance agreements are one example of a collaboration regime to resolve a dilemma of common aversions. Note that David K. Lewis would not consider Chicken to be a coordination problem because the two equilibria in Chicken are not coordination equilibria. I believe that it *is* a coordination problem, but one that collaboration can also solve.

32. For background and analysis of the most recent World Administrative Radio Conference of 1979, see the articles in *Foreign Policy* 34 (Spring 1979): 139–64, and those in the *Journal of Communication* 29 (Winter 1979): 143–207. See also "Scramble for the Waves" *Economist*, September 1, 1979): 37; "The Struggle Over the World's Radio Waves Will Continue," *Economist* (December 8, 1979): 83; and "Policing the Radio," *New Statesman* (December 14, 1979), p. 924.

33. The absence of regimes does not mean, however, that the actors are independent of one another.

34. The conditions in which misperception matters, and the ways in which it matters, are delineated in Arthur A. Stein (1982b).

35. Goodin (1976:26) puts it this way: "Joint decision making is said to occur when all actors participate in determining the decisions of each actor. It implies that there was interaction between all the actors prior to the decisions and that this interaction shaped the decision of each actor." It is not surprising, then, that two recent formulations both stress the importance of agreement as part of their definition of regimes: see Young (1980) and Ernst B. Haas (1980:358). For interesting delineations of the range of decision-making procedures, see Knut Midgaard (1976) and I. William Zartman (1977). Both of these authors, however, heavily emphasize the bargaining process. Various forms of international cooperation can also be seen as forms of decision making; see Jan Tinbergen (1978:224–25).

36. Although I do not define regimes by reference to their degree of institutionalization, it is the case that collaboration regimes are more likely to be institutionalized than coordination regimes, because of the requirements of enforcement.

37. Difference maximization is discussed by Charles G. McClintock (1972:271–92). Taylor calls them pure difference games and designates them a subtype of games of difference generally; see (1976:73–74). See also Martin Shubik (1971).

38. Those who argue that world politics constitutes a zero-sum game cannot, of course, sustain their position at the extremes. After all, it is impossible for all dyadic relationships to be zero-sum or constant-sum in a world of more than two actors. Thus even if some relationships in international

politics are zero- or constant-sum, there must also exist some subset of relationships that are nonconstant-sum and therefore provide a basis for regime formation among this subset of nations. Yet Robert Gilpin still claims that "in power terms, international relations is a zero-sum game" (1975).

39. Recent exponents of the predominance model of stability, as opposed to the classical balance-of-power model of stability, include A. F. K. Organski (1968:338–76) and George Modelski (1978). The international political economy variant of the argument is provided by Stephen D. Krasner (1976); see also Stein (1981).

40. Note that this is precisely the way in which Krasner develops his argument (1976).

41. The quotation and the substantive discussion are from Charles O. Pannenberg (1979:179–80).

42. Regulations founded on health reasons and scientifically based can still become the basis of political disagreement, as the Japanese response to the California medfly spraying in 1981 demonstrates.

43. Note that this clearly distinguishes domestic sectoral from international structural approaches. Although both approaches can be seen as delineating the determinants of actor preferences, the international structural perspective can be claimed to determine the constellation of all actors' preferences. Thus, the existence of offensive weapons creates a PD situation for any pair of nations. On the other hand, the sectoral approach explains one actor's preferences at a time, and thus must be linked with an analysis of the interaction between actors to explain outcome. This is, of course, why the analysis of foreign policy is not equivalent to the analysis of international relations. Thus the works of Allison, Gourevitch, Katzenstein, and Kurth, among others, which explain foreign policy by reference to domestic economic or bureaucratic interests, remain incomplete precisely because they do not incorporate relations *between* nations.

44. The recognition of the multiple determination of actor interests also makes possible an issue approach to international politics that is not necessarily issue-structural.

45. One can, of course, expect there to be lags between changes in interests and actor behavior; see Michael Nicholson (1972). Schick distinguishes realization lags from adaptation lags (1977:790).

46. One can argue that regimes actually change actor preferences. The property rights argument about dealing with externalities through changes in liability rule is an example of a situation in which prearranged agreements are specifically devised in order to change utilities in subsequent interaction; see John A. C. Conybeare (1980).

3

INTERNATIONAL COOPERATION IN ECONOMIC AND SECURITY AFFAIRS

Charles Lipson

The study of international political economy is distinguished not only by its substantive focus but also by its continuing attention to cooperative, or at least rule-guided, arrangements. These cooperative arrangements are defined variously: as an open world economy by Robert Gilpin and Stephen Krasner, and as strong international regimes by Robert Keohane and Joseph Nye (Gilpin 1975; Krasner 1976; Keohane and Nye 1977). But in either case, the problems of cooperation and order are not approached simply as tactical alliances or as limiting cases of international anarchy. Instead close attention is paid to the possibilities for rule making and institution building, however fragile and circumscribed they may be. By this view, the absence of a Hobbesian "common power to keep them all in awe" does not preclude the establishment of some effective joint controls over the international environment. Elaborating on this perspective, Brian Barry argues that "international affairs are not a pure anarchy in which nobody has any reason for expecting reciprocal relations to hold up. In economic matters, particularly, there is a good deal of room for stable expectations."[1]

These stable expectations, which arise in the context of repeated transactions, are critically important since they can serve as the basis for international rules and conventions. Indeed legal theorist Lon Fuller argues that this is exactly how *all* customary law develops. It grows, he says, out of stable, complementary expectations and serves as both a "language of interaction" and a "base line for human interaction" (Fuller 1978:61, 76). Along the same lines, recent studies of international regimes emphasize the centrality of interactional expectancies.[2]

What has not been answered satisfactorily is why convergent expectations characterize some issues but not others. Why do some issues admit of extensive regulation whereas others do not? Put another way, the problem is to go beyond a reassertion of the distinctive subject matter of international political economy and to construct *a theoretically principled account of why significantly different institutional arrangements are associated with international economic and security issues.* An answer to this fundamental question could well lie in the different forms of strategic interaction (including expectations) that typify these two broad issues.

THE PRISONER'S DILEMMA AS A POLITICAL DILEMMA

The most direct and systematic approach to questions of strategic interaction is through game theory (and, relatedly, through theories of simulated gaming). In this section I shall consider one particularly important game, the Prisoner's Dilemma (PD), which helps clarify some basic features of international conflict and cooperation. In the following sections, I shall argue that the situational context is crucial to achieving cooperation in a repeatedly played PD, and, further, that this context is significantly different in economic and security issues.

The Prisoner's Dilemma, in its simplest form, involves two players. Each is assumed to be a self-interested, self-reliant maximizer of his own utility, an assumption that clearly parallels the Realist conception of sovereign states in international politics. Each player can move only once per game, and each faces a simple choice: to cooperate or to defect. Under these conditions, each player can maximize his own reward by defecting, *regardless of what the other does.* Note, however, that if both defect, each receives a smaller reward than if they had cooperated. The formal result is that the game's equilibrium, in which both players defect, is stable but not Pareto-optimal.[3]

Unfortunately, it is not easy to move toward the collectively rational solution or to maintain it, were it ever achieved. If a "nice" player were to try to cooperate, for example, his counterpart could play him for a "sucker" and reap greater rewards by defecting than by reciprocating.

No player has any incentive to take the first step toward a cooperative solution, and if it could be achieved, every player would have strong individual incentives to depart from it.[4] The dilemma, then, is the ineluctable failure to coordinate despite the obvious possibility of joint gains.

Because the PD highlights both the potential gains from cooperation and the temptations that prevent it, it has been taken as an elegant expression of the most profound *political* dilemmas, including that of the social contract. Indeed Jon Elster once defined politics as "the study of ways of transcending the Prisoner's Dilemma" (1976:249). Social-exchange theories take up this problem quite directly. The central explanatory issue in such theories, according to Russell Hardin, is to determine "how relationships are ramified in relevant ways to make cooperation of exchange rationally secure" (1982:215). This issue is obviously pertinent to the study of international political economy, with its emphasis on the emergence of cooperation and exchange in an anarchic world of sovereign states.

Actually, cooperation under the PD would be relatively simple were it not for several restrictions that define the game in its fundamental form. One is that players cannot rely on any outside assistance. There is no external mechanism to enforce threats or promises.[5] Nor can any player know what the other will do on a given move, so reputation is worthless. This restriction also prohibits me-

FIGURE 3.1	Player 2	
The Prisoner's Dilemma	*Cooperate*	*Defect*
Player 1 *Cooperate*	R=3 R=3	S=1 P=4
Defect	T=4 S=1	P=2 P=2

Note: Payoffs are given as ordinal rankings, with 4 as most preferred; for each player T > R > P > S, where
T = temptation to defect
R = reward for mutual cooperation
P = punishment for mutual defection
S = sucker's payoff for unreciprocated cooperation

tagame strategies in which either player can choose "the same move as the other player."[6] Finally, there is no way for a player to change the other's payoff ranking.[7] The game is thus rigid (all its rules are completely specified and defined in advance) and "environment poor" (all players understand the rules, the number of variables is highly limited, and the emphasis is on abstract structure rather than on institutional or environmental detail) (Shubik 1975:3–4).

These restrictions, and the ability to vary them, permit the PD to be simulated in interesting ways. At the same time, they suggest that in situations resembling the PD an inhospitable social context and the absence of certain institutions may block cooperative solutions. In fact, the restrictions imposed by gaming theorists point to practical devices used to resolve real-life PDs. Metagame solutions are possible, for example, if escrow mechanisms are available (since they permit simultaneous, contingent decisions) or if third parties such as the state can guarantee contracts. Such institutional devices are common domestically but rare internationally. Indeed the absence of reliable guarantees is an essential feature of international relations and a major obstacle to concluding treaties, contracts, and agreements. Thus the constraints on opportunism are weak.

If cooperation is to arise in the institutionally arid setting of the Prisoner's Dilemma, its sources often lie in the game's environmental context or its repeated play. The mere fact of repetition changes several key features of the game, especially if the players can communicate.[8] These subtle but important changes are one reason why Martin Shubik speaks of a "class" of PD games, which are often mistaken for a single game (Shubik 1970:191). Not only does repetition permit players to make threats and commitments, it also makes reputation important—all the more so since there is no external guarantee that promises will be kept. Beyond developing a reputation, a player can also make his strategy explicitly contingent on the choices of others, including their willingness to cooperate for joint gains.

TIT-for-TAT is one such contingent strategy (and a very important one, as we shall see later). Using this strategy, a player always cooperates on the first move. This "nice" strategy receives either the reward for mutual cooperation or the sucker's payoff if it is not reciprocated. From then on, the TIT-for-TAT player does whatever the other player did on the previous move. This strategy simultaneously offers to cooperate, to retaliate, and to resume cooperation after punishing defection. Like all strategies in iterated games, this one has a present (discounted) value, which players try to maximize. To calculate this value, we assume that earlier payoffs are worth more than later ones, either because future consumption is valued less or because the game's continuation is uncertain (Axelrod 1981:308). Then, using each player's discount for the future, we can cumulate the present value of all payoffs.

To illustrate, let us assume that both players choose the strategy, TIT-for-TAT. Each then wins the payoff R (the reward for cooperation) for every round of the game. Since the first round is played immediately, its present value to each player is R. If the game continues for a second round, each player will again receive R. But he will receive it only when that round is played—sometime in the future. The present value (before round one) of this second payoff is wR, some fraction of the immediate reward. This fraction reflects the player's discount for future rewards and his uncertainty about the game's continuing to this point. (Thus the discount parameter, w, will approach 1.0 if the game's continuation is likely or if future consumption is relatively important.) For a potentially infinite game, the present value for the stream of cooperative payoffs is

$$V = R + wR + w^2R + w^3R + \ldots$$

$$V = \frac{R}{1 - w,}$$

where $0 \leq W \leq 1$.

Robert Axelrod has shown that if the discount parameter, w, is sufficiently large, there is no one best strategy independent of the other player's choice.[9] If the future is very important, in other words, the players' optimal strategies are interdependent.

Even more important, Axelrod has shown that a strategy of cooperation based on reciprocity (TIT-for-TAT) can foster the emergence of stable cooperation among egoists.[10] He assumes that many individuals are playing separate games against each other, one at a time. In such a world, even if many players refuse to cooperate, small clusters of discriminating players can still profit from playing TIT-for-TAT as long as they have even a small fraction of their interactions with each other. Axelrod's conclusion is striking and evocative: "Mutual cooperation can emerge in a world of egoists without central control, by starting with a cluster of individuals who rely on reciprocity."[11]

These findings obviously bear on a central issue in international relations theory: the emergence and maintenance of cooperation among sovereign, self-interested states, operating without any centralized authority. If the time horizon is long enough, then the best strategy for individual actors is some initial generosity (that is, cooperating unilaterally on the first move), followed by tough-minded reciprocity. The more general result, as Hardin observes, is that "when there is even tacit opportunity for making one's choices contingent on those of one's adversary-partner, that is, of threatening the partner with defection in return for defection, rationality can become strategic" (1982:145).

It is now generally recognized that cooperation can be strategically rational if the PD is potentially infinite or if it is simultaneously linked to a wide variety of other games with the same players. Under these conditions, players can *individually* benefit from coordination conventions—whether they arise spontaneously, by following a leader, or through centralized efforts. In international relations, such conventions, which are typically grounded in ongoing reciprocal exchange, range from international law to regime rules. They form "baselines for interaction" and are extensive despite the chronic condition of international anarchy.[12]

INTERNATIONAL COOPERATION UNDER THE PRISONER'S DILEMMA

This analysis of iterated PDs suggests several vital elements of stable cooperation in international affairs: (1) the actors' perceptions that they are interdependent and that their decisions are mutually contingent; (2) a timely capacity to monitor and react to one another's decisions; (3) a strong interest in the long haul; and (4) moderate differences between the payoffs for cooperation and defection.

These general conditions highlight the most significant issues in forging international cooperation. Consider, for example, the actors' interdependence. If they play the same game repeatedly or several games contemporaneously, then defections can be punished and coordination conventions can develop.

Of course, if decisions are to be made contingent (over time or across several games), then the actors' moves must be reasonably transparent. Timely monitoring is especially important if the "sucker" pays a high price for unwitting and unreciprocated cooperation.[13] In its absence, he will be reluctant to cooperate. In general, when players share a conditional preference for cooperative solutions (as they do in the Prisoner's Dilemma), then confidence in monitoring capacity can foster cooperation.

Knowledge about other players' payoffs and strategies is important because a player who offers to cooperate runs real risks. These risks are minimized, however, if the sucker's penalty (for unreciprocated cooperation) is not grievous and if any gains from immediate defection are modest when compared to the value of long-term cooperation. There are two distinct issues here. One is how much future payoffs are discounted. If the future is highly valued, then a player might prudently risk the sucker's payoff now in hopes of fostering reciprocal cooperation over the long term. The other is the relative costliness of the sucker's payoff *in any single game*, compared to rewards for mutual cooperation and the temptations to defect. Experimental studies show that players are much more likely to cooperate when the immediate gains from defection (against a cooperating opponent) are small and the costs of mutual defection are high. Consider the two games in figure 3.2, both of which are PDs. If the payoffs are ranked ordinally, the two games are identical. Yet Anatol Rapoport and Albert M. Chammah found that if pairs of students played one variant hundreds of times, they were almost three times as likely to choose cooperative strategies in Game 2 (Rapoport and Chammah 1965:33–39).

In cases involving jointly supplied goods (where consumption by

FIGURE 3.2
Prisoner's Dilemmas with Differing Cardinal Payoffs

	Game 1				Game 2	
	C	D			C	D
C	1, 1	-50, 50		C	9, 9	-10, 10
D	50, -50	-1, -1		D	10, -10	-1, -1

one party does not diminish that of others), cooperation may also be impeded by free riders and communicative difficulties. The size and structure of the group are critical. Is the group able to determine its own membership? Can it exclude or punish defectors? A small group, or a larger one composed of overlapping small groups with extensive interactions, may be important for the establishment and diffusion of conventions, for the detection and sanction of defectors, and, in the case of truly public goods, for the formation of a viable coalition.[14]

These game-theoretic issues have profound implications for the maintenance of political cooperation among open economies. The ramifications of contingent decision making are a good example. The basic question here is whether key actors really consider their decisions mutually contingent and can convey that point effectively. This issue is especially important, and problematic, in the case of rising economic powers like modern Japan or interwar America. Once minor players, they may be slow to recognize the full implications of their new international status. Formerly allowed to defect with impunity, they may fail to recognize that their defections are now considered pernicious and that others' decisions are now contingent upon them. They assume, in effect, that others act completely independently. Elster terms this "parametric rationality" since it assumes that the actor's environment is a parametric constant rather than the product of strategic interaction.[15]

To its trading partners, Japanese commercial policy appears to be an unfortunate example of parametric rationality and an illustration of the threat it poses to stable cooperation in small groups.[16] Although Japan has recently made substantial efforts to open its internal market, its official policies and corporate practices still make Japan harder to penetrate than other major markets. The issue is one of long standing, but it has become increasingly acute because Japan's domestic market has grown and its manufacturing trade surplus has increased at a time when many of its trading partners suffer from overcapacity. Its trade policies have never been truly reciprocal (indeed they are more forthcoming now than ever), but the combination of Japan's size and world economic conditions has drawn attention to Japan's implicit (and parametric) assumption that its export markets will remain accessible even though its own market is still laced with restrictions. Japan's major trading partners are now challenging this assumption quite directly—by threatening trade retaliation. Responding to these credible threats, Japan has accelerated the selective opening of its domestic market even though these changes in trade barriers erode the electoral base of the ruling LDP party.

Threats of retaliation are not always taken so seriously, especially when they would be costly to carry out. Perhaps that is why less developed countries have ignored recent U.S. warnings that the Congress will raise trade barriers unless they open their markets substantially. "Oh, you won't do anything," India's trade minister told U.S. officials. "I have confidence in America, and I would be terribly disappointed if America went the protectionist route."[17] Referring to this candid statement, the *Wall Street Journal* concluded that the 1982 multilateral trade talks ended "without much progress, in part because no one believed the U.S. warning."

What was in doubt was America's willingness to act strategically, and therefore its capacity to threaten such action effectively. The Indian minister may ultimately be proven wrong (the U.S. continues to press the point), but there is certainly a reasonable basis for his doubts. A sharp increase in American protectionism would carry high costs for the U.S. economy,[18] would be difficult to contain and later reverse, and would have major repercussions in Europe, legitimating and encouraging protectionism there. Trade policy-making is an open, fragmented process, especially in America, and is far too cumbersome to plausibly threaten adroit strategic action. These difficulties encourage parametric thinking in all trading countries—this despite a shared recognition that the major actors' policies are fundamentally interdependent.

This discussion of trade policy-making suggests some limits in our earlier treatment of strategic interaction under the PD. Our analysis, like most stylized treatments of international bargaining, presumes that states are coherent, unitary, rational actors. This strong assumption is, of course, descriptively inaccurate. Governments do not choose between alternative tactics, as single decision makers might, to maximize expected returns or to assure some minimum payoff. Rather such choices are typically the product of politically mediated coalition bargaining.

Such descriptive inaccuracy is hardly damning—spare, simple models can seize essential elements of the problem at hand—but it does highlight the stylized framework of most bargaining models and the inherent limitations of their empirical application. For example, a national policy that appears irrational *as an international bargaining strategy* may actually be preferred by some domestic actors or may be the product of internal compromise. International bargaining models could then be used to analyze the implications of this suboptimal strategy. Equally important, the process of building and sustaining domestic coalitions necessarily limits the capacity of modern states to devise and execute sophisticated strategies, which may require plausible threats to change policy sharply or to stick to one policy resolutely. Although contingent strategies are often used—in the START talks, for instance, or in the GATT trade rounds—the negotiators' threats and promises may be more or less credible because of domestic political constraints.

More generally, at least four objections can be made to using the PD as a model of international interaction. The first, already indicated, is that it oversimplifies the nature of the actors and distorts both their goals and policy processes. The second is that it fails to acknowledge the cognitive and perceptual elements of strategic interactions. The third is that it fails to capture subtle interactions: the give-and-take of bargaining, the creation of new alternatives, and the search for symmetry and joint gains. And finally, it compresses a variety of bargaining situations into a single type of game when, in fact, several analytically distinct games are being played.

These objections, each significant in its own right, indicate the properly circumscribed uses of gaming models in the analysis of international relations. Such models cannot adequately describe the actual play of experimental subjects, much less the play of actors as complex as states. Still, as Henri Theil once remarked, "models are to be used but not to be believed." [19] Certainly that is true of gaming models, which are useful, despite their limitations, for the analytic exposition of bargaining relationships. They can be used to explore (1) the pattern of structural constraints on players' choices; (2) the varied inducements and punishments they represent; (3) the role of environmental variables, including time horizons, in modifying the players' interactions; and (4) the relationship between the choice of each and the outcome for all. As Glenn Snyder and Paul Diesing observe in their study of crisis bargaining, "A 2x2 model can be used to describe the *basic structure of the crisis situation*. . . . The 2x2 alternatives are not specific strategies but general directions that specific strategies may take. They represent the two basic modalities of ac-

commodation and coercion that run through all crisis bargaining"
(Snyder and Diesing 1977:83; emphasis in original)—through all bargaining, one might say.

Nor do gaming models depreciate the importance of cognition,
perception, and information processing (Stein 1982b). As Thomas
Schelling's work illustrates, gaming can be used to consider the role
of expectations and the complex motivational structures associated
with particular games.[20] These cognitive and communicative issues
are central to the analysis of coordination games, for instance. In
pure coordination games, including contract by convention, neither
player has any reason to defect. But because there may be more than
one equilibrium, the solution may fall short of Pareto optimality if
players cannot communicate adequately. These informational requirements are especially important because, for small numbers of
actors, an iterated PD of indeterminate length is essentially equivalent to a coordination game.

STRATEGIC INTERACTION IN SECURITY
AND ECONOMIC ISSUES

This extended treatment of the Prisoner's Dilemma and its variations lays the groundwork for reconsidering the basic question with
which we started: why are significantly different institutional arrangements associated with international economic and security issues? The answer lies, I think, in sharply differing ideal-typical forms
of strategic interaction in these two broad issues.

Conflict and cooperation are, of course, comingled in both issues,
but there are still important and systematic differences: economic
issues are characterized far more often by elaborate networks of
rules, norms, and institutions, grounded in reasonably stable, convergent expectations. Security regimes, on the other hand, are very
rare indeed, as Robert Jervis and others have concluded (Jervis 1982).
One might object that a reasonably stable set of rules and norms
(although virtually no permanent, formal organization) does exist in
certain carefully defined areas such as nuclear proliferation, weapons
testing, and so forth. Reaching back to the early nineteenth century,
some would even call the Concert of Europe a generalized security
regime since it encompassed a range of basic national security concerns among the major powers. But the basic point still stands.

Generalized security regimes are exceptional, even though alliances are not. There are few equivalents in the security field to the comprehensive, rule-guided arrangements in trade and money. *The real question is why security regimes—but not economic ones—are so rare and so limited in scope.*

One straightforward answer is that security issues and economic issues lend themselves to quite different types of strategic interaction. According to this view, economic games often involve relatively simple coordination or mutually beneficial exchange. Security issues, by contrast, are inherently more conflictual and their equilibria less stable. The recurrent attention paid by security analysts to the game of Chicken is testimony to this view.[21]

This answer is both illuminating and misleading. It resists, quite properly, any conflation of international affairs into one or two simple games. Certainly the PD is not a prototype for all interactions. It also underscores the sharper conflicts that surround security issues and implies that the skillful use of gaming approaches must pay close attention to payoff matrices, as the actors themselves understand them.

Yet it is seriously misleading to assume that security issues do not present the opportunity for significant joint gains, or at least the prevention of joint losses. Even adversaries like the United States and the Soviet Union wished to avoid nuclear war. And both could profit from restraints on arms racing: limits on the number of launchers and warheads, reduction of conventional forces in Europe, and so forth. Fundamental opposition, colored by mistrust, is thus tempered by the chance for genuine joint gains. This complex mix of motives was captured in Nikita Khrushchev's comment about John Kennedy: "He was, so to speak, both my partner and my adversary" (quoted in Russett 1983:99).

This mix of motives suggests a broad analogy to the PD. Each nation would undoubtedly prefer military superiority; that is, it would prefer to defect opportunistically while the other state accommodated. Similarly, the worst alternative for each is to play the sucker while the other state builds its arsenal and extends its military reach. To minimize these grave risks, each may avoid cooperation, or sharply limit its scope, producing a result no one really wants: a competitive escalation of military research, expenditures, and deployments. If the analogy to the PD holds, both countries consider this competitive escalation inferior to a cooperative, negotiated solution, but better than unilateral restraint. In this important sense, the major powers are, in Bruce Russett's phrase, prisoners of insecurity (Russett 1983).

This dilemma is not a static, one-shot affair, but a game played repeatedly. The United States and the Soviet Union are militarily interdependent on a continuing basis, just as the United States, Japan, and Western Europe are economically interdependent. The superpowers also recognize that their decisions are mutually contingent, even if they habitually portray their own actions as prudent *responses* and gloss over their own impact on others. In all these respects, including the opportunity to avoid joint losses, security issues share significant common features with economic issues.

Where contingent decision making is the rule, cooperative solutions are possible in iterated PDs. But if both economic and security issues can be understood, in part, as iterated PDs, then why are cooperative arrangements rare in one, recurrent in the other? The answer lies in the conditions that foster cooperation in games of indefinite iteration. Cooperation is most likely if (1) the future is not highly discounted, and (2) the penalty for unreciprocated cooperation is not devastating.

What is typically different in economic and security affairs is:

- the immediate and potentially grave losses to a player who attempts to cooperate without reciprocation; and
- the risks associated with inadequate monitoring of others' decisions and actions.

If a security game is indefinitely iterated, cooperation (including a generous effort to begin cooperation) may well be rational individually as well as collectively. But if one player, by defecting, can reap rewards by placing the other player at an immediate and overwhelming disadvantage, then there is little hope for stable, extensive cooperation.

It is this special peril of defection, not the persistence of anarchy as such, that makes security preparation such a constant concern.[22] In "placid peacetime," write Snyder and Diesing, the expectation of war (the worst defection) remains in the background, its effects muted and hard to observe. In a crisis, however, "the expectation [of war] is dramatically elevated and its behavioral effects stand starkly revealed" (Snyder and Diesing 1977:4). But a crisis is too late to begin serious military preparation, too late to discover that one's cooperative efforts have been dashed. Knowing these risks, prudent states are reluctant to cooperate with adversaries unless they can monitor with confidence, prepare in time to meet a prospective defection, and circumscribe the arrangements to minimize vulnerability.

In game-theoretic terms, this danger of defection has two complementary elements: the immediate gains from defection and the long-term costs. The costs, which stem from diminished cooperation in the future, can be given a present value. If these prospective payoffs are deeply discounted, or if one's opponent is likely to defect anyway, then the game resembles a finite PD and there is a best strategy: defection. We have also seen how, in experimental settings, defections are encouraged when the immediate gains are high.

This deadly logic of noncooperation lies behind Rousseau's fundamental insight:

> It is quite true that it would be much better for all men to remain always at peace. But so long as there is no security for this, everyone, having no guarantee that he can avoid war, is anxious to begin it at the moment which suits his own interest and so forestall a neighbor, who would not fail to forestall the attack in his turn, at any moment favourable to himself, so that many wars, even offensive wars, are rather in the nature of unjust precautions for the protection of the assailant's own possessions than a device for seizing those of others. However salutary it may be in theory to obey the dictates of public spirit, it is certain that, politically and even morally, those dictates are liable to prove fatal to the man who persists in observing them with all the world when no one thinks of observing them towards him (Rousseau 1917:78–79; quoted in Jervis 1976:63).

Thus, the high costs of unreciprocated cooperation, together with uncertainty about others' intentions, fuels suspicion and fosters anxiety to strike first.[23] Under these difficult conditions, all interactions with potential adversaries may come to be seen as purely competitive, or may be plausibly depicted that way in political discourse. In the extreme case, termed "status games," each player aims exclusively to maximize the *difference* between his own score and that of his opponent (Shubik 1971; Stein 1982a:319). This harsh perspective transforms a variable-sum game like Prisoner's Dilemma into a strictly competitive struggle with no possibility for joint gains.

In practice, two factors dampen this tendency and encourage modest collusion between the superpowers. First, as long as there is little prospect of a successful first strike, the confrontation is likely to remain a deterrent standoff. This prospect of continuity (as we have observed) encourages further cooperation, at least to diminish the risks of a clear common aversion such as nuclear war.[24] Second, although competitive status concerns are important, they are typically combined with welfare goals, leaving some room for joint maximization. Even so, the tendency to convert variable-sum games into constant-sum struggles is a persistent feature of security issues and an impediment to cooperative conventions.

This mixture of status and welfare calculations can be found in both security and economic negotiations, but in economic negotiations status goals are seldom a significant end in themselves. Rather they are instrumental—a rough measure of balance among the parties in extending trade concessions, for example. In security matters, on the other hand, status calculations are often critical to the overall value of the agreement to either side. Opponents of SALT II, for instance, argued that the treaty gave the Soviets certain advantages, so the U.S. was necessarily the loser *even if there were significant joint benefits.*[25]

This recurrent image of competitive struggle, and the anarchic conditions in which it is rooted, naturally limits the scope and durability of security agreements between potential adversaries. In spite of the risks, however, agreements are still possible if each side has reasonable grounds for confidence and if defection does not threaten devastation (Schelling 1984:56). The specific environment is crucial. Surveillance capabilities, weapons characteristics, the scope of the proposed agreement, and the pace of technological change all matter a great deal. So, too, do actors' perceptions about one another's willingness to act in bad faith—and the likely consequences.

If it takes time to execute a really damaging defection, and if good-faith cooperators can detect violations promptly, then agreements are quite possible. They are possible, at least, if adversaries are confident about their monitoring and their ability to withstand a surprise defection.[26] Similarly, agreements are more likely if both sides have a significant margin of security, a "surplus" allowing each to proffer cooperation with some protection in case the agreement fails.[27] Finally, if defensive forces are considered preeminent, the risks of any breakdown are surely lessened and the opportunities for agreement significantly broadened. The most fragile and dangerous situation by far is when offensive forces are believed to hold the advantage and when an offensive posture cannot be reliably distinguished from a defensive one.[28]

A margin of safety may be necessary for arms control, but it is not sufficient. The essential dilemma, unresolvable in the abstract, is whether to make an initial concession and them promise still more if properly reciprocated. This is the TIT-for-TAT strategy once again. Its aim is to promote reciprocal cooperation by initially lowering tension and by supplying evidence of nonaggressive intent. Clear and seemingly simple, it is actually a complex mixture of inducements and implied threats, generosity and possible retribution.

Unfortunately, it is extremely difficult for states to conceive and make credible such a sophisticated strategy. It requires a durable yet precise commitment, one that must be executed with consistency over many years.[29] Even more troublesome, an aggressive, expansive power may consider an adversary's initial concession to be a sign of weakness and irresolution rather than a carefully designed inducement to cooperate (Jervis 1976, chap. 3). It is precisely these problems of mistrust, which spring from cognitive uncertainty and the danger of surprise, that make cooperation so difficult and unstable.

The dangers of swift, decisive defection simply do not apply in most international economic issues.[30] Timely monitoring is important but rarely vital since most economic actions are reasonably transparent. A few, such as nontariff barriers or short-term Mexican debt, may be opaque, but most are matters of public record.[31] Second, although defection would (by definition) injure others, the prospect of immediate, critical damage is quite unusual. As a result, states know that they can readily verify compliance with economic agreements and will have time to discuss possible violations and, if need be, adjust to them. These favorable conditions facilitate trust and diminish the risks of cooperating.

The luxury of time is especially important. Evidence from experimental gaming suggest how it may aid cooperation. If a player is given the chance to change his mind after seeing another's choice, he is much more likely to switch his move toward cooperative reciprocity than toward exploitation or betrayal.[32] Thus transparency and the absence of immediate peril encourage mutual accommodation.

In the most fundamental security matters, this luxury of time may not exist. The classic instance was the rush to full mobilization after the assassination of Archduke Francis Ferdinand. In retrospect, those days in August 1914 seem positively languid when compared to the eight minutes it would take a Pershing II or SS20 to fly across the terrain of Western civilization and change it forever.

To summarize, then, my analysis has emphasized the possibilities for strategic cooperation that foster the development of rules, norms, and political institutions in the world economy, and the more impoverished possibilities in security affairs. We have argued that *both* economic and military issues are often characterized by the opportunity for joint gains and by interdependent but autonomous decision making, so these factors cannot adequately differentiate their regulation. The crucial differences appear to lie in the costs of betrayal, the difficulties of monitoring, and the tendency to comprehend security issues as strictly competitive struggles.

It is these environmental conditions that transform otherwise similar iterated PDs into distinctive games. Speaking of such environment-rich games, Shubik concludes that considerable attention should be paid "to institutional detail, to context, and to the problem of 'realistic representation,' " including the problems of devising and interpreting rules (Shubik 1975:4). Indeed the development of rule systems and common interpretations can serve as crucial signposts, as informational devices to coordinate expectations in a murky, complex environment. In security issues, though, the risks severely constrain reliance upon such conventions. They also highlight the importance of an undisturbed margin of safety and a reliable warning system for any significant security agreement.

HEGEMONS, RECESSIONS, AND THE EVOLUTION OF COOPERATION

This analysis shows how, in the context of international economic relations, cooperation can be sustained among several self-interested states. Thus it provides a theoretically principled and empirically plausible account of sustained economic cooperation among advanced capitalist states. What it does *not* show is how such cooperation can emerge in the first place. In practice, the rise of economic cooperation and commercial openness among industrial states has been associated with the rising power of hegemons: Victorian Britain and postwar America. I shall concentrate here on how America fostered economic cooperation in the Atlantic community. Its policies can be understood, I think, as institutionalizing a relatively open world economy through a TIT-for-TAT strategy.

To build the postwar order, the United States not only gave essential economic assistance and security guarantees to Western Europe, it also sponsored a network of multilateral institutions committed to liberalizing trade and long-term capital flows. It founded the International Monetary Fund, the World Bank, and the General Agreement on Tariffs and Trade (GATT), and funded the Organization for European Economic Cooperation. Beyond that, the U.S. offered prominent solutions to the most serious coordination issues, made side payments when necessary,[33] and promoted relevant conventions of cooperation. In the same way, the United States set the limits on cooperation. When it defected from cooperative commercial arrangements, as it did in agriculture, liberal trade was stymied in the sector involved (Kock 1969, chap. 7; Curzon 1965, chap. 7). Similarly, when the International Trade Organization failed to win congressional support, it died stillborn.

These limitations are important, but the basic U.S. policy was to foster greater openness in trade and capital flows. At the broadest level. the United States was deeply engaged in the political, economic, and military reconstruction of Western Europe as a whole. Less obviously, it stimulated a discourse among parallel national bureaucracies, offering them opportunities for joint gains—but only if they could cooperate.[34]

Early on, key European economic ministries were caught up in a web of collaborative enterprises. As a consequence, bureaucratic membership in the basic postwar economic regimes was solidified by the late 1940s. Repeated intercourse among these bureaucracies was to forge transgovernmental alliances in trade, money, and finance.[35]

American leadership and the shared experiences of war and depression ultimately shaped a transatlantic policy community with common values, perspectives, and language. Evidence from postwar negotiations reveals broadly shared standards for categorizing action and evaluating possible violations of embryonic rules and norms. Robert Hudec, in his study of *The GATT Legal System and World Trade*

Diplomacy, concludes that such shared standards were crucial to the success of trade adjudication in the 1950s (Hudec 1975, especially chap. 17).

America's hegemonic system, like that of Victorian Britain, began with unilateral initiatives designed to spur multilateral cooperation (on the hegemon's terms, of course). In Britain's case, however, the opening of her domestic market was considered advantageous in its own right, regardless of what others did. The United States, which reluctantly acknowledged greater state economic controls, never aimed at such openness at home and was willing to tolerate the slow dismantling of trade and capital restrictions abroad.

The United States thus reconstituted the Atlantic community in a particular fashion, established its central institutions, and nurtured a dense array of relationships that was to ensure broad and deep interdependence. But even though the United States gave economic aid and allowed discrimination against the dollar, it was ultimately committed to a TIT-for-TAT strategy in which U.S. concessions would be fully reciprocated by the opening of foreign markets. The opening phase of this strategy established the possibility of stable, long-term cooperation. The aims were large and the efforts strikingly successful (even though the very strength of U.S. commitments created some incentives to cheat on joint activities).[36]

After the difficulties of postwar reconstruction were over, the moment of greatest strain lay in the transition from hegemonic unilateralism to multilateral reciprocity. The problem is *not* that multilateral reciprocity is inherently unstable, although hegemonic systems may be more stable yet, especially when the supply of truly collective goods is involved.[37] It is rather that a difficult learning period must be traversed.

This is truly a moment of passage—what, in another context, cultural anthropologists call a liminal period (from the Latin for "threshold"). The parties' relative status and obligations shift from fixity to ambiguity, and once-customary classification and routinized spheres of action become problematic.[38]

In the world economy, this liminal period, with its special cognitive uncertainties, began in the late 1960s. By then it was clear that American economic and military capacities were diminishing, at least in relative terms. Hence, hegemonic diplomacy was no longer appropriate, as all the major actors understood in their own self-serving ways. The United States wanted to retain its leadership while bearing fewer costs. Europe wanted a larger voice in joint policies without incurring significantly greater responsibilities. These positions encapsulate what is so intriguing about moments of liminality—their implicit redescription of structure, away from a differentiated hierarchical model toward a substantially more equal community. In trade relations, this period began with the onset of the Kennedy Round, negotiated on a fully reciprocal basis and successfully concluded in 1967. In monetary relations, it began with the unraveling of the asymmetric dollar-exchange standard in the late 1960s, culminating in the breakdown of fixed exchange rates in 1971.

At the conclusion of liminal periods, in which roles are necessarily ambiguous and conventional relationships less determinate, the actors are normally reintegrated on new terms (Turner 1969:94–95). The transition from a hegemonic system, however, was especially difficult because it was followed by a series of economic catastrophes. Unfortunately, we still have an inadequate understanding of the relationship between the decline of American hegemony and the decade of instability that followed. There is a tight nexus (but not necessarily a causal chain) linking U.S. military overcommitments, U.S. monetary expansion, the resulting excess of global liquidity, the oil shocks, and the ensuing recession.

That recession, the worst since the Depression, confronted all Western states with the same severe problems: high unemployment, surplus capacity, and significant inflation. It also strained, but did not break, multilateral arrangements for economic openness.

Why do recessions and depressions create such powerful incentives to defect from collective agreements and cooperative conventions? First, a recession heightens calls for *immediate* solutions to crushing problems. Since the value of collusion often lies in the longer run, and since some gains from defection might seem to be available immediately, the incentives for collusion will be weakest when economic crises are at hand. In the language we used earlier, the discount parameter for future rewards has shifted. Second, given the already difficult circumstances, the sucker's payoff may be disastrous. In short, cooperation becomes riskier in the short run and less valued over the long haul.

The surest obstacle to this dissolution is the mutual recognition by key actors that any defection will be met swiftly and surely be reciprocal punishment, eliminating any potential short-term gains for the "cheater." This has been an underlying theme of economic summitry, for example. So, too, has been the public recommitment to long-standing cooperative conventions. Given the scale of economic problems in the 1970s and 1980s, and the continuing shift in underlying power distributions, the continuity of cooperation through these times is far more striking than its imperfections or frailty.

Cooperation is, indeed, a fragile enterprise in the world economy. Yet rule-guided and norm-governed arrangements are far more common than the usual insistence on an international "state of nature" would suggest. The idea of anarchy is, in a sense, the Rosetta stone of international relations: a heuristic device for decoding its basic grammar and syntax. But what was once a blinding insight— profound and evocative—has ossified and so become blinding in the other sense of the word—limiting and obscuring.

Theory construction and theoretically principled accounts must incorporate this fundamental notion of deep structure, but they must also move beyond even compelling metaphors to consider the subtle ways that environmental conditions shape interactions in particular issues, the patterned incentives and disincentives for national choice, and the processes by which individual choices affect the rewards for all. This task is largely a matter of reconstructing the ways in which these rewards are structured and understood and the uneven role played by convergent expectations, which can reduce the uncertainties generated when *interdependent* players make *independent* decisions.

That states are independent actors, as the Realist tradition insists, is a durable truth. That their choices are interdependent, at least in their consequences, is equally important. It is precisely the juxtaposition of these two compelling features that defines the fundamental problems of international relations. Our theories must cope with both.

Nor should the centrality of policy choice be masked by an exaggerated distinction between the international political environment (Waltz's Third Image) and the internal structure and actions of state (the Second Image) (Waltz 1959, chaps. 4 and 6). Although this distinction is a useful clarification, it should not be extended to treat international structure as an analog of competitive markets, which are a much more profound limitation on actors' choices (Waltz 1979:89–98). Thus the two images are analytically distinct but need not be treated as mutually exclusive, even in ideal-typical form. *The real problem, again, is to integrate choice and structure,* not to depreciate or conflate the distinction.

To stress interdependence is not to minimize conflict. In different contexts, interdependent decision making can produce Hobbes's "warre of all against all" or a nexus of cooperative conventions. As Louis Hartz once remarked of the debate between liberal and progressive historians, "The argument over whether we should 'stress' solidarity or conflict misleads us by advancing a false set of alternatives" (1955:20). Our goal, instead, should be to understand the checkered pattern of rule construction and anomie in international relations.

NOTES

1. Brian Barry (1981:30). Barry's use of the term "anarchy" obviously differs from its more typically circumscribed meaning in international relations: "the absence of an international sovereign."
2. See the definition of regimes given by Krasner in his introductory essay and used by most contributors to Krasner (1983a:1).
3. The Prisoner's Dilemma is the only two-player game with such a deficient equilibrium in which both players have dominant strategies.
4. In Jon Elster's terms, a cooperative solution is not "individually accessible" or "individually stable" (1979:21). The problems of the "nice" egoist, who takes the first step toward cooperation, are explored in Robert Axelrod (1981).
5. Thus any promises (such as "I will cooperate if you will cooperate") cannot be relied upon. If, however, a player feels ethically obliged to keep such promises, then his payoff structure must be modified accordingly, and the game is no longer a PD.
6. Such metastrategies permit synchronic reciprocity and leave no room for being a "sucker" unless only one side can play a metastrategy. Metagames and their strategies are treated in depth in Nigel Howard (1971).
7. Axelrod (1981:308); see also Axelrod's (1970) innovative treatment of changes in players' utilities.
8. Repeated moves *within* a single game can have similar effects. As

R. Harrison Wagner (1983) has shown, cooperation can arise in single-play games resembling the Prisoner's Dilemma (that is, where conditional cooperation is Pareto-optimal) when the players must make an indefinite sequence of moves.

9. Axelrod (1981:309). As we already know, if the game is played only once, then $w = 0$ (since all future payoffs are worth zero), and defection is always the best individual strategy.

10. These arguments are summarized in Robert Axelrod (1984).

11. Axelrod (1981:317); also see Robert Axelrod and William D. Hamilton (1981). The stability of this strategy depends on prompt retaliation: the TIT-FOR-TAT player is "nice," but he is not a patsy. It is also important to recognize that Axelrod's treatment is limited to players who can discriminate, not to the provision of public goods as such.

12. Such conventions and tacit contracts can even embrace large groups if they are built up from the overlapping interactions of smaller groups. These smaller groups are critical because they permit low-cost sanctions, such as exclusion, against defectors and because they help disseminate the knowledge required for conventional behavior (Hardin 1982:174, 191–93).

13. Thomas C. Schelling offers a perceptive discussion of these surveillance issues and their significance for U.S.-Soviet relations. When facing a potentially hostile enemy, says Schelling, "what one wants is not to be confident, but to be as confident as the true state of affairs justifies. What one wants is grounds for confidence, evidence that confidence is justified" (1984:56).

14. The problem of creating and sustaining a viable group of cooperators is treated imaginatively (as a multiperson PD) in Thomas C. Schelling (1978b).

15. The *strategically* rational actor makes a much more complex calculation. Unlike the parametric actor, he assumes that his environment is made up of other calculating actors, that he is part of their strategic environment, that they know this, and so on (Elster 1979:18).

16. America's protectionist Smoot-Hawley tariff, passed in 1930, is an equally good example.

17. Shiv Raj Patil's private statement to U.S. Trade Representative William Brock at the 1982 GATT ministerial conference (quoted in the *Wall Street Journal*, January 17, 1983, p. 31).

18. To threaten trade protection as a strategic act amounts to blackmail. The reason is straightforward: blackmail involves a threat to do something that one does not really want to do for its own sake, but will refrain from doing only if compensated. See Kenneth Oye (1979:14).

19. Henri Theil (1971:vi). I am indebted to Adam Przeworski for this quotation.

20. Schelling, for example, finds three distinct motivational structures associated with the game of Chicken. Chicken can be a "pure test case" in which the only stakes are the players' reputations; it can be a "conven-

tional case" in which the nominal stakes take on special importance by virtue of the actors' own commitments to winning them; and finally the "real case" in which the ostensible stakes are intrinsically valuable to the players (1966:118–19).

21. Steven J. Brams, for instance, treats the Cuban Missile Crisis as a game of Chicken in *Game Theory and Politics* (1975:39ff.).

22. Anarchy is a necessary condition for the security dilemma, but it is misleading to stress it exclusively, since anarchy and extensive cooperation coexist in international economics.

23. It will be especially difficult to allay these suspicions when the offense is considered dominant.

24. Note that as both sides' fear of a preemptive strike increased, cooperation on strategic issues became more difficult—precisely when it was most needed.

25. Opponents of SALT II also emphasized the difficulties of monitoring compliance—a recurrent obstacle to security cooperation, as we have already noted. In this case, the difficulties are related to the characteristics of specific weapons systems, the nature of treaty provisions, and the limits of technical surveillance (in the absence of on-site inspection).

26. The best situation, as Jervis notes, is one in which "a state will not suffer greatly if others exploit it, for example, by cheating on an arms-control agreement . . . but it will pay a high long-run price if cooperation with others breaks down." Such situations are more common, I think, in economic issues. See Jervis (1978:173).

27. The idea of surplus security is developed in Bruce Andrews (1978).

28. Jervis (1978:173, 189, 211). Therein lies much of the current debate over the deployment of new land-based ICBM's, which the Reagan administration portrays as a catch-up deterrent force but which others view as a potential first-strike weapon. See Herbert Scoville, Jr. (1981).

29. These issues are not germane in formal game theory since strategies are viewed as absolute commitments and all strategies are considered equally plausible. According to Shubik, "the concept of *plausibility* is at the crux of the relationship between a strict game-theoretic formulation . . . and the treatment of conflict by a mixture of 'gamemanship,' bargaining and strategic theories, and behavioral models of man" (Shubik 1970:188; emphasis in original).

30. There are exceptions, of course, mainly in monetary affairs. The most notable was the United States' suspension of gold convertibility on August 15, 1971.

31. Making nontariff barriers more visible to foreign producers was a major accomplishment of the Tokyo round of trade negotiations.

32. Russett (1983:109). These experimental results suggest a significant gap in game theory: the treatment of speech acts and symbolic interaction. "Much of the confusion and misapplication of game theory," according to Shubik, "has been caused by the failure to perceive that the formal theory of games makes no claims to having solved the critical problem of

how to represent verbal acts as moves. Many aspects of negotiation depend upon trust, interpretation, and evaluation. These factors and precommitments are implicitly assumed in game theoretic analysis" (Shubik 1975:15).

33. Japan's entry into the GATT, for instance, was "bought" by U.S. trade concessions to several European states (Charles Lipson 1982:250–51).

34. The best example is the postwar distribution of Marshall Plan aid to a unitary Western European institution, which then had to distribute the funds.

35. The fact that specific bureaucracies, with their particular interests, control national participation in different regimes tends to strengthen issue-specific interdependence over time but attenuates the connections across issues. The fragmentation of national decision making thus systematically favors longitudinal (diachronic) interdependence, issue by issue, over simultaneous interdependence across many issues, which requires more centralized national control.

36. This suggests that there may well be an optimal level of weakness in collective arrangements—a level that, by making the strategies of others appear contingent and the outcome uncertain, diminishes the likelihood of parametric rationality and encourages strategically based cooperation.

37. The reason is that the hegemon alone may find it worthwhile to supply the collective good, bypassing the difficulties of forming and sustaining a group of joint providers. Remember, however, that such collective goods are rare internationally and certainly do not include all cases of cooperation for joint benefit (since, in many cases, noncooperators can be excluded).

38. See, for example, Victor Turner's analysis of rites of passage (1969, chap. 3).

4

ACHIEVING COOPERATION UNDER ANARCHY: STRATEGIES AND INSTITUTIONS

Robert Axelrod
Robert O. Keohane

Achieving cooperation is difficult in world politics. There is no common government to enforce rules, and by the standards of domestic society, international institutions are weak. Cheating and deception are endemic; yet cooperation is sometimes attained. World politics is not a homogenous state of war: cooperation varies among issues and over time.

Before trying to draw conclusions about the factors that promote cooperation under anarchy, let us recall the definitions of these key terms. Cooperation is not equivalent to harmony. Harmony requires complete identity of interests, but cooperation can only take place in situations that contain a mixture of conflicting and complementary interests. In such situations, cooperation occurs when actors adjust their behavior to the actual or anticipated preferences of others. Cooperation, thus defined, is not necessarily good from a moral point of view.

Anarchy also needs to be defined clearly. As used here, the term refers to a lack of common government in world politics, not to a denial that an international society—albeit a fragmented one—exists. Clearly, many international relationships continue over time and engender stable expectations about behavior. To say that world politics is anarchic does not imply that it entirely lacks organization. Relationships among actors may be carefully structured in some issue areas, even though they remain loose in others. Likewise, some issues may be closely linked through the operation of institutions while the boundaries of other issues, as well as the norms and principles to be followed, are subject to dispute. Anarchy, defined as a lack of common government, remains a constant; but the degree to which interactions are structured, and the means by which they are structured, vary.

It has often been noted that military-security issues display more of the characteristics associated with anarchy than do political-economic ones. Charles Lipson, for instance, has recently observed that political-economic relationships are typically more institutionalized than military-security ones (1984:1–23). This does not mean, however, that analysis of these two sets of issues requires two separate analytical frameworks. Indeed one of our major purposes is to show that a single framework can throw light on both.

Mutuality of interests, the shadow of the future, and the number of players help us to understand the success and failure of attempts at cooperation in both military-security and political-economic relations. The first section of this essay synthesizes some of the findings of various case studies and thereby helps to specify some of the most important ways in which these three factors affect world politics. It deals with issues in isolation from one another, as separate games or as a series of games, in order to clarify some basic analytic points.

In this section, we follow the lead of game theorists, who have tried to avoid complicating their models with extraneous material in order to reach interesting conclusions. If the problem is a small event, such as a duel between two airplanes, our analysis of it may not depend on our knowledge of the context (e.g., the purpose of the war). If the issue is of very high salience to the participants, such as the 1914 crisis or the Cuban missile crisis, the extraneous issues (such as tariffs, or pollution of the Caribbean) may be so insignificant that they can be ignored. Either way, the strategy of focusing only on the central interaction is clearly justified.

Yet if the issue is neither isolated nor all-consuming, the context within which it takes place may have a decisive impact on its politics and its outcomes. As the case studies illustrate, world politics includes a rich variety of contexts. Issues arise against distinctive backgrounds of past experience; they are linked to other issues being dealt with simultaneously by the same actors; and they are viewed by participants through the prisms of their own expectations about the future. To ignore the effects of context would be to overlook many of the most interesting questions raised by a game-theoretic perspective on the problem of cooperation.

In the second section, we therefore consider the context of issues; in so doing, we move outward from the three dimensions discussed above (mutuality of interests, the shadow of the future, and the number of players), toward broader considerations, including linkages among issues, multilevel games, complications encountered by strategies of reciprocity in complex situations, and the role of international institutions. Analysis of the context of games leads us to regard context as malleable: not only can actors in world politics pursue different strategies within an established context of interaction, they may also seek to alter that context through building institutions embodying particular principles, norms, rules, or procedures for the conduct of international relations. In the concluding section, we will argue that a contextual approach to strategy—by leading us to see the importance of international institutions—helps us to forge necessary links between game-theoretic arguments and theories about international regimes.

THE EFFECTS OF STRUCTURE ON COOPERATION

Three situational dimensions affect the propensity of actors to cooperate: mutuality of interest, the shadow of the future, and the number of actors.

Payoff Structure: Mutual and Conflicting Preferences

It is well established that the payoff structure for a game affects the level of cooperation. For comparisons within a given type of game, this idea was first formalized by Axelrod, who established a measure of conflict of interest for specific games, including the Prisoner's Dilemma (Axelrod 1967; 1970). Experimental evidence demonstrated that the greater the conflict of interest between the players, the greater the likelihood that the players would in fact choose to defect. Jervis has elaborated on these theories and shown that different types of games, such as Stag Hunt and Chicken, have different potentials for cooperation (Jervis 1978:167–214). He has also applied his strategic analysis to historical and contemporary problems related to the security dilemma. His work clearly indicates that international cooperation is much easier to achieve in some game settings than in others.

Payoff structures often depend on events that take place outside the control of the actors. The economic depressions of 1873–96 and of the early 1930s stimulated demands for protection by firms and individuals in distress, and therefore reduced the incentives of governments to cooperate with one another. The weakness and vacillation of the British and French governments before 1939 reduced the potential value of anti-German alliances with those countries for the Soviet Union, making a Nazi-Soviet pact seem relatively more attractive.

This is obvious enough. Slightly less obvious is another point about mutuality of interests: the payoff structure that determines mutuality of interests is not based simply upon objective factors, but is grounded upon the actors' perceptions of their own interests. Perceptions define interests. Therefore, to understand the degree of mutuality of interests (or to enhance this mutuality), we must understand the process by which interests are perceived and preferences determined.

One way to understand this process is to see it as involving a change in payoffs, so that a game such as Prisoner's Dilemma becomes either more or less conflictual. To start with, PD is a game in which both players have an incentive to defect no matter whether the other player cooperates or defects. If the other player *cooperates* (C), the first player prefers to defect (D): DC > CC. On the other hand, if the other player *defects*, the first player still prefers to defect: DD > CD. The dilemma is that, if both defect, both do worse than if both had cooperated: CC > DD. Thus PD has a preference ordering for both players of DC > CC > DD > CD.[1]

Now consider a shift in the preferences of both players, so that mutual cooperation is preferred to unilateral defection. This makes the preference ordering CC > DC > DD > CD, which is a less conflictual game called Stag Hunt.

Jervis's (1985) study of the shift from the balance-of-power systems to concerts suggests that after world wars, the payoff matrix for the victors may temporarily be one of Stag Hunt: fighting together results in a short-lived preference for staying together. After a war against a hegemonic power, the other great powers often perceive a mutual interest in continuing to work together in order to ensure that the defeated would-be hegemon does not rise again. They may even feel empathy for one another and take an interest in one another's welfare. These perceptions seem to have substantial momentum, both among the mass public and in the bureaucracy. Yet the cooperation that ensues is subject to fairly easy disruption. As recovery from the war proceeds, one or both parties may come to value cooperation less and relative gains more. And if one side believes that its counterpart prefers to defect, its own preference will shift to defection in order to avoid the worst payoff, CD.

Actors can also move from Prisoner's Dilemma to more conflictual games. If both players come to believe that mutual cooperation is worse than mutual defection, the game becomes Deadlock, with both sides having preferences of DC > DD > CC > CD. Since the dominant strategy of each player is to defect regardless of what the other player does, the likely outcome is DD. Players in Deadlock, unlike those in Prisoner's Dilemma, will not benefit from repeated plays since mutual cooperation is not preferred to mutual defection.

Kenneth Oye (1985) provides a fine example of the movement from Prisoner's Dilemma to Deadlock in his essay on monetary diplomacy in the 1930s. Shifts in beliefs, not only about international regimes but particularly about desirable economic policy, led leaders such as Franklin D. Roosevelt to prefer unilateral, uncoordinated action to international cooperation on the terms that appeared feasible. Oye argues that the early 1930s do not mark a failure of coordination where common interests existed (as in PD); rather they indicate the decay of these common interests, as perceived by participants. Downs, Rocke, and Siverson (1985) argue that arms races are often games of Deadlock rather than Prisoner's Dilemma, making them much more difficult to resolve.

Beliefs are as important in the military area as in economics. Consider, for example, Van Evera's (1985) study of the beliefs leading to World War I. By 1914, what Van Evera labels "the cult of the offensive" was universally accepted in the major European countries. It was a congenial doctrine for military elites everywhere, since it magnified the role of the military and reduced that of the diplomats. It also happened to be disastrously wrong, since its adherents failed to appreciate the overwhelming advantage that recent technological change had given to the defensive (in what was soon to become trench warfare), and overlooked the experiences of the American Civil War and the Russo-Japanese War.

Gripped by this cult of the offensive, European leaders sought to gain safer borders by expanding national territories, and took more seriously the possibility of successful aggressive war; hence Germany and (to a lesser extent) other European powers adopted expansionist policies that brought them into collision with one another. European leaders also felt greater compulsion to mobilize and strike first in a conflict, since the penalty of moving late would be greater in an offense-dominant world; this compulsion then fueled the spiral of mobilization and countermobilization that drove the July 1914 crisis out of control. Had Europeans recognized the actual power of the defense, expansionism would have lost much of its appeal, and the compulsion to mobilize and countermobilize would have diminished. Put differently, the European payoff structure actually would have rewarded cooperation; but Europeans perceived a payoff structure that rewarded *non*cooperation, and responded accordingly. Beliefs, not realities, govern conduct.

The case of 1914 also illustrates a point made above: subjective interpretations by one side become objective reality for the other side. When a European state adopted expansionist policies, those nearby found themselves with an expansionist neighbor and had to adjust accordingly. For instance, Germany's expansionism, though largely based on illusions, led to a genuine change in Russia's environment. Russia adopted its inflexible war plan (which required mobilization against Germany as well as against Austria) partly because the Russians feared that Germany would strike into Russia's northern territories once the Russian armies were embroiled with Austria. Thus the Russian calculus was importantly affected by Russia's fear of German bellicosity. German expansionism was premised largely on illusions, but for Russia this expansionism was a real danger that required a response.

This discussion of payoff structures should make it clear that we do not assume that PDs are typical of world politics. More powerful actors often face less powerful ones, yielding asymmetric payoff matrices. Furthermore, even symmetrical games can take a variety of forms, as illustrated by Stag Hunt, Chicken, and Deadlock. What is important for our purposes is not to focus exclusively on PD per se, but to emphasize the fundamental problem that it (along with Stag Hunt and Chicken) illustrates. In these games, myopic pursuit of self-interest can be disastrous. Yet both sides can potentially benefit from cooperation—if they can only achieve it. Thus choices of strategies and variations in institutions are particularly important, and the scope for the exercise of intelligence is considerable.

Our review of payoff structures also illustrates that political-economic and military-security issues can be analyzed with the same analytic framework. Admittedly, economic issues usually seem to exhibit less conflictual payoff structures than do those of military security. Coordination among bankers, as described by Lipson (1985), has been more extensive and successful than most arms control negotiations, as analyzed by Downs and his colleagues (1985); and the patterns of trade conflict and cooperation described by Conybeare (1985) are hardly as conflictual as Van Evera's story of World War I. On the other hand, the great power concerts discussed by Jervis (1985), as well as several of the arms control negotiations, were more cooperative than the trade and monetary measures of 1930–33 delineated in Oye's essay (1985). And postwar economic relations between the United States and Japan have been more conflictual than military-security relations. As an empirical matter, military issues may more often have payoff structures involving a great deal of conflict of interest; but there is no theoretical reason to believe that this must always be the case.[2]

The Shadow of the Future

In Prisoner's Dilemma, concern about the future helps to promote cooperation. The more future payoffs are valued relative to current payoffs, the less the incentive to defect today—since the other side is likely to retaliate tomorrow (Axelrod 1984). The cases discussed support this argument and identify specific factors that help to make the shadow of the future an effective promoter of cooperation. These factors include:

1. Long time horizons
2. Regularity of stakes

3. Reliability of information about the others' actions
4. Quick feedback about changes in the others' actions

The dimension of the shadow of the future seems to differentiate military from economic issues more sharply than does the dimension of payoffs. Indeed its four components can be used to analyze some of the reasons why issues of international political economy may be settled more cooperatively than issues of international security, even when the underlying payoff matrices are similar—for example, when PD applies. Most important is a combination of the first two factors: long time horizons and regularity of stakes. In economic relations, actors have to expect that their relationships will continue over an indefinite period of time—that is, the games they play with each other will be iterated. Typically, neither side in an economic interaction can eliminate the other or change the nature of the game decisively in a single move. In security affairs, by contrast, the possibility of a successful preemptive war can sometimes be a tempting occasion for the rational timing of surprise (Axelrod 1979). Another way to put this is that, in the international political economy, retaliation for defection will almost always be possible; therefore a rational player, considering defection, has to consider its probability and its potential consequences. In security affairs, it may be possible to limit or destroy the opponent's capacity for effective retaliation.

To illustrate this point, let us compare the case of 1914 with contemporary international debt negotiations. In 1914 some Germans, imbued with the cult of the offensive, thought that a continental war would permanently solve Germany's security problems by restructuring power and territorial relations in Europe. For these German leaders, the temptation to defect was huge, largely because the shadow of the future seemed so small. Indeed it seemed that future retaliation could be prevented, or rendered ineffective, by decisive German action. Moreover, in the opening move of a war the stakes would be far greater than usual because of the value of preempting before the other side was fully mobilized. This perceived irregularity in the stakes further undercut the potential for sustained cooperation based upon reciprocity.

By contrast, contemporary negotiations among banks, and between banks and debtor countries, are heavily affected by the shadow of the future. That is not to say that the stakes of each game are the same; indeed there are great discontinuities since deadlines for rescheduling take on importance for regulators, banks, and the reputations of borrowers. But the banks know that they will be dealing with both the debtor countries and with one another again and again. Continuing interbank relationships imply, as Lipson (1985) points out, that small banks will think twice before double-crossing large banks by refusing to participate in rescheduling. This is particularly true of the small banks that are closely tied, in a variety of ways, to the large banks. Continuing relations between banks and debtor countries give the banks incentives to cooperate with the debtor countries, not merely in order to facilitate debt servicing on loans already made, but to stay in their good graces—looking toward a more prosperous future. The fact that Argentina, Brazil, and Mexico are so large, and are perceived to be potentially wealthy, is a significant bargaining asset for them now, since it increases the banks' expected profits from future lending, and therefore enlarges the shadow of the future. Indeed if these governments could credibly promise to favor, in the future, banks that help them now, and to punish or ignore those that defect in these critical times, they could further improve their bargaining positions; but, as sovereign governments whose leaders will be different in the future, they cannot effectively do so.

Reliability of information about the others' actions and promptness of feedback are also important in affecting the shadow of the future, although they do not seem to differentiate military-security from political-economic issues so clearly. Because of the absence of military secrecy, actors may sometimes have more reliable information on political-economic than on military-security issues. Banks thrive on differential access to information and therefore hold it closely. Furthermore, since the systemic effects of political-economic actions are often difficult to judge, and "cheating at the margin" is frequently easy, feedback between policy and results may be slow. For instance, the distribution of benefits from the Tokyo Round of trade negotiations is still a matter of conjecture and political contention rather than economic knowledge. By contrast, the superpowers publish lists of the precise number of missiles in each other's inventories, and we can assume that the information about the effect of a military action by either side—short of a devastating surprise attack

—would be communicated almost immediately to the leaders of both states.

The length of the shadow of the future, like the character of payoff structures, is not necessarily dictated by the objective attributes of a situation. On the contrary, as we have just seen, expectations are important. International institutions may therefore be significant, since institutions embody, and affect, actors' expectations (Krasner 1983a; Keohane 1984). Thus institutions can alter the extent to which governments expect their present actions to affect the behavior of others on future issues. The principles and rules of international regimes make governments concerned about precedents, increasing the likelihood that they will attempt to punish defectors. In this way, international regimes help to link the future with the present. This is as true of arms control agreements, in which willingness to make future agreements depends on others' compliance with previous arrangements, as it is in the General Agreement on Tariffs and Trade, which embodies norms and rules against which the behavior of members can be judged. By sanctioning retaliation for those who violate rules, regimes create expectations that a given violation will be treated not as an isolated case but as one in a series of interrelated actions.

Number of Actors: Sanctioning Problems

The ability of governments to cooperate in a mixed-motive game is affected not only by the payoff structure and the shadow of the future but also by the number of players in the game and by how their relationships are structured. Axelrod has shown that reciprocity can be an effective strategy to induce cooperation among self-interested players in the iterated, bilateral PD, where the values of each actor's options are clearly specified (Axelrod 1984). However, effective reciprocity depends on three conditions: (1) players can identify defectors; (2) they are able to focus retaliation on defectors; and (3) they have sufficient long-run incentives to punish defectors. When there are many actors, these conditions are often more difficult to satisfy. In such situations, it may be impossible to identify, much less punish, defection; even if it is possible, none of the cooperators may have an incentive to play the role of policeman. Each cooperator may seek to be a free rider on the willingness of others to enforce the rules.

We may call the difficulty of preventing defection through decentralized retaliation the "sanctioning problem." Its first form, the inability to identify defectors, is illustrated by the terrorist bombings against American installations in Lebanon in 1983. The United States did not know, at the time the bombings took place, who was responsible. The only state that could plausibly have been held responsible was Syria; but since the Syrians denied responsibility, retaliation against Damascus could have spread and deepened the conflict without punishing the terrorist groups themselves. The issue of identifying defectors is one aspect of a fundamental problem besetting efforts to cooperate in world politics: acquiring, in a timely fashion, adequate amounts of high-quality information. In order to maintain cooperation in games that reward unreciprocated defection, such as Prisoner's Dilemma, governments must have confidence in their ability to monitor their counterparts' actions sufficiently well to enable them to respond effectively to betrayal. As Lipson (1984) pointed out, the greater perils of betrayal (to the side that is betrayed) in military-security than in political-economic relations put more sever demands on gathering information in the former than in the latter area.

The second form of the sanctioning problem occurs when players are unable to focus retaliation on defectors. This difficulty is illustrated by Conybeare's (1985) analysis of the Anglo-Hanse trade wars. The Hanseatic League was unable to punish English privateers for their depredations, and instead retaliated against English merchants in Hanseatic towns. This produced escalation rather than cooperation.

The third form of the sanctioning problem arises when some members of a group lack incentives to punish defectors. This obstacle to cooperation often arises where there are many actors, some of which fail to cooperate in the common effort to achieve some collective good. Oye (1985) observes that although British devaluation in 1931 hurt other countries, no single government had the incentive to devote its own resources to bring about a revision of British policy. This form of the sanctioning problem—lack of incentives to punish defectors—also arose in the debt negotiations of the 1980s. To prevent default, it was necessary to arrange rescheduling agreements involving additional bank lending. Smaller banks were tempted to refuse to provide new funds. Only the fact that the large banks had strong incentives to put pressure on smaller ones to ante up prevented rescheduling agreements from unraveling "like a cheap sweater."

When sanctioning problems are severe, cooperation is in danger of collapsing. One way to bolster it is to restructure the situation so that sanctioning becomes more feasible. Sometimes this is done unilaterally. Oye (1985) points out that external benefits or costs may be "privatizable"; that is, changes can be made in the situation so that the benefits and costs of one's actions are directed specifically at those with whom one has negotiated. He argues that in the early 1930s Britain eventually succeeded in privatizing its international currency relationships by adopting exchange controls and attaching conditions, negotiated bilaterally, to new loans. This transformation of the game permitted a modest revival of international lending, based not on open access to British capital markets but on bilateral reciprocity.

As our examples indicate, sanctioning problems can occur both in the international political economy and on military-security issues. They tend to be more severe on military-security than on political-economy issues, due to the high cost of punishing defections, the difficulties of monitoring behavior, and the stringent demands for information that are imposed when successful defection can dramatically shorten the shadow of the future. But since sanctioning problems occur on both types of issues, issue area alone cannot account for their incidence or severity. To explain the incidence and severity of sanctioning problems, we need to focus on the conditions that determine whether defection can be prevented through decentralized retaliation: the case of identifying sources of action; the ability of governments to focus retaliation or reward on particular targets; and the incentives that exist for members of a group to punish defectors.

While the likelihood that these problems will arise may be enhanced by an increase in the number of actors involved, difficulties may also appear on issues that seem at first glance to be strictly bilateral. Consider, for instance, the example of 1914. In the Balkan crisis, Austria sought to impose sanctions against Serbia for its support of revolutionaries who tried to destroy the ethnically heterogeneous Austro-Hungarian empire. But sanctions against Serbia implied punishment for Russia, Serbia's ally, since Russian leaders were averse to accepting another Balkan setback. Russian mobilization, however, could not be directed solely against Austria, since Russia only had plans for general mobilization (Osgood and Tucker 1967, especially chap. 2). Thus neither Austria nor Russia was able to focus retaliation on the defector; the actions of both helped to spread rather than to contain the crisis. With more clever and moderate leadership, Austria might have found a way to punish Serbia without threatening Russia. And a detailed plan for mobilization only against Austria could have provided Russia with a more precisely directed measure to retaliate against Austria's ultimatum to Serbia.

Privatization is not the only way to maintain cooperation. Moreover, as some of our examples indicate, it can be difficult to achieve. Another way to resolve sanctioning problems is to construct international regimes to provide standards against which actions can be measured, and to assign responsibility for applying sanctions. Regimes provide information about actors' compliance; they facilitate the development and maintenance of reputations; they can be incorporated into actors' rules of thumb for responding to others' actions; and they may even apportion responsibility for decentralized enforcement of rules (Keohane 1984:49–132).

Charles Lipson's discussion of the international lending regime that has been constructed by bankers reveals how regimes can promote cooperation even when there are many actors, no dominant power, and no world central bank. Creditor committees were established under the leadership of large money-center banks. Each money-center bank then took responsibility for a number of relatively large regional banks, which in turn were assigned similar responsibilities for smaller banks (Lipson 1985). As a result, a hierarchy of banks was created, isolating smaller banks from one another and establishing responsibility for enforcing sanctions. Small banks displaying tendencies toward defection were threatened with being outside the flow of information in the future and, implicitly, with not being offered participation in lucrative future loans. This informal hierarchy, of course, was reinforced by the presence of the U.S. Federal Reserve System looming in the background: stories, whether apocryphal or not, of small bankers being told to "cough up" by high officials of the Fed circulated in banking circles during the early

1980s. It would have taken a bold president of a small bank to ignore both the banking hierarchy and the danger of arousing the Fed's wrath by not participating in a rescheduling.

This reference to the role of institutions in transforming *N*-person games into collections of two-person games suggests once again the importance of context within which games are played. In isolation, the basic concepts discussed earlier—payoff structures, iteration, and the number of players—provide only a framework for analysis. They take on greater significance, as well as complexity, when they are viewed within the broader context of other issues, other games, and the institutions that affect the course of world politics. We now turn to the question of how the context of interaction affects political behavior and outcomes.

THE CONTEXT OF INTERACTION

Whether cooperation can take place without central guidance depends not merely on the three game-theoretic dimensions we have emphasized so far but also on the context within which interaction takes place. Context may, of course, mean many different things. Any interaction takes place within the context of norms that are shared, often implicitly, by the participants. John Ruggie (1983a) has written of the "deep structure" of sovereignty in world politics and also of the ways in which shifting values and norms of state intervention in society—the emergence and legitimation of the welfare state —affected the world political economy between 1914 and 1945. International political-economic bargaining was fundamentally changed by the shift, during this period, from laissez-faire liberalism as a norm to what Ruggie calls "embedded liberalism" (1982; Hirsch 1978:263–84).

Interactions also take place within the context of institutions. Robert Keohane has argued elsewhere that even if one adopts the assumption that states are rational and self-interested actors, institutions can be shown to be important in world politics (1984). Institutions alter the payoff structures facing actors, they may lengthen the shadow of the future, and they may enable *N*-person games to be broken down into games with smaller numbers of actors.

Using our game-theoretic perspective, another way of looking at context may be especially revealing. This aspect has to do with what we call multilevel games. In such situations, different games affect one another, so that their outcomes become mutually contingent. Three such situations are particularly important for world politics: issue-linkage, domestic-international connections, and incompatibilities between games among different sets of actors. After considering these situations, we will turn to the implications of these multilevel games for the efficacy of a strategy of reciprocity in fostering cooperation.

Multilevel Games

Issue-linkage. Most issues are linked to other issues. This means that games being played on different issues—different "chessboards," in Stanley Hoffmann's phrase (1970)—affect one another. Connections between games become important when issues are linked.

Issue-linkage in this sense involves attempts to gain additional bargaining leverage by making one's own behavior on a given issue contingent in others' actions toward other issues.[3] Issue-linkage may be employed by powerful states seeking to use resources form one issue area to affect the behavior of others elsewhere; or it may be employed by outsiders attempting to break into what could otherwise be a closed game. Linkage can be beneficial to both sides in a negotiation and can facilitate agreements that might not otherwise be possible (Tollison and Willett 1979). Actors' resources may differ, so that it makes sense to trade one for the other: the United States, for instance, may provide economic aid to Egypt in exchange for Egyptian support for American policy in the Middle East. Furthermore, different players may have different preferences of different intensities: thus, in a log-rolling game, each party trades its "vote," or policy position, on an issue it values less highly for the other's vote on one it values more highly. The outstanding example of a successful bargaining linkage in the case studies mentioned here is that of the Washington Naval Treaty of 1922. As Downs, Rocke, and Siverson (1985) show, these arms control negotiations were successful in part because they linked bargaining over arms with bargaining over other issues. As part of an agreement to limit battleship construction, Japan gave Britain and the United States guarantees regarding trade in China and limitations of fortification on certain Pacific islands; Japan received legal recognition of its right to certain territory taken form Germany after World War I. Bringing these issues into the negotiations to limit the building of battleships helped to make cooperation possible, not only on these specific issues but on the whole package.

Of course, not all issue-linkages promote agreement, any more than each exercise of power can be expected to lead to cooperation. Oye has distinguished between "backscratching," which he regards as welfare-enhancing, and "blackmailing," which may reduce welfare levels (1979). The "backscratcher" merely offers, in return for compensation, to refrain from acting in what would otherwise be its own best interest. For instance, a debtor country, unable to make its payments on time without facing severe hardship or political revolution, may offer to continue servicing its debts only if compensated with new loans and an easier payment schedule. If this offer is rejected, the debtor does what it would have done without the offer: it defaults.

Backscratching entails a promise. Blackmailing, by contrast, implies a threat. As Schelling has pointed out, "The difference is that a promise is costly when it succeeds, and a threat is costly when it fails" (1960:177). Blackmailers threaten to act against their own interests unless compensated. Thus a debtor country that would be hurt by defaulting may nevertheless threaten to do so unless compensation is offered. This threat, if carried out, would leave both the debtor (the blackmailer, in this case) and its creditors worse off than if it had merely acted in its own interest without bargaining at all. If the blackmailing strategy works, on the other hand, the effect will be to transfer resources from the creditors to the debtor, an action that will not necessarily improve overall welfare.

Although it may be difficult to differentiate between backscratching and blackmailing in practice, the distinction helps us to recognize that issue-linkages have dangers as well as opportunities. One side may demand so much of the other in other areas that cooperation will not take place even in the area of shared interests. This accusation is frequently made against Henry Kissinger's version of linkage. Kissinger insisted that the Soviets exercise great restraint in the Third World in return for American cooperation on arms control (Breslauer 1983:319–40; Gaddis 1983–84; Hoffmann 1984:231–64). In Oye's terms (1979), Kissinger was trying to "blackmail" the Soviets by threatening to act against the United States' own interests (delay arms control) unless the Soviets compensated the United States with unilateral restraint.

The most intriguing point about linkage that is highlighted by the case studies we have discussed is the existence of what could be called "contextual" issue-linkage. In such a situation, a given bargain is placed within the context of a more important long-term relationship in such a way that the long-term relationship affects the outcome of the particular bargaining process. Two cases of contextual issue-linkage show that this form can often work to reduce conflict even without affecting the preferences of the participants on the specific issues being discussed. Oye (1985) notes that in 1936 the United States, Britain, and France were able to reach an agreement on international monetary reform because of the common security concern over a rising Nazi Germany. And as Downs and his colleagues point out (1985), by far the most important cause of cooperation in arms races that ended peacefully has been the activity of a third power. For example, the Anglo-French naval arms race of 1852–53 was resolved when the two states formed an alliance in order to fight the Russians in the Crimean War.

International Relations and Domestic Politics. Similar analytic questions arise in considering connections between international relations and domestic politics. Arms control negotiations involve not merely bargaining between governments, but within societies as well; the Carter administration was able to resolve the SALT II game with the Soviet Union, but not with the U.S. Senate. Trade issues typically also involve both international and domestic games. In the Tokyo Round, the Carter administration—this time with a different responsible party, Robert Strauss—was able to mesh international and domestic games, playing them simultaneously rather than sequentially (international first), as had been done on some issues in the Kennedy Round a decade earlier. The result in this case was that the Tokyo Round trade agreements with other countries were all ratified overwhelmingly by Congress, in contrast to the rejection of some of the international agreements made in the Kennedy Round (Winham 1980).

Such domestic-international connections are commonplace. Frequently, the incentives provided by domestic bargaining games inhibit effective foreign policy and may exacerbate international conflict. A well-known case is that of American decision making during the early months of the Korean War. General MacArthur was such a formidable figure in American politics that even his military superiors were reluctant to challenge his judgment in marching toward the Yalu River in the fall of 1950; yet this maneuver was so questionable that, if it had not been for the domestic political games taking place, serious reservations would have been expressed in the Pentagon and the White House (George and Smoke 1974).

Another type of domestic-international linkage is discussed by Conybeare (1985). During the fifteenth century, the Hanseatic League responded to naval setbacks at the hands of Britain by financing and equipping Edward IV who, upon defeating the Lancastrians in the Wars of the Roses, signed a treaty that was one-sidedly favorable to the Hanse's trading interests. By intervening in British domestic politics, the Hanse was thus able to triumph despite military weakness. This technique—intervening in a domestic political game as compensation for weakness at the international level—has recently been employed in more subtle ways by small powers with strong interest in American foreign policy (Keohane 1971).

Compatibilities and Incompatibilities Among Games. Many different games take place in world politics, involving different but overlapping sets of actors. Sometimes the existence of more than one game makes it easier to attain cooperation, but related games may also create difficulties for one another. That is, games in world politics can be compatible or incompatible with each other.

One example of a set of compatible games is provided by cooperation in international economic negotiations among the major industrialized countries. After World War II, such cooperation was facilitated by the fact that these countries were military allies. In contrast to Britain's situation in the nineteenth century, America's ability to persuade other major trading states to accept the rules that it preferred was greatly enhanced by the fact that in the military-political game the United States was a senior partner, rather than an adversary, of the other major actors in the world economy. To take another example: Lipson's (1985) analysis of debt negotiations suggests that the negotiating game among large banks was rendered compatible with games between large and small banks by structuring the situation so that small banks could not coordinate with each other. That is, two sets of negotiations were made compatible by precluding a third one.

The case of 1914 illustrates the problem of incompatibility among games. In noncrisis periods, loyalty within an alliance was compatible with friendly relations across alliances. But when the 1914 crisis occurred, loyalty within an alliance—such as Germany's support for Austria, Russia's for Serbia, and France's for Russia—implied defection across alliances. The increased cooperativeness of intra-alliance games destroyed broader patterns of cooperation.

In the contemporary international political economy, problems of incompatibility may also arise. For instance, negotiations on questions such as tariffs or energy policies are most likely to yield positive results for the advanced industrialized countries when only a few major players are involved in the initial negotiation. Friction with others, however, especially the less developed countries, may produce conflict on a larger scale. Or, to take a different example from the politics of international debt, close and explicit collaboration among debtor countries could, some fear, disrupt relations between debtor governments and banks in the richer countries.

The contrast between the fate of Soviet-American arms control in the 1970s and the Tokyo Round of trade negotiations illustrates the importance of multilevel games. In the face of linkages to other contentious issues, complex domestic political games, and a lack of reinforcement between political-economic and military-security games, even shared interests, a long shadow of the future, and bilateralism may be insufficient to promote cooperation. If the interaction happens to be an iterated game of Chicken, the problem is even worse because each player has a strong incentive to avoid cooperation in the short run in order to develop a reputation for firmness in the long run. Conversely, even when there are quite severe conflicts of interest, these may be overshadowed by more important mutual interests, perhaps institutionalized in organizations such as NATO. Once again, it is not sufficient to analyze a particular situation in isolation from its political context. We must also analyze the patterns of expectations, and the institutions created by human beings, within which particular negotiations are located and in light of which they are interpreted by participants.

Reciprocity as a Strategy in Multilevel Games

Robert Axelrod has employed computer tournaments and theoretical analysis of the iterated, two-player PD to show that a strategy based on reciprocity—such as TIT-for-TAT—can be remarkably effective in promoting cooperation (Axelrod 1984). Even among pure egoists, cooperation can "emerge" if a small initial cluster of potential cooperators exists.

This argument suggests that governments may have incentives to practice reciprocity in a variety of situations that are characterized by mixtures of conflicting and complementary interests—that is, in certain non-zero-sum games. Evidence for this proposition is established best for the particular game of Prisoner's Dilemma. Axelrod's theory suggests that in this game a strategy based on reciprocity can yield relatively high payoffs against a variety of other strategies. Furthermore, such a strategy helps the whole community by punishing players who use uncooperative strategies. When payoff structures are those of PDs, therefore, we can expect practitioners of reciprocity to attempt to institutionalize it as a general practice, so that they will benefit from others' use of the strategy as well as their own.

As we have noted above, not every situation in which conflict or cooperation may occur can be categorized as Prisoner's Dilemma. Games such as Chicken and Stag Hunt are also significant. Evidence on these cases is not as extensive as on PD. Yet, as Oye (1985) points out, there are good reasons to believe that reciprocity is an attractive strategy in a variety of non-zero-sum situations. The key conditions for the successful operation of reciprocity are that mutual cooperation can yield better results than mutual defection, but that temptations for defection also exist. In such situations, reciprocity may permit extensive cooperation without making cooperative participants inordinately vulnerable to exploitation by others. Furthermore, it may deter uncooperative actions.[4]

It is not surprising, therefore, that reciprocity is a popular strategy for practical negotiators as well as for analysts in the laboratory. Oye's (1985) analysis of monetary policies in the 1930s reveals that Britain developed such a strategy in its relations with the Scandinavian countries. Contemporary discussions of international trade provide another case in point. U.S. officials have frequently defended reciprocity in trade relations on the grounds that pursuit of this strategy would deter discrimination against American products by other countries, and that relaxation of reciprocity would invite retaliation by others. Even observers skeptical about reciprocity often agree. In a policy-oriented article critical of current proposals that the

United States should practice "aggressive reciprocity" in trade negotiations, William Cline argues that such action is rendered less effective by a high probability of foreign counterretaliation (1982:25). In
Axelrod's terms, TIT-for-TAT (which begins by cooperating and then
retaliates once for each defection by the other player) discourages
exploitative strategies—"aggressive reciprocity."

Thus the applicability of TIT-for-TAT does not seem to be limited
to PD. Yet it is not a perfect strategy. In the first place, it can
perpetuate conflict through an "echo effect": "if the other player
defects once, TIT-for-TAT will respond with a defection, and then if
the other player does the same in response, the result would be an
unending echo of alternating defections" (Axelrod 1984:176). In real-
world politics as well as in the laboratory, reciprocity can lead to
feuds as well as to cooperation, particularly when players have different perceptions of past outcomes.[5] Soviet-American détente collapsed partly because each side concluded that the other was not
practicing reciprocity, but was, on the contrary, taking unilateral
advantage of its own restraint (Breslauer 1983; Gaddis 1983–84; Hoffmann 1984). Second, even when many shared interests exist and
judgments of equivalence are not distorted, reciprocity may lead to
deadlock. John W. Evans has pointed out that in tariff negotiations
conducted according to the principle of reciprocity, potential concessions may become "bargaining chips" to be hoarded: "Tariffs that
have no intrinsic economic value for a country that maintains them
have acquired value because of the insistence of other countries on
reciprocity in the bargaining process." As a result, "tariff levels may
be maintained in spite of the fact that a lower level would raise the
country's real income" (1971:31–32). Third, when several actors negotiate separately and sequentially over issues that are substantively
interdependent, subsequent bargains may call previous agreements
into question by altering the value of concessions that have been
made. This "issue interdependent problem" bedeviled trade negotiations under the conditional most-favored-nation clause prior to the
institution of multilateral trade negotiations after World War II. Conditional most-favored-nations treatment permitted discrimination
among suppliers. Later agreements between an importer and other
suppliers therefore eroded the value of earlier concessions. This led
to complex, acrimonious, and frustrating patterns of bargaining
(Keohane 1986c).

Despite these difficulties, reciprocity remains a valuable strategy for decentralized enforcement of cooperative agreements. Players who are aware of the problems of echo effect, bargaining deadlock, and issue interdependence can compensate for these pitfalls. Axelrod observes that a better strategy than TIT-for-TAT "might be to return only nine-tenths of a TIT for a TAT" (Axelrod 1984:138). The Tokyo Round dealt with the deadlock problem by beginning negotiations not on the basis of current tariff rates, but rather on the basis of a formula for hypothetical large across-the-board tariff cuts, with provisions for withdrawing offers on sensitive products, or if adequate compensation was not received. The problem of issue interdependence was dealt with in the trade area through multilateralization of tariff negotiations and adoption of unconditional most-favored-nation treatment.

These difficulties in applying reciprocity, and the responses of players to them, illustrate the significance of the institutions within which reciprocity is practiced. As noted above, multilateral trade negotiations are a case in point. In the military-security area, reciprocity has also been institutionalized. For example, stationing of American troops in Europe is linked to purchases of American military equipment by European governments. NATO as an institution has helped member governments achieve a variety of such reciprocal arrangements.

The debt negotiations discussed by Lipson (1985) also illustrate how reciprocity can be institutionalized in an *N*-person game. First, the major actors are identified, and bilateral negotiations take place between them or their agents. The International Monetary Fund (IMF) and committees of banks negotiate with debtor countries. At a second stage, smaller banks are given the opportunity to adhere to these bargains, but not to influence their terms. At this stage, emphasis is placed on reciprocity at a different level: although the smaller actors have the potential to act as free riders, efforts are made to ensure that they have incentives not to do so for fear that they may suffer in a larger game. Small banks face the threat of being excluded from crucial relationships with big banks, and from future lending consortia, if they fail to provide funds for rescheduling loans. As in the other cases described above, strategies of reciprocity for debt rescheduling are adapted creatively to avoid the problems of issue interdependence that arise when there are many actors.

CONCLUSION

The Importance of Perception

The contributors to *Cooperation Under Anarchy* (Oye 1986) did not specifically set out to explore the role of perception in decision making, but the importance of perception has kept asserting itself. The significance of perception, including beliefs and cognition, will come as no surprise to students of international politics (Jervis 1976). Yet it is worth pointing out once again that decision making in ambiguous settings is heavily influenced by the ways in which the actors think about their problem.

While this point has been made in laboratory studies many times (for example, Tversky and Kahneman 1974; Nisbet and Ross 1980), there is an important twist in international politics that does not get sufficient attention from the psychologists who study decision making in the laboratory. Leaders of one state live far away from the leaders of other states. They are far away not only in space but also in their cognitive framework: their tacit assumptions differ about what is important, what needs to be done, and who bears the responsibility for change. Put simply, those acting on behalf of states often do not appreciate how their own actions will affect others and how they will be interpreted by others. As Van Evera (1985) concludes from his study of World War I, preventing that war would have required dispelling extensive misperceptions that were prevalent in Europe before 1914.

Other striking examples of the importance of perceptions also come from the security area. For example, Downs, Rocke, and Siverson (1985) have found that even when nations in arms races built defensive rather than offensive weapons, it was usually done not to defuse the arms race, but simply because they believed that such weapons offered the greatest amount of security per dollar. Even more to the point is that many arms races were started or accelerated without serious appreciation of the consequences. For example, when the Soviet leaders deliberately exaggerated their bomber strength in 1955 and their ICBM capabilities several years later, they did so for short-term political advantages; there is no evidence that they fully appreciated the long-term consequences that would follow when the United States geared up to take the threat seriously. In general,

Downs, Rocke, and Siverson find that arms races are not often perceived as the result of actions chosen by others. In the events leading to the outbreak of war, national leaders may completely misunderstand the consequences of their acts. Van Evera (1985) notes, for example, that in 1914 the Russian government did not realize that Russia's mobilization would lead directly to Germany's mobilization, and to war. Another example of the impact of biased interpretations of events is provided by Jervis (1985) in his discussion of the decay of great-power concerts, which were undermined by divergent views of which side had made greater concessions to maintain cooperation.

While security issues provide the most dramatic examples, governments may be no better at understanding how their actions in the realm of political economy will be seen by others. Conybeare's (1985) study shows that trade wars have sometimes begun when states held mistaken beliefs that other countries would be reluctant to raise tariffs on imported food in retaliation for new tariffs placed on their exported manufactured goods. Trade wars have begun when states have exaggerated expectations about the tolerance of others for attempts at minor exploitation in widely accepted terms of trade.

Groping Toward New Institutions and Norms

Our project began with a set of hypotheses about how specific features of an international setting would affect the chances for the development of cooperation (Oye 1986). Factors included were mutuality of interests, the shadow of the future, and the number of actors. These hypotheses have been supported by a broad set of cases that began in the fourteenth century, and covered trade disputes, monetary policy, and debt rescheduling as well as arms races, the outbreak of war, and diplomatic concerts. The three factors did, in fact, help to account for both cooperation and conflict.

We also discovered something else: over and over again we observed that the actors were not satisfied with simply selecting strategies based upon the situation in which they found themselves. In many cases we saw deliberate efforts to change the very structure of the situation by changing the context in which each of them would be acting. Decision makers themselves perceived (more or less consciously) that some aspects of the situations they faced tended to make cooperation difficult. So they worked to alter these background conditions. Among the problems they encountered were the following:

1. How to provide incentives for cooperation so that cooperation would be rewarded over the long run, and defection punished;
2. How to monitor behavior so that cooperators and defectors could be identified;
3. How to focus rewards on cooperators and retaliation on defectors;
4. How to link issues with one another in productive rather than self-defeating ways and, more generally, how to play multi-level games without tripping over their own strategies.

A fundamental strategic concept in attaining these objectives is that of reciprocity. Cooperation in world politics seems to be attained best not by providing benefits unilaterally to others, but by conditional cooperation. Yet reciprocity encounters many problems in practice. As Axelrod (1984) has demonstrated, and as Van Evera's (1985) discussion of 1914 illustrates, payoff structures in the strategic setting may be so malign that TIT-for-TAT cannot work. Reciprocity requires the ability to recognize and retaliate against a defection. And retaliation can spread acrimoniously.

Actors in world politics seek to deal with problems of reciprocity in part through the exercise of power. Powerful actors structure relationships so that countries committed to a given order can deal effectively with those that have lower levels of commitment. This is done by establishing hierarchies, as one would expect from Herbert Simon's assertion that complex systems will be hierarchic in character (Simon 1982, chap. 4). The construction of hierarchy for the sake of cooperation is best illustrated by Lipson's (1985) discussion of interbank networks to facilitate rescheduling of Third World debts; but it is also evident in Jervis's (1985) discussion of great-power concerts.

Another way to facilitate cooperation is to establish international regimes. Regimes can be defined as "sets of implicit or explicit principles, norms, rules, and decision-making procedures around which actors' expectations converge in a given area of international relations" (Krasner 1983a:3). International regimes have been extensive in the post-1945 international political economy, as illustrated by the international trade regime (centered on the GATT) and the international monetary regime (including the IMF as well as other organizations and networks) (Keohane 1984, chaps. 8–9). Since the use of power can facilitate the construction of regimes, this approach should be seen as complementary to, rather than in contradiction with, an emphasis on hierarchical authority. Regimes do not enforce rules in a hierarchical sense, but they do change patterns of transaction costs and provide information to participants, so that uncertainty is reduced. Jervis (1985) argues that the Concert of Europe helped to facilitate cooperation by making it easier for governments to understand one another. Lipson (1985) shows how, in the regime for debt rescheduling, the control of information is used to facilitate cooperation on terms favored by the big banks. He also indicates that one weapon in the hands of those banks is their ability to structure transaction costs: the costs of negotiations involving major money-center banks are reduced while the costs of coordinating resistance by small banks are not. Conybeare's (1985) analysis implies that if England and the Hanseatic League had been able to form an international trade regime, they might have been able to make mutually advantageous bargains and to discipline some of their more unruly constituents.

International regimes do not substitute for reciprocity; rather they reinforce and institutionalize it. Regimes incorporating the norm of reciprocity delegitimize defection and thereby make it more costly. Insofar as they specify precisely what reciprocity means in the relevant issue area, they make it easier to establish a reputation for practicing reciprocity consistently. Such reputations may become important assets, precisely because others will be more willing to make agreements with governments that can be expected to respond to cooperation with cooperation. Of course, compliance is difficult to assure; and international regimes almost never have the power to enforce rules. Nevertheless, since governments with good reputations can more easily make agreements than governments with bad ones, international regimes can help to facilitate cooperation by making it both easier and more desirable to acquire a good reputation (Keohane 1984, especially chaps. 5–7).

International regimes may also help to develop new norms, as Ruggie has argued (1982). Yet few such examples are evident in the cases we have discussed. The great-power concerts discussed by Jervis embodied new norms, but these did not last long; and the new norms of the 1930s monetary system described by Oye were largely uncooperative and connected with the breakdown rather than the institutionalization of a regime. Major banks today are trying mightily to strengthen norms of repayment (for debtors) and of relending (for banks), but it is not at all clear that this will be successful. Better examples of creating norms may be provided by the evolution of thinking on chemical and biological warfare, and by the development, under GATT, of norms of nondiscrimination—which are now, as we have seen, under pressure. Evidently, it is difficult to develop new norms, and they often decay in reaction to conspicuous violations.

Establishing hierarchies, setting up international regimes, and attempting to gain acceptance for new norms are all attempts to change the context within which actors operate by changing the very structure of their interaction. It is important to notice that these efforts have usually not been examples of forward-looking rationality. Rather they have been experimental, trial-and-error efforts to improve the current situation based upon recent experience. Like other forms of trial-and-error experimentation, they have not always worked. Indeed it is instructive to enumerate the variety of ways in which such experiments can fail.

1. The most important source of failure is that efforts to restructure the relationships may never get off the ground. As Downs, Rocke, and Siverson (1985) note, there was an active peace movement in the years before 1914, and World War I was preceded by a series of conferences designed to secure arms control and strengthen international law; but these efforts did not significantly affect the nature of world politics. Similarly, the shakiness of monetary arrangements in the 1920s was perceived by many of the participants, but conferences to deal with these weaknesses, such as that at Genoa in 1922, failed to cope with them effectively. The great-power concerts discussed by Jervis (1985) seemed to get somewhat farther, but were never sufficiently institutionalized to have much prospect of longevity.

2. Some agreements are instituted, but turn out to be self-contradictory. We have noted that sequential bilateral negotiations under conditional most-favored-nation treatment may lead to a problem of infinite regress; each bargain tends to require the renegotiation of

many others. Bilateral arms control agreements, whose restraints could encourage third parties to increase their armaments in order to catch up with the major powers, face a similar difficulty.

3. Even successful arrangements are subject to decay. Decay can result from actors' attempts to find loopholes in established rules. The very success of GATT in reducing tariff rates contributed to an expansion of nontariff barriers; and efforts to evade those barriers led to their progressive extension and tightening (Aggarwal 1983; Yoffie 1983). Likewise, successful cooperation in the area of security may lead governments to believe that their partners' cooperation is not based on reciprocity but is unconditional. Insofar as this belief is incorrect, discord may ensue.

4. In some cases, changes that have nothing to do with the arrangements make them obsolete. Thus the international debt regime in place before the crisis of August 1982 was manifestly ill-equipped to handle a situation in which most Third World debts had to be rescheduled. In this instance, the old regime was adapted to meet new needs. The Depression of the 1930s made the monetary orthodoxy of the gold-exchange standard obsolete. Indeed Oye (1985) argues that the cooperative international monetary arrangements of the 1920s hindered attempts at monetary cooperation during the 1930s. The collapse of the old regime was a necessary condition for creation of a new one.

Eventually, any institution is likely to become obsolete. The question is under what conditions international institutions—broadly defined as "recognized patterns of practice around which expectations converge" (Young 1982)—facilitate significant amounts of cooperation for a period of time. Clearly, such institutions can change the incentives for countries affected by them, and can in turn affect the strategic choices governments make in their own self-interest.

This interaction between incentives and institutions suggests the importance of linking the upward-looking theory of strategy with the downward-looking theory of regimes. The strategic approach is upward-looking in that it examines what individual actors will choose to do, and derives consequences for the entire system based on these choices. Most of the analysis discussed here has followed the upward-looking approach. On the other hand, much regime analysis has been downward-looking in that it examines the implications, for actors, of the way the entire system is organized. Some recent work has attempted to combine these two approaches,[6] but it has not yet been done in either a formally rigorous or an empirically comprehensive way.

The experimental groping by policymakers does not necessarily lead to stronger and ever more complex ways of achieving cooperation. The process proceeds by fits and starts. The success of each step is uncertain, and there is always danger that prior achievements will come unstuck. New experiments are often tried only under obvious pressure of events (as in debt rescheduling). And they are often dependent upon the active leadership of a few individuals or states who feel a serious need for change and who have the greatest resources.

We are beginning to understand the structural conditions that affect strategic choices leading to cooperation or discord. These factors are mutuality of interests, the shadow of the future, and the number of actors. Over a wide range of historical cases, these three dimensions of situations do help account for the emergence, or nonemergence, of cooperation under anarchy.

But in the course of this research we have also found that states are often dissatisfied with the structure of their own environment. We have seen that governments have often tried to transform the structures within which they operate so as to make it possible for the countries involved to work together productively. Some of these experiments have been successful, others have been stillborn, and still others have collapsed before fully realizing the dreams of their founders. We understand the functions performed by international regimes, and how they affect strategies pursued by governments, better than we did a number of years ago. What we need now are theories that account for (1) when experiments to restructure the international environment are tried, and (2) whether a particular experiment is likely to succeed. Even within a world of independent states that are jealously guarding their sovereignty and protecting their power, room exists for new and better arrangements to achieve mutually satisfactory outcomes, in terms both of economic welfare and military security.

This does not mean that all endeavors to promote international cooperation will yield good results. Cooperation can be designed to help a few at the expense of the rest; and it can accentuate as well as alleviate injustice in an imperfect world. Yet the consequences of failure to cooperate—from warfare to the intensification of depressions—make us believe that more cooperation is often better than less. If governments are prepared to grope their way toward a better-coordinated future, scholars should be prepared to study the process. And in a world where states have often been dissatisfied with international anarchy, scholars should be prepared to advance the learning process—so that despite the reality of anarchy, beneficial forms of international cooperation can be promoted.

NOTES

1. The definition of Prisoner's Dilemma also includes one additional restriction: CC > (DC + CD)/2. This is to ensure that it is better to have mutual cooperation than to have an even chance of being the exploiter or the exploited.
2. For an earlier discussion of contemporary events, using a common analytic framework to examine both economic and security relations, see Kenneth A. Oye (1979:3–33).
3. Ernst B. Haas refers to this as "tactical" issue-linkage, contrasting it with "substantive" issue-linkage resulting from causal knowledge; see Haas (1980:372). For a sophisticated analysis of tactical issue-linkage, see Michael McGinnis (1986).
4. Consider the example of Stag Hunt, defined by the preference ordering of both players as CC > DC > DD > CD. If player A is credibly committed to a strategy of reciprocity, beginning with cooperation, B's incentives to cooperate are enhanced. A's commitment to cooperate ensures that B will not be double-crossed (which would leave B with the worst payoff). Furthermore, A's commitment to retaliate against defection ensures that any defection by B would lead, after the first move, not to B's second-best outcome (DC) but to its third-best outcome (DD).

   The game of Chicken provides another appropriate case in point. In Chicken, mutual cooperation is only the second-best outcome for both players, but mutual defection is worst for both. Thus, DC > CC > CD > DD. A credible strategy of reciprocity by player A in Chicken ensures B of its second-best outcome if it cooperates, and guarantees that continual defection will in the long run provide it with its worst payoff. Assuming that B's shadow of the future is sufficiently long, it should respond to A's strategy of reciprocity by cooperating.
5. For an analysis of the spiral mode of conflict, see Robert Jervis (1976:58–113).

6. In *After Hegemony* (1984), Robert Keohane sought to show how game theory (which is "upward-looking") can be combined fruitfully with the "downward-looking" theories of public goods and market failure to develop a functional theory of international regimes. But he has not formalized his theory, and has applied it only to post–World War II international political economy.

5

ANARCHY AND THE LIMITS OF COOPERATION: A REALIST CRITIQUE OF THE NEWEST LIBERAL INSTITUTIONALISM

Joseph M. Grieco

Realism has dominated international relations theory at least since World War II.[1] For realists, international anarchy fosters competition and conflict among states and inhibits their willingness to cooperate even when they share common interests. Realist theory also argues that international institutions are unable to mitigate anarchy's constraining effects on interstate cooperation. Realism, then, presents a pessimistic analysis of the prospects for international cooperation and of the capabilities of international institutions.[2]

The major challenger to realism has been what I shall call liberal institutionalism. Prior to the current decade, it appeared in three successive presentations—functionalist integration theory in the 1940s and early 1950s, neofunctionalist regional integration theory in the 1950s and 1960s, and interdependence theory in the 1970s.[3] All three versions rejected realism's propositions about states and its gloomy understanding of world politics. Most significantly, they argued that international institutions can help states cooperate. Thus, compared to realism, these earlier versions of liberal institutionalism offered a more hopeful prognosis for international cooperation and a more optimistic assessment of the capacity of institutions to help states achieve it.

International tensions and conflicts during the 1970s undermined liberal institutionalism and reconfirmed realism in large measure. Yet that difficult decade did not witness a collapse of the international system, and in the light of continuing modest levels of interstate cooperation, a new liberal institutionalist challenge to realism came forward during the early 1980s (Stein 1983:115–40; Axelrod 1984; Keohane 1984; Lipson 1984; Axelrod and Keohane 1985). What is distinctive about this newest liberal institutionalism is its claim that it accepts a number of core realist propositions, including, apparently, the realist argument that anarchy impedes the achievement of international cooperation. However, the core liberal arguments—that realism overemphasizes conflict and underestimates the capacities of international institutions to promote cooperation—remain firmly intact. The new liberal institutionalists basically argue that even if the realists are correct in believing that anarchy constrains the willingness of states to cooperate, states nevertheless can work together and can do so especially with the assistance of international institutions.

This point is crucial for students of international relations. If neoliberal institutionalists are correct, then they have dealt realism a major blow while providing the intellectual justification for treating their own approach, and the tradition from which it emerges, as the most effective for understanding world politics.

This essay's principal argument is that, in fact, neoliberal institutionalism misconstrues the realist analysis of international anarchy and therefore it misunderstands the realist analysis of the impact of anarchy on the preferences and actions of states. Indeed, the new liberal institutionalism fails to address a major constraint on the willingness of states to cooperate which is generated by international anarchy and which is identified by realism. As a result, the new theory's optimism about international cooperation is likely to be proven wrong.

Neoliberalism's claims about cooperation are based on its belief that states are atomistic actors. It argues that states seek to maximize their individual *absolute* gains and are indifferent to the gains achieved by others. Cheating, the new theory suggests, is the greatest impediment to cooperation among rationally egoistic states, but international institutions, the new theory also suggests, can help states overcome this barrier to joint action. Realists understand that states seek absolute gains and worry about compliance. However, realists find that states are *positional*, not atomistic, in character, and therefore realists argue that, in addition to concerns about cheating, states in cooperative arrangements also worry that their partners might gain more from cooperation that they do. For realists, a state will focus both on its absolute and relative gains from cooperation, and a state that is satisfied with a partner's compliance in a joint arrangement might nevertheless exit from it because the partner is achieving relatively greater gains. Realism, then, finds that there are at least two major barriers to international cooperation: state concerns about cheating and state concerns about relative achievements of gains. Neoliberal institutionalism pays attention exclusively to the former and is unable to identify, analyze, or account for the latter.

Realism's identification of the relative gains problem for cooperation is based on its insight that states in anarchy fear for their survival as independent actors. According to realists, states worry that today's friend may be tomorrow's enemy in war, and fear that achievements of joint gains that advantage a friend in the present might produce a more dangerous *potential* foe in the future. As a result, states must give serious attention to the gains of partners. Neoliberals fail to consider the threat of war arising from international anarchy, and this allows them to ignore the matter of relative gains and to assume that states only desire absolute gains. Yet in doing so, they fail to identify a major source of state inhibitions about international cooperation.

In sum, I suggest that realism, its emphasis on conflict and competition notwithstanding, offers a more complete understanding of the problem of international cooperation than does its latest liberal challenger. If that is true, then realism is still the most powerful theory of international politics.

REALISM AND LIBERAL INSTITUTIONALISM

Realism encompasses five propositions. First, states are the major actors in world affairs (Morgenthau 1973:10; Waltz 1979:95). Second, the international environment severely penalizes states if they fail to protect their vital interests or if they pursue objectives beyond their means; hence, states are "sensitive to costs" and behave as unitary-rational agents (Waltz 1986:331). Third, international anarchy is the principal force shaping the motives and actions of states (Waltz

1959:224–38; 1979:79–128; Hoffmann 1965:27, 54–87, 129; Aron 1973a:6–10). Fourth, states in anarchy are preoccupied with power and security, are predisposed toward conflict and competition, and often fail to cooperate even in the face of common interests (Aron 1966:5; Gilpin 1986:304). Finally, international institutions affect the prospects for cooperation only marginally (Waltz 1979:115–16; Morgenthau 1973:512; Hoffmann 1973b:50).

Liberal institutionalists sought to refute this realist understanding of world politics.[4] First, they rejected realism's proposition about the centrality of states.[5] For functionalists, the key new actors in world politics appeared to be specialized international agencies and their technical experts; for neofunctionalists, they were labor unions, political parties, trade associations, and supranational bureaucracies; and for the interdependence school, they were multinational corporations and transnational and transgovernmental coalitions (Haas 1958:16–31, 113–239, 283–340; 1964:32–40; Mitrany 1966:17, 85–87, 133–34; Nye 1971:195–206; Keohane and Nye 1972:ix–xxix, 371–98). Second, liberal institutionalists attacked the realist view that states are unitary or rational agents.[6] Authority was already decentralized within modern states, functionalists argued, and it was undergoing a similar process internationally (Mitrany 1966:54–55, 63, 69–73, 88, 134–38). Modern states, according to interdependence theorists, were increasingly characterized by "multiple channels of access," which, in turn, progressively enfeebled the grip on foreign policy previously held by central decision makers (Mitrany 1966:20, 32–38; Haas 1968:152, 155–56; Morse 1970:387–89; Cooper 1972:177, 179; Keohane and Nye 1972:xxv, 375–78, 1977:33–35, 226–29).

Third, liberals argued that states were becoming less concerned about power and security. Internationally, nuclear weapons and mobilized national populations were rendering war prohibitively costly (Mitrany 1966:13; Morse 1970:380–81; Keohane and Nye 1977:27–29, 228). Moreover, increases in internation economic contacts left states increasingly dependent upon one another for the attainment of such national goals as growth, full employment, and price stability (Mitrany 1966:131–37; Haas 1968:161–62; Cooper 1972:161–68, 173–74; Keohane and Nye 1977:26, 228). Domestically, industrialization had created the present "social century": the advanced democracies (and, more slowly, socialist and developing countries) were becoming welfare states less oriented toward power and prestige and more toward economic growth and social security (Mitrany 1966:41–42, 95–96, 136–37, 144–45; Haas 1968:155–58; Morse 1970:383–85; Keohane and Nye 1977:227). Thus liberals rejected realism's fourth proposition that states are fundamentally disinclined to cooperate, finding instead that states increasingly viewed one another not as enemies but instead as partners needed to secure greater comfort and well-being for their home publics.[7]

Finally, liberal institutionalists rejected realism's pessimism about international institutions. For functionalist theory, specialized agencies like the International Labor Organization could promote cooperation because they performed valuable tasks without frontally challenging state sovereignty (Mitrany 1966:133–37, 198–211; Haas 1968). For neofunctionalist theory, supranational bodies like the European Economic Community were "the appropriate regional counterpart to the national state which no longer feels capable of realizing welfare goals within its own narrow borders" (Haas 1968:159). Finally, interdependence theory suggested that "in a world of multiple issues imperfectly linked, in which coalitions are formed transnationally and transgovernmentally, the potential role of international institutions in political bargaining is greatly increased" (Keohane and Nye 1977:35; see also 36, 232–34, 240–42. For an example, see 1977:186).

Postwar events, and especially those of the 1970s, appeared to support realist theory and to invalidate liberal institutionalism. States remained autonomous in setting foreign policy goals; they retained the loyalty of government officials active in "transgovernmental networks"; and they recast the terms of their relationships with such seemingly powerful transnational actors as high-technology multinational corporations (Russell 1973; Krasner 1978; Grieco 1984). Industrialized states varied in their economic performance during the 1970s in the face of similar challenges (oil shortages, recession, and inflation). Scholars linked these differences in performance to divergences, and not convergence, in their domestic political-economic structures (Zysman 1977, 1983; Katzenstein 1978, 1985; Gourevitch 1986:181–217). A number of events during the 1970s and early 1980s also demonstrated that the use of force continued to be a pervasive future of world politics: increases in East-West tensions and the continuation of the Soviet-American arms competition; direct and indirect military intervention and counterintervention by the superpowers in Africa, Central America, and Southwest Asia; and the Yom

Kippur and Iran-Iraq wars.[8] International institutions appeared to be unable to reshape state interests; instead they were often embroiled in and paralyzed by East-West and North-South disputes.[9] Finally, supranationalism in West Europe was replaced by old-fashioned intergovernmental bargaining, and the advanced democracies frequently experienced serious trade and monetary conflicts and sharp discord over economic relations with the Soviet Union.[10]

And yet, international cooperation did not collapse during the 1970s as it had during the 1930s (Krasner 1983:viii). In finance, private banks and governments in developed countries worked with the International Monetary Fund to contain the international debt crisis (Lipson 1985; Kahler 1986). In trade, the advanced states completed the Tokyo Round negotiations under the GATT (Finlayson and Zacher 1983:273–314; Lipson 1983:233–72; Winham 1986). In energy, the advanced states failed to coordinate responses to the oil crises of 1973–74 and 1979, but cooperated effectively—through the International Energy Agency—following the outbreak of the Iran-Iraq war in 1980 (Badger and Belgrave 1982; Lieber 1983; Keohane 1984:217–40). Finally, in high technology, the European states initiated and pursued during the 1970s a host of joint projects such as Airbus Industrie, the ARIANE rocket program, and the ESPRIT information technology effort (McDougall 1985; Smith 1986). Governments had not transformed their foreign policies, and world politics were not in transition, but *states* achieved cooperation through *international institutions* even in the harsh 1970s. This set the stage for a renewed, albeit truncated, liberal challenge to realism in the 1980s.

THE NEW LIBERAL INSTITUTIONALISM

In contrast to earlier presentations of liberal institutionalism, the newest liberalism accepts realist arguments that states are the major actors in world affairs and are unitary-rational agents. It also claims to accept realism's emphasis on anarchy to explain state motives and actions. Robert Axelrod, for example, seeks to address this question: "Under what conditions will cooperation emerge in a world of egoists without central authority?" (1984:3; see also 4, 6). Similarly, Axelrod and Robert Keohane observe of world politics that "there is no common government to enforce rules, and by the standards of domestic society, international institutions are weak."[11]

Yet neoliberals argue that realism is wrong to discount the possibilities for international cooperation and the capacities of international institutions. Neoliberals claim that, contrary to realism and in accordance with traditional liberal views, institutions can help states work together.[12] Thus, neoliberals argue, the prospects for international cooperation are better than realism allows.[13] These points of convergence and divergence among the three perspectives are summarized in table 5.1.

Neoliberals begin with assertions of acceptance of several key realist propositions; however, they end with a rejection of realism and with claims of affirmation of the central tenets of the liberal institutionalist tradition. To develop this argument, neoliberals first observe that states in anarchy often face mixed interests and, in particular, situations that can be depicted by Prisoner's Dilemma (see Axelrod 1984:7; Keohane 1984:66–69; Axelrod and Keohane 1985:231; Lipson 1984:2; Stein 1983:120–24). In the game, each state prefers mutual cooperation to mutual noncooperation (CC > DD), but also successful cheating to mutual cooperation (DC > CC) and mutual defection to victimization by another's cheating (DD > CD); overall, then, DC > CC > DD > CD. In these circumstances, and in the absence of a centralized authority or some other countervailing force to bind states to their promises, each defects regardless of what it expects the other to do.

However, neoliberals stress that countervailing forces often do exist—forces that cause states to keep their promises and thus to resolve the Prisoner's Dilemma (PD). They argue that states may pursue a strategy of TIT-for-TAT and cooperate on a conditional basis —that is, each adheres to its promises so long as partners do so. They also suggest that conditional cooperation is more likely to occur in PD if the game is highly iterated, since states that interact repeatedly in either a mutually beneficial or harmful manner are likely to find that mutual cooperation is their best long-term strategy. Finally, conditional cooperation is more attractive to states if the costs of verifying one another's compliance, and of sanctioning cheaters, are low compared to the benefits of joint action. Thus conditional cooperation among states may evolve in the face of international anarchy and mixed interests through strategies of reciprocity, extended time horizons, and reduced verification and sanctioning costs.

Neoliberals find that one way states manage verification and sanc-

TABLE 5.1

Liberal Institutionalism, Neoliberal Institutionalism, and Realism: Summary of Major Propositions

Proposition	Liberal Institutionalism	Neoliberal Institutionalism	Realism
States are the only major actors in world politics	No; other actors include: —specialized international agencies —supranational authorities —interest groups —transgovernmental policy networks —transnational actors (MNCs, etc.)	Yes (but international institutions play a major role)	Yes
States are unitary–rational actors	No; state is fragmented	Yes	Yes
Anarchy is a major shaping force for state preferences and actions	No; forces such as technology, knowledge, welfare-orientation of domestic interests are also salient	Yes (apparently)	Yes
International institutions are an independent force facilitating cooperation	Yes	Yes	No
Optimistic/pessimistic about prospects for cooperation	Optimistic	Optimistic	Pessimistic

tioning problems is to restrict the number of partners in a cooperative arrangement (Keohane 1984:77; Axelrod and Keohane 1985:234–38; for a demonstration, see Lipson 1985). However, neoliberals place much greater emphasis on a second factor—international institutions. In particular, neoliberals argue that institutions reduce verification costs, create iterativeness, and make it easier to punish cheaters. As Keohane suggests, "In general, regimes make it more sensible to cooperate by lowering the likelihood of being double-crossed" (1984:97). Similarly, Keohane and Axelrod assert that "international regimes do not substitute for reciprocity; rather, they reinforce and institutionalize it. Regimes incorporating the norm of reciprocity delegitimize defection and thereby make it more costly" (Axelrod and Keohane 1985:250). In addition, finding that "coordination conventions" are often an element of conditional cooperation in PD, Charles Lipson suggests that "in international relations, such conventions, which are typically grounded in ongoing reciprocal exchange, range from international law to regime rules" (1984:6). Finally, Arthur Stein argues that, just as societies "create" states to resolve collective action problems among individuals, so too "regimes in the international arena are also created to deal with the collective suboptimality that can emerge from individual [state] behavior" (1983:123). Hegemonic power may be necessary to establish cooperation among states, neoliberals argue, but it may endure after hegemony with the aid of institutions. As Keohane concludes, "When we think about cooperation after hegemony, we need to think about institutions" (1984:246).

REALISM AND THE FAILURE OF THE NEW LIBERAL INSTITUTIONALISM

The new liberals assert that they can accept key realist views about states and anarchy and still sustain classic liberal arguments about institutions and international cooperation. Yet in fact, realist and neoliberal perspectives on states and anarchy differ profoundly, and the former provides a more complete understanding of the problem of cooperation than the latter.

Neoliberals assume that states have only one goal in mixed-interest interactions: to achieve the greatest possible individual gain. For example, Axelrod suggests that the key issue in selecting a "best strategy" in PD—offered by neoliberals as a powerful model of the problem of state cooperation in the face of anarchy and mixed inter-ests—is to determine "what strategy will yield a player the highest possible score."[14] Similarly, Lipson observes that cheating is attrac-tive in a single play of PD because each player believes that defecting "can maximize his own reward," and, in turning to iterated plays, Lipson retains the assumption that players seek to maximize individ-ual payoffs over the long run (1984:2, 5). Indeed reliance upon con-ventional PD to depict international relationships and upon iteration to solve the dilemma unambiguously requires neoliberalism to ad-here to an individualistic payoff maximization assumption, for a player responds to an iterated conventional PD with conditional cooperation *solely out of a desire to maximize its individual long-term total payoffs.*

Moreover, neoliberal institutionalists assume that states define their interests in strictly individualistic terms. Axelrod, for example, indicates that his objective is to show how actors "who pursue their own interests" may nevertheless work together (1984:9). He also notes that PD is useful to study states in anarchy because it is as-sumed in the game that "the object is to do as well as possible, regardless of how well the other player does" (22). Similarly, Lipson suggests that PD "clearly parallels the Realist conception of sovereign states in world politics" because each player in the game "is assumed to be a self-interested, self-reliant maximizer of his own utility" (1984:2).

Finally, Keohane bases his analysis of international cooperation on the assumption that states are basically atomistic actors. He suggests that states in an anarchical context are, as microeconomic theory assumes with respect to business firms, "rational egoists." Rational-ity means that states possess "consistent, ordered preferences, and . . . calculate costs and benefits of alternative courses of action in order to maximize their utility in view of these preferences." In turn, he defines utility maximization atomistically; egoism, according to Keohane, "means that their [i.e., state] utility functions are indepen-dent of one another: they do not gain or lose utility simply because of the gains or losses of others" (1984:27).

Neoliberalism finds that states attain greater utility—that is, a higher level of satisfaction—as they achieve higher individual pay-offs. Also, in keeping with the concept of rational egoism, a utility function specified by the new theory for one state would not be "linked" to the utility functions of others. Hence, if a state enjoys utility (U) in direct proportion to its payoff (V), then the neoliberal institutionalist specification of that state's utility function would be $U = V.$[15]

Overall, "rational egoist" states care only about their own gains. They do not care whether partners achieve or do not achieve gains, or whether those gains are large or small, or whether such gains are greater or less than the gains they themselves achieve. The major constraint on the cooperation in mixed-interest international situations is the problem of cheating.

And yet realist theory rejects neoliberalism's exclusive focus on cheating. Differences in the realist and neoliberal understanding of the problem of cooperation result from a fundamental divergence in their interpretations of the basic meaning of international anarchy. Neoliberal institutionalism offers a well-established definition of anarchy, specifying that it means "the lack of common government in world politics" (Axelrod and Keohane 1985:226; see also Stein 1983:116; Axelrod 1984:3–4; Keohane 1984:7; Lipson 1984:1–2). Neoliberalism then proceeds to identify one major effect of international anarchy. Because of anarchy, according to neoliberals, individuals or states believe that no agency is available to "enforce rules," or to "enact or enforce rules of behavior," or to "force them to cooperate with each other" (Axelrod and Keohane 1985:226; Keohane 1984:7; Axelrod 1984:6). As a result, according to neoliberal theory, "cheating and deception are endemic" in international relations.[16] Anarchy, then, means that states may wish to cooperate, but, aware that cheating is both possible and profitable, *lack a central agency to enforce promises.* Given this understanding of anarchy, neoliberal institutional theory correctly identifies the problem of cheating and then proceeds to investigate how institutions can ameliorate that particular problem.

For realists, as for neoliberals, international anarchy means the absence of a common interstate government. Yet according to realists, states do not believe that the lack of a common government only means that no agency can reliably enforce promises. Instead, realists stress, states recognize that, in anarchy, *there is no overarching authority to prevent others from using violence, or the threat of violence, to destroy or enslave them.* As Kenneth Waltz suggests, in anarchy wars can occur "because there is nothing to prevent them," and therefore "in international politics force serves, not only as the *ultima ratio*, but indeed as the first and constant one."[17] Thus some states may sometimes be driven by greed or ambition, but anarchy and the danger of war cause all states always to be motivated in some measure by fear and distrust (Gilpin 1986:304–5).

Given its understanding of anarchy, realism argues that individual well-being is not the key interest of states; instead it finds that *survival* is their core interest. Raymond Aron, for example, suggested that "politics, insofar as it concerns relations among states, seems to signify—in both ideal and objective terms—simply the survival of states confronting the potential threat created by the existence of other states" (1973a:7, 64–65). Similarly, Robert Gilpin observes that individuals and groups may seek truth, beauty, and justice, but he emphasizes that "all these more noble goals will be lost unless one makes provision for one's security in the power struggle among groups."[18]

Driven by an interest in survival, states are acutely sensitive to any erosion of their relative capabilities, which are the ultimate basis for their security and independence in an anarchical, self-help international context. Thus realists find that the major goal of states in any relationship is not to attain the highest possible individual gain or payoff. Instead *the fundamental goal of states in any relationship is to prevent others from achieving advances in their relative capabilities*. For example, E. H. Carr suggested that "the most serious wars are fought in order to make one's own country militarily stronger, or, *more often*, to prevent another from becoming militarily stronger" (1964:111; emphasis added). Along the same lines, Gilpin finds that the international system "stimulates, and may compel, a state to increase its power; at the least, it necessitates that the prudent state prevent relative increases in the power of competitor states" (1981:87–88). Indeed states may even forgo increases in their absolute capabilities if doing so prevents others from achieving even greater gains. This is because, as Waltz suggests, "The first concern of states is not to maximize power but to maintain their position in the system" (1979:126; see also Waltz 1986:334).

States seek to prevent increases in others' relative capabilities. As a result, states always assess their performance in any relationship in terms of the performance of others.[19] Thus I suggest that states are positional, not atomistic, in character. Most significantly, *state posi-*

tionality may constrain the willingness of states to cooperate. States fear that their partners will achieve relatively greater gains; that, as a result, the partners will surge ahead of them in relative capabilities; and, finally, that their increasingly powerful partners in the present could become all the more formidable foes at some point in the future.[20]

State positionality, then, engenders a "relative gains problem" for cooperation. That is, a state will decline to join, will leave, or will sharply limit its commitment to a cooperative arrangement if it believes that partners are achieving, or are likely to achieve, relatively greater gains. It will eschew cooperation even though participation in the arrangement was providing it, or would have provided it, with large absolute gains. Moreover, a state concerned about relative gains may decline to cooperate even if it is confident that partners will keep their commitments to a joint arrangement. Indeed if a state believed that a proposed arrangement would provide all parties absolute gains, but would also generate gains favoring partners, then greater certainty that partners would adhere to the terms of the arrangement would only accentuate its relative gains concerns. Thus a state worried about relative gains might respond to greater certainty that partners would keep their promises with a lower, rather than higher, willingness to cooperate.

I must stress that realists do not argue that positionality causes all states to possess an offensively oriented desire to maximize the difference in gains arising from cooperation to their own advantage. They do not, in other words, attribute to states what Stein correctly calls a mercantilist definition of self-interest (1983:134). Instead realists argue that states are more likely to concentrate on the danger that relative gains may advantage partners and thus may foster the emergence of a more powerful potential adversary.[21] Realism, then, finds that states are positional, but it also finds that state positionality is more defensive than offensive in nature.

In addition, realists find that defensive state positionality and the relative gains problems for cooperation essentially reflect the persistence of uncertainty in international relations. States are uncertain about one another's future *intentions*; thus they pay close attention to how cooperation might affect relative *capabilities* in the future.[22] This uncertainty results from the inability of states to predict or readily to control the future leadership or interests of partners. As Robert Jervis notes, "Minds can be changed, new leaders can come to power, values can shift, new opportunities and dangers can arise" (1978:168).

Thus realism expects a state's utility function to incorporate *two distinct terms*. It needs to include the state's individual payoff, V, reflecting the realist view that states are motivated by absolute gains. Yet it must also include a term integrating both the state's individual payoff and the partner's payoff, W, in such a way that gaps favoring the state add to its utility while, more importantly, gaps favoring the partner detract from it. One function that depicts this realist understanding of state utility is $U = V - k (W - V)$, with k representing the state's coefficient of sensitivity to gaps in payoffs either to its advantage or disadvantage.[23]

This realist specification of state utility can be contrasted with that inferred from neoliberal theory, namely $U = V$. In both cases, the state obtains utility from the receipt of absolute payoffs. However, while neoliberal institutional theory assumes that state utility functions are independent of one another and that states are indifferent to the payoffs of others, realist theory argues that state utility functions are at least partially interdependent and that one state's utility can affect another's.[24] We may also observe that this realist-specified function does not suggest that any payoff achieved by a partner detracts from the state's utility. Rather *only gaps in payoffs to the advantage of a partner do so*.

The coefficient for a state's sensitivity to gaps in payoffs—k—will vary, but it will always be greater than zero. In general, k will increase as a state transits from relationships in what Karl Deutsch termed a "pluralistic security community" to those approximating a state of war.[25] The level of k will be greater if a state's partner is a long-term adversary rather than a long-term ally; if the issue involves security rather than economic well-being; if the state's relative power has been on the decline rather than on the rise; if payoffs in the particular issue area are more rather than less easily converted into capabilities within that issue area; or if these capabilities and the influence associated with them are more rather than less readily transferred to other issue areas.[26] Yet given the uncertainties of international politics, a state's level of k will be greater than zero even in interactions with allies, for gaps in payoffs favoring partners will always detract from a state's utility to some degree.[27]

Faced with both problems—cheating and relative gains—states

seek to ensure that partners in common endeavors comply with their promises and that their collaboration produces "balanced" or "equitable" achievements of gains. According to realists, states define balance and equity as distributions of gains that roughly maintain precooperation balances of capabilities. To attain this balanced relative achievement of gains, according to Hans Morgenthau, states offer their partners "concessions"; in exchange, they expect to receive approximately equal "compensations." As an example of this balancing tendency, Morgenthau offers the particular case of "cooperation" among Prussia, Austria, and Russia in their partitions of Poland in 1772, 1793, and 1795. He indicates that in each case, "The three nations agreed to divide Polish territory in such a way that the distribution of power among themselves would be approximately the same after the partitions as it had been before" (1973:179). For Morgenthau, state balancing of joint gains is a universal characteristic of the diplomacy of cooperation. He attributes this to the firmly grounded practice of states to balance power, and argues that "given such a system, no nation will agree to concede political advantages to another nation without the expectation, which may or may not be well founded, of receiving *proportionate* advantages in return" (1973:180; emphasis added).

In sum, neoliberals find that anarchy impedes cooperation through its generation of uncertainty in states about the compliance of partners. For neoliberals, the outcome a state most fears in mixed-interest situations is to be cheated. Yet successful unilateral cheating is highly unlikely, and the more probable neoliberal "worst case" is for all states to defect and find themselves less well off than if they had all cooperated. For neoliberal institutionalists, then, anarchy and mixed interests often cause states to suffer the opportunity costs of not achieving an outcome that is mutually more beneficial. Keohane and Axelrod argue that games like Prisoner's Dilemma, Stag Hunt, Chicken, and Deadlock illustrate how many international relationships offer both the danger that "the myopic pursuit of self-interest can be disastrous" and the prospect that "both sides can potentially benefit from cooperation—if they can only achieve it" (Axelrod and Keohane 1985:231; see also Stein 1983:123–24).

Realists identify even greater uncertainties for states considering cooperation: which among them could achieve the greatest gains, and would imbalanced achievements of gains affect relative capabilities? In addition, a state that knows it will not be cheated still confronts another risk that is at least as formidable: perhaps a partner will achieve disproportionate gains and, thus strengthened, might someday be a more dangerous enemy than if they had never worked together. For neoliberal theory, the problem of cooperation in anarchy is that states may fail to achieve it; in the final analysis, the worst possible outcome is a lost opportunity. For realist theory, state efforts to cooperate entail these dangers plus the much greater risk, for some states, that cooperation might someday result in lost independence or security.

Realism and neoliberal institutionalism offer markedly different views concerning the effects of international anarchy on states. These differences are summarized in table 5.2. Compared to realist theory, neoliberal institutionalism understates the range of uncertainties and risks states believe they must overcome to cooperate with others. Hence, realism provides a more comprehensive theory of the problem of cooperation than does neoliberal institutionalism.

CONCLUSION

Neoliberal institutionalism is not based on realist theory; in fact, realism specifies a wider range of systemic-level constraints on cooperation than does neoliberalism. Thus the next scholarly task is to conduct empirical tests of the two approaches. It is widely accepted —even by neoliberals—that realism has great explanatory power in national security affairs. However, international political economy would appear to be neoliberalism's preserve. Indeed economic relationships among the advanced democracies would provide opportunities to design "crucial experiments" for the two theories.[28] That is, they would provide the opportunity to observe behavior confirming realist expectations in circumstances least likely to have generated such observations unless realism is truly potent, while at the same time they might disconfirm neoliberal claims in circumstances most likely to have produced observations validating neoliberal theory.[29]

According to neoliberal theory, two factors enhance prospects for the achievement and maintenance of political-economic cooperation among the advanced democracies. First, these states have the broadest range of common political, military, and economic interests (Keohane 1984:6–7). Thus they have the greatest hopes for large absolute gains through joint action. This should work against realism and its specification of the relative gains problem for cooperation. That is, states that have many common interests should have the fewest worries that they might become embroiled in extreme conflicts in the future and, as a result, they should have the fewest concerns about

TABLE 5.2

Anarchy, State Properties, and State Inhibitions About Cooperation: Summary of Neoliberal and Realist Views

Basis of Comparison	Neoliberal Institutionalism	Political Realism
Meaning of anarchy	No central agency is available to enforce promises	No central agency is available to enforce promises *or* to provide protection
State properties		
Core interest	To advance in utility defined individualistically	To enhance prospects for survival
Main goal	To achieve greatest possible absolute gains	To achieve greatest gains *and* smallest gap in gains favoring partners
Basic character	Atomistic ("rational egoist")	Defensively positional
Utility function	Independent: $U = V$	Partially interdependent: $U = V - k(W - V)$
State inhibitions concerning cooperation		
Range of uncertainties associated with cooperation	Partners' compliance	Compliance *and* relative achievement of gains *and* uses to which gaps favoring partners may be employed
Range of risks associated with cooperation	To be cheated and to receive a low payoff	To be cheated *or* to experience decline in relative power if others achieve greater gains
Barriers to cooperation	State concerns about partners' compliance	State concerns about partners' compliance *and* partners' relative gains

relative achievements of gains arising from their common endeavors. Neoliberal theory emphasizes another background condition: the economic arrangements of advanced democracies are "nested" in larger political-strategic alliances. Nesting, according to the theory, accentuates iterativeness and so promotes compliance (Keohane 1984:90–91; Aggarwal 1985). This condition should also place realist theory at a disadvantage. If states are allies, they should be unconcerned that possible gaps in economic gains might advantage partners. Indeed, they should take comfort in the latter's success, for in attaining greater economic gains these partners become stronger military allies.

We can identify a number of efforts by advanced democracies to cooperate in economic issue areas that were characterized by high common interests and nesting. In the trade field, such efforts would include the Tokyo Round codes on nontariff barriers and efforts by the Nordic states to construct regional free-trade arrangements. In the monetary field, there are the experiences of the European Community with exchange-rate coordination—the Economic and Monetary Union and the European Monetary System. Finally, in the field of high technology, one might examine European collaboration in commercial aviation (Airbus Industrie) or data processing (the Unidata computer consortium).[30] If these cooperative arrangements varied in terms of their success (and indeed such variance can be observed), and the less successful or failed arrangements were characterized not by a higher incidence of cheating but by a greater severity of relative gains problems, then one could conclude that realist theory explains variation in the success or failure of international cooperation more effectively than neoliberal institutional theory. Moreover, one could have great confidence in this assessment, for it would be based on cases that were most hospitable to neoliberalism and most hostile to realism.

However, additional tests of the two theories can and should be undertaken. For example, one might investigate realist and neoliberal expectations as to the *durability* of arrangements states prefer when they engage in joint action. Neoliberal theory argues that cheating is less likely to occur in a mixed-interest situation that is iterated; hence, it suggests that "the most direct way to encourage cooperation is to make the relationship more durable."[31] If, then, two states that are interested in cooperation could choose between two institutional arrangements that offered comparable absolute gains but that differed in their expected durability—one arrangement might, for example, have higher exit costs than the other—neoliberalism would expect the states to prefer the former over the latter, for each state could then be more confident that the other would remain in the arrangement. Realism generates a markedly different hypothesis. If two states are worried or uncertain about relative achievements of gains, then each will prefer a less durable cooperative arrangement, for each would want to be more readily able to exit from the arrangement if gaps in gains did come to favor the other.

A second pair of competing hypotheses concerns the *number of partners* states prefer to include in a cooperative arrangement. Advocates of neoliberalism find that a small number of participants facilitates verification of compliance and sanctioning of cheaters. Hence, they would predict that states with a choice would tend to prefer a smaller number of partners. Realism would offer a very different hypothesis. A state may believe that it might do better than some partners in a proposed arrangement but not as well as others. If it is uncertain about which partners would do relatively better, the state will prefer more partners, for larger numbers would enhance the likelihood that the relative achievements of gains advantaging (what turn out to be) better-positioned partners could be offset by more favorable sharings arising from interactions with (as matters develop) weaker partners.

A third pair of competing empirical statements concerns the effects of *issue-linkages* on cooperation. Neoliberalism's proponents find that tightly knit linkages within and across issue areas accentuate iterativeness and thus facilitate cooperation (Keohane 1984:91–92, 103–6; Axelrod and Keohane 1985:239–43). Realism, again, offers a very different proposition. Assume that a state believes that two issue areas are linked, and that it believes that one element of this linkage is that changes in relative capabilities in one domain affect relative capabilities in the other. Assume also that the state believes that relative achievements of jointly produced gains in one issue area would advantage the partner. This state would then believe that cooperation would provide additional capabilities to the partner not only in the domain in which joint action is undertaken but also in the linked issue area. Cooperation would therefore be unattractive to this state in direct proportion to its belief that the two issue areas were interrelated. Thus issue-linkages may impede rather than facilitate cooperation.

These tests are likely to demonstrate that realism offers the most effective understanding of the problem of international cooperation.[32] In addition, further analysis of defensive state positionality may help pinpoint policy strategies that facilitate cooperation. If relative gains concerns do act as a constraint on cooperation, then we should identify methods by which states have been able to address such concerns through unilateral bargaining strategies or through the mechanisms and operations of international institutions. For example, we might investigate states' use of side-payments to mitigate the relative gains concerns of disadvantaged partners.[33] Thus, with its understanding of defensive state positionality and the relative gains problem for collaboration, realism may provide guidance to states as they seek security, independence, and mutually beneficial forms of international cooperation.

NOTES

1. Major realist works include: E. H. Carr (1964), Hans J. Morgenthau (1973), Raymond Aron (1966), Kenneth N. Waltz (1959; 1979), and Robert Gilpin (1975; 1981). This essay does not distinguish between realism and "neorealism," because on crucial issues—the meaning of international anarchy, its effects on states, and the problem of cooperation—modern realists like Waltz and Gilpin are very much in accord with classical realists like Carr, Aron, and Morgenthau. For an alternative view, see Richard Ashley (1986:255–300).

2. Richard Rosecrance provided the insight that realism presents an essentially pessimistic view of the human condition: this is noted by Robert Gilpin (1986:304). This pessimism in realist theory is most clearly evident in Hans J. Morgenthau (1946:187–203).

3. For functionalist international theory, see David Mitrany (1966); see also Ernst B. Haas (1964). On neofunctionalism, see Haas (1958; 1968:149–76); and Joseph S. Nye, Jr. (1971:192–231). On interdependence theory, see Edward S. Morse (1970); Richard C. Cooper (1972); and Robert O. Keohane and Joseph S. Nye, Jr. (1977).

4. Liberal institutionalist theories may be distinguished from three other variants of liberal theory. One of these, trade liberalism, articulated by Richard Cobden and John Bright, finds that international commerce facilitates greater interstate cooperation: for Cobden, see Arnold Wolfers and Laurence W. Martin (1956:192–205); with respect to both Cobden and Bright, see also Waltz (1959:98–99, 103–107). A second variant, democratic structural liberalism, posited by Immanuel Kant and Wood-

row Wilson, finds that democracies based on national self-determination
are conducive to greater international cooperation. For Wilson, see Wolfers and Martin (1956:263–79); for Kant and Wilson, see Waltz (1959:101–
103, 109–11, 117–19), and Michael W. Doyle (1986). Finally, a liberal
transactions approach suggests that private international interactions
promote international integration: see Karl Deutsch et al. (1957); and
Bruce Russett (1963). Citing an unpublished study by Keohane, Nye
refers to the first two variants as commercial and democratic liberalism,
respectively, and suggests that the third might be termed sociological
liberalism. See Joseph S. Nye, Jr. (1988:246).

5. In a way quite different from liberal institutionalist theories, world systems analysis also challenges realism's focus on states. It suggests that
they are not ultimate causes of world events but instead are themselves
resultants of the development of a single world capitalist economy. See
Immanuel Wallerstein (1979:1–37; and 1974).

6. A substantial body of literature that is not based on liberalism nevertheless shares the latter's skepticism about the unity and rationality of
states. It finds that subsystemic forces, such as organizational and bureaucratic politics, small group dynamics, crisis decision making, and
individual psychology, all undermine state coherence and rationality.
See Alexander L. George and Juliette L. George (1964); Ole R. Holsti
(1970); Graham T. Allison (1971); John D. Steinbruner (1974); Robert
Jervis (1976); and Irving J. Janis (1980).

7. Neofunctionalists suggested that, for West European states, "the argument is no longer over the slice of the pie to go to each; it is increasingly
over the means for increasing the overall size of the pastry" (Haas
1968:158; see also 1968:160–62, 166–67). See also Mitrany (1966:92–93);
Morse (1970:383–85); and Cooper (1972:164–67, 170–72, 179).

8. On the continuing utility of force in the nuclear age, see Alexander L.
George and Richard Smoke (1974); Barry M. Blechman and Stephen S.
Kaplan (1978); Stephen S. Kaplan (1981); and Richard Betts (1987).

9. East-West disputes in a specialized international agency are examined in
Walter Galenson (1981). North-South struggles within international institutions are discussed in Stephen D. Krasner (1985).

10. On the problem of European integration, see Donald J. Puchala, (1975)
and Paul Taylor (1983). Trends toward a "new protectionism" supported
realist arguments that the erosion of America's hegemonic position would
produce a less open international economy. See Gilpin (1975) and Stephen D. Krasner (1976). On trade conflicts during the 1970s, see John H.
Jackson (1978); Bela and Carol Balassa (1984); and Miles Kahler (1985).
On monetary disputes, see Susan Strange (1976:320–53) and Benjamin J.
Cohen (1979). On disputes over economic ties with the Soviet Union, see
Stephen Woolcock (1982) and Bruce W. Jentleson (1986).

11. Axelrod and Keohane (1985:226); Stein argues that his theory of international regimes "is rooted in the classic characterization of international
politics as relations between sovereign entities dedicated to their own
self-preservation, ultimately able to depend only upon themselves, and

prepared to resort to force" (1983:116). Lipson notes that Axelrod's ideas are important because they "obviously bear on a central issue in international relations theory: the emergence and maintenance of cooperation among sovereign, self-interested states, operating without any centralized authority" (1984:6).

12. Keohane notes (1984:9) that "I begin with Realist insights about the role of power and the effects of hegemony" but that "my central arguments draw more on the Institutionalist tradition, arguing that cooperation can under some conditions develop on the basis of complementary interests, and that institutions, broadly defined, affect the patterns of cooperation that emerge." Keohane also notes that "what distinguishes my argument from structural Realism is my emphasis on the effects of international institutions and practices on state behavior" (26).

13. Keohane (1984:14, 16) indicates that he does not seek the wholesale rejection of realism. However, on the issue of the prospects for cooperation, like the question of international institutions, he does seek to refute realism's conclusions while employing its assumptions. He notes that "starting with similar premises about motivations, I seek to show that Realism's pessimism about welfare-increasing cooperation is exaggerated" (29), and he proposes "to show, on the basis of their own assumptions, that the characteristic pessimism of Realism does not follow" (67). Keohane also suggests that rational-choice analysis "helps us criticize, in its own terms, Realism's bleak picture of the inevitability of either hegemony or conflict" (84). Finally, he asserts that rational-choice theory, "combined with sensitivity to the significance of international institutions," allows for an awareness of both the strengths and weaknesses of realism, and in so doing "we can strip away some of the aura of verisimilitude that surrounds Realism and reconsider the logical and empirical foundations of its claims to our intellectual allegiance" (84).

14. Axelrod (1984:6; see also 14). Stein acknowledges that he employs an absolute-gains assumption and that the latter "is very much a liberal, not mercantilist, view of self-interest; it suggests that actors focus on their own returns and compare different outcomes with an eye to maximizing their own gains" (1983:134). It is difficult to see how Stein can employ a "liberal" assumption of state interest and assert that his theory of regimes, as noted earlier in note 11, is based on the "classic [realist?] characterization" of international politics.

15. On payoffs and utility functions, see Anatol Rapoport (1960:121) and Michael Taylor (1976:70–74).

16. Axelrod and Keohane (1985:226). Similarly, Lipson notes that while institutionalized mechanisms (such as governments) that guarantee the enforcement of contracts are available in civil society, "the absence of reliable guarantees is an essential feature of international relations and a major obstacle to concluding treaties, contracts, and agreements"; the resulting problem, according to Lipson, is that "constraints on opportunism are weak"(1984:4). Also see Keohane (1984:93) and Stein (1983:116).

17. Waltz (1959:232; 1979:113). Similarly, Carr suggests that war "lurks in

the background of international politics just as revolution lurks in the background of domestic politics" (1964:109). Finally, Aron observes that international relations "present one original feature which distinguishes them from all other social relations: they take place within the shadow of war" (1973a:6).

18. Gilpin (1986:305). Similarly, Waltz indicates that "in anarchy, security is the highest end. Only if survival is assured can states safely seek such other goals as tranquility, profit, and power" (1979:126; also see Waltz 1979:91–92 and 1986:334).

19. On the tendency of states to compare performance levels, see Oran Young (1986:118). Young suggests that realists assume that states are "status maximizers" and attribute to states the tendency to compare performance levels because each seeks "to attain the highest possible rank in the hierarchy of members of the international community." The present writer offers a different understanding of realism: while realism acknowledges that *some* states may be positional in the sense noted by Young, its fundamental insight is that *all* states are positional and compare performance levels because they fear that *others* may attain a higher ranking in an issue area.

20. As Waltz suggests, "When faced with the possibility of cooperating for mutual gains, states that feel insecure must ask how the gain will be divided. They are compelled to ask not 'Will both of us gain?' but 'Who will gain more?' If an expected gain is to be divided, say, in the ratio of two to one, one state may use its disproportionate gain to implement a policy intended to damage or destroy the other" (1979:105).

21. In her review of Axelrod, Joanne Gowa cites the Waltz (1979) passage employed in note 20 and, following Taylor's terminology (1976:73–74), suggests that a state may display "negative altruism." Furthermore, according to Gowa, a state "may seek to maximize a utility function that depends both on increases in its own payoffs *and* on increases in the difference between its payoffs and those of another state" (1986:178). This portrays realist thinking in a manner similar to that suggested by Young and cited above in note 19. However, this understanding of state utility cannot be readily based on Waltz, for his core insight, and that of the realist tradition, is not that all states necessarily seek a balance of advantages in their favor (although some may do this) but rather that all fear that relative gains may favor and thus strengthen others. From a realist viewpoint, some states may be negative altruists, but *all* states will be "defensive positionalists." Waltz emphasizes that he does not believe that all states necessarily seek to maximize their power: see especially Waltz (1979:126; 1986:334).

22. Waltz, for example, observes that "the impediments to collaboration may not lie in the character and the immediate intention of either party. Instead, the condition of insecurity—at the least, the uncertainty of each about the other's future intentions and actions—works against their cooperation" (1979:105).

23. Similar to the concept of a state "sensitivity coefficient" to gaps in jointly produced gains is the concept of a "defense coefficient" in Lewis Richardson's model of arms races. The latter serves as an index of one state's fear of another: the greater the coefficient, the stronger the state's belief that it must match increases in the other's weapons inventory with increases in its own. See Richardson (1960:14–15).
24. Robert Jervis also argues that realist theory posits at least partially interdependent state utility functions. See Jervis (1988:334–36).
25. A pluralistic security community, according to Deutsch and his associates, "is one in which there is real assurance that the members of that community will not fight each other physically, but will settle their disputes in some other way," and in which the members retain separate governments; the examples they provide are Canada–United States and Norway-Sweden. See Deutsch et al. (1957:5–7).
26. Contextual influences on state sensitivities to gaps in gains are explored in Joseph M. Grieco (1988b:600–24).
27. In contrast, Keohane finds that relative gains concerns may impede cooperation only in cases in which states pursue "positional goods" such as "status" (1984:54). Similarly, Lipson expects that states will be sensitive to relative gains only in security relationships (1984:14–16).
28. A crucial experiment seeks real-world observations confirming one theory's empirical expectations in circumstances most unlikely to have done so unless the theory is very powerful, while simultaneously disconfirming a competitive theory's empirical expectations in circumstances most likely to have provided such confirming observations. On the methodology of crucial experiments, see Arthur L. Stinchcombe (1968:20–28) and Harry Eckstein (1975:118–20).
29. Such a crucial experiment would demonstrate realism's superiority over neoliberalism. On the other hand, if neoliberal theorists wanted to design a crucial experiment to demonstrate the superiority of their approach, they would focus not on North-North economic relations but rather on North-South relations or, better still, on East-West military interactions.
30. I am completing a study of the relative gains problem in the case of the Tokyo Round trade codes. Available studies suggest that the Economic and Monetary Union broke down during 1972–76 as a result of concerns by Britain, France, Ireland, and Italy that they had taken on disproportionate burdens and that West Germany was achieving disproportionate gains: see Loukas Tsoukalis (1977:157). Its successor, the European Monetary System, was designed to ensure greater balance in the gains and losses among partners: see Peter Coffey (1984:21–26, 126–27). In the case of Scandinavian trade cooperation, Norway shifted from opposition during the 1950s and much of the 1960s to support at the end of the latter decade as it became less concerned about its capacity to achieve a satisfactory share of trade gains with Sweden: see Barbara Haskel (1976:124–27). Much of the literature on the problem of regional integration among

developing countries also emphasizes the importance of relative gains issues. See, for example, Lynn K. Mytelka (1973); W. Andrew Axline (1977); and Constantine V. Vaitsos (1978). For case studies of the problem of relative gains in developing country regional efforts to cooperate, see Richard I. Fagan (1970); Arthur Hazelwood (1979:44–48, 53–54); and Lynn Krieger Mytelka (1979:39–61).

31. Axelrod (1984:129); also see Keohane (1984:257–59), in which he argues that there are "costs of flexibility" and that states commit themselves to regimes and thereby forgo a measure of flexibility in the future to attain cooperation in the present; and Axelrod and Keohane (1985:234), in which they argue that international regimes promote cooperation because they "link the future with the present."

32. This, however, would certainly not mark the end of the liberal institutionalist challenge to realism. There are at least two related clusters of modern literature that are firmly rooted in the liberal institutionalist tradition, that attempt no compromise with realism, and that present an understanding of world politics markedly at odds with realist theory. The first cluster argues that international institutions embody and reinforce norms and beliefs that are held in common among states and that facilitate and guide their cooperative endeavors. The key works in this cluster include John Gerard Ruggie (1975; 1982); Donald J. Puchala and Raymond F. Hopkins (1983:61–92); Friedrich Kratochwil (1984); and Friedrich Kratochwil and John Gerard Ruggie (1986).

    The second cluster suggests that international institutions help states develop, accept, and disseminate consensual theoretical and empirical knowledge that can reinforce or introduce international norms leading to cooperation. Haas presented this argument (1964:12–13, 47–48, 79–85; also see Haas 1975; 1980; 1983:23–59); Ernst B. Haas, Mary Pat Williams, and Don Babai (1977); and Beverly Crawford and Stefanie Lenway (1985).

33. On the general concept of side-payments, see R. Duncan Luce and Howard Raiffa (1957:168–69); and William H. Riker (1962:34, 108–23). Deutsch and his associates determined that the capacity of advantaged regions to extend symbolic and material side-payments to disadvantaged regions was essential to national integration and amalgamation in such cases as Switzerland and Germany (see Deutsch et al. 1957:55). Similarly, special subsidies were provided to Italy and Ireland to attract them to the European Monetary System; see George Zis (1984:58). In addition, Norway was attracted to the proposed Nordek arrangement during 1968–70 partly because Sweden offered to provide the bulk of the funds for a Nordic development bank that would be used in large measure to support Norwegian industrial projects; see Claes Wiklund (1970:322) and Haskel (1976:127). Finally, West Germany has sought to ameliorate U.S. concerns about relative burden-sharing in NATO through special "offset" programs aimed at reducing U.S. foreign exchange expenditures associated with its European commitment; see Gregory F. Treverton (1978).

III EXTENSIONS OF THE DEBATE

6

THE ASSUMPTION OF ANARCHY IN INTERNATIONAL RELATIONS THEORY: A CRITIQUE

Helen Milner

Anarchy is one of the most vague and ambiguous words in language.
—George Cornewall Lewis, 1832 (1970:226)

In much current theorizing, anarchy has once again been declared to be the fundamental assumption about international politics. Over the last decade, numerous scholars, especially those in the neorealist tradition, have posited anarchy as the single most important characteristic underlying international relations. This essay explores implications of such an assumption. In doing so, it reopens older debates about the nature of international politics. First, I examine various concepts of "anarchy" employed in the international relations literature. Second, I probe the sharp dichotomy between domestic and international politics that is associated with this assumption. As others have, I question the validity and utility of such a dichotomy. Finally, this article suggests that a more fruitful way to understand the international system is one that combines anarchy and interdependence.

Many of the points made in this essay have been made individually by other scholars, especially those in the early 1960s such as Inis Claude and James Rosenau. But today these points need to be reiterated, as recent theorizing focuses ever more on anarchy and divorces international politics and domestic ones. It is once again time for a reminder that anarchy is an ambiguous concept and that dangers exist when it is exaggeratedly seen as the central fact of world politics.

Critiques of the assumption that international politics is anarchic are not lacking. John Ruggie has argued against Kenneth Waltz's neorealist theory of the anarchic international system, claiming that it cannot explain change and that it must incorporate other variables —such as "dynamic density"—to do this (1983a:261–85). Richard Ashley has charged that Waltz's structural model based on anarchy loses sight of politics and of the original insights of the realists; he has also attacked Waltz's epistemology (1984). For Hayward Alker, the conception of international politics as anarchic presents a value-laden interpretation of the system (1986). Despite the criticisms made by these authors, all of them have assumed that anarchy is a well-understood concept. Their attacks have not focused on what international relations scholars mean when using the term. Moreover, while these authors have criticized the positivist epistemology used by neorealists, they have not challenged the claim that the anarchy assumption is fruitful within a positivist research design.

This essay addresses both of these points. It argues that the notion of anarchy is not so well understood as is commonly implied. It suggests that an emphasis on the assumption of anarchy can be misleading and may have heuristic disadvantages. Even within a positivist framework, this assumption may be degenerative, posing anomalies and inhibiting new insights by separating international politics too radically from other politics.[1] Clarification of this central concept in international relations is important since such a key term should not be used without knowing what is meant by it.

CONCEPTS OF ANARCHY

Anarchy has been accorded a central role in international politics, especially in recent theoretical writings. Robert Art and Robert Jervis, for instance, assert that "anarchy is the fundamental fact of international relations" (Art and Jervis 1986:7). For them, any understanding of international politics must flow from an understanding of this fact. Robert Gilpin defines the fundamental nature of international politics as "a recurring struggle for wealth and power among independent actors in a state of anarchy" (1981:7). For Kenneth Waltz, anarchy is the first element of structure in the international system

(1979:88). It is for him the structural feature from which all other consequences derive. Recent studies of international cooperation have also started from the assumption that the international system is anarchic. Robert Axelrod defines his central question as being "under what conditions will cooperation emerge in a world of egoists without central authority?" (1984:3). He believes anarchy is especially relevant to international politics since "today nations interact without central authority" (4). The condition of anarchy provides the baseline for his game-theoretic analysis. As he concludes: "Today, the most important problems facing humanity are in the area of international relations, where independent, egoistic nations face one another in a state of near anarchy. Many of the problems take the form of an iterated Prisoner's Dilemma" (190).

Other scholars have used this analogy between anarchy and the Prisoner's Dilemma (PD) as well. In *After Hegemony*, Robert Keohane begins his effort to explain international cooperation by assuming that anarchy is the fundamental fact about international politics. He describes the initial international environment as one peopled by egoistic, anomic states, pursuing their self-interests in a self-help system without any centralized authority. He shows that even in this environment, which resembles single-play PD, states can find cooperation to be in their narrow self-interest.[2]

This view of anarchy as the central condition of international politics is also apparent in the explanation of cooperation that emerges in editor Kenneth Oye's *Cooperation Under Anarchy*. As the title suggests, this volume's fundamental premise about international politics is that it is anarchic. Indeed the first sentence asserts that "Nations dwell in perpetual anarchy, for no central authority imposes limits on the pursuit of sovereign interests" (1986:1). Moreover, the authors view their central question as being "What circumstances favor the emergence of cooperation under anarchy?" and see the structure of the international system as resembling PD. Assuming anarchy to be primary, they then proceed to diagnose what factors make cooperation possible in such an environment. For all these authors then— although less so for Keohane—anarchy is taken to be the central background condition of international politics. All their analyses flow from this assumption. But what do these authors mean by anarchy?

Anarchy has at least two meanings. The first meaning that anarchy carries is a lack of order. It implies chaos or disorder. The *Oxford*

English Dictionary, for instance, lists political disorder as its primary definition. Such lack of order is often associated with the existence of a state of war. It is thus linked to the Hobbesian analogy of politics in the absence of a sovereign, which realists use as a model of international politics. As Hedley Bull describes the realist view,

> The Hobbesian tradition describes international relations as a state of war of all against all, an arena of struggle in which each state is pitted against every other. International relations, on the Hobbesian view, represent pure conflict between states and resemble a game that is wholly distributive or zero-sum. . . . The particular international activity that, on the Hobbesian view, is most typical of international activity as a whole . . . is war itself. (1977:24–25)

In this view then, the international system is a chaotic arena of war of all against all.

But are chaos, lack of order, and constant threat really what scholars mean by the anarchic nature of the system? It does not seem to be. Persistent elements of order in international politics have been noted by many. International order, defined in a strong sense as "a pattern of activity that sustains the elementary or primary goals of a society of states, or international society" (Bull 1977:8) is not lacking in international relations. Such order implies the existence of a common framework of rules and institutions guiding international practices, and some such framework has existed among states at many times (Bull 1977:15–16, and chap. 2). For Hedley Bull, order in the form of "international society has always been present in the modern international system because at no stage can it be said that the conception of the common interests of states, of common rules accepted and common institutions worked by them, has ceased to exert an influence" (42).

Others as well have noted the elements of order and society that mark international politics. Much of the recent literature on international regimes makes this point. Regimes serve to constrain and guide states' behavior according to common norms and rules, thereby making possible patterned, or orderly, behavior. Indeed the authors of *Cooperation Under Anarchy* seek to explain such order. While initially seeing international politics in the Hobbesian image of a system marked by persistent war and lacking limits on states' behavior, they eventually note that

> an international society—albeit a fragmented one—exists. . . . To say that world politics is anarchic does not imply that it entirely lacks

organization. Relationships among actors may be carefully structured in some issue-areas, even though they remain loose in others. (Oye 1986:226)

In this strong sense of a set of patterned behavior promoting various goals or norms, order is not what the international system lacks.

In a weaker sense, order is also apparent. Discovery of the orderly features of world politics amidst its seeming chaos is perhaps the central achievement of neorealists. For example, Gilpin points out that "the relationships among states have a high degree of order and that although the international system is one of anarchy (i.e., absence of formal governmental authority), the system does exercise an element of control over the behavior of states" (1981:28). Waltz also finds order in the regularized patterns of state behavior that he observes. The timeless and recurrent formation of balances of power constitutes such a pattern.

Balancing gives order to the system in two ways. First, if effected properly, it may prevent war. Here power is used to create a structure that inhibits war and thus provides a means for organizing the international system. Other realists also see power and its distribution as providing for order in international politics. Robert W. Tucker, for example, sees power differentials among Northern and Southern states creating a hierarchy of relations that make for an orderly system (1977). Unlike Waltz, who focuses on balances of power, Tucker emphasizes the inequalities in power. But both see the distribution of power as creating the means for producing order—i.e., regularized, predictable patterns of behavior—among states. Second, recurrent balancing by states suggests the order lurking in the seeming chaos of international politics. While states themselves may not realize it, like firms in a perfect market their behavior is being constrained into an orderly outcome. Again, the behavior of states is being influenced to produce unintended order. In this case, however, states' behavior is not guided by their norms or goals, but rather by structures beyond their control. In this weaker sense then, as well, lack of order does not seem to be the distinguishing feature associated with the system's anarchy. Thus although anarchy may refer to a lack of order in international politics, such a conception is not what most international relations scholars mean by it.

The second definition of anarchy is the lack of government. It is the first meaning of anarchy given in the *Oxford English Dictionary* and is common among political scientists. Among the many uses

Waltz makes of anarchy, the notion of an absence of government is central (1979:102). In *Cooperation Under Anarchy*, anarchy is also defined as a "lack of common government" (see Axelrod and Keohane in Oye 1986:226). Earlier writers concur in this; for instance, Martin Wight sees "the international system [as] properly described as an anarchy—a multiplicity of powers without a government."[3] Frederick Dunn in 1948 also writes that "international politics is concerned with the special kind of power relationships that exist in a community lacking an overriding authority" (1948:144). Again, the analogy to Hobbes's state of nature is evoked. States in the international system are seen as being in a state of nature, in a state prior to the creation of Leviathan (i.e., without a common authority keeping them in awe). This meaning of anarchy then relates to the lack of something, the time to a common government or authority.

But what exactly is lacking? What is meant by government or authority? Many discussions in international politics fail to define government and/or authority or define them in very different ways. They tend also to use government and authority interchangeably. But the two are distinct concepts. Waltz, for instance, associates anarchy with lack of government, which deals with the means used to organize how and when force can be employed. Government, for him, has a Weberian cast to it; it implies a monopoly on the legitimate use of force:

> The difference between national and international politics lies not in the use of force but in the different modes of organization for doing something about it. A government, ruling by some standard of legitimacy, arrogates to itself the right to use force. . . . A government has no monopoly on the use of force, as is all too evident. An effective government, however, has a monopoly on the *legitimate* use of force, and legitimate means here that the public agents are organized to prevent and to counter the private use of force. (Waltz 1979:103–4)

For others, government denotes something different. It is less associated with force than with the existence of institutions and laws to maintain order. Lack of government means the absence of laws, a legislature to write them, a judiciary to enforce them, and an executive to administer them. For example, Martin Wight notes,

> Anarchy is the characteristic that distinguishes international politics from ordinary politics. The study of international politics presupposes absence of a system of government, as the study of domestic politics presupposes the existence of one. . . . But it is roughly the case that,

while in domestic politics the struggle for power is governed and circumscribed by the framework of law and institutions, in international politics law and institutions are governed and circumscribed by the struggle for power. (1978:102)

Others suggest that it is a particular function of government that the international system lacks. For the contributors to *Cooperation Under Anarchy*, anarchy means the absence of a central authority to enforce states' adherence to promises or agreements (Oye 1986:1–2). The means for hierarchical rule enforcement are missing. The emphasis here is on institutions and authority, rather than force, as central to governance. Different definitions of government are thus used in the literature.

These three notions of government offer different visions of what is lacking in international politics. Which of these best fits standard notions of government? The definition of government as a monopoly over the legitimate use of force has three problems. The first involves the issue of monopoly. How much of a monopoly of force must a government have to exist? Most governments do not possess an absolute monopoly over the legitimate use of force. For instance, the U.S. government does not; citizens have the right to self-defense, and they have the constitutional right to bear arms. When the right to use force legitimately (under certain circumstances) is diffused to 240 million people, can a government in Waltz's terms be said to exist? The difficulties with this definition are also apparent since it would not allow us to recognize even Hobbes's Leviathan as a government. While individuals give up nearly all their rights to it, even Leviathan does not possess a monopoly over the use of force. As Hobbes states emphatically, "A covenant not to defend myself from force by force is always void" (1958:117, chap. 14). The right to self-defense through the legitimate use of force weakens any monopoly over legitimate coercion possessed by a government. A *monopoly* over the use of force then is probably not the distinguishing feature of a government.[4]

Perhaps the defining feature of government in this definition is the legitimacy of using force. This, though, raises the issue of what legitimacy means and how it is determined. A sense of legitimacy allows a government to use force without prompting the resistance of (or use of force by) society. Lack of such a sense is conducive to civil war. But does not the issue of the legitimacy of force arise internationally as well? The use of force in international politics is not always considered illegitimate; some uses seem legitimate to a majority of states. Even Morgenthau notes the range of legitimate and illegitimate uses of force in international politics:

> Legitimate power, that is power whose exercise is morally or legally justified, must be distinguished from illegitimate power. . . . The distinction is not only philosophically valid but also relevant for the conduct of foreign policy. Legitimate power, which can invoke a moral or legal justification for its exercise, is likely to be more effective than equivalent illegitimate power, which cannot be justified. That is to say, legitimate power has a better chance to influence the will of its objects than equivalent illegitimate power. Power exercised in self-defense or in the name of the United Nations has a better chance to succeed than equivalent power exercised by an "aggressor" nation or in violation of international law. Political ideologies . . . serve the purpose of endowing foreign policies with the appearance of legitimacy. (1985:34)

The use of force internationally then can be legitimate—or more or less legitimate—just as can its use domestically. This conception of what international politics lacks—a monopoly on the legitimate use of force—is not as clear as it seems, since governments lack such monopolies and since the legitimacy issue arises in international as well as domestic politics.

Third, this conception of government reveals a narrow notion of politics. It reduces both international and domestic politics to the use of force. Government ultimately depends on the threat of force, as does international politics (Waltz 1979:88). This is implicit in the Weberian definition of government. As Weber himself notes, "The threat of force, and in the case of need its actual use, is the method which is specific to political organization and is always the last resort when others have failed."[5] It is difficult in terms of this definition to see much distinction between international and domestic politics.

Other notions of government stress the existence of institutions and laws that maintain order. Government is based on more than coercion; it rests on institutionalized practices and well-accepted norms. Governments legislate, adjudicate, resolve PDs, and provide public goods, for example—all of which require more than mere coercion to accomplish. This broader institutional definition conforms more to standard notions of government than does the conception linked to force. The *International Encyclopedia of the Social Sciences* defines government as a system of social control which has "acquired a definite institutional organization and operate[s] by means of legal mandates enforced by definite penalties."[6] As a clarification, the entry states

that "Whenever·a group of human beings actuated by common interests and desires creates an organized institutional mechanism for the
furtherance of these ends and for the adjustment and control of their
relationships, there is government" (8). Similarly, in discussing why
politics is not coterminous with government, Harry Eckstein defines
government as "those formally organized structures of societies that
specialize in the exercise of 'sovereignty,' as that term has been
understood since, roughly, the early seventeenth century: specialized organizations that make laws, implement them, and resolve
conflicts arising under them, and have a uniquely 'legitimate' right
to do so" (1973:1, 142). Government in this standard definition centers on three notions: institutions, law, and legitimacy.

Institutions are valued in this definition not for themselves but for
the functions they perform and the way in which they perform them.
Governing institutions provide social order through their legal institutions and sense of legitimacy. But as noted earlier, the provision of
order is not unique to governments. Order exists in the international
system; it is simply provided through different means. David Easton
makes this point:

> The fact that policies recognized as authoritative for the whole society
> must exist does not imply or assume that a central governmental
> organization is required in order to make decisions and effectuate
> them. Institutional devices for making and executing policy may take
> an infinite variety of forms. The clarity and precision with which the
> statuses and roles of legislators and administrators are defined will
> depend upon the level of development of a particular society. Societies
> could be placed on a continuum with regard to the degree of definition
> of such roles. Well-defined organizations, which we call government,
> exist in the national societies of western Europe; scarcely discernible
> statuses and roles of which a governmental organization is constituted
> exist in international society and in non-literate societies. . . . Not all
> [international] disputes are automatically settled through the efforts of
> individual nations along customary lines. As in the domestic sphere,
> the solution of differences is in large measure left to the individual
> national units through bilateral or wider negotiations. . . . The general
> atmosphere or set of relations within which the individual national
> units are able to conduct their private negotiations about the distribu-
> tion of values is dominated and supervised by the great powers. In the
> last resort, if any specific pattern of distribution of values, or if the
> general pattern emerging from individual private negotiations over
> time, does not accord with their conception of a desirable distribution
> of resources internationally, it has been normal for the great powers to
> step in to speak with the voice of international society. (1965:137–38)

The provision of order may not require formal institutions or laws. But supposedly the manner in which order is provided is what distinguishes the two areas. Within the state, law and hierarchy prevail; within the international system, power without legitimate authority dominates. Anarchy is equated with lawlessness.

But international governing institutions and a body of international laws do exist. It seems not to be their existence that matters but their capacity for commanding obedience. This capacity depends much on their perceived legitimacy, as it does for domestic institutions. These institutions will have little influence internationally or domestically if they lack legitimacy. It is an actor's belief that an institution's commands or a law are binding or valid that gives them much of their force. As Weber recognized, an order that is seen as legitimate is far more likely to be obeyed than one that appeals only to self-interest or habit. "But custom, personal advantage, purely affectual or ideal motives of solidarity, do not form a sufficiently reliable basis for a given domination. In addition, there is normally a further element, the belief in legitimacy" (Weber 1978:231, 31). Many studying domestic politics have realized this. Dahl and Lindblom, for instance, note that there are many goals that cannot be achieved by command (i.e., threatening deprivation to get someone to do something) and that command is not the primary mechanism used to achieve almost any goal in politics (Dahl and Lindblom 1953:99–123). A sense of legitimacy is essential to the maintenance of any order.

Legitimacy then appears to be the linchpin upon which conceptions of government rest. It, more than institutions or laws, is what distinguishes domestic and international politics. Lack of legitimacy seems in the end to be what many international relations scholars have in mind when they talk about anarchy. Anarchy as a lack of government is for them transformed into a discussion of lack of authority, or legitimacy. Both Waltz and the contributors to *Cooperation Under Anarchy* end up here. But government and authority should not be conflated. Not all governments have de facto authority over their subjects. Authority is often tied to the notion of legitimacy; it implies a belief in the validity or bindingness of an order (see, for example, Easton 1965:132–33; Eckstein 1973). It is not just laws or governing institutions that international politics may lack, but most importantly a sense of legitimacy.

But does the absence of authority provide a firm basis for the distinction between domestic and international politics? May not some domestic systems lack centralized authority and legitimacy, while certain international systems (e.g., the Concert of Europe)[7] enjoy high levels of legitimacy? Can and should we draw a rigid dichotomy between the two on the basis of anarchy defined this way?

ANARCHY AND THE DICHOTOMY BETWEEN DOMESTIC AND INTERNATIONAL POLITICS

The renewed focus on anarchy in international politics has led to the creation of a sharp distinction between domestic and international politics. Politics internationally is seen as characterized primarily by anarchy, while domestically centralized authority prevails. One of the most explicit statements of this position is in Waltz's *Theory of International Politics*. His powerful articulation of this dichotomy is interesting to examine closely since it is the clearest logical statement of the consequences of the anarchy assumption.

Waltz makes three separate claims about the distinction between the two areas. First, anarchy as a lack of central authority implies that international politics is a decentralized competition among sovereign equals. As he says,

> The parts of domestic political systems stand in relations of super- and subordination. Some are entitled to command; others are required to obey. Domestic systems are centralized and hierarchic. The parts of international political systems stand in relations of coordination. Formally, each is the equal of all the others. None is entitled to command; none is required to obey. International systems are decentralized and anarchic. (1979:88)

A second distinction flows from the assumption of anarchy. As a lack of centralized control over force, anarchy implies that world politics is a self-help system reliant primarily on force. This also distinguishes international from national politics.

> Nationally, the force of a government is exercised in the name of right and justice. Internationally, the force of a state is employed for the sake of its own protection and advantage. . . . Nationally, relations of authority are established. Internationally, only relations of strength result. (1979:112)

Finally, international politics is seen as the only true "politics":

National politics is the realm of authority, of administration, and of law. International politics is the realm of power, of struggle, and of accommodation. The international realm is preeminently a political one. The national realm is variously described as being hierarchic, vertical, centralized, heterogeneous, directed, and contrived; and international realm, as being anarchic, horizontal, decentralized, homogeneous, undirected, and mutually adaptive. (1979:113)

A very sharp distinction is drawn between the two political arenas on a number of different grounds, all of which flow from the assumption of anarchy. While some societies may possess elements of both ordering principles—anarchy and hierarchy—the conclusion of many is that such a rigid dichotomy is empirically feasible and theoretically useful (Waltz 1979:115–16). In this section the utility of such a distinction is examined. Is it empirically and heuristically helpful? To answer this question, it is important to examine Waltz's three distinctions because they represent the logical outcome of adopting the assumption of anarchy as the basis of international politics. While his views are the most explicit and perhaps extreme statement of this dichotomy, they do reflect the implicit understanding of neorealist theory in general.

The first line of demarcation between domestic and international politics is the claim that centralization prevails in the former and decentralization in the latter. What is meant by centralization or its opposite? Centralization seems related to hierarchy. As Waltz notes, "The units—institutions and agencies—stand vis-à-vis each other in relations of super- and subordination" (1979:81). Apparently, it refers to the number of, and relationship among, recognized centers of authority in a system. Domestic politics has fewer, more well-defined centers that are hierarchically ordered, while in international politics many centers exist and they are not so ordered. What counts as a center of authority, however? Waltz resorts to the legalistic notion of sovereignty to make his count internationally. He also assumes that domestically a well-defined hierarchy of authority exists. While qualifying his point, he asserts that

Domestic politics is hierarchically ordered. . . . In a polity the hierarchy of offices is by no means completely articulated, nor are all ambiguities about relations of super- and subordination removed. Nevertheless, political actors are formally differentiated according to the degrees of their authority, and their distinct functions are specified. (1979:81)

Such a view of domestic politics is hard to maintain. Who is the highest authority in the United States? The people, the states, the Constitution, the executive, the Supreme Court, or even Congress. De jure, the Constitution is; but de facto, it depends upon the issue. There is no single hierarchy of authority, as in some ideal military organization. Authority for deciding different issues rests with different groups in society. Authority is not highly concentrated; it is diffused. This was the intention of the writers of the Constitution, who wanted a system where power was not concentrated but rather dispersed. It was dispersed not only functionally through a structure of countervailing "checks and balances" but also geographically through federalism.[8]

Moreover, this decentralization is not unique to the United States. One of the main concerns in comparative politics has been to locate the centers of authority in different nations and relate their different degrees of political centralization and decentralization along some continuum. Authority in some states may be fairly centralized, while in others it is highly decentralized, as in the debate over "strong" and "weak" states (see, for example, Katzenstein 1978). But the central point is that states exhibit a very broad range of values along this continuum, and not all of them—or perhaps even the majority —may be more centralized than the international system.

A second issue is to what extent the international system is decentralized. The point made above that the concentration of authority in any system is best gauged along a continuum, and not a dichotomy, is relevant. Where along the continuum does the international system fit? The answer to this depends on two factors: what issue we are discussing (e.g., fishing rights, the use of nuclear weapons, or control of the seas) and what time period we have in mind. The first factor raises the issue of the fungibility of power. Curiously, Waltz assumes it is highly fungible: force dominates and a hierarchy of power exists internationally—i.e., "great powers" are identifiable. This view centralizes power much more than does assuming it is infungible. The issue of change over time is important. The international system may evince different levels of centralization and decentralization (e.g., the nineteenth-century Concert of Europe versus the post–World War II system).[9]

To deal with these issues, Waltz has to relinquish his more legalistic notion of the international system as one of sovereign equals. At times, he indeed does this. In discussing anarchy, he posits that all states are equal and thus that authority internationally is highly decentralized. But when talking of the distribution of capabilities, he recognizes that states are not equal and that only a few great powers count. In this latter discussion, he implies that capabilities are highly centralized in the international system. Waltz himself then does *not* find the assumption that all states are equal and thus that power is highly decentralized to be either empirically true or heuristically useful. As a "good" realist, he focuses upon the few strong powers in the system.

John Ruggie argues that this apparent contradiction between the system's anarchic structure and the distribution of capabilities is not real. He attributes to Waltz a "generative model" in which the "deep structure" of anarchy influences the more superficial structure of the power distribution (Ruggie 1983a:266). But Ruggie concludes that Waltz has failed to develop such a generative model, and Waltz agrees (Ruggie 1983a:148–52; Waltz 1986:328). It is unclear how Waltz intends to reconcile anarchy with its metaphor of a decentralized, perfectly competitive market and hierarchy established through the distribution of capabilities with its metaphor of an oligopolistic market (Waltz 1979:89–90, 129–36). As the conflicting metaphors reveal, the two structural principles work against one another, and their impact on one another and their causal priority are unclear.

The issue of the centralization of power internationally touches on another distinction between domestic and international politics. Waltz, for instance, claims that

> In anarchic realms, like units coact. In hierarchic realms, unlike units interact. In an anarchic realm, the units are functionally similar and tend to remain so. Like units work to maintain a measure of independence and may even strive for autarky. In a hierarchic realm, the units are differentiated, and they tend to increase the extent of their specialization. Differentiated units become closely interdependent. (1979:104)

The argument is that states are sovereign, implying that they are functionally equal and hence not interdependent. They are duplicates, who do not need one another. Domestically, the units within states are differentiated, each filling some niche in the chain of command. For many domestic systems, this is not accurate. For instance, in federal systems each state is functionally equal, and no generally agreed upon chain of command between the states and the national government exists. On some issues at some times, states have the final say; on others, the central government.

On the other hand, there is the question of whether all nation-states are functionally equivalent. If states are "like units," why only examine the great powers? Waltz realizes this is a problem. He admits that "internationally, like units sometimes perform different tasks." Moreover, "the likelihood of their doing so, varies with their capabilities" (1979:47). Thus he acknowledges that states with different capabilities perform different functions; hence, they are not all "like" units. Later he takes the point further:

> Although states are like units functionally, they differ vastly in their capabilities. Out of such differences something of a division of labor develops. . . . The division of labor across nations, however, is slight in comparison with the highly articulated division of labor within them. (1979:105)

His position is that states do not perform the same tasks, that some international division of labor exists, but that this differentiation is *empirically* unimportant relative to that domestically. The dilemma is that two of Waltz's three central assumptions/ordering principles conflict. It is difficult to assume both that all states are equal (the first and second principles) *and* that all states are not equal as a result of the distribution of their capabilities (the third principle). Waltz might claim that they are equal in function but not in capabilities; however, as he himself states, one's capabilities shape one's functions. The point is, as others have noted before, the distribution of resources internationally creates a division of labor among states; differentiation and hierarchy exist and provide governing mechanisms for states, just as they do for individuals within states. Most importantly, the distinction among different international systems and within nation-states over the degree of centralization of authority as well as over the degree of differentiation among their units is variable and should be viewed along a continuum, rather than as a dichotomy.[10]

A second means of separating domestic and international politics is to differentiate the role and importance of force in the two arenas. For Waltz, domestically force is less important as a means of control and is used to serve justice; internationally, force is widespread and serves no higher goal than to help the state using it. But is the importance of force so different in the two realms? As noted before, for theorists like Waltz, Carr, and Weber the threat of the use of force

—in effect, deterrence—is ultimately the means of social control domestically. Threats of sanctions are the state's means of enforcement, as they are internationally. When norms and institutions fail to maintain social control, states internally and externally resort to threats of force. It may be that norms and institutions are more prevalent forms of control domestically than internationally. But this depends on the state in question. In some countries, belief in the legitimacy of government and institutions, being widespread and well-developed, might suffice to maintain control. However, the fact that more civil wars have been fought in this century than international ones and that since 1945 more people have died in the former should make one pause when declaiming about the relative use of force in the two realms (Small and Singer 1979:63, 65, 68–9).

Since at times the frequency of violence domestically is acknowledged, perhaps the point is that force is legitimate and serves justice domestically and not internationally (Waltz 1979:103). Again, this depends upon the perceived legitimacy of the government and the particular instance of use. Have the majority of people in the former Soviet Union, Poland, Ethiopia, South Africa, Iran, or the Philippines —to name just a few—felt that the state's use of force serves justice (all the time? some of the time?)? Whether force serves justice domestically is an issue to be studied, not a given to be assumed. On the other hand, is it never the case that force serves justice internationally? Is it always, or most of the time, "for the sake of [the state's] own protection and advantage"? States have been known to intervene forcefully for larger purposes. The fight against Germany in World War II by the United States and others, for example, helped serve justice regardless of whether America's own protection was a factor. The distinction between international and domestic politics on this issue does not appear as clear as is claimed.

A third dichotomy between the two arenas asserts that power and politics operate internationally. Domestically, authority, administration, and law prevail; internationally, it is power, struggle, and accommodation. For some, the latter alone is politics. This distinction is the hardest to maintain. Disputes among political parties, local and national officials, the executive and the legislature, different geographic regions, different races, capital and labor, industry and finance, organized and unorganized groups, and so on over who gets how much and when occur constantly within the nation. Morgenthau recognizes this:

> The essence of international politics is identical with its domestic counterpart. Both domestic and international politics are a struggle for power, modified only by the different conditions under which this struggle takes place in the domestic and in the international spheres.
>
> The tendency to dominate, in particular, is an element of all human associations, from the family through fraternal and professional associations and local political organizations, to the state. . . . Finally, the whole political life of a nation, particularly of a democratic nation, from the local to the national level, is a continuous struggle for power. (1985:39–40)

E. H. Carr, another realist, also disagrees with Waltz. Like Morgenthau, he sees the national and world arenas as being based on the same principles and processes: power politics. In talking of domestic politics, he echoes Thucydides' Melian dialogue: "The majority rules because it is stronger, the minority submits because it is weaker" (Carr 1964:41). He maintains that the factors that supposedly distinguish domestic politics—e.g., legitimacy, morality, ideology, and law—are just as political nationally as internationally:

> Theories of social morality are always the product of a dominant group which identifies itself with the community as a whole, and which possesses facilities denied to subordinate groups or individuals for imposing its view of life on the community. Theories of international morality are, for the same reason and in virtue of the same process, the product of dominant nations or groups of nations. (1964:79)

As an example of this, Carr notes that "laissez-faire, in international relations as in those between capital and labor, is the paradise of the economically strong" (60). He points out that even law, another factor that is supposed to make politics within the nation different, is merely a manifestation of power: "Behind all law there is this necessary political background. The ultimate authority of law derives from politics" (180).

Others would reject Carr's insistence that law and morality spring from power, but would nonetheless agree that politics within nations and among them are similar. These authors see authority, law, and morality as being as important to international relations as to domestic ones. For instance, Inis Claude holds that international order is maintained by a balance of power among opposing forces, just as it is domestically. In attacking the notion that governments maintain peace through some monopoly of force, Claude returns to Morgenthau to make his point:

> Morgenthau's espousal of the concept of the state's "monopoly of organized violence" is contradicted by his general conception of politics: "Domestic and international politics are but two different manifestations of the same phenomenon: the struggle for power." In his terms, "The balance of power . . . is indeed a perennial element of all pluralistic societies." (Claude 1962:231)

For him, as for Morgenthau, societies are pluralistic, and thus the role of government is "the delicate task of promoting and presiding over a constantly shifting equilibrium" (Claude 1962:231). Politics domestically and internationally is about balancing power. To assume that a state has a monopoly of power and that this is "the key to the effectiveness of [it] as an order-keeping institution may lead to an exaggerated notion of the degree to which actual states can and do rely upon coercion" (234). Unlike Morgenthau and other realists, Claude sees factors other than coercion—such as, norms and institutions—as being more important both domestically and internationally to the maintenance of order, but like them he views the balance of power as fundamental to the two realms. Unlike Waltz, all these authors find relations within nations and among them to be political and to be based on similar political processes.

Overall, the sharp distinctions between the two realms are difficult to maintain empirically. More importantly, any dichotomous treatment of domestic and international politics may have heuristic disadvantages.[11] Two heuristic problems exist with the radical separation of international and domestic politics. First, the isolation of international politics as a realm of anarchy with nothing in common with other types of politics is a step backward conceptually. Throughout the 1950s and 1960s, political scientists worked to incorporate international relations into the main body of political science literature. They strove to end the prevailing conception of international relations as a *sui generis* field of study and to apply methods of analysis to it from other branches of political science, mainly domestic politics (see, for example, Spiro 1966, chap. 1). Writing in the early 1960s, James Rosenau decried the tendency to treat international relations as a *sui generis* branch of inquiry:

We must avoid the widespread tendency to assume rather than to conceptualize the nature of the politics which occur at the international level. One reason for the lack of conceptual links is that most students in the international field have not treated their subject as local politics writ large. Instead, like advocates of bipartisanship in foreign policy, most students tend to view politics as "stopping at the water's edge" and consider that something different, international politics and foreign policy, takes place beyond national boundaries. Consequently, so much emphasis has been placed on the dissimilarities between international and other types of politics that the similarities have been overlooked and the achievement of conceptual unity has been made much more difficult. For example, because of their stress upon the fact that international political systems are lacking in authoritative decision-making structures, many analysts have largely overlooked unifying concepts developed in areas where the focus is upon sovereign actors. (1963:2–3)

Heeding the advice of these and other writers, scholars began applying techniques and ideas from other fields of political inquiry and asking new questions about international relations. The problem with reverting back to a situation where international politics is seen as unique is that one is less likely to use the hypotheses, concepts, and questions about politics developed elsewhere. International politics must then reinvent the wheel, not being able to draw on other political science scholarship. The radical dichotomy between international and domestic politics seems to represent a conceptual and theoretical step backward.

A second and related heuristic problem is the tendency implicit in this separation of the two fields to view all states as being the same. Waltz, for one, wants us to conceive of states as like units and to avoid looking within them at their internal arrangements. His is a systemic-level theory. But the issue is whether it is possible and/or fruitful to abstract from all of domestic politics. All states are not the same; and their internal characteristics, including their goals and capabilities, affect international politics importantly, as Waltz is forced to admit. This is reflected in the tension between his ordering principles, the first two of which give primacy to structural pressures while the third makes certain agents key. Using systemic theory, he wants to "tell us about the forces the units are subject to," but he also notes that "in international politics, as in any self-help system, the units of greatest capability set the scene of action for others as well as for themselves" (1979:72). The units do matter.

Moreover, the difference among states—even the strongest—are not trivial and may be useful to conceptualize for understanding international relations better. Developing continuums along which all politics—domestic and international—are understandable can be fruitful. Some, such as Roger Masters, Chadwick Alger, and Ernest Gellner, have compared international politics with primitive political systems and developing countries and have produced interesting insights about the international system from this comparison (Gellner 1958:579–83; Alger 1963:406–19; and Masters 1964:595–619). Using hypotheses and concepts from comparative politics can enrich international relations theory, while limiting this cross-fertilization is likely to hurt the field. As argued, politics in the two arenas are similar. William T. R. Fox stated long ago that:

> Putting "power" rather than "the state" at the center of political science makes it easier to view international relations as one of the political sciences. So conceived, it is possible for some scholars to move effortlessly along the seamless web which connects world politics and the politics of such less inclusive units as the state or the locality, and to emphasize the political process, group behavior, communications studies, conflict resolution, and decision-making. (1968:20)

The argument here concurs with those who would add to this focus on power a concern with norms and institutions, which also may play similar roles in the domestic and international arenas. Conceptions unifying, and not separating, these two arenas are heuristically fruitful.

THE ASSUMPTION OF INTERDEPENDENCE

The current tendency to overemphasize the centrality of anarchy to world politics may not be the most useful way to conceptualize international politics. As other scholars have pointed out, such reductionism overlooks another central fact about international politics —namely, the interdependence of the actors. This section explores the notion of interdependence, suggests why it is also a key *structural* feature of the international system, and notes some of its implications for world politics. Other scholars have made some of these points before but, in this time when anarchy reigns supreme in the discipline, a reminder of the importance of other aspects of the international system can be valuable.

What do we mean by interdependence? There are two related notions of interdependence. First, the notion of "strategic interdependence" implies, as Schelling puts it, a situation in which "the ability of one participant to gain his ends is dependent to an important degree on the choices or decisions that the other participant will make" (1960:5). In this situation, an actor cannot get what he/she wants without the cooperation of other actors. This notion fits the conventional definition of the term, which refers to a situation in which the actors face mutual costs from ending their relationship.[12] In other words, breaking a relationship means that each actor that was party to it can no longer obtain some value he/she wanted. Interdependence implies nothing about the degree of equality among the actors; it merely denotes a situation where all the actors suffer costs from terminating their relationship. Interdependence also implies that satisfaction of the actors' utilities is *not* independent. The actors are still sovereign—that is, able to make decisions or choices autonomously. But to realize their goals they must be concerned with the choices other actors make.

Interdependence is *not* the opposite of anarchy as we have defined it—i.e., an absence of central authority. The two concepts represent different aspects of the international system. As with anarchy, the definition of interdependence says nothing about the degree of order, the likelihood of war, the inherency of conflicting interests, or the primary means used to achieve one's goals in the international system. Links between these latter variables and either anarchy or interdependence are empirical, *not* conceptual, statements. Anarchy and interdependence do not conflict on these dimensions, as is often supposed, since neither concept says anything about them a priori. The two concepts are not opposite ends of some single continuum. The extent of hierarchical authority relations—i.e., of anarchy—does not necessarily affect the degree of interdependence present. Two coequal actors can be in a situation of strategic interdependence (i.e., can be unable to attain their goals without the cooperation of the other) just as easily as can two actors in a hierarchical relationship. A priori one cannot determine the extent of their interdependence from the degree of hierarchy/anarchy present in their relationship, and vice versa. The two concepts are logically independent.[13]

This definition of interdependence also does *not* imply either that the actors' interests are in harmony or that power relations are unimportant. The assumption that interdependence implies harmony or cooperation is widespread.[14] In part this is a consequence of the links between international trade theory and interdependence. An interdependent situation is seen as one where an extensive division of labor exists so that each part performs a different role and thus has complementary interests. Everyone gains from such a situation; it is a positive-sum game. But, as Schelling, among others, has pointed out, interdependent situations are really mixed-motive games. Both conflicting and harmonious interests are evident. Each gains from continuing the relationship, but the distribution of these gains involves struggle. Harmony is not the result of interdependence; rather a mix of conflict and cooperation is. A priori it is impossible to tell which will prevail.

Interdependence does not imply that power is unimportant. Indeed, as analysts like Schelling, Keohane and Nye, Baldwin, and Hirschman, have shown, power is an intrinsic element of interdependence (Schelling 1960; Keohane and Nye 1977; Baldwin 1980; Hirschman 1980). An actor involved in such relations can manipulate them in order to prompt the other actors involved to do what he/she wants. For instance, relations involving asymmetric interdependence provide an essential means of exercising influence; the less vulnerable side can threaten, however subtly, to end the relationship in order to induce changes in the other side's behavior. Relative gains and losses from ending the relationship are here the central means of exercising leverage. But interdependence need not refer only to asymmetric relations. A symmetric relationship between two actors may also be interdependent and allow each to exercise power over the other, often through anticipated reactions as the U.S.-Soviet nuclear-deterrence relationship since the 1950s has shown.[15] Power, in fact, is much more evident in interdependent relations than in situations where actors are independent or autarkic. To return to our market metaphor, power is a constant in oligopolistic or monopolistic markets, while it can be depicted as absent from purely competitive ones.

Reasons why interdependence is a central feature of the international system are connected with its implications for the system. Empirically, the international system has structural features that imply interdependence is important; moreover, viewing the system as interdependent may generate useful theoretical insights. Two important points can be made. First, interdependence means that the actors are linked. While states remain sovereign, their actions and attainment of their goals are conditioned by other actors' behavior and their expectations and perceptions about this. In a situation of strategic interdependence, one's best choice depends on the choice others make. Thus the game is about anticipating others' behavior. One's expectations and perceptions of their behavior shape one's own choices. Scholars using game-theoretic models of international politics recognize this. For instance, contributors to *Cooperation Under Anarchy* use the image of an iterated PD to explore international interactions, but they tend not to note that this implies that strategic interdependence is as fundamental to the actors as is anarchy.

Much of international relations involves this type of strategic game. One's best choice of how to spend one's resources—e.g., on guns or on butter—depends on one's expectations about how others are spending theirs. This understanding of international politics leads to a focus on states' expectations about and perceptions of others, as seen in Robert Jervis's works (1970, 1976). Structural imperatives—such as changes in some objective distribution of capabilities—are not the sole guide to behavior. Furthermore, this strategic focus leads to an interest in factors that shape expectations and perceptions—factors like past behavior patterns, institutions, and cognitive processes. Finally, emphasizing interdependence draws attention to issues involving communication and information. In situations of strategic interdependence, the more one knows about the true preferences of other actors, ceteris paribus, the better off one may be. The gathering of reliable information and the reduction of costs associated with this then become key problems for states, a point Robert Keohane among others has made (Keohane 1984). Additionally, control over communication becomes imperative in this situation. How one's preferences are revealed and to what extent they are become very important in obtaining one's goals because of the influence this process has on the other side's expectations of one's behavior. If, on the other hand, some set of objective structural factors shapes states' behavior, then issues of communication and information exchange among states are relatively unimportant. Viewing the international system as a web of interdependencies necessitates a focus on the linkages among actors; it directs attention to their perceptions and knowledge of one another and their communications.

Second, if the international system is viewed as characterized by structural interdependence, then the mechanisms of the system look different from those in the neorealist model. For this model, the anarchic international system is like a perfect market. Many similar actors coact in such a way that some equilibrium results. Communication, concern about other actors' likely behavior, institutionalized practices—none of these matter. The structure of the system, through some invisible hand, selects behavior appropriate for the states. This metaphor can be misleading for international politics. As Waltz's third ordering principle argues, at any time only a few states count —the great powers. The number of important actors, or the number of important actors each state interacts with, in international politics is small. The metaphor that is more relevant, then, is *not* a perfectly competitive market but an oligopolistic or monopolistic one.[16] These markets are defined as having only a few large actors. Such markets are characterized by extensive interdependence; how each firm maximizes its profits depends on the choices (about price and quantity produced) other firms make. The behavior of others then shapes the best strategy for each, as is true for states in the international system.

A second interesting feature of these markets is that they tend to be unstable. They bring forth a mixture of conflictual and cooperative behavior. Periods marked by stable collusive monopoly pricing where all are enriched tend to be followed by bitter competitive price wars where some may be ruined. Such unstable, mixed behavior seems more characteristic of international politics than does the steady-state equilibrium of a perfectly competitive market. In these oligopolistic markets, periods of cooperation depend upon the establishment of various means of tacit communication as well as of norms and institutionalized practices that elicit cooperative behavior by signaling and/or constraining the behavior of others.[17] On the other hand, periods of price warfare are usually the result of attempts to manipulate the relationship in order to redistribute the gains from it. Fights over cheating and ultimately who gets how much are commonplace. The mechanisms by which cooperation is established and the reasons that conflict occurs in these markets appear very similar to those in international politics.

In addition, these markets feature a subtle balancing mechanism. No firm wants to let any other gain so much it can become dominant and drive the others out of business; relative gains matter. Survival dictates that the attempts of any one to dominate be met by cooperative behavior on the part of others to prevent this. Balancing behavior is thus engendered, much as in international politics. These imperfect markets, which are characterized by strategic interdependence, may then function more like the international system than do perfect markets. Furthermore, the study of these types of markets is likely to contribute to our understanding of international relations.

A final point about imperfect markets is that they produce indeterminate outcomes as well as unstable ones. They are rarely single-exit situations; a unique solution is not structurally given.[18] Instead outcomes depend upon the interaction of different actors, each making different assumptions about the others' likely behavior. Some range of outcomes, is, however, possible to identify; it lies between the outcomes predicted by perfect markets and monopoly. This indeterminacy may be frustrating, but it too may more adequately represent politics. Focusing on actors' interdependence can alleviate the strong structural determinism associated with metaphors using perfect markets, such as Waltz's. Politics seems ultimately to be about choice—choice in the presence of uncertainty, incomplete information, and guesses about the intentions of other actors. Seeing the international system as one characterized by strategic interdependence among sovereign states and thus modeled on these imperfect or oligopolistic markets can provide many empirically and heuristically useful ways of looking at international politics, as some of the recent work using game theory has shown.

The recent tendency in international relations theory to view anarchy as *the* fundamental background condition of international politics underestimates the ambiguity of the concept and lends it an exaggerated importance. While anarchy is an important condition of world politics, it is not the only one. Strategic interdependence among the actors is at least as fundamental. An exclusive focus on anarchy may be overly reductionist. A reminder of the complexities involved in the notion of anarchy and of the dangers involved in overemphasizing it—namely, the radical separation between domestic and international politics and the aura of oversimplification it creates—seems worthwhile repeating in this period when anarchy reigns.

NOTES

1. The assumption is not progressive in the sense that Lakatos proposes. The propositions it generates do not lead to new questions and their answers; see Imre Lakatos (1970).
2. Robert Keohane (1984, chaps. 5 and 6, esp. pp. 73, 85, 88). He later relaxes this restrictive assumption, citing various forms of interdependence which may mitigate this anarchy (chap. 7, esp. pp. 122–23).
3. Martin Wight (1978:101). The essays here were originally written in 1946.
4. Robert Dahl deals with this issue of monopoly by adding a new dimension to the definition of monopoly. He sees government as having a monopoly over the regulation of what constitutes the legitimate use of force. See Dahl (1984:17).
5. Max Weber (1978:54). Weber, unlike Waltz, emphasizes elsewhere institutions and legitimacy as well as force to explain politics.
6. (1968:13). The *Dictionary of Political Science* provides a similar definition: government is "the agency which reflects the organization of the statal (politically organized) group. It normally consists of an executive branch, a legislative branch, and a judicial branch" (1964:217).
7. See Robert Jervis (1982) for a discussion of the legitimate order formed under this system.
8. Waltz recognizes this; see Waltz (1979:81–82). But it never influences his very sharp distinction between the order in domestic and international politics.
9. Waltz does note the differences in systems in terms of the number of great powers, or poles. He suggests the consequences of this are different levels of stability in the system. Ruggie (1983a) also sees differences in systems over time. But his focus is on the divide between the medieval and the modern (post-seventeenth-century) systems.
10. Waltz admits that anarchy and hierarchy are ideal types. But he rejects their use as a continuum, preferring for theoretical simplicity to see them as dichotomies (see 1979:115). Moreover, he simply posits that the anarchic ideal is associated with international politics more than it is with domestic politics.
11. For Waltz this is the ultimate test of an assumption (see Waltz 1979:6).
12. See David Baldwin (1980). This conception of interdependence does not include the notion of sensitivity, as employed by Robert Keohane and Joseph Nye (1977). The notion of vulnerability is the most well-accepted definition.
13. Waltz is confusing on this point. He sees the two as opposed but linked; however, he cannot decide which way the linkage runs. Anarchy for him implies equality, sameness, and hence independence of actors, on the one hand. On the other, he claims interdependence is highest when states are equal. If this is true, then anarchy may well be characterized by very high levels of interdependence, since all states are equal.
14. See Carr (1964), for example; also see the discussion of neoliberal institutionalism in Joseph Grieco (1988a:485–508).

15. Richard Little makes this point about symmetric relations and suggests that this is an understudied area; see Little (1984:121–26). Waltz claims that only symmetric relations can be interdependent, but this position seems untenable (see 1979:143–46).
16. A metaphor Waltz resorts to later (1979:129–36).
17. The rules of thumb that Schelling discusses (1960) are one type of tacit communication.
18. Solutions in oligopolistic markets are possible to identify if one assumes away strategic interdependence. For instance, Cournot-Nash and Stackleberg equilibria are identifiable if one holds constant the other's behavior in price or quantity decisions.

7

RELATIVE GAINS AND THE PATTERN OF INTERNATIONAL COOPERATION

Duncan Snidal

Recent international theorizing continues the long-standing contest between realists who argue that prospects for international cooperation are quite limited and institutionalists who argue that cooperation is possible among states. At the risk of caricature, the relevant strands of this debate can be stated simply. Since Thucydides, realists have proposed that international anarchy makes cooperation difficult because agreements cannot be centrally enforced. In the past decade, institutionalists have found their countervailing case greatly strengthened by analytical results demonstrating, under plausible circumstances, the possibility of decentralized enforcement of cooperation. Recently, realists have replied that this result does not apply to international politics because it is a realm where states seek relative gains, rather than the absolute gains analyzed by institutionalists. I examine this last claim analytically to determine the implications of relative gains for international cooperation.

Relative gains do not provide a sufficient response to the institutionalist claim about cooperation. Only in the very special case of the two-state interaction, with high concern for relative gains and near disregard for absolute gains, is the realist case compelling. For a broad range of more realistic problems, where there are more than two states or where states care about a mixture of absolute and relative gains, the institutionalist case for the possibility of decentralized cooperation remains strong.

My results have a broader relevance for other important social and political settings. Whenever individuals seek status or victory, whenever they engage in contests or tournaments, and whenever goods are "positional" in nature, relative gains are at stake. Since international anarchy, where states seek power or security, is often compared to a Hobbesian state of nature where individuals seek eminence or safety, my results on international cooperation apply equally to contractual theories of the state. Relative gains analysis may also contain insights for understanding certain aspects of bureaucratic or electoral competition. I leave the exploration of these general similarities to the reader, however, and focus instead on relative gains in the specific context of international politics.

I begin with a brief discussion of why realists believe states seek relative gains. Next I examine the strongest part of the realist case concerning the impact of relative gains in interactions involving two states. When two states care only about relative gains, their relations can be modeled as a zero-sum game with no room for cooperation. When states are largely, though not exclusively, motivated by relative gains, their relations are shown to be equivalent to the Prisoner's Dilemma (PD) regardless of the structure of the underlying absolute gains game. This supports the standard realist construction of international anarchy as PD and suggests why cooperation is problematic. If the initial absolute game is not PD, however, the relative gains PD will be fairly mild and susceptible to decentralized cooperation. But if the absolute gains game is already PD, then incorporating relative gains considerations makes this PD more intense and decentralization cooperation more difficult. In effect, I establish the limited circumstances under which relative gains incentives turn two-actor international situations into either zero-sum games or such intensely conflictual PDs that cooperation is well-nigh impossible. Relative gains do not matter nearly so much in less restrictive, more realistic circumstances. I develop a model to examine relative gains in PD situations with more than two actors. The general result is that *a small increase in the number of actors dramatically decreases the impact of relative gains in impeding cooperation*. This effect is augmented by interaction with anything less than a total concern for relative gains. The realist case is thereby shown to be quite weak outside the pure relative gains, tight bipolar world.

Finally, I explore the implications of relative gains for international politics. Although relative gains do not eliminate cooperation, they do predict specific patterns for international cooperation. These predictions provide novel explanations for standard "stylized facts," including why the small exploit the large, why cooperation leads to hegemonic decline, and why particular patterns of cooperation prevail in a bipolar world. Other implications address long-standing disputes in the field, including a surprising finding that relative gains advocates should prefer multipolarity to bipolarity. While the analytical basis for these specific conclusions deserves further refinement, they illustrate the testable propositions that would allow us to evaluate the relative gains hypothesis as an explanation of international behavior.

Thus the relative gains hypothesis cannot salvage the general pessimism of realism but has interesting implications deserving further careful analytical and empirical investigation. It clearly has important consequences for two-actor situations and, where there are small numbers or important asymmetries among larger numbers, it may modify conclusions obtained from the absolute gains model. In this way the relative gains argument may find an important place in international relations theory.

WHY ASSUME THAT STATES SEEK RELATIVE GAINS?

The assumption that states seek relative gains influences a wide variety of scholarship on international politics. A number of scholars have discussed the inhibiting effect of relative gains on cooperation (Waltz 1979; Gilpin 1981, 1987; Stein 1982a; Lake 1984; Lipson 1984; Gowa 1986; Kennedy 1987; Krasner 1987; Grieco 1988a, 1988b, 1990; Jervis 1988; Larson 1988). Realists argue that the general insecurity of international anarchy leads states to worry not simply about how well they fare themselves (absolute gains) but about how well they fare compared to other states (relative gains). States that gain disproportionately in relations with other states may achieve a superiority that threatens the goals or even the very security of their cooperative partners. Kenneth Waltz summarizes this perspective well:

> When faced with the possibility of cooperating for mutual gain, states that feel insecure must ask how the gain will be divided. They are compelled to ask not "Will both of us gain?" but "Who will gain more?" If an expected gain is to be divided, say, in the ratio of two to

one, one state may use its disproportionate gain to implement a policy intended to damage or destroy the other. Even the prospect of large absolute gains for both parties does not elicit their cooperation so long as each fears how the other will use its increased capabilities. (1979:105)

Thus states are seen to seek relative gains, and the inference is drawn that this inhibits cooperation.

The relative gains hypothesis applies to economy as well as security. In part, this is because economic gains can ultimately be transformed into security gains, so that in the long run, security and economics are inseparable. But relative gains thinking occurs independently in economics. Pure mercantilism, where states seek to accumulate specie, entails relative gains aspirations that pit state against state. Similar implications emerge from neomercantilism and the new theory of "strategic trade," with its emphasis on how economies of scale in industries present states with incentives to interfere in trade to gain market shares. This suggests that the pursuit of relative gains can interfere with economic as well as military cooperation.

I do not address the plausibility of relative gains seeking as a description of international behavior, I stipulate it as an assumption. My reason is that I am ambivalent as to how much such aspirations or fears motivate states. I do not believe that relative gains pervade international politics nearly enough to make the strong realist position hold in general. In some circumstances, however, relative gains can help explain certain aspects of international behavior. Rather than debate its merits a priori, I evaluate the relative gains assumption by exploring its implications, which are not yet correctly understood. By accepting the assumption of relative gains maximization, I show that it does not have the general inhibiting effect on international cooperation widely ascribed to it.

Relative gains seeking can inhibit cooperation in two ways. The less important way is by limiting the range of viable cooperative agreements because states will not accept deals that provide disproportionately greater benefits to others.[1] This understanding of relative gains seeking does not clearly distinguish relative from absolute gains. Intense bargaining for greater absolute benefits also leads to a concern with the distribution of joint gains from cooperation. Indeed in the pure zero-sum case there is no analytic or substantive difference between seeking a greater absolute amount and seeking a greater relative share. More importantly, if distribution is the primary relative gains problem, states can alter the terms of a cooperative agreement or offer side-payments until the distribution of gains is sufficiently proportionate.[2] Ironically, this relative gains problem might even facilitate cooperation by narrowing the range of viable cooperative agreements and thereby reducing the absolute gains bargaining problem.[3]

Therefore I focus on the second, more general, way in which relative gains affect international cooperation—namely, by changing states' incentives.[4] Common interests created by the prospect of joint absolute gains become increasingly conflictual as relative comparisons are introduced. This alters the strategic structure of interstate relations and thereby decreases the prospects for cooperation. As I shall show, even purely harmonious absolute gains situations between two actors approximate zero-sum conflictual contests when relative gains are important. If room for cooperation remains, agreements are often less viable, since states' incentives to violate them increase under relative gains. Thus relative gains decrease states' interests in cooperation as well as their ability to maintain self-enforcing agreements in anarchy.

It should be noted that the hypothesis of relative gains seeking can be criticized as a misspecification of an argument that could be better expressed in absolute gains terms. When Waltz argues that states do not cooperate when others will gain more than them and threaten their security, he is implicitly describing a trade-off between short-term absolute gains (i.e., immediate payoffs from cooperation) and long-term absolute gains (i.e., security over the long haul). This choice problem is perfectly amenable to absolute gains analysis, including effects over time, without recourse to relative gains. Similarly, if states forgo immediate economic benefits to capture market share and score relative gains, their ultimate goal is monopoly profits as a long-run absolute benefit of their short-run sacrifice. Even if competition among states prevents any of them from realizing these long-run absolute benefits, that does not diminish the importance of these incentives in motivating states. Thus it is possible to substitute a more complicated absolute gains maximization problem for the relative gains hypothesis (Powell 1990).

There are several reasons why it makes sense to investigate implications of the prevailing relative gains hypothesis rather than translate it into absolute gains terms. First, despite the foregoing comments, perhaps states really do care about relative gains independent of these other considerations. To the extent that goals such as prestige, status, or winning motivate states, relative gains are basic elements of their preferences.[5] Second, relative gains may serve as a useful proxy for state goals just as in the realist's view power may serve as a proxy for states' more specific goals (Morgenthau 1978). Finally, because realists have failed to produce a model presenting the goals of states in a more explicit and complete way, I am loath to undertake that task for them. Any alternative model I proposed could be rejected as not a fair or true depiction of their arguments. Therefore I take the relative gains hypothesis as it stands and use a specification for relative gains that is analytically equivalent to Grieco's (1990:41).

RELATIVE GAINS WITH TWO STATES

Relative gains considerations convert a wide variety of absolute gains situations into PD. Since PD is the typical depiction of the international anarchy associated with relative gains, this may not seem surprising. But other strategic situations, including Chicken and Assurance games, are also often discussed in connection with international anarchy. Furthermore, liberals who challenge the realist conception of international anarchy sometimes argue that the circumstances of international politics (or at least some international issues) are best represented as Coordination or even Harmony games. Choosing among such different analytic representations consequently poses a tough problem at the foundations of international relations theory. The assumption of relative gains provides an escape from this quandary by offering a substantive motivation for the analytic presumption that PD is the archetypical international problem.[6]

Relative Gains Create Prisoner's Dilemmas

To investigate the impact of relative gains, consider a standard two-actor game matrix where each actor faces a decision to cooperate (C) or defect (D) from cooperation.[7] Payoffs are initially defined in absolute terms. If both states cooperate, each receives payoff M from *mutual* cooperation. If one state cooperates *unilaterally*, it receives payoff U while the other state receives the *free-ride* payoff F. If neither cooperates, each receives a zero payoff (0), as the normalized payoff associated with *noncooperation*. Figure 7.1 depicts these four possible outcomes in a simple game matrix.

Three substantively motivated restrictions on the payoffs focus the analysis on the most relevant subset of the seventy-eight ordinal game situations implied by this two-by-two (2 X 2) structure (Rapoport and Guyer 1966; Hardin 1983). First, assume that the game is symmetric (as is implicit in the absence of subscripts on the payoffs). This means that two states are equally well situated to benefit or hurt one another and fashion their cooperative agreement to provide equal absolute gains. Later I shall relax this assumption to examine interactions among multiple states of different sizes and with different relative gains concerns for one another.[8] Second, assume that states prefer mutual cooperation to mutual defection, so that $M > 0$. This follows from a commonsense understanding of what we mean by cooperation. It is not a significant restriction on the analysis, since it affects only naming conventions for behaviors C and D and not the forms of strategic interdependence allowed. Interchanging C and D for each state converts any game where $0 > M$ into a strategically equivalent game, with only the labels changed, where $M > 0$. Third, assume that states prefer a free ride over unilateral cooperation, so that $F > U$. This fosters individual incentives not to cooperate which, in conjunction with the previous assumption of a collective incentive to cooperate, results in an interesting set of cooperation problems.

FIGURE 7.1
Absolute Gains

	D	C
D	0, 0	F, U
C	U, F	M, M

Since the contrary assumption $U > F$ typically facilitates cooperation, we are effectively limiting the analysis to cases where relative gains have a negative impact on cooperation.[9]

These three restrictions produce six strategic situations spanning the range of cooperation problems as shown in table 7.1. One possible game is appropriately described as Harmony because both sides have dominant strategies resulting in an equilibrium where each gets its maximal outcome. Two other possibilities correspond to versions of the Assurance or Stag Hunt game, where one of two equilibria is mutually preferred. Although joint cooperation provides the best outcome for both, it is not guaranteed. Fear that the other will fail to cooperate may lead risk-averse actors not to cooperate and thereby to the deficient equilibrium outcome. A fourth possibility is a Coordination game, where both states have incentives to coordinate on either of two equilibria but differ over which one to select.[10] Next is Chicken, where states differ strongly over which equilibrium is preferred and where a Pareto-optimal but nonequilibrium compromise outcome is available to cooperating states, and disaster occurs in the form of the mutually worst outcome if neither cooperates. Finally, our three restrictions can also lead to PD where individually rational defection results in an equilibrium leaving states collectively worse off. This game turns out to be of increasing relevance with the introduction of relative gains considerations.

Corresponding to each of these absolute gains games is a relative gains game defined by the difference between actor's payoffs (Taylor 1987; Grieco 1988a, 1988b, 1990).[11] Figure 7.2 shows the payoff matrix for the pure relative gains model. The resulting game is zero-sum, with the same ordinal structure for all six absolute gains games. Since $F > U$, defection (D) is always a dominant strategy for both actors. Thus pure relative gains considerations eliminate all prospects for cooperation in two-actor strategic interactions.

Only in the most extreme case would we expect states to care only about relative gains and totally disregard absolute gains. A more realistic presumption is that states seek relative gains in combination with absolute gains, with the pure absolute and relative gains models seen as limiting cases. This continuum is represented by a weighting parameter r for the importance of relative gains, and $(1 - r)$ for the importance of absolute gains, where $0 \leq r \leq 1$. Larger r means that

Preference Ordering for Each Side	Ordinal 2x2 Game	Popular Name

M>F>U>O

	D	C
D	1,1	3,2
C	2,3	(4,4)

Harmony

M>F>O>U

	D	C
D	(2,2)	3,1
C	1,3	(4,4)

Assurance I
(Stag Hunt)

M>O>F>U

	D	C
D	(3,3)	2,1
C	1,2	(4,4)

Assurance II
(Stag Hunt)

F>U>M>O

	D	C
D	1,1	(4,3)
C	(3,4)	2,2

Coordination

F>M>U>O

	D	C
D	1,1	(4,2)
C	(2,4)	3,3

Chicken

F>M>O>U

	D	C
D	(2,2)	4,1
C	1,4	3,3

Prisoner's Dilemma

states care more about relative gains and less about absolute gains. Combining relative and absolute gains considerations in this way leads to the payoff matrix shown in figure 7.3.[12]

This framework allows us to investigate the consequences of increased concern for relative versus absolute gains for the game structure. Recall the impact of relative gains in figure 7.2. Relative gains provide a negative payoff for unilateral cooperation (since $F > U$), a positive payoff for free-riding, and zero payoff where states gain equally through either mutual cooperation or mutual defection. In addition, increased emphasis on relative gains means that absolute payoffs are less important, so that the value of cooperation itself

FIGURE 7.2
Relative Gains

	D	C
D	0, 0	F-U, U-F
C	U-F, F-U	0,0

FIGURE 7.3
Mixture of Absolute and Relative Gains

	D	C
D	0, 0	$F^*=F-rU$, $U^*=U-rF$
C	$U^*=U-rF$, $F^*=F-rU$	$M^*=(1-r)M$, $M^*=(1-r)M$

drops. These two effects produce transformed U^*, F^*, and M^* payoffs (where the asterisk represents the combination of absolute and relative gains considerations) while not affecting the normalized non-cooperation payoff of 0. For example, increasing r decreases M^* unconditionally and decreases U^* provided $F > 0$. In turn, changes in these values change the rank order of states' preferences and thereby transform the game structure.

The transformation of the Harmony game illustrates how relative gains calculations change game structures. The initial preference ordering for each state is $M > F > U > 0$. As relative gains considerations become more important, the first three payoffs in this ordering decrease but at different rates. When $U > M - F$, as in the left half of figure 7.4, the Harmony ordering is maintained until $r > (M - F)/(M - U)$. Beyond this, the preference orderings become $F^* > M^* > U^* > 0$, and the structure of the game is changed to Chicken (see table 7.1). If relative gains concerns increase further, so that $r > U/F$, the individual orderings become $F^* > M^* > 0 > U^*$ and the structure of the game converts to PD. This structure persists until $r = 1$ and the pure relative gains, zero-sum game of figure 7.2 pertains. Conversely, when $U < M - F$, as in the right half of figure 7.4, the Harmony ordering is maintained until $r > U/F$, at which point the structure of the game is transformed to Assurance I. As r increases further, the structure of the game converts to PD once $r > (M - F)/(M - U)$. Again, this structure persists until $r = 1$.[13]

Only one scenario is possible for each of the other five symmetric games, as shown in figure 7.5. Assurance I is transformed into PD once the weighting of relative gains exceeds $(M - F)/(M - U)$. Assurance II passes through an intermediate phase, first being transformed into Assurance I when $r > R/U$ and then into PD once $r > (M - F)/(M - U)$. The Coordination game passes through an intermediate phase of Chicken before becoming PD as r increases. Chicken is transformed directly into PD once $r > U/F$.[14] Finally, PD maintains its same structure for all relevant values of r.[15] However, this PD structure becomes more intense with increasing r, since the temptation to free-ride increases, the consequences of unilateral cooperation are more severe, and the advantages of mutual cooperation over mutual defection decrease.[16] In all situations, the limiting case where only relative gains matter (i.e., $r = 1$) is the zero-sum game where both sides have a dominant strategy not to cooperate.

This tendency to convert absolute gains situations into PD can be summarized in terms of the impact of relative gains motives on states' payoffs. Since $F > U$, $F^* = F - rU$ must become positive as r increases toward 1. Therefore, free-riding is eventually preferred to mutual cooperation (i.e., $F^* > M^*$), since $M^* = (1 - r)M$ becomes a

FIGURE 7.4
Different Relative Gains Transformations of Harmony to PD

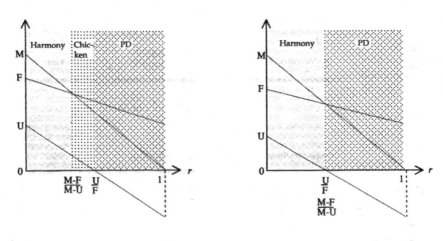

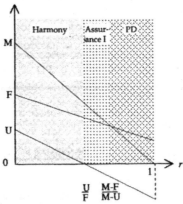

a. $M > F > U > 0$ with $U > M - F$
b. $M > F > U > 0$ with $U = M - F$
c. $M > F > U > 0$ with $U < M - F$
Note that $U < M - F$ implies $U/F < (M - F)/(M - U)$ since $F, U > 0$.

FIGURE 7.5

Relative Gains Transformation of Absolute Gains Games into Prisoner's Dilemmas

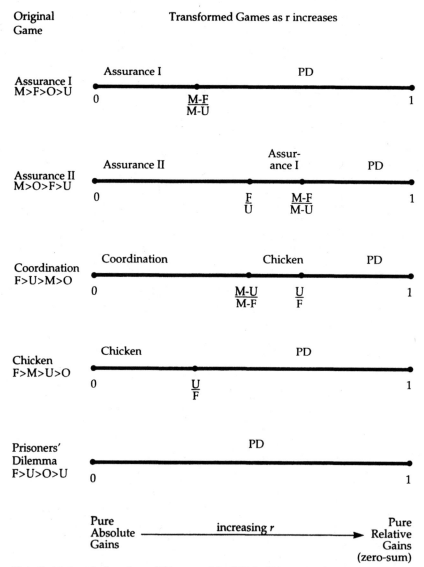

Note that intervals for r (e.g., $F/U \leq r \leq (M - F)/(M - U)$) are not directly comparable across cases because the stipulated orders of M, F, U, and 0 are not the same.

progressively smaller positive payoff as relative gains become more important. Until $r = 1$, however, mutual cooperation provides a greater payoff than the normalized 0 payoff from mutual defection (i.e., $M^* > 0$). Finally, relative gains pressures necessarily make $U^* = U - rF$ negative and the least preferred payoff as r increases (i.e., $0 > U^*$). Thus, as r increases, the preference orderings of states are eventually transformed to $F^* > M^* > 0 > U^*$, which defines PD. In the limiting case where $r = 1$, the game becomes zero-sum with $F^* > M^* = 0 > U^*$ and $F^* = -U^*$. Whatever the initial absolute gains circumstance, relative considerations augment incentives for states not to cooperate for familiar reasons associated with PD and zero-sum games.[17]

Thus we see how the substantive intuition of realism that states care about relative gains maps into its implicit analytic presumption that international anarchy can be characterized as a PD. Relative gains calculations transform each of the various absolute gains circumstances presented in table 7.1 into PD. This makes cooperation problematic even when absolute gains conditions are congenial as in Harmony or Assurance. The greater the concern for relative gains, the more intense is the resulting PD, until $r = 1$, when all two-actor interactions become zero-sum. In these circumstances, realists argue, cooperation is much more difficult or even impossible.

Prospects for Cooperation in a Two-Actor Relative Gains World

How much do relative gains considerations impede cooperation in a two-actor world? When states are exclusively relative gains seekers, the two-actor world is zero-sum and cooperation is impossible. Because such an extreme assumption is rarely warranted, I shall briefly examine the impact of more realistic, intermediate levels of relative gains aspirations. First, I consider how mixtures of relative and absolute considerations affect cooperation within PD. Second, I evaluate the tendency for relative gains aspirations to transform non-PD absolute gains games into PD. Finally, I measure the intensity of the resulting PDs. The conclusion is that moderate levels of relative gains reinforce the characterization of international politics as PD, but that only quite high levels of r produce intense PDs from other absolute gains situations.

First, what is the differential impact of low, medium, and high levels of relative gains ambitions in PD? If small degrees of relative gains make any PD very intense, the deleterious implications for cooperation are enormous. Conversely, if only an extreme relative gains preoccupation makes PD very intense, relative gains considerations are important only in rare circumstances.

Changes in the *minimum discount factor* ($0 \leq \phi < 1$) required to support cooperation provide a useful measure of the impact of relative gains in inhibiting cooperation in the PD. The discount factor measures the extent to which a state values future benefits relative to current benefits. For example, a discount factor of .8 means that a state values a unit of benefit in the next period as worth only .8 units in the current period and, generally, values a unit of benefit p periods in the future at only $.8p$ units today. Since decentralized cooperation in PD can be supported by ongoing future incentives offered by mutual cooperation (e.g., through joint choice of TIT-for-TAT strategies), it is more likely to be stable when a lower discount factor is required of states. The reason is that smaller future benefits of continuing cooperation are then sufficient to outweigh larger immediate gains from noncooperation (Axelrod 1984). Minimum ϕ is the lowest discount factor for states at which cooperation is stable; increases in minimum ϕ indicate the deleterious impact of relative gains on cooperation. A related measure used below is the increase in minimum discount factor induced by a given level of relative gains seeking as a proportion of the total change in the discount factor caused by a shift from pure absolute gains to pure relative gains seeking.[18]

Figure 7.6 shows that cooperation in PD is most greatly affected when relative gains concerns increase from low levels (i.e., $\delta\phi/\delta r > 0$ and $\delta^2\phi/\delta r^2 < 0$). The top curve clearly illustrates this concave relation between r and ϕ. Here r has had nearly 80 percent of its impact on ϕ by the time $r = .25$, and over 90 percent by the time $r = .5$. This is an extreme case, however, where the difference between unilateral cooperation (U) and no cooperation (0) is twenty times as great as the difference between cooperation (M) and no cooperation (i.e., $\{F, M, 0, U\} = \{2, 1, 0, -20\}$). In general, low levels of r have their greatest impact when U is low compared to the other payoffs. The bottom curve presents a possibly more typical PD game based on the "standard" preference ordering (i.e., $\{4, 3, 2, 1\}$ normalized to $\{2, 1, 0, -1\}$). Here the impact of low levels of relative gains on ϕ is much more modest. Nevertheless, the proportional impact of low levels of relative gains is greater at lower levels of *r* with 33 percent of their impact on ϕ occurring for levels of *r* = .25, and 60 percent of their impact occurring when *r* = .5. The middle curve shows similar results for an intermediate case {2, 1, 0, -5}. These results indicate that small degrees of relative gains motivations are important, though not necessarily decisive, in impeding cooperation in PD games.

The second issue is how quickly relative gains transform other absolute games into PD. Since *F, M,* 0, and *U* can vary widely within the minimal constraints imposed on them, it is difficult to generalize as to the level of relative gains pressures necessary to convert various absolute gains games into PD. Very low levels of *r* are sufficient to transform different situations into PD whenever the payoff from unilateral cooperation (*U*) is significantly lower than the gains from free-riding (*F*). Conversely, when unilateral cooperation is almost as beneficial as free-riding (i.e., *U* is close to *F*), games become PD only when *r* is close to unity. And where mutual cooperation is preferred

FIGURE 7.6
The Relationship Between ϕ and *r* for Three Prisoner's Dilemmas of Increasing severity

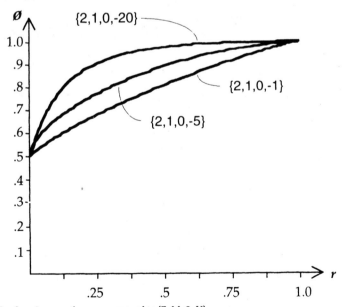

Note: Numbers in parentheses correspond to {F, M, 0, U}.

to free-riding, low levels of relative gains considerations inhibit co-operation only if the difference (i.e., $M - F$) is small. Most importantly, it is obviously easy to concoct particular examples where small or large doses of relative gains are needed to have an impact.

A way to appreciate the impact of relative gains is in terms of the "standard" 2 X 2 game preferences with the best outcome equal to four and the worst outcome equal to one. These interval-level payoffs are normalized so that mutual noncooperation is equal to zero. In this case, Assurance I and Chicken turn into PD when $r > \frac{1}{3}$; Harmony turns into PD when $r > \frac{1}{2}$ and Assurance II and Coordination turn into PD when $r > \frac{2}{3}$. The PD, of course, remains PD throughout but becomes more intense with increasing r.[19] We can conclude that under the typical specification of 2 X 2 game payoffs, a moderate (i.e., $\frac{1}{3}$) to high (i.e., $\frac{2}{3}$) level of r is necessary to transform non-PD games into PD.

An important caveat follows: *PD results significantly overstate the deleterious impact of relative gains on cooperation in other absolute gains circumstances.* The reason is that the initial impact of relative gains is used up in first converting these other games to PD. Only then can increasing relative gains pressures make the resulting PD progressively more intense. Figure 7.7 shows these differential results for the standard preference rankings described. Consider a comparison of the minimal discount factor (ϕ) required to support cooperation in various games when $r = .5$. Cooperation in PD requires $\phi > .8$, whereas Chicken requires $\phi > .6$ and Assurance I requires $\phi > .33$. The cooperative equilibrium in Harmony is stable for any positive discount factor when $r = .5$, since it is at this point that it has just converted to PD.[20] Assurance II possesses a stable cooperative outcome for $r < \frac{2}{3}$ and is not greatly affected by relative gains considerations of this magnitude. Indeed except for a minor exception in the Coordination game, the minimum discount factor (ϕ) required for a stable cooperative equilibrium is higher for PD than for the other games until $r = 1$. Therefore, relative gains findings for PD significantly overstate their impact on other initial absolute gains games. Relative gains make other games PD, but not especially intense ones.[21]

Thus the intuition of realism is confirmed but qualified whenever there are substantial relative gains concerns between two states. Although relative gains transform other absolute gains situations into PD, PD results significantly overstate the impact of relative gains for these other games. Within PD, the impact of increasing relative gains is greatest at low levels of r and increases at a decreasing rate until all prospects for cooperation are eliminated at $r = 1$. This lends some credence to the realist conclusion that cooperation is more difficult when states are relative gains seekers and are in absolute gains PD situations.

Because this realist pessimism is predicated on the two-actor case, it cannot be uncritically transferred to the multiactor world—as it has been—without careful scrutiny. I now stipulate that the initial absolute gains situation is PD—the most favorable assumption for the relative gains case—and examine the further limitations to the realist position when there are more than two states and they care about both relative and absolute gains.

FIGURE 7.7
The Relationship Between ϕ and r for All Six 'Standard" Games

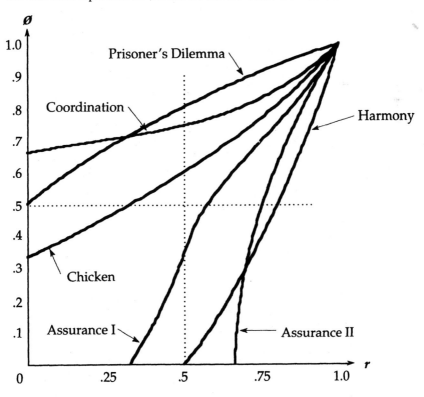

RELATIVE GAINS WITH MORE THAN TWO STATES

A separate paper analyzes cooperation among different numbers of identical states that care only about relative gains (Snidal 1991a). It shows that relative gains do *not* affect prospects for cooperation whenever the number of states (n) is large. Because those results depend on large n, however, that analysis is inconclusive as to the effect of relative gains involving small numbers of states. It also assumes symmetry (in that states are of equal importance) and does not allow for mixtures of relative and absolute gains objectives.

I explore here the impact of relative gains among small numbers of states, especially when they are not all identical. The logic is to examine the conditions under which cooperation is a stable equilibrium outcome in an iterated relative gains PD, using the minimum discount factor (ϕ) as an indicator of the difficulty of cooperation. This equilibrium is examined to see how it is affected by variations in overall concerns for relative gains as well as differential concerns with relative gains vis-à-vis particular other states. Because the analysis is generalized to include states of different sizes, I shall first examine how the costs and benefits of cooperation are distributed among states of different sizes.

Why Cooperative Gains Are Equally Distributed Between States

The central result derived is that small and large states share equally in costs and benefits of international cooperation; that is, when Canada and the United States cooperate, each bears equal costs and earns equal benefits even though Canada is roughly one-tenth as populous as the United States. This seemingly surprising conclusion follows from an assumption of constant returns to scale: cooperating with q states of equal size provides a state with q times the cooperative benefits of cooperating with one state. Similarly, cooperating with a state that is q times as large as another provides q times as many benefits. When such conditions apply, different-sized states gain equally from cooperation.

Constant returns to scale is a reasonable, though imperfect, assumption for analyzing international cooperation. Cooperative returns are surely increasing in some range, playing an important role in the formation of the nation-state itself, as well as in the development of any international division of labor in either economic or security affairs. Returns are probably decreasing at some later stage, at least for states that are large and well integrated into the international system. But for an important range of intermediate levels of international cooperation, constant returns to scale is a useful initial approximation.[22]

To demonstrate that constant returns imply an equal division of costs and benefits between states, consider different-sized states as composed of different integral numbers of equal units. These units are the accounting measures for the relevant attributes constituting the "size" of a state for international cooperation. Because units are identical, cooperation between any two of them entails identical costs (c) and benefits (b) for each. Constant returns to scale means that the costs and benefits of any dyadic interaction are independent of other cooperative interactions in which either of those two units is engaged. Thus the total net benefit to any unit from cooperation equals $b - c$ times the number of cooperative dyads to which it belongs. The total collective benefit summed over a group of S units all cooperating with one another equals $b - c$ times twice the number of dyads in the population or $[(b - c)(S!)/(S - 2)!]$.

If S represents the number of units in the international system, then state sovereignty is a partition of the system into n mutually exclusive and exhaustive subsets $\{s_1, \ldots, s_n\}$ where s_i is the size of the ith state, individual states may be of different sizes, and $\Sigma s_i = S$. By expanding the measure of collective cooperative gains in terms of this sovereignty partition and rearranging terms, we obtain

$$(b-c) \frac{S!}{(S-2)!} = (b-c) \sum_{\substack{i=1 \\ s_i \geq 2}}^{n} \frac{s_i!}{(s_i-1)!} + (b-c) \sum_{i=1}^{n} s_i \left\{ \sum_{j \neq i} s_j \right\}.$$

The left-hand side represents total benefits from global cooperation, while the right-hand side terms partition these into benefits from domestic and international cooperation, respectively. The first term represents the sum of domestic cooperative benefits within each of n states (i.e., the aggregate cooperative benefits among the s_i units constituting a particular state).[23] This domestic cooperation is taken as unproblematic from an international perspective and will not be discussed here. The second term on the right-hand side represents the benefits of complete international cooperation. Each state i receives $s_i s_j(b - c)$ from cooperation with state j, while state j simultaneously receives $s_j s_i(b - c)$ from cooperating with state i. Thus the assumption of constant returns to scale implies that the gains of international cooperation between two states are proportional to the product of their "sizes" and are equally divided between the two states. Although I use the specific form $s_i s_j(b - c)$ below, the conclusion concerning the equality of the gains is most important in the general argument.

An example is cooperation between Canada and the United States. On the one hand, the United States is ten times the size of Canada, so each Canadian unit benefits from cooperation with ten times as many U.S. units as does each U.S. unit with Canadian units. On the other hand, ten times as many U.S. units benefit from cooperation. Since the aggregate national gain from bilateral cooperation is the sum of the gains of their respective units, it is straightforward to see that these sums are equal for the two states. The key assumption here is of constant returns to scale. The Canadian units represent the 101st–110th cooperative partners for the U.S. units, whereas the U.S. units represent the 11th–110th partners for Canadian units. If cooperation with the eleventh partner provides more benefits than cooperation with the 101st partner (i.e., declining returns), then aggregate Canadian gains will exceed U.S. gains from cooperation.

Under a constant returns assumption, gains from cooperation are proportional to the size of the involved states and are shared equally between them. In *absolute* terms, states have the same interest in cooperation regardless of their respective sizes. Because the potential benefits of international versus domestic cooperation are proportionately greater for small states, asymmetric interdependence places them in a more vulnerable bargaining position. I do not address such considerations except to show why relative gains create incentives for larger states *not* to take advantage of this bargaining strength and, if anything, to offer sweeter deals to smaller states. In terms of *relative* position (as measured by absolute gaps between states), cooperation does not lead to relative gains.[24] But relative considerations do provide additional incentive to break agreements, since states seek not only to do well for themselves but also to do better than others.

The Limited Impact of Relative Gains
in Multilateral Settings

Now we can examine relative gains maximization among a set of states $\{s_1, \ldots, s_n\}$ where s_i represents the size of state i. As I have shown, cooperation between two states leads to an equal payoff $s_i s_j(b - c)$ for each. This is an absolute payoff, however, and we want to consider states that worry about relative gains as well. Let the parameter r (with $0 \leq r \leq 1$) represent the weight states place on relative gains and $(1 - r)$ the weight of absolute gains in their overall evaluation of outcomes. When $r = 1$, we have the special case where states care exclusively about relative gains; when $r = 0$, they care only about absolute gains. Thus variations in r allows us to examine the impact of relative gains considerations on cooperation.[25]

We need to address the possibility that states are concerned with relative gains compared to specific other states. Certain states are more threatening for geopolitical reasons, including proximity or competition for key resources, or because of their seemingly aggressive character or ideological differences or a history of grievances between the two states. Or a state may be inherently more threatening simply because it has greater capabilities. Conversely, another state is typically less threatening when it is far away, has no reason to be hostile, or is small. To incorporate different evaluations of different states, let every state have a set of weights $\{w_{i1}, \ldots, w_{in}\}$, where $0 \leq w_{ij} \leq 1$ indicates the emphasis state i places on state j's performance in evaluating its relative gains position.

Assume that states distribute their relative gains concerns across other states so that $\Sigma w_{ij} = 1$. This restriction follows straightforwardly from a standard intuition of international balancing: it is at least as dangerous to suffer a unilateral loss in a world with fewer actors as in a world with more actors.[26] The reason is that more actors enhance the possibilities of protecting oneself through forming coalitions; and, generally, the less well united one's potential enemies, the safer one is. For example, the United States would be less adversely affected (or at least no more affected) by a drop in its power if the Soviet Union had first disintegrated into its separate republics than otherwise. This assumption has the substantive implication that states are not paranoid in the sense of magnifying relative gains losses versus other states without regard to their importance for overall power or security considerations. Conversely, states cannot be deluded by artificially inflating their relative gains performance through comparisons to strategically insignificant states.

Denoting state i's absolute payoff from international interactions as P_{ia}, its payoff incorporating relative gains concerns (defined as differences between its absolute payoff and the absolute payoff of other states) is

$$P_{ir} = (1 - r)P_{ia} + r \sum_{j=1}^{n} w_{ij} (P_{ia} - P_{ja}). \tag{1}$$

Index r reflects state i's degree of concern with relative gains. The first term on the right-hand side indicates the importance of its own absolute gains, and the second term its evaluation of relative gains versus every other state. This is the objective function that state i seeks to maximize.[27]

To investigate the impact of relative gains on cooperation, consider the circumstances under which state i would maintain a cooperative agreement with state k. Here cooperation involves a dichotomous choice to cooperate (by providing the other a benefit at a cost to oneself) or not-cooperate at each play of a repeated interaction. Repeated play situations are of primary interest because self-enforcing cooperation requires that the incentives provided by future cooperation be sufficient to maintain ongoing cooperation against current incentive to not-cooperate. For simplicity, states consider only two supergame strategies—TIT-for-TAT starting with cooperation or *never cooperate*. Third-party states are assumed to maintain their current behavior and do not react to the outcome between i and k. The possibility for cooperation then depends on whether the joint choice of TIT-for-TAT strategies is an equilibrium or whether states have an incentive to not-cooperate (never cooperate) when others cooperate (TIT-for-TAT).[28]

If both states choose TIT-for-TAT, then, with constant returns to scale, each receives $(b - c)s_i s_k$ on every play of the game. With a discount factor of ϕ the current value of this stream of absolute gains is $s_i s_k (b - c)/(1 - \phi)$. Incorporating relative gains considerations, the payoff to state i from a joint TIT-for-TAT strategy choice is

$$P_{ir} + (1-r)\frac{b-c}{1-\phi}s_i s_k + r\frac{b-c}{1-\phi}s_i s_k \sum_{j\neq k} w_{ij}. \qquad (2)$$

The first term represents the value of the preexisting situation (as shown in equation 1), while the second term is the absolute gains value of cooperation with k. The third term represents the relative advantage achieved over other states through cooperation with k. Since i and k gain equally from cooperation, neither achieves any relative gain over the other through joint cooperation.[29]

The stability of cooperation depends on whether an individual state i does better by breaking the agreement for immediate gains at the expense of destroying the longer-run cooperative agreement. If state i defects, it receives a first-round payoff of $s_i s_k b$ from its free ride on k's unilateral cooperation. This ends bilateral cooperation, since k will reciprocate in the next round and no further benefits will be received from the interaction. Meanwhile, state k incurs a one-period loss of $s_i s_k c$ from unilateral cooperation. After this loss, state k will cease cooperation and realizes no further costs or benefits from the dyad. Again, these are all absolute gains payoffs, and state i's overall evaluation—including relative gains considerations—can be seen in the light of equation 1 to be

$$P_{ir} + (1-r)s_i s_k b + rs_i s_k b \sum_{j\neq k} w_{ij} + rs_i s_k(b+c)w_{ik}. \qquad (3)$$

The first term is again the value of the preexisting situation, while the second term reflects the absolute gains from a free ride on state k's unilateral cooperation for one period. The third term represents the relative advantage achieved over third-party states through this free ride. The final term is i's relative gain over k, due not only to the value of i's free ride but also to the loss sustained by k through unilateral cooperation.

The stability of cooperation between i and k depends on whether the value of continuing cooperation in equation 2 exceeds the value of defection in equation 3. This will be the case if

$$\phi > \phi_{rw} = \frac{c + rw_{ik}b}{b + rw_{ik}c}, \qquad (4)$$

where ϕ_{rw} is the minimum discount factor that will support cooperation when state i places an overall weight of r on relative gains and a specific relative gains weight of w_{ik} on state k. Note that neither the absolute nor relative sizes of two interacting states directly affect their propensity to cooperate. Insofar as size affects relative gains weights (e.g., s_k partly determines w_{ik}), however, it indirectly makes cooperation more difficult among larger states and dampens the willingness of smaller states to cooperate with larger states. I pursue possible implications of this below.

The key factors determining the impact of relative gains are r and w_{ik}. If either is zero, then equation 4 reduces to $\phi_{rw} = c/b$, the condition for cooperation when states care only about absolute gains (ϕ_a). That is, if state i either does not care about relative gains in general ($r = 0$) or its relative gains concerns do not involve state k in particular ($w_{ik} = 0$), then cooperation is not impeded.[30] At the other extreme, cooperation is impossible if r and w_{ik} are both unity since equation 4 reduces to the impermissible $\phi > \phi_{rw} = 1$. That is, if a state cares only about relative gains ($r = 1$) and evaluates them only with respect to one other state ($w_{ik} = 1$), there is no room for cooperation with that state. This is unsurprising, since it reduces the interaction to a two-actor pure relative gains situation that is strictly zero-sum, as shown earlier. Such a world is doubly unrealistic, since it assumes both that states do not care at all about absolute gains and that they inhabit a bipolar system so tight that no regard is paid to third parties.

Understanding the impact of relative gains in the multilateral setting requires analysis of the joint impact of r and w_{ik}. As in the two-actor case, the impact of increasing r is greatest at low levels, with positive but decreasing additional impact as r increases. The same is true for w_{ik} (i.e., $\delta\phi/\delta w > 0$ and $\delta^2\phi/\delta w^2 < 0$). Although this suggests that low levels of concern for relative gains have a significant impact on cooperation, as shown for the two-state case above, the interactive relation of these two factors decreases that impact dramatically. Figure 7.8 shows this relation for $\phi_a = .5$. The axes represent different levels of r and w_{ik} while the rectangular hyperboles are isograms for equal levels of ϕ_{rw} required to support cooperation. The origin is the point where there are no relative gains considerations so that $\phi_{rw} = \phi_a$. Finally, the horizontal axis indicates the cases of bipolarity, tripolarity, and classical balance of power involving two, three, and five states, respectively.[31]

Both r and w_{ik} must be large for relative gains to matter. Figure 8

FIGURE 7.8

Isogram Curves for ϕ_{rw} Under Different Values of r and w

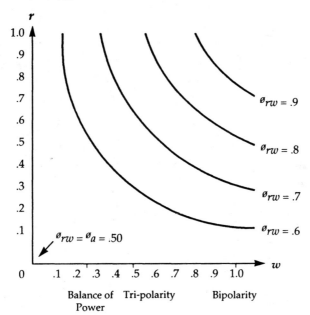

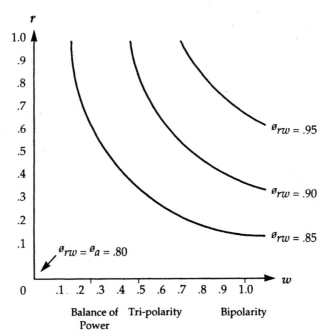

shows that if either r or w_{ik} is small, then ϕ_{rw} is not substantially larger than ϕ_a. More importantly, unless both r and w_{ik} are large, the impact on ϕ_{rw} is at most moderate. Consider a tripolar system where relative and absolute gains are weighted equally, so that $r = w_{ik} = .5$. Relative gains considerations increase ϕ from an initial absolute gains $\phi_a = .5$ to $\phi_{rw} = .67$. This increase is substantially less than the extreme relative gains case, with ϕ increasing only one-third as much. The increase in ϕ is slightly greater for higher values of ϕ_a, but relative gains considerations still do not necessarily impede cooperation. Thus the tripolar case already indicates a very different situation from the pure bipolar relative gains situation. Whenever there are more than three significant states or relative gains are weighted less heavily, the impact of relative gains is even smaller, as can be seen clearly in figure 7.8.

Table 7.2 highlights this relationship numerically for this case and also for $\phi_a = .8$. The bipolar system with $r = 1$ represents the case

TABLE 7.2

Percentage Impact of Relative Gains Under Different Combinations of r and w

System type (n,w)	\multicolumn{11}{c}{*Impact of Relative Gains (%)*}

	\multicolumn{5}{c}{$\phi_a = .5$}	\multicolumn{5}{c}{$\phi_a = .8$}
System type (n,w)	\multicolumn{10}{c}{General Weighting of Relative Gains (r)}
	0	.25	.50	.75	1.0	0	.25	.50	.75	1.0
Bipolar $n=2; w=1$	0	33	60	82	100	0	38	64	84	100
Tripolar $n=3; w=.5$	0	18	33	47	60	0	20	38	52	64
Balance of Power $n=5; w=.25$	0	10	18	26	33	0	11	20	29	38
Ten Countries $n=10; w=.11$	0	4	8	12	16	0	5	10	14	18
Twenty Countries $n=20; w=.05$	0	2	4	6	8	0	2	5	7	9
Large n $n\to\infty; w\to0$	0	0	0	0	0	0	0	0	0	0

where relative gains have 100 percent of their impact and fully inhibit cooperation. With large numbers of relevant actors or $r = 0$ (corresponding to the vertical and horizontal axes of figure 7.8, respectively), relative gains have no impact (0 percent). Intermediate cases show the percentage of relative gains impact under the stipulated circumstances.

The impact of relative gains drops off rapidly whenever r and w are not *both* high. Again, the tripolar case is most dramatic. Adding a third actor to the pure bipolar relative gains world is equivalent to cutting the concern for relative gains in half (e.g., $n = 3$, $r = 1$ is equivalent to $n = 2$, $r = .5$) and reduces the impact of relative gains by about 40 percent. When both $n = 3$ and $r = .5$, the impact of relative gains is reduced by roughly two-thirds. Similarly, a move to a balance-of-power system (even with $r = 1$) is equivalent to a reduction of relative gains concerns by 75 percent and reduces their impact by two-thirds. In general, whenever $n > 2$ and $r < .5$, relative gains have no more than 40 percent of their potential impact, regardless of the initial value of ϕ_a. The drop-off is even greater for lower levels of r and w. [32]

Thus the relative gains argument cannot provide a decisive response to the institutionalist claim that decentralized cooperation is possible under anarchy. Relative gains can save the realist case only in the two-actor world and perhaps demonstrate that institutionalists underestimate the difficulty of cooperation in other very-small-n cases. But these are much weaker claims than realists have made in uncritically transferring relative gains arguments from the two-actor world to international politics more generally.

IMPLICATIONS OF RELATIVE GAINS FOR CONTEMPORARY INTERNATIONAL RELATIONS THEORY

Although the general claim that relative gains prevent international cooperation is not correct, some potentially interesting implications follow from the assumption. As I have shown, relative gains have their greatest impact when the number of states is small or (equivalently in terms of the model) there are asymmetries among them. I shall informally sketch out some plausible explanations that relative gains may provide for key aspects of the interaction between large and small states, hegemonic cooperation and decline, cooperation patterns in a bipolar system, and the possibility of increasing cooperation under multipolarity.

Why Do the Small Exploit the Large?

A common claim about international politics is that small states fare better than large states from their interactions. Examples include unequal burden-sharing in military alliances (Olson and Zeckhauser 1966) and the need for some large country to absorb the costs of leading the international economy (Kindleberger 1973). The standard explanation for this putative phenomenon is that international cooperation is a public goods problem where large actors make the group privileged by unilaterally providing the collective good (Olson 1965). Difficulties with this account include such questions as whether the relevant international goods are truly public and why relative decline of the largest state does not always result in the collapse of public goods provision (Keohane 1984; Snidal 1985b). These objections are not necessarily fatal, but they require complicated supplementary arguments regarding the role of international institutions in promoting and maintaining cooperation.

The relative gains explanation is simpler and arguably more elegant. Although I did not assume it earlier, it is reasonable to believe that states are warier of larger states with regard to relative gains. Thus, for any pair of states, the smaller state will be more concerned with the relative gains consequences of their interaction (i.e., $w_{ij} > w_{ji}$ if $s_i < s_j$, ceteris paribus). The larger state may overcome the smaller state's greater reluctance to cooperate by offering it more than an equal share of the benefits. It is in the large state's interest to do so because it prefers an unequal cooperative arrangement to no cooperation. Therefore an asymmetric distribution of absolute gains may be a requisite for striking cooperative agreements among different-sized states concerned about relative gains.

Hegemonic Cooperation and Decline

Cooperative arrangements favoring smaller states contribute to relative hegemonic decline. As the unequal distribution of benefits in favor of smaller states helps them catch up to the hegemonic actor, it also lowers the relative gains weight they place on the hegemonic actor. At the same time, declining relative preponderance increases the hegemonic state's concern for relative gains with other states, especially any rising challengers. The net result is increasing pressure from the largest actor to change the prevailing system to gain a greater share of cooperative benefits.[33]

This relative gains argument may better explain changes in economic relations among Western states than in security relations where the public goods nature of defense spending (especially deterrence) is more compelling. Shifting concern over foreign trade and investment is one indicator of perceived changes in relative advantage. Whereas in the 1950s and 1960s Europe, Canada, and the Third World complained of U.S. dominance in trade and investment, in the 1970s and 1980s it was the United States that worried about foreign —especially Japanese—relative advantage. The United States now actively seeks to alter international trading rules in its favor whereas in the early postwar period it accepted special exceptions for European and less-developed states.

Cooperation Patterns in a Loose Bipolar World

The hegemony argument overlooks the obvious fact that the postwar international system combined two superpowers with a handful of secondary powers and a multitude of small states. As a first approximation, consider the relative gains consequences in a system with two great powers and many small ones. The large states weight one another heavily on relative gains and weight the small states barely at all. The many small states weight the great powers heavily and one another not very much at all. (Again, I set aside geopolitical, historical, and other factors that affect this pattern.) Therefore, small states find it easier to cooperate with one another than with large states. Large states find it difficult to cooperate with one another, but their willingness to cooperate with smaller states is not impeded by relative gains. Because small states are reluctant to cooperate with them, the great powers may offer favorable terms to small states as noted above. Indeed competition between them for cooperative relations with small states seems likely. The result is the relative decline of the superpowers and therefore increased possibilities for cooperation between them.

This approximation to bipolarity explains many stylized facts of the postwar period. The superpowers found it very difficult to cooperate with one another. They competed to establish good relations with small states, especially in the Third World, where spheres of influence were more fluid. Cooperation among smaller states was evidenced in the early successes of the European Community. The greatest anomaly is perhaps relations among Third World states, where a number of major cooperative initiatives—including the Andean Pact, the Association of Southeast Asian Nations (ASEAN), nonalignment, or the Organization of African Unity—met limited success. Only in the late 1960s did Third World cooperation emerge in forums such as the Law of the Sea and the United Nations Conference on Trade and Development (UNCTAD), and some of this was more rhetorical than real. Finally, if the relative gains hypothesis is correct, it helps explain how competition between the two superpowers led to their mutual decline and improved prospects for cooperation between them. (See Snidal 1991a for a related discussion of the instability of bipolarity under relative gains.)

Multipolarity Versus Bipolarity

Some realists argue that bipolarity is preferable to multipolarity because states care about relative gains. Waltz, for example, proposes that it is easier to keep track of relative capabilities in a bipolar world and that the resulting reduction in uncertainty increases stability (1979:168). However, the preceding analysis shows why it is less necessary to keep track of relative gains in a multipolar world. Because rational state behavior is less affected by relative gains, cooperation is easier under multipolarity. Therefore realists who premise their arguments on relative gains should prefer multipolarity over bipolarity.[34]

This contrasts sharply with standard absolute gains arguments that increasing the number of states limits cooperation. Increasing n impedes retaliation against noncooperators whenever states cannot perfectly discriminate their behavior with respect to particular other states. It therefore limits the possibilities for decentralized enforcement of cooperative agreements. These problems have been set aside in the current analysis by treating interactions as dyadic, although the broader n-actor environment is crucial to each state's behavior in the dyad. Limiting the ability of states to differentiate their behavior across dyads also makes relative gains cooperation more difficult under increasing n. When discrimination is possible, however, increasing n has the opposite impact of promoting cooperations in the relative gains world.

It is premature to conclude that recent trends toward multipolarity have facilitated international cooperation. To be sure, there has been a short-run blossoming of cooperative East-West relations; and it is possible to point to recent successes in intra-West relations. However, this follows a period of intense rivalry between the superpowers and is accompanied by continuing tensions over the management of the Western economy. In brief, there is insufficient evidence to support the claim that multipolarity has increased cooperation. What we can say is that relative gains arguments do not support claims that the increasing importance of other actors will be unsettling for the international system.

Defensive Cooperation Versus Defensive Positionality

Grieco (1990) argues that the possibility of *some* states' seeking relative gains leads *all* states to forgo cooperative opportunities out of fear that others will take advantage of them. He labels this *defensive positionality*. But relative gains need not have this effect and instead can lead states to *defensive cooperation*. As we have seen, concern for relative gains in respect to some states is consistent with cooperation with other states. More surprisingly, cooperation with relative gains adversaries can be the best choice in a multilateral world, especially as the number of states increases. States that do not cooperate fall behind other relative gains maximizers that cooperate among themselves. This makes cooperation the best defense (as well as the best offense) when your rivals are cooperating in a multilateral relative gains world (Snidal 1991a).

CONCLUSION

The realist argument that relative gains seeking greatly diminishes possibilities for international cooperation is not generalizable. It applies in the special case of tight bipolarity between states that care only about relative gains. Its truth diminishes rapidly if concerns for relative gains are less than total, or if the initial absolute gains game between states is not PD, *or* (especially) if the number of states increases to three or more. Since one or more of these conditions characterizes most international political phenomena, relative gains do not limit international cooperation in general.

Yet relative gains hold other interesting implications for international politics. I have not addressed the veracity of the assumption that states aspire to relative gains, only examined its consequences. The resulting conclusions connect relative gains to prevailing hypotheses about international relations theory and are plausible in light of postwar experience. Many of these implications should be unsurprising to both institutionalists and realists, since they correspond to prevailing academic folk wisdom. Others do not fit well with realist beliefs — for example, the claim that relative gains seeking makes multipolarity preferable. All of them are fairly casual and require tighter analytical specification and closer empirical analysis. But they point toward the sorts of testable implications that will ultimately be the proof or disproof of the relative gains hypothesis.

Finally, the analysis suggests a moral for international relations theorizing more generally. The realist argument is guided by an intuition that relative gains transform issues into highly conflictual — even zero-sum — situations where cooperation is not viable. The intuition is correct when there are just two states. The error lies in uncritically mistaking conclusions from a two-actor model for general claims about international politics with any number of actors. One thing we increasingly know about theoretical claims is that they are sensitive to particular changes and contexts. Only a more careful working through of the analytical argument will enable us to understand their consequences.

NOTES

1. Grieco (1990) stresses this as a distinctive aspect of relative gains. As I point out, distributional concerns neither differentiate realism from liberal institutionalism as markedly as he would wish nor place the relative gains argument on its strongest footing. Much of Grieco's empirical evidence for relative gains is contestable because he cannot distinguish it from absolute gains bargaining over the distribution of cooperative benefits. Finally, his differentiation of the two models is biased, since his relative gains model includes absolute gains considerations but not the other way around. For a further discussion of these issues, see Snidal (1991a).

2. I develop a simple model based on constant returns to scale where gains from cooperation are equal even among different-sized states. The point is that even if this were not the "natural" result, it could be achieved by renegotiating the terms of cooperation.

3. Misperception or uncertainty among risk-averse actors could still explain the failure of such deals. Although references to uncertainty are common in the relative gains literature (e.g., see the implicit reference to the quotation from Waltz in the text), it is not systematically developed as part of the relative gains argument. Moreover, uncertainty and risk aversion play a similar role under absolute gains and thus are not a distinctive part of the relative gains argument. Finally, as Andrew Moravcsik (personal communication dated June 28, 1990) has reminded me, relative gains analysts who wish to incorporate the risk of cooperation must also be attentive to the risks of the status quo of noncooperation in anarchy. Risk and uncertainty may also promote cooperation and are part of the standard explanation for international regimes. These considerations would be even more important in the *n*-actor situation.

4. This second aspect of relative gains seeking effectively incorporates the first, since cooperative agreements are evaluated in terms of relative payoffs. Now, however, the relative gains problem cannot be resolved by changing the terms of the agreement, since relative gains are fundamental to states and not a property of particular cooperative agreements.

5. Joanne Gowa (personal communication dated September 26, 1989) states this case succinctly: "Security gains, whenever they enter utility functions, are always relative." Rather than argue the point, I investigate its implications.

6. Elsewhere I argue that there is no reason to presume that all international issues are adequately represented by PD or any other single strategic structure (Snidal 1985a). But that argument assumes states care about absolute gains, whereas the present one demonstrates how relative gains provide a basis for arguing that PD is a sufficient description for international issues.

7. Labeling particular behaviors as *cooperation* or *defection* independent of their consequences runs the danger of persuasive definition. This is exemplified by the peculiar definition of *mutual cooperation* in the Deadlock game as an outcome where both sides are worse off than they would have been through *mutual defection* (Oye 1985; Downs and Rocke 1990). Such problems are avoided here by the stipulation that $M > 0$. Note, however, that in the two-actor situation, gains from cooperation diminish to zero as relative gains concerns increase to unity.

8. Here we are interested primarily in the ordinal symmetry (i.e., same order of payoffs) necessary to define a two-by-two (2 X 2) game; subsequently, the symmetry condition will be extended to entail interval-level symmetry with the algebraic comparisons of payoffs inherent to relative gains. This evaluation of relative gains requires that states compare gains

but does not require interstate comparisons of utility. Thus, payoffs could be "objective" factors such as gains from trade or increases in military strength. Grieco argues against symmetry as an assumption because it entails equal payoffs from mutual cooperation (1990:42). I have argued that this can be readily achieved by adjusting the terms of cooperation and is not central to the relative gains argument. Concerns for relative gains do help determine the mutually acceptable cooperative agreements—although that role is indistinguishable from bargaining over the distribution of absolute gains.

9. Four of the six games excluded by the $F > U$ restriction are strictly harmonious in that each side has a dominant strategy to cooperate. The remaining two games are variants of the included Assurance and Coordination games. In addition, in all six of these games where $U > F$, relative gains reinforce absolute incentives to cooperate. Note 17 below expands on this point. Finally, an alternate third assumption to restrict the number of games is that free-riding is preferred to mutual cooperation, $F > M$. This produces four 2 X 2 games. Three of these ($F > U > M > 0$, $F > M > U > 0$, and $F > M > 0 > U$) have $F > U$ and so are included here. The fourth, $U > F > M > 0$, offers a minor variation on the included coordination game with $F > U > M > 0$, where relative gains facilitate cooperation.

10. Defining cooperative behavior in this game is difficult. One state cooperates by acceding to the other state's preferred equilibrium outcome. The other state sacrifices nothing. Cooperation is therefore not well defined at the individual level but is defined at the collective level in terms of avoiding noncoordinated outcomes. When relative gains matter, cooperation is effectively redefined as choosing the mutually preferred noncoordination point. For this reason, this game fits awkwardly at several stages in the analysis. I give more detailed discussion of the contrast between PD and coordination elsewhere (Snidal 1985a).

11. Treating relative gains as differences in absolute gains is standard in the formal literature. Verbal discussions are often ambiguous, sometimes also referring to relative gains in terms of ratios or proportions. (See Waltz [1979:105]) The alternative formulation is easily handled here by treating absolute payoffs as the impact of cooperation on growth rates of payoffs and relative gains as differential growth rates.

12. This formulation is equivalent to Grieco's (1990), where $r = k/(1 + k)$ and k is his weighting parameter.

13. In the intervening case where $U = M - F$, there is no transition zone between harmony and the PD. Finally, games that are symmetric in ordinal but not interval terms undergo a similar transition except that the two ordinal payoff structures are transformed at different rates. This leads to some additional and nonsymmetric intermediate games during the transition.

14. See Taylor (1987). The transformation of Chicken reminds us of the peculiar consequences of relative gains: once $r > U/F$, players in Chicken

prefer mutual noncooperation (or "disaster") to unilateral cooperation.

15. Grieco incorrectly reports that increasing relative gains concerns can transform PD into Deadlock (1990:43). Examination of Grieco's equation 4 shows that both sides cannot simultaneously have Deadlock preferences.

16. Taylor (1987) develops this result. With two minor exceptions, the PDs that emerge in other games also become progressively more intense with the increasing importance of relative gains. The temptation to defect from mutual cooperation increases with r, provided $M > U$, which is true for all games considered here except coordination. The sucker cost of unilateral cooperation similarly increases with r, provided $F > 0$, which is true for all the games here except Assurance. The advantages of mutual cooperation over mutual defection always decrease with increasing r.

17. This logic confirms that the assumption $F > U$ is appropriate for examining how relative gains affect cooperation. When $U > F$, the preference ordering under relative gains ultimately becomes $U^* > M^* > 0 > F^*$. This harmonious Deadlock game offers each side a dominant strategy leading to a Pareto-efficient equilibrium. Now, relative gains incentives reinforce cooperative incentives in the initial absolute gains game. Thus, to study how relative gains impede cooperation, it is reasonable to restrict analysis to cases where $F > U$. This means, moreover, that the present analysis is constructed to be favorable to the relative gains case.

18. Formally, this measure is $(\phi - \phi_a)/(\phi_r - \phi_a)$, where ϕ_a and ϕ_r are the minimum discount rates required to support cooperation under pure absolute and pure relative gains, respectively.

19. These values are used in figure 7.5 to locate the transition points between games. They are not used in figure 7.4 because, with $U = M - F$, these two scenarios collapse into one, with no transition zone between Harmony and PD.

20. This is the case for other games, except Chicken, at their point of transformation to PD. Chicken poses its own cooperation problem that can sometimes be resolved if states' concern for future benefits is sufficiently high. Coordination and Harmony (when $U > M - F$) pass through an intermediate Chicken phase, where the discount factor matters even before PD is reached at higher r.

21. The discussion in this paragraph is based on a "vertical" reading of figure 7.7 to see the value of ϕ indicated by a given level of r. An alternative "horizontal" reading shows the level of r necessary to make a given ϕ the lowest discount factor amenable to cooperation. This allows a comparison of the different levels of relative gains necessary to create a PD as intense as the standard PD when $r = 0$ and $\phi = .5$. Chicken requires $r = .33$; Assurance I requires $r = .6$; Assurance II requires $r = .75$; and harmony requires $r = .8$. Coordination always

requires a higher ϕ, regardless of r, reflecting the peculiarities it raises for the concept of cooperation as discussed above. These results strongly confirm the limited impact of relative gains in creating intense PDs from other absolute gains situations.

22. A variety of returns-to-scale assumptions appear in the literature. In economics, the standard trade model assumes constant returns, whereas analyses of the international division of labor and the "new" theory of international trade consider increasing returns to scale. On the security side, returns will be increasing with respect to alliance membership for public goods aspects of security provision (Olson and Zeckhauser 1966). Friedman (1977) explains the size and shape of nations by increasing returns to tax collection on trade and labor with constant returns to taxation on expanding territory.

23. The restriction $s_i \geq 2$ reflects the assumption that at least two units are required for cooperation as defined here. If $s_i = 1$, there is no domestic cooperation as measured in terms of these units. The measure of domestic cooperative benefits depends on the definition of units because some cooperative activity that occurs *within* larger units is external to (i.e., occurs *between*) the smaller units. The measure of international cooperation is not affected by changes in units.

24. The situation is different if we consider gains from purely domestic cooperation. Under constant returns and autarky, larger states grow by absolutely larger amounts and therefore achieve relative gains. The situation is also different if we define relative gains in terms of the ratio of sizes. With constant returns and full global cooperation—that is, all domestic and international cooperative interactions occur—all states grow at the same rate and there are no relative gains. Because small states depend on international cooperation for a larger portion of their growth, large states could achieve relative gains by breaking off international cooperation. This ratio measure of relative position is not used here— but it is straightforward to see that increasing numbers of states decrease these incentives for noncooperative behavior for similar reasons as when states care about relative gains defined as differences.

25. Because we assume a PD situation, note that "r" is overstated if the absolute gains is not PD. Assurance I, for example, only becomes PD when $r > .5$ and the impact of relative gains on it is less than for PD until $r = 1$. Thus the results are biased toward the relative gains hypothesis for the other five absolute gains games.

26. The key part of the restriction is $\Sigma w_i \leq 1$, since higher sums favor the relative gains position. This follows directly from the balancing intuition for the symmetric case. If a state suffers an absolute gains loss of π in a world with n other states, each weighted w_n, its relative gains payoff decreases by $(1 - r)\pi + r\pi n w_n$, as will be seen in equation 1. Since this is preferable to suffering the same absolute loss in a world of $n - 1$ other states, each weighted $w_n - 1$, it is straightforward to show $w_n \leq ((n - 1)/n)w_n - 1$. Because $w_1 = r \leq 1$, $w_2 \leq \frac{1}{2}$. It follows by forward induction

that $w_3 \leq \frac{1}{3}$ and, in general, that $w_n \leq 1/n$. Therefore, it must be that $\Sigma w_i \leq 1$. A parallel proof leads to the same conclusion regarding the sum of weightings when gains in relative power are more valuable in a world with fewer states.

27. We ignore payoffs from domestic cooperation, since these are not affected by international cooperation under constant returns. Note that if $r = 1$ and all states weight all other states equally in relative gains (i.e., $w_{ij} = w_{kl}$ for all i, j, k, l) then $\Sigma P_{ir} = 0$ (Snidal 1991a). Unequal w's allow the sum of relative gains in the system to be positive or negative.

28. This comparison establishes the necessary conditions for a stable cooperative equilibrium. If joint TIT-for-TAT strategies are stable, there will be a multitude of other cooperative equilibria. Showing the minimum requirements for the existence of one such equilibrium is sufficient for present purposes of investigating how much more difficult cooperation is under relative gains. For a more detailed exposition, see Snidal (1991a).

29. Unequal gains diminish the incentives of one side to cooperate (and increase the incentives of the other side) for both absolute and relative gains reasons. I have discussed how this aspect of relative gains can be handled by changing the terms of bilateral cooperation—notwithstanding the more important point that the two states still evaluate outcomes in terms of relative gains. Later I shall discuss circumstances under which an asymmetric distribution of benefits actually improves prospects for cooperation.

30. This parallels the finding cited above that relative gains have no impact in symmetric large-n situations, since large n implies small w_{ik} for all i, k. For a more detailed discussion with special attention to tipping points and the stability of the cooperative equilibrium, see Snidal (1991a).

31. This assumes that other states are weighted equally in terms of relative gains (i.e., $w_{ik} = w_{ij}$, for all j, k) so $w_{ij} = 1/(n - 1)$. That is unproblematic for bipolarity where there is only one other state and for balance of power defined as a rough equality of the great powers. A perfect tripolar system would also have this property, although it is easy to imagine one state placing different weights on the other two major powers. Such a "two-and-a-half-power" system would fall between tripolarity and bipolarity as depicted here.

32. The maximum impact of r in percentage terms occurs when ϕ_a approaches unity and equals $(2rw/rw + 1)$ (100 percent). An example of the continuing drop-off of relative gains effects is the five-actor balance-of-power system ($w = .25$) with $r = .25$ where the impact of relative gains must be less than 12 percent. The increase in n is defined in terms of significant actors, as I have discussed. A tripolar system, for example, has three significant actors regardless of the number of minor actors. These pure cases never exist but provide appropriate benchmarks for my arguments.

33. The relation between size and relative gains weights may be more complicated than the monotonic relation used here. A plausible curvilinear

specification is that relative gains concerns peak when states are roughly equal and drop off when one state is either far behind, or far ahead of, the other. This would seem particularly appropriate for analyses of inter-actions between a rising challenger and a declining hegemon. It would alter the explanation for the posthegemonic breakdown of cooperation from that in the text to emphasize rising tensions between these two central actors. Finally, relative gains concerns may vary across issue dimensions. It makes little sense for small states such as Canada and Finland to worry about relative gains in security against their militarily formidable neighbors. But they may worry about other dimensions such as economic relations where they are better able to counteract relative gains.

34. This supports Kaplan's view of multipolarity as fostering a complemen-tarity between states (1957:23). (Kaplan assumes that states measure relative gains against the system, not against each other.) Grieco argues that under relative gains, cooperative deals are easier when they involve larger numbers of states (1988a:506). I show that what is important is the number of states that affect relative gains calculations, not how many participate in any particular cooperative deal.

8

ABSOLUTE AND RELATIVE GAINS IN INTERNATIONAL RELATIONS THEORY

Robert Powell

The problem of absolute and relative gains divides two of the most influential approaches to international relations theory. *Neoliberal institutionalism* assumes that states focus primarily on their individual absolute gains and are indifferent to the gains of others. Whether cooperation results in a relative gain or loss is not very important to a state in neoliberal institutionalism so long as it brings an absolute gain. In terms of preferences, this focus on absolute gains is usually taken to mean that a state's utility is solely a function of its absolute gain. In contrast, *neorealism,* or *structural realism,* assumes that states are largely concerned with relative rather than absolute gains. In the anarchy of international politics, "relative gain is more important than absolute gain" (Waltz 1959:198). A state's utility in structural realism is at least partly a function of some relative measure like power.[1] These differing assumptions about states' preferences lead to different expectations about the prospects for international conflict and cooperation. The more states care about relative gains, the more a gain for one state will tend to be seen as a loss by another and the more difficult, it seems, cooperation will be.[2]

However, tracing different expectations about the likelihood of conflict and cooperation to different assumptions about states' preferences poses an important theoretical difficulty for international relations theory.[3] Stein (1983, 1984), Keohane (1984), Lipson (1984), the contributors to Oye (1986), and Jervis (1988) have called for trying to bring at least some aspects of the study of international political economy (which is usually taken to be the province of neoliberal institutionalism) and the study of security affairs (which is usually taken to be the province of structural realism) within a single analytic framework. But if neoliberal institutionalism and structural realism really do make fundamentally different assumptions about states' preferences, then efforts to unify these approaches with a third-image explanation cannot succeed.

To use Waltz's analogy (1979:89–91) between political structures and economic market structures, it will be impossible to explain the differences between neoliberal institutionalism and structural realism over, say, the prospects for international cooperation in the same way that economists explain the differences between outcomes in a perfectly competitive market and a monopoly. In that explanation, economists assume that the goals or preferences of the unit—in this case the firm—are the same in both a perfectly competitive market and in a monopoly: a firm seeks to maximize its profits. What varies in moving from one market structure to the other are the constraints under which a firm attempts to maximize its profits. Thus changes in the market constraints and not in the units' preferences account for the variation in a firm's behavior in the two different market structures. If, however, neoliberal institutionalism and structural realism are actually based on fundamentally different assumptions about states' preferences, then moving from a neoliberal institutional to a structural realist setting would see a change in the attributes of states —that is, their preferences. In this sense, neoliberal institutionalism and structural realism would be about essentially different types of units, one primarily concerned with absolute gains, the other with relative gains. Consequently, the locus of the differences between neoliberal institutional and structural realist explanations of international behavior would be in the first or second images. A third-image unification of these approaches, which would explain changes in states' behavior in terms of changes in the constraints facing the states and not in terms of changes in the type or nature of states' preferences, would be impossible.

I offer a reformulation of the problem of absolute and relative gains and take a step toward bringing the study of international conflict and cooperation within a single analytic framework.[4] I show that many important aspects of neoliberal institutionalism and structural realism may be seen as special cases of a very simple model of the international system in which changes in the states' behavior, the feasibility of cooperation, and especially the states' concern for relative versus absolute gains are explicitly linked not to different assumptions about the states' preferences but to changes in the constraints facing the states. The model thus shifts the focus of analysis away from preferences to constraints.[5]

In the model, states are assumed to be trying to maximize their absolute gains. That is, a state's utility depends solely on the absolute level of economic welfare it attains. This is in keeping with neoliberal institutionalism. But the states are trying to maximize their economic welfare within the constraints imposed by an anarchic international system in which the use of force, in keeping with structural realism, may be at issue. When the cost of using force is sufficiently low that the use of force actually is at issue, cooperative outcomes that offer unequal absolute gains cannot be supported as part of an equilibrium even though the states' preferences are defined only over their absolute level of economic welfare. This inability to cooperate is in accord with the expectations of structural realism, though the assumption that states are maximizing their absolute gains is not in keeping with its usual formulations. If the use of force is not at issue because fighting is too costly, then the results are more in accord with neoliberal institutionalism. For example, cooperative outcomes that could not be sustained when the use of force was at issue now become feasible. Thus many aspects of neoliberal institutionalism and structural realism appear as special cases of the model.

The model developed below is extremely simple. It aims primarily at conceptual clarification, not empirical application. To this end, it has been deliberately designed to show, in the simplest possible well-defined game-theoretic model, that many of the differences between neoliberal institutionalism and structural realism can be traced explicitly to the constraints facing states, rather than to their preferences. The extreme simplicity of the model clarifies the relation between constraints and the problem of absolute and relative gains that, although present in more complicated models, would be more difficult to discern there. The development of more complicated and less contrived models awaits future work.[6] But despite the model's simplicity, its analysis makes three new points that are relevant to international relations theory. Most narrowly, it suggests that cooperation in some circumstances may be even more difficult to achieve than has been previously appreciated. Some agreements that offer equal absolute gains—and therefore no relative gain—cannot be sustained in equilibrium. The reason is that cheating on the agreement would bring large relative gains.

The second and third points address two other broader issues in international relations theory. The model offers a simple formal example showing that Waltz's notion of political structure is unable to account for important changes in the feasibility of international cooperation. The political structure as Waltz defines it (1979:79–101) remains constant throughout the analysis; but the feasibility of cooperation varies. Thus variations in what Waltz takes to be the structure of the political system cannot explain the variation in the feasibility of cooperation in the model.

The second issue is the relation between anarchy and cooperation. Structural realism generally associates anarchy with a concern for relative gains and a lack of cooperation (Waltz 1979:105). Neoliberal institutionalism, however, argues that anarchy in the sense of a "lack of a common government" (Keohane 1984:7; Axelrod and Keohane 1986:226) does not imply a lack of cooperation (Keohane 1984:65–84). The present analysis helps to elucidate the sources of this difference. The ability or inability to enforce rules of behavior is relevant only if the physical environment defined by the system's constraints is such that one of the possible behaviors is to use one's relative gain to one's advantage and to the disadvantage of others. If there are no such opportunities, then the inability to commit oneself to a promise not to use a relative gain to one's advantage is moot. Thus the concern for relative gains arises from both anarchy and the constraints that define the range of possible behavior. Although such a system is clearly implicit in structural realism, neither neoliberal institutionalism nor structural realism fully appreciates the significance of the system's constraints in the origins of the concern for relative gains.

One consequence of the failure of both structural realism and neoliberal institutionalism to appreciate the role of the system's constraints in the problem of absolute and relative gains is the use of repeated games in both of these approaches to model the international system implicit in structural realism (e.g., Jervis 1978:171; Keohane 1984; Oye 1986). As will be shown, relative gains in repeated games, including the repeated Prisoner's Dilemma (PD), cannot be used to one's advantage. Thus even if states are unable to make binding agreements in these models, relative gains in repeated games do not matter. This renders any analysis of structural realism's understanding of the relation between anarchy, relative gains, and cooperation based on these models problematic.

Finally, a more complete understanding of the relation between the system's constraints and the origins of the concern for relative gains also shows there is nothing theoretically special about the possible use of force. If the nature of military technology is such that one state can turn a relative gain to its advantage and the disadvantage of others, then these constraints will induce a concern for relative gains, and this may impede cooperation absent any superior authority to ensure that these gains not be used in this way. But if, for example, the nature of an oligopolistic market is such that a firm can use a relative gain in market share to increase its long-run profits at the expense of other firms, then this system will also induce a concern for relative gains that may make cooperation difficult. The concern for relative gains may characterize many domains, and a more refined understanding of the origins of this concern helps to identify them.[7]

I will examine a very simple neoliberal institutional model of the problem of cooperation. The examination shows that the repeated games offer poor models of the problem of conflict and cooperation in structural realism. I will then modify the model so that the constraints of the modified model create opportunities for a state to turn relative gains to its advantage, which in turn, induces a concern for relative gains. I then use this model to study how changes in these constraints affect the feasibility of cooperation.

A SIMPLE NEOLIBERAL INSTITUTIONAL MODEL

The essence of the neoliberal institutional analysis of the problem of cooperation is that the shadow of the future may lead the egoistic states hypothesized in structural realism to cooperate. Repeated interaction gives each actor the ability to punish uncooperative behavior today with future sanctions. If the shadow of the future looms sufficiently large, then the future costs to uncooperative behavior will outweigh the immediate gains; and, weighing costs against benefits, even egoistic states will cooperate. This logic is, in turn, formalized in the neoliberal institutional analysis with a repeated PD in which mutual cooperation can be sustained as an equilibrium outcome with a strategy of punishing defection should it occur.[8]

First, I will present a simple neoliberal institutional model of the problem of conflict and cooperation. The model has been explicitly designed to capture the essence of the neoliberal institutional analysis in the simplest possible formal setting and to be as similar to a repeated PD as possible. This similarity helps to clarify the relation between the formalization used here and that employed in other work on neoliberal institutionalism. Second, I will demonstrate that the model actually does capture the essence of the neoliberal analysis problem of cooperation. Finally, repeated games are shown to be poor models of the problem of absolute and relative gains and cooperation in structural realism.

The simple neoliberal institutional model is a three-by-three game that is played twice. The states, in keeping with neoliberal institutionalism, will try to maximize the absolute sum of their first- and second-period payoffs. The second play of the game casts a shadow of the future onto the first play of the game. But because the game is only played twice, there is no shadow of the future to affect the prospects of cooperation in the second period. Thus the problem of cooperation reduces to seeing if the shadow of the future makes cooperation possible in the first period. In this way, the two-period repeated game provides a formal setting for studying the problem of conflict and cooperation that is simpler than the infinitely repeated PD.[9]

The three-by-three game, which will be played twice, will be called E and is derived from the Prisoner's Dilemma by adding a third strategy to the two-by-two PD. There are two states, S_1 and S_2, in this game; and each has three strategies: F, T, and C. Figure 8.1 shows the payoffs to the various possible outcomes. The four cells at the upper left form a simple PD in which each state strictly prefers playing T to F regardless of whether the other state is playing T or F. But if both states play T, they are worse off than if both had played F. The outcome (T,T) is Pareto-inferior to (F,F). If one state plays C, then that state's payoffs are zero regardless of what the other state does—while the other state obtains 0, $-1/2$, or -1 if it plays C, T, or F, respectively.

It is important to emphasize that the game composed of two plays of E is an extreme theoretical simplification. E has been explicitly designed so that it captures the essence of an infinitely repeated PD and the neoliberal institutional analysis of the problem of cooperation in the simpler formal setting of a two-period repeated game. At this level of abstraction, E serves as a substantive model of the international system or of the international economy only in the very general ways that the repeated PD does in neoliberal institutional or structural realist analyses of the problem of cooperation. Nevertheless, E may be given a more concrete interpretation that is roughly based on an optimal tariff model, and describing this interpretation may help to make the analysis clearer. Building on Harry Johnson's (1953) seminal work on optimal tariffs, the strategies F, T, C may denote free and open trading policies, imposition of the optimal tariff, and closure of the economy by trade prohibition, respectively. By assumption, there are only two states; consequently, the option of closing the economy is equivalent to imposing an embargo.[10] The game E, then, represents the case in which a state gains if it is the only state to impose a tariff, but both states lose if they both impose tariffs; that is, the outcome in which both states impose tariffs (T,T) leaves both states worse off than the free trade outcome, (F,F). If

FIGURE 8.1
A Neoliberal Institutional Model

		S_2		
		F	T	C
	F	3, 3	1, 4	-1, 0
S_1	T	4, 1	2, 2	1/2, 0
	C	0, -1	0, 1/2	0, 0

both states close their economies and effectively embargo one another by playing C, there will be no trade. The payoffs in this case
are less than the payoffs obtained if both states had imposed an
optimal tariff.[11] If only one of the states closes its economy, there will
still be no trade regardless of what the other state does; and the state
that closed its economy receives the same payoff regardless of what
the other state does. But the state that had expected to trade, either
freely or with tariffs, suffers a loss due to a misallocation of its
productive resources. Accordingly, each state prefers to close its
economy if the other does. For the sake of clarification, the neoliberal
institutional model composed of playing E may be loosely interpreted as a very rudimentary model of strategic trade.[12]

The formal aspects of the neoliberal institutional critique of structural realism's analysis of the problem of cooperation are based on a
repeated PD in which the shadow of the future is large enough to
induce cooperation. In order to relate the present formalization to
that employed in the neoliberal institutional critique, the payoffs of
the model developed here have been constructed so that the shadow
of the future does induce cooperation in the model. More formally,
the neoliberal institutional model has been explicitly designed so that
(F,F) is a first-period equilibrium outcome.[13]

To show that (F,F) can be a first-period equilibrium outcome, the
equilibria of the neoliberal institutional model will be determined. In
equilibrium, the outcome on the last play of a repeated game must
be an equilibrium of the stage game that is being repeated.[14] In
particular, the second-period outcome of the game composed of two
plays of the stage game E must be an equilibrium of E. E, in turn,
has two pure-strategy equilibria.[15] In the first equilibrium, each state
imposes the optimal tariff and receives a payoff of 2. In the second
equilibrium, each state embargoes the other by closing its economy
to trade. This yields the payoffs $(0,0)$. Thus in the game in which E is
played twice, the only second-period outcomes that can be part of an
equilibrium are (T,T) and (C,C).[16]

Playing E twice does, however, affect the first-period outcomes
that can be sustained in equilibrium. Indeed the free trade outcome
(F,F) as well as the outcomes in which one state imposes a tariff,
(T,F) and (F,T), can occur in equilibrium. For example, the equilibrium strategies that lead to (F,F) in the first period are for S_1 to play F
in the first period and T in the second period if (F,F) is the first-

period outcome and C if not and, similarly, for S_2 to play F in the first period and T in the second period if (F,F) is the first-period outcome and C if not. In essence, the state that remained faithful to free trade during the first period by playing F is punishing the defector in the second period by imposing an embargo. Clearly, (F,F) is the first-period outcome if both states follow these strategies. These strategies also constitute an equilibrium if neither state can improve its payoff by deviating from its strategy, given that the other player is following its strategy. If both states follow these strategies, each receives three in the first period and two in the second for a total payoff of five. If, however, a state deviates in the first period by playing T, it will do better in that period by realizing a payoff of four. But given the other state's strategy of imposing an embargo in the second period by playing C if (F,F) was not the first-period outcome, the most that a defector can attain is a second-period payoff of zero. This yields a total payoff of four; that is, the future cost of defection, which is to obtain zero rather than two in the second period, outweighs the immediate gain to defecting, which is four rather than three in the first period. No player has any incentive to deviate from the strategies just described, so these strategies constitute an equilibrium whose first-period outcome is (F,F).[17] Thus threats to punish can be used to sustain cooperation in this model. Similar strategies will also support (F,T) and (T,F) as equilibrium outcomes.[18]

As in the neoliberal institutional critique of structural realism, anarchy does not imply a lack of cooperation. The equilibria of this model are consistent with the lack of a common government in the sense that they are subgame perfect.[19] This means that carrying out the threatened punishment of imposing an embargo in equilibrium is in the threatener's own self-interest. Neither state can improve its payoff by backing down and not following through on its threat, given the other state's strategy.[20] Because implementing the threat to punish deviation is in the threatening state's own interest, the equilibria supporting (F,F), (T,F), or (F,T) do not implicitly require that some external authority exists to enforce threats or promises that are in a state's interest to make but not necessarily to implement should the time come to do so. In this sense, these equilibria are in keeping with the notion of international anarchy as the absence of a central authority. Cooperation, even in anarchy, is possible.[21]

In sum, the repeated PD has been widely used to provide the

formal underpinnings of the neoliberal institutional analysis of the problem of international conflict and cooperation. The repeated game composed of twice playing E formalizes much of the essence of the neoliberal institutional critique of structural realism in a simpler setting. The shadow of the future makes cooperation possible even in an anarchic system in which each state judges "its grievances and ambitions according to the dictates of its own reason" (Waltz 1959:157) because there is no authority that is superior to the states. In particular, the cooperative outcome in which both states maintain open economies and receive equal absolute gains can be supported in equilibrium. This equilibrium offers each state a payoff of five in the repeated game. The absolute gains are equal, so there are no relative losses. There are, however, also equilibrium outcomes in which the states' absolute gains are unequal and, therefore, one of the states suffers a relative loss. For example, in the equilibrium in which (F,T) is the outcome in the first period, S_1 receives four in the first period and two in the second for a total of six. S_2 receives one in the first period and two in the second for a total of three. Because these are equilibrium payoffs, the state suffering a relative loss, while certainly preferring a higher payoff, cannot improve its payoff by altering its strategy. In this sense, this state is unconcerned by its relative loss.

Although the repeated PD provides the formal foundations for the neoliberal institutional critique of structural realism's pessimistic assessment of the prospects for cooperation in anarchic systems, repeated games, including the repeated PD and the simple neoliberal institutional model developed here, formalize structural realism's understanding of the international system and, especially the role of force in that system very badly. This, in turn, significantly weakens any analysis of the problem of relative gains and the feasibility of cooperation based on this type of formalization. Repeated games are poor models for two reasons.

The first is more readily apparent but less directly related to the problem of absolute and relative gains and the effects of the concern for relative gains on the problem of cooperation. Structural realism, as well as realism,[22] focuses on a system in which states have the option of using force if that seems to them to be in their best interest and in which the use of force may transform the system. For Aron, international relations "present one original feature which distinguishes them from all other social relations: they take place within the shadow of war" (Aron 1966:6). For Waltz, force in international relations "serves, not only as the ultima ratio, but indeed as the first and constant one. . . . The constant possibility that force will be used limits manipulations, moderates demands, and serves as an incentive for the settlement of disputes" (1979:113). And for Gilpin, hegemonic war is a principle means of systemic change (1981:42–49).

Given the central role that the possible use of force plays in structural realism, it would seem that any model of the international system envisioned in structural realism would have to satisfy two requirements: (1) the option of using force should be represented in the model; and (2) the model should allow for the possibility that the use of force might, whether intentionally or not, change the system. For a repeated-game model, the first requirement means that one of the options in the stage game that is being repeated should correspond to the option of using force. If, for example, the system is being formalized with a repeated PD, then defecting should be taken to represent the option of attacking. Repeated games can satisfy this requirement.

But repeated games cannot satisfy the second requirement, and this renders them poor models of the international system implicit in structural realism. If the international system is modeled as a repeated game, then the state of the system (i.e., the actors, the options available to the actors in each period, and the payoffs to the various possible combinations of actions) remains constant. Every period looks like every other period in a repeated game. Nothing the actors do can change the state of the system. Fighting a hegemonic war in one period does not affect the constraints facing the actors in the next period. If, for example, both states defect in any round of a repeated PD and this is interpreted as fighting a hegemonic war, then a hegemonic war can never change the system; for immediately after the war, the same states simply play the Prisoner's Dilemma again and the game continues on as if nothing had happened. Put another way, using a repeated game to model the international system is to say that the system in 1939 was formally equivalent to the system that emerged in 1945. Because force can never change the system if this system is formalized as a repeated game, formalizing the international system inherent in structural realism in this way is quite problematic.

The second reason that repeated games formalize structural realism's conception of the international system poorly is more subtle but also more directly related to the problem of absolute and relative gains and the feasibility of cooperation. The concern for the relative gains in structural realism arises because a state's relative loss to another state may be turned against it as that other state pursues its own ends: "If an expected gain is to be divided, say, in the ratio of two to one, one state may use its disproportionate gain to implement a policy intended to damage or destroy the other" (Waltz 1979:105). If, therefore, a model is to provide a good formalization of structural realism's conceptualization of the problem of relative and absolute gains, there should be some way for a state in that model to use a relative gain to its advantage and to the detriment of the other state. Unless such an option exists in the model, there is no reason for a state to be troubled by a relative loss, and the model is not capturing what structural realism sees as the essence of the problem of relative gains and cooperation. But no such option exists in repeated games; consequently, they assume away what structural realism takes to be the essence of the problem of relative gains and cooperation.

That there is no way for a state's relative loss to be turned against it in a repeated game is easiest to see by considering how actors sustain cooperation in repeated games and then showing that a state's ability to induce the other state to cooperate is unaffected by any relative losses. To sustain cooperation in any two-actor game, each actor must be able to make the long-run costs of defection for the other actor outweigh the immediate gains. The future costs that each actor can impose on the other determine whether or not the actors can sustain cooperation. But in a repeated game, an actor's ability to make the future costs of defection higher than the immediate gain does not depend on how well that actor has done in the past relative to the potential defector. If, for example, a sanction must be imposed for five periods in a repeated game to make the cost of defection exceed the gain, then it will always take five periods to do this regardless of how well the actors have done in relation to one another before the sanction is imposed. Because the ability to impose future costs does not depend on how well the states have done relative to one another, achieving a relative gain or suffering a relative loss does not affect a state's ability to induce cooperation with threats of future punishment. A state that has suffered a series of relative losses can threaten to impose just as much future punishment on the other state as it would have been able to threaten had it not suffered these relative losses. Relative losses do not impede a state's ability to enforce cooperation in a repeated game. There is, therefore, no reason to be concerned with relative gains or losses. Thus the formalism of a repeated game omits what structural realism sees as the very essence of the problem of absolute and relative gains. For this reason, repeated games formalize the international system implicit in structural realism very badly.[23]

A more satisfying analysis of the problem of relative gains and the feasibility of cooperation requires a model in which the option of using force is represented explicitly and in which a state's relative loss may be turned against it. Using the neoliberal institutional model analyzed here as a point of departure, I next develop a model that satisfies these two requirements. In that model, each state's ability to use force successfully to achieve its ends will depends on how well it has previously done relative to the other state.

A STRUCTURAL MODEL OF THE PROBLEM OF ABSOLUTE AND RELATIVE GAINS

I develop a very simple and highly stylized formalization of the problem of absolute and relative gains. States will now have the explicit option of using force if that seems to them to be in their best interest. More importantly, the model has been explicitly designed so that relative gains and losses matter because they affect a state's ability to use force successfully to further its interests. As will be seen, these constraints actually do induce a concern for relative gains. For this reason, this model offers a better formalization of structural realism's understanding of the problem of absolute and relative gains.

Because the constraints in the model formally induce a concern for relative gains, the model may be used to examine how changes in these constraints affect the states' relative concern for absolute and relative gains and the feasibility of cooperation. This examination shows that many important aspects of neoliberal institutionalism and structural realism emerge as special cases of the model. If the use of force is at issue because the cost of fighting is sufficiently low, cooperation collapses in the model. This is in keeping with the expectations of structural realism. But if the use of force is no longer at issue, cooperation again becomes feasible. This is more in accord with neoliberal institutionalism. The model thus offers a synthesis of the apparently conflicting perspectives of neoliberal institutionalism and structural realism on the problem for relative gains and the feasibility of cooperation in terms of changes in the constraints facing the states and not in terms of the attributes of the states.

The model also addresses two other issues in international relations theory. First, the structure of the international system as Waltz defines it will be shown to remain constant throughout the analysis. Yet the feasibility of cooperation varies. This means that Waltz's notion of structure is unable to account for these changes in the feasibility of cooperation. Second, the model clarifies the relation between anarchy and cooperation by helping to explain why anarchy does not imply a lack of cooperation in some systems but does impede cooperation in others as neoliberal institutionalism has shown.

The specter of war is introduced into the model by assuming that each state must decide whether or not to attack between the two plays of E. As illustrated in figure 8.2, after the first play of E, S_1 chooses between attacking, A, or not attacking, NA. If S_1 attacks, there is war. If S_1 does not attack, then S_2 must decide between attacking or not. If S_2 attacks, there will also be war. If S_2 does not attack, then there is no war and the game ends with the second play of E.

To complete the specification of the modified game, the payoffs to attacking must be defined. This specification depends, in turn, on making a fundamental assumption about the nature or technology of warfare; and it is at this point that relative gains formally enter the analysis. The very simple, highly stylized assumption about the na-

FIGURE 8.2
The Option of Fighting

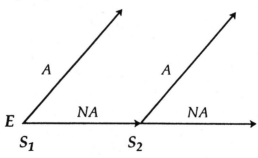

ture of warfare underlying this analysis is that the stronger a state is economically, the more likely it is to prevail in war. Thus relative gains matter because they affect how the states are likely to fare in the event of war and thus affect the states' future expected payoff. It is important to emphasize, however, that relative gains are significant not because a state's utility is a function of them—the states are still trying to maximize their absolute gains—but because the constraints imposed by the underlying technology of war makes it possible for a state to use its relative gains to its advantage and to the disadvantage of the other state.[24]

To formalize a stylized technology of warfare in which relative gains and losses affect a state's ability to prevail in the event of war, the payoffs to attacking will be taken to depend on what happened on the first play of E. The states are assumed to be roughly equal before the game begins, so that the states will fight to a stalemate if there is war and if the difference between the first-period payoffs is too small to give one state a significant military advantage. More specifically, if one state attacks and the difference between the first-period payoffs is less than 3, then both states will fight to a draw, paying a fighting cost of 3.5, and then play E for a second time. These payoffs are shown in figure 8.3, where E - {3.5} is the payoff matrix obtained by subtracting 3.5 from each payoff in E. If the difference between the first-period payoffs is at least 3, then the state with the higher payoff will be assumed to be sufficiently strong economically that it will prevail if there is war. If a state prevails, then its payoff to the entire game is what it received on the first play of E, which must have been 4 (for otherwise the difference between

FIGURE 8.3
The Payoffs if Fighting Brings Stalemate

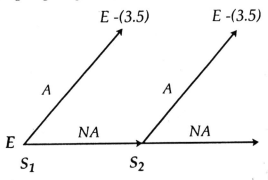

its payoff and the other state's payoff would have been less than 3) less the cost of fighting, 3.5, plus the payoff to victory, which will be taken to be 6. In sum, the total payoff to prevailing is 6.5. Defeat means a loss of 3.5 due to the cost of fighting plus 0, which will be taken as the payoff to defeat. Thus the total payoff if a state is defeated is the first-period payoff, which must have been 1 if the difference between the states' first-period payoffs was at least 3, less the cost of fighting, 3.5, for a net of -2.5. These payoffs are depicted in figure 8.4.

The prospect of war renders cooperation in the first play of E impossible. Clearly, the outcome (T,F) cannot be sustained as a first-period equilibrium outcome. If S_1 imposes a tariff and S_2 maintains an open economy, then S_1 is sure to attack and defeat S_2 because this maximizes S_1's payoff. The game would end with payoffs (6.5, -2.5). S_2, however, can do better than this by playing T in the first period. This will give S_2 a first period payoff of 2; and, because war would mean stalemate, neither state will attack. S_2 will therefore end the game with at least two. Thus S_2 has an incentive to deviate from F in the first period in order to deprive S_1 of its relative gain; and this means that (T,F) cannot be part of an equilibrium. A similar argument shows that (F,T) cannot be an equilibrium outcome.

The effects of the specter of war on the outcome in which both states maintain open economies (F,F) illustrate a point that suggests cooperation may even be more difficult than has been previously appreciated. Because (F,F) offers both states equal absolute gains and consequently no relative gains, it might seem that it would be possible to sustain this outcome in equilibrium. This, however, is not the case. Although this outcome offers no relative gain, deviating

FIGURE 8.4
The Payoffs if S_1 Will Prevail

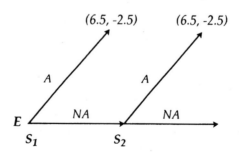

from it does; and this means that it cannot be an equilibrium outcome. If one state plays *F* and the other cheats with *T*, then the latter will secure a large relative gain and then attack and prevail. Each state, therefore, has an incentive to deviate from *F* if the other player is playing *F*, so (*F*,*F*) cannot be an equilibrium outcome. Anarchy and the possible use of force may even prevent the realization of agreements that provide equal absolute gains if deviating from the agreement would yield large relative gains.

These results are in keeping with the expectations of structural realism. Although each state in the model is trying to maximize its absolute level of economic welfare, it is doing so within an anarchical structure whose underlying technology of warfare means that the relative gains of another can be turned against it so as to reduce its future level of economic welfare. These constraints force the states to be concerned about relative gains in the sense that outcomes that offer unequal absolute gains or the prospect of unequal absolute gains should one state cheat on an agreement cannot be sustained in equilibrium. The only first-period equilibrium outcomes in the model are those in which both states impose tariffs (*T*,*T*) or close their economies (C,C).

But if the constraints facing the states change, the conclusions are more in accord with the expectations of neoliberal institutionalism. In particular, cooperation reemerges once the use of force is not at issue. To formalize this, suppose that the cost of fighting rises from 3.5 to 7. Then the payoff to victory is $4 - 7 + 6 = -1$, to defeat, $1 - 7 + 0 = -6$. In these circumstances, a state prefers not to attack even if it has secured a relative gain on the first play of E. Even if sure of prevailing, no state will resort to force; and cooperation again becomes feasible in the model. To sustain (*F*,*F*), for example, the state's equilibrium strategies would be to play *F* in the first play of E, not attack, and then play *T* in the second period if both states played *F* in the first period. If a state deviated from *F* in the first period or if a state attacked and the war ended in a stalemate, then the states would sanction one another during the second period by playing C. To see that these are, in fact, equilibrium strategies that do support (*F*,*F*) in the first period, note that if both states follow them, then each receives 3 in the first period, does not attack, and then obtains 2 in the second period for a total of 5. If S_1 deviates from *F* by playing *T*, it will receive 4 in the first round and then must decide whether or not to go to war. If it does, it will prevail, but its total payoff will be the first-period payoff of 4, less the cost of war, 7, plus the payoff to victory, 6. The overall payoff of deviating in this way is 3. This, however, is less than S_1 would have obtained had it followed the original strategy. S_1, therefore, has no incentive to deviate by playing T and then attacking. S_1 also has no incentive to deviate by playing T in the first period and then not attacking, for S_2 will be playing C in the second period because of S_1's deviation from F. In this case, S_1's payoff will be $4 + 0 = 4$. S_1, therefore, has no incentive to deviate from the strategy specified; nor, by a symmetric argument, has S_2. These strategies thus constitute an equilibrium that leads to the co-operative first-period equilibrium outcomes.

In brief, cooperation collapses in the model when the use of force is at issue. This is in keeping with structural realism. But if the cost of war is sufficiently high that the use of force is no longer at issue, then cooperation again becomes possible; and this is in accord with neoliberal institutionalism. Thus the simple model developed here integrates much of structural realism and neoliberal institutionalism within a common analytic framework, in that many aspects of these two approaches appear as special cases of the present model.

The structural model illuminates two other issues in international relations theory. First, it formally shows that Waltz's notion of a political structure (1979:79–101) cannot explain the variation in the feasibility of cooperation considered here. The political structure, as Waltz defines it, remains constant and unchanged throughout the analysis. Consequently, structural changes as Waltz conceives of them cannot account for the variations in the likelihood of coopera-tion. Explaining the range of cooperative behavior examined here requires a more detailed examination of the system's constraints than Waltz's definition of structure permits.

To see that the three characteristics that define a political structure for Waltz (i.e., the distribution of capabilities, the functional differ-entiation or nondifferentiation of the units, and the ordering princi-ple) remain constant, note that the game is completely symmetric. There are only two states, and the only difference between them is that one is labeled S_1 and the other is labeled S_2. Thus, as the cost of fighting varies, there is no change in the distribution of capabilities or in the functional differentiation of the states. The ordering princi-ple also remains that of anarchy, in that the games are always analyzed in terms of subgame perfect equilibria. The political structure, therefore, remains constant, although the feasibility of cooperation varies.

The second issue in international relations theory is the relation between anarchy and cooperation. Cooperation collapses when the use of force is at issue. But anarchy in the sense of a "lack of common government" to enforce agreements is not in and of itself the cause of this collapse. No such authority exists in the neoliberal institutional model in which E was simply repeated twice or in the structural model. Yet cooperation was an equilibrium outcome in the former and in the latter when the use of force was sufficiently costly. Anarchy, as neoliberal institutionalism argues, does not logically imply a lack of cooperation (Keohane 1984:65–84).

What accounts for the lack of cooperation is not anarchy, for this is present in all of the models. Rather the explanation lies in the different sets of constraints that define what the states can do in anarchy. In the structural model when the use of force is at issue, as it is in the international system envisioned in structural realism, relative gains matter. In these circumstances, the constraints in the structural model formally create an opportunity for each state to exploit its relative gain to its own advantage and to the detriment of the other state. Such constraints will then induce a concern for relative gains unless there is a central authority that can ensure that no state will exploit the opportunity afforded by these constraints. Cooperation, therefore, collapses for two reasons. The constraints create opportunities for a state to exploit its relative gains to its advantage and to the disadvantage of the other state; and there is no common government to ensure that states do not exploit these opportunities. In contrast with the structural model, anarchy does not imply a lack of cooperation in the neoliberal institutional model, because relative gains do not matter in that model. As I have shown, each state's ability to deter defection with the threat of future punishment does not depend on how well that state has done relative to the other in a repeated game. The constraints in the neoliberal institutional model do not offer the states a way to exploit a relative gain. Consequently, there is no need for a common government to ensure that the states do not exploit opportunities to turn a relative gain to their advantage, because there are no such opportunities in the model.

In sum, two factors combine to induce a concern for relative gains and make cooperation difficult. The first factor, which heretofore has only been implicit in structural realism's description of the international system, is that the constraints defining the system create opportunities for one state to turn relative gains to its advantage and to the disadvantage of other states. The second factor, on which both structural realist and neoliberal institutional analyses of the problem of relative gains and cooperation have focused, is anarchy.[25] If opportunities to exploit relative gains exist, then the absence of a common government to ensure that the states do not exploit these opportunities may impede cooperation.

By emphasizing that structural realism implicitly assumes that the nature of military conflict means that the potential use of force creates a set of constraints in which states can exploit their relative gains, I may have obscured a more general point. The general problem confronting a state in this system is one of constrained optimization in which the units are trying to maximize their absolute level of economic welfare subject to a set of constraints in which a unit's current relative gain may be translated into a future absolute gain for that unit and a future absolute loss for the other units. If this more general description also applies to other systems, then the present analysis may also help to explain why cooperation may be difficult to achieve in those systems even though the units in those systems are attempting to maximize their absolute gains and the possible use of military force is not a relevant part of the problem. If, for example, long-run profit maximization within an oligopolistic market structure depends on relative gains in terms of, say, market share, then this analysis would suggest that it may be very difficult to achieve international cooperation and collaboration even if national security concerns are not at issue.[26] Describing the problem faced by states in the international system in the more abstract terms of the optimization problem confronting them may suggest previously unappreciated parallels between this and other problems where the possible use of force is not the source of the concern for relative gains.

The problem of absolute and relative gains divides neoliberal institutionalism and structural realism. The former assumes that states are primarily concerned with absolute gains while the latter assumes that states are primarily concerned with relative gains. What to assume about states' preferences is a theoretical question, not an empirical one. States as rational unitary actors do not exist. They are a theoretical construct. Thus the question of whether states maximize absolute gains or are concerned about relative gains is empirically meaningless. The real question is, which assumption about state preferences is more useful? Which in the context of a broader theory gives rise to better insights? Any firm judgment about this must await further work. As a first step toward this judgment, I have begun to describe some of the insights that follow from examining a simple model in which states are assumed to be attempting to maximize their absolute level of economic welfare in an anarchic international system in which an absolute gain but relative loss today can become an absolute loss tomorrow.

This simple model takes a step toward bringing neoliberal institutionalism and structural realism within a single analytic framework by showing that many aspects of these two approaches can be seen as special cases of the model. In keeping with the expectations of structural realism, states are concerned about relative gains when the possible use of force is at issue. Cooperative outcomes that offer unequal absolute gains cannot be an equilibrium in this system. Indeed even some agreements that offer equal absolute gains, and therefore no relative gain, cannot be sustained in equilibrium, because one state can achieve a relative gain by defecting from the agreement. The prospects for cooperation are, however, sensitive to the costs of fighting. If the use of force is no longer at issue, then a state's relative loss will not be turned against that state. Relative gains no longer matter, and cooperation now becomes feasible. This is in keeping with the expectations of neoliberal institutionalism.

The model also furthers the analysis of two other issues in international relations theory. First, it provides a simple formal example showing that Waltz's characterization of a system's political structure in terms of its ordering principle, the functional differentiation of its units, and the distribution of capabilities across the units cannot account for the variations in the feasibility of cooperation examined here. Changes in the cost of war do not affect the system's structure in Waltz's formulation but do affect the potential for cooperation in the model. Second, the model helps to clarify the relation between anarchy and cooperation. Anarchy, as neoliberal institutionalism has shown, does not imply a lack of cooperation. Rather two factors combine to make cooperation difficult. The first is anarchy, defined as a lack of a common government that can enforce commitments. The second factor (crucial to structural realism but only implicit in it) is that the system be characterized by a set of constraints that present the states with opportunities in which they can use relative gains to their advantage and to the disadvantage of others. Absent such opportunities, relative gains cannot be exploited, and there is no need for a central authority to ensure that these nonexistent opportunities are not exploited.

NOTES

1. For discussions of neoliberal institutionalism's emphasis on absolute gains and realism's (or structural realism's) emphasis on relative gains, see Viner (1948:1–29); Waltz (1959:34–36, 196–98, 219–21; 1979:102–28); Wolfers (1962:67–115); Morgenthau (1967); Hoffmann (1973a:6–12); Keohane and Nye (1977:23–37; 1987:728–33) Gilpin (1981:18–25); Rosecrance (1981:705–707; 1986:44–63); Snidal (1981b:3–6); Krasner (1983b:356); Stein (1983:134; 1984:383–86); Keohane (1984); Lipson (1984:12–18); Gowa (1986:172–79); Grieco (1988a; 1988b; 1990); Jervis (1988:334–36); and Mearsheimer (1990a:11, 44–45).
2. Discussions of absolute and relative gains and the problem of cooperation include Lipson (1984); Gowa (1986); Grieco (1988a; 1988b; 1990); and Snidal (1991b).
3. For specific examples characterizing the concern about relative gains in terms of preferences, see Gilpin (1981:18–21); Stein (1983:134; 1984:382); Keohane (1984:66); Lipson (1984:15); Grieco (1988a; 1988b; 1990); Jervis (1988:335); Mearsheimer (1990a:11, 44–45); and Snidal (1991b). Keohane also claims that many aspects of neoliberal institutionalism can be based on the same set of assumptions about states' preferences that structural realism employs (1984:67). However, Gowa (1986) in general and Grieco (1988a) in particular argue that the repeated Prisoner's Dilemma on which Keohane bases much of his analysis (1984:65–84) is not consistent with structural realism.
4. For other attempts to integrate the analysis of conflict and cooperation, see Lipson (1984), Stein (1984), and Oye (1986).
5. Explaining states' concern for relative gains in terms of constraints rather than preferences is incidentally more in keeping with the original notions of structural realism. Indeed what makes structural realism structural and distinguishes structural realism from realism is that the concern for relative gains is induced by the system's structural constraints (Waltz 1959:34–36).
6. See Powell (1991b) for an effort in this direction.
7. For Waltz the concern for relative gains also extends beyond the inter-

national system to other self-help systems (1979:91). But it is difficult to define self-help precisely.

8. For examples using the repeated PD to formalize the problem of cooperation see Axelrod (1984), Keohane (1984), and Oye (1986).

9. As is well known, if the PD is repeated a known finite number of times and there is complete information, there is no cooperation in equilibrium. There must be infinitely many repetitions for there to be cooperation in equilibrium. If, therefore, one is to study the problem of cooperation formally in the context of a repeated PD, one must focus on an infinitely repeated PD. The present formulation permits the formal study of cooperation in the simpler setting of a two-period repeated game.

10. One of the weaknesses of this interpretation is that the states in E are choosing their policies simultaneously and must endure significant losses before they can change their policies in the second period. A better substantive model would not entail simultaneous decisions or would allow the states to change their policies before suffering significant losses.

11. Johnson (1953) shows that if both states impose optimal tariffs, then, depending on the elasticities of demand, one or both states will suffer compared to the free trade outcome. Optimal tariffs cannot make both states better off. (In this analysis, optimal tariffs are assumed to leave both states worse off relative to the free trade outcomes. Consequently, the payoffs to (F,F) are larger than those to (T,T) in E.) He also establishes that there will be a positive volume of trade even if both states have imposed an optimal tariff. This implies that the states obtain higher payoffs even with mutual tariffs than they would if there were no trade. Thus, payoffs to (T,T) are higher than the payoffs to an outcome in which at least one of the states plays C.

12. For an introduction to, and survey of, some of the recent work on strategic trade, see Krugman (1986), Stern (1987), Stegemann (1989), Cohen (1990), and Richardson (1990).

13. Recall that the problem of cooperation reduces to what can happen in the first period because E is only played twice, which implies that there is no shadow of the future in the second period.

14. If the equilibrium of a repeated game did not require the states to play an equilibrium of the stage game in the last period, then one of the states would have an incentive to deviate from the purported equilibrium strategy in the last period of the game. This implies that the purported equilibrium strategies cannot actually be equilibrium strategies because no actor can ever have any positive incentive to deviate from an equilibrium strategy.

15. I will focus exclusively on pure-strategy equilibria and disregard mixed strategies.

16. The combination of strategies (T,T) is an equilibrium of E because no state has any incentive to deviate from its strategy, given the other state's strategy. If S_1 plays T, then playing T offers S_2 its highest payoff. Conversely, if S_1 plays β, then $\dot{c}$ also offers S_2 its highest payoff. Similarly,

(C,C) is an equilibrium even though it is Pareto-dominated by (T,T) because no state has any incentive to deviate from its strategy, given the other state's strategy. If S_1 plays C, then playing C offers S_2 its highest payoff; conversely, if S_1 plays C, then C also offers S_2 its highest payoff.

17. The reason that cooperation can arise in equilibrium in the game composed of a finite number of repetitions of E but not in a finite number of repetitions of the Prisoner's Dilemma has to do with a very peculiar characteristic of the PD, which is that the minmax payoff equals the equilibrium payoff. This is true of very few other games; and when the minmax payoff does not equal the equilibrium payoff, cooperative outcomes, as well as any other individually rational outcome, can be supported in equilibrium in a finitely repeated game if the number of repetitions is sufficiently large and the actors do not discount the future too much. Indeed the technical reason for adding the strategy C to the Prisoner's Dilemma formed by the strategies F and T is to make the minmax payoff unequal to the equilibrium payoff. This makes it possible to sustain cooperation in the first period and thus to capture the essence of the infinitely repeated PD in a simpler setting. For further discussion of the equilibria of repeated games, see Kreps et al. (1982), Benoit and Krishna (1985), Fudenberg and Maskin (1986).

18. The problem of multiple equilibria frequently plagues repeated games. Indeed almost any outcome can be supported in equilibrium. More formally, any individually rational payoffs can be approximated in the limit if the game is repeated sufficiently often and the actors do not discount the future too much (Benoit and Krishna 1985; Fudenberg and Maskin 1986).

   The existence of multiple equilibria suggests that one purpose of institutions and regimes may be to focus expectations on a particular equilibrium. This is certainly in keeping with the notion that regimes are "sets of implicit or explicit principles, norms, rules, and decision-making procedures around which actors' expectations converge in a given area of international relations" (Krasner 1983b:2). Although suggestive, this is formally rather ad hoc. Ideally, one would like to formalize the institution within the model with the result that the model has a unique equilibrium. For an important effort along these lines see Morrow (1990).

19. See Rasmusen (1989:83–89) for a discussion of subgame perfection.

20. To see that the equilibrium supporting the (F,F) is subgame perfect, let S_1's strategy be to play F in the first period and T in the second period if (F,F) is the first-period outcome and C if not. Similarly, S_2's strategy is to play F in the first period and T in the second period if (F,F) is the first-period outcome and ' if not. As shown above, neither state has any incentive to deviate from its strategy, given the other state's strategy, so this combination of strategies constitutes a Nash equilibrium in which (F,F) is the first-period outcome. To establish subgame perfection, it must also be shown that neither state has any incentive to deviate from carrying out the threatened embargo, given the other state's strategy and

that (F,F) was not the first-period outcome. Suppose that S_1 played T, rather than F, in the first period. Given S_1's strategy of playing C in the second period if, as is assumed, (F,F) was not the first-period outcome, then S_2 has no incentive to deviate from its strategy of embargoing S_1; that is, S_2 cannot improve its payoff by playing something other than C, given S_1's strategy of playing C. Similarly, given S_2's strategy of playing C in the second period if (F,F) was not the first-period outcome, then S_1 has no incentive to change its strategy by playing something other than C, given that S_2 is playing C. Neither state has any incentive not to carry out its threat, given the other's strategy; and the equilibrium is subgame perfect.

21. Although the equilibria of the neoliberal institutional model are subgame perfect, the desire to conduct this analysis in the simplest formal setting possible creates some difficulties. These equilibria are not renegotiation-proof (Farrell and Maskin 1989). Surmounting this would require moving to a more complicated formal setting that would tend to obscure the basic points the model is intended to illustrate.

22. See note 5, above.

23. Gowa (1986) and Grieco (1988a, 1988b, 1990) have also criticized the use of the repeated PD to model structural realism's conception of the problem of cooperation. Their criticisms, however, focus on the states' preferences and the assumption that states are trying to maximize their absolute gain.

24. The phrase "technology of warfare" is used here because the nature of military technology in this formalization constrains the states in the international system in much the same way that the technology of production constrains firms in an oligopolistic market.

25. For examples of this focus, see Oye (1986).

26. Indeed Grieco (1990) studies the problem of relative gains in the context of negotiations between the European Community and the United States over nontariff barriers, a context in which it is difficult to attribute any concern for relative gains to the effects that a relative loss may have on the probability of survival. This analysis helps explain why this concern may nevertheless still be present at least at the level of firms and why they may try to induce the government to reflect these concerns.

9

GLOBAL COMMUNICATIONS AND NATIONAL POWER: LIFE ON THE PARETO FRONTIER

Stephen D. Krasner

There is no single international regime for global communications. Radio and television broadcasting, electromagnetic spectrum allocation, telecommunications (telephone, telegraph, communications satellites, transborder data flows), and remote sensing are governed by a variety of principles, norms, rules, and decision-making procedures, or, in some cases, no regime at all. The variation in outcomes can be explained by the interests and relative power capabilities of actors.

Global communications have not been characterized by Nash equilibria that are Pareto suboptimal, but rather by disagreements over which point along the Pareto frontier should be chosen: by distributional conflicts rather than market failure. Changes in the relative power of states have led to changes in international regimes. The apparatus of economics, which has been so heavily deployed in regime analysis, has focused on information and monitoring rather than power, implying, if not explicitly arguing, that intelligence (figuring out the right institutional structure) is more important than the underlying distribution of capabilities. Regime analyses based upon market failure inevitably obscure issues of power because, given a Pareto suboptimal situation and a concern with absolute not just relative gains, it is possible to make at least one actor better off without making others worse off; an outcome that can be resolved through cleverness rather than power, threat, and coercion.

Information flows and knowledge have been less important for international communications regimes, or the lack thereof, than relative power capabilities. Where there have been disagreements about basic principles and norms, and where the distribution of power has been highly asymmetrical, international regimes have not developed. Stronger states have simply done what they pleased. Radio broadcasting and remote sensing offer the clearest examples.

Where there are coordination problems and the distribution of power has been more symmetrical, however, regimes have been established. The level of conflict has varied according to whether states were dealing with pure coordination problems or with coordination problems that had distributional consequences. The resolution of the former has caused little conflict because the purpose of the regime has been to avoid mutually undesirable outcomes. The allocation of the radio spectrum before the 1970s and the telecommunications regime before the 1980s offer two examples.

By contrast, in cases that have had distributional consequences, conflict has been more intense because, while states agreed on mutually undesirable outcomes, they disagreed on their preferred outcome. Controversies were triggered by changes in power, usually resulting from the development of new technologies. In recent years, distributional questions have precipitated conflict over the allocation of the radio spectrum and international telecommunications. The outcome of these disputes has been determined primarily by the relative bargaining power of states. Previous institutional choices have not imposed much constraint. New interests and power capabilities conferred by new technologies have led to new institutional arrangements.

This is not to say that institutional arrangements were irrelevant, they were necessary to resolve coordination problems and to establish stability. Without regimes all parties would have been worse off. There are, however, many points along the Pareto frontier: the nature of institutional arrangements is better explained by the distribution of national power capabilities than by efforts to solve problems of market failure.

EXPLAINING INTERNATIONAL REGIMES

The consequences of different configurations of interests for the creation and maintenance of international regimes has been elaborated in a number of studies over the last decade. There are four possible configurations of interests, two of which can give rise to international regimes. Regimes are irrelevant for situations characterized by either harmony or pure (zero - sum) conflict. Regimes can arise under what Arthur Stein has called dilemmas of common aversions or dilemmas of common interests (Stein 1983; see also Snidal 1985a).

Under zero-sum conditions there is no basis for regimes, no reason to coordinate policies, because one actor's loss is another's gain.[1] Harmony is also a situation in which there is no reason to create a regime; each individual player, acting without regard for the behavior of others, maximizes both its own utility and that of the system as a whole. Purely self-regarding behavior produces both a Nash and Pareto optimal equilibrium (Keohane 1984:51).

By contrast, dilemmas of common aversions and dilemmas of common interests are distributions of preferences that do create incentives to establish and maintain international regimes. Both involve strategic interaction. Dilemmas of common aversions refer to situations in which actors must coordinate their policies to avoid mutually undesirable outcomes. Coordination requires that actors agree on some set of rules or conventions. The specific content of these rules will only matter if the actors disagree about which is the most desirable outcome. If there is no disagreement, then the outcome is a Nash equilibrium and is Pareto optimal; there is no incentive for any actor to defect, and no opportunity to increase any actor's utility without damaging that of another. Cheating is therefore not a problem. There is no need to develop elaborate information generating and monitoring information, because there is no sucker's payoff to worry about. One set of rules is as good as any other, provided that all states agree to do the same thing. For instance, starting from a situation in which no prior investments have been made, it does not matter whether cars drive on the left or right side of the road provided that all drivers adopt the same rule. It may not matter to a couple whether they go to the mountains or the ocean for vacation, provided that they go to the same place. Such a configuration of interests is shown in figure 9.1.

With a minimal level of coordination (actors need only avoid switching back and forth at the same time when one starts from the right and the other from the left), actors will end up driving on either the left or the right; or both members of a couple will go to either the mountains or the ocean.[2]

Dilemmas of common aversions, however, can also involve questions of distribution as well as coordination. Actors may recognize that they would all be worse off without some agreement, but they may disagree about precisely what the terms of that agreement ought to be. There are many points along the Pareto frontier.

Such a distribution of interests is shown in figure 9.2. This game is commonly referred to as the Battle of the Sexes. The story line here is as follows: both members of a couple prefer to do something together, but they disagree on their preferred outcome, vacationing in the mountains or at the ocean. With such a distribution of interests, the choice of mountains or ocean, or left or right, matters, for vacationing in the mountains gives the column player a higher payoff than going to the ocean and vice versa. Both parties are averse to an absence of coordination in which they take different vacations, but the payoff matrix itself provides no information about which of the two equilibrium points will be chosen. The problem is not how to get

FIGURE 9.1
Simple Coordination Problem

	Mountains Left	Ocean Right
Mountains Left	1 1	0 0
Ocean Right	0 0	1 1

FIGURE 9.2
Battle of the Sexes

	Mountains Left	Ocean Right
Mountains Left	3 2	0 0
Ocean Right	0 0	2 3

to the Pareto frontier but which point along the frontier will be chosen.

In the international relations literature that has evolved since Schelling, commitment has been the analytic device that has most commonly been used to understand which outcome will be chosen, and commitment has usually referred to cleverness (such as throwing a steering wheel out the window in a game of Chicken).[3] The resolution of distributional conflicts could, however, be resolved through a very different route: the exercise of state power, which could be manifest in at least three ways.

1. Power may be used to determine who can play the game in the first place. In international relations less powerful actors are often never invited to the table.[4]

2. Power may also be used to dictate rules of the game—for instance, who gets to move first; in figure 9.2, the player who moves first can dictate the outcome provided that the other player is convinced that the first player's strategy is irrevocable.

3. Power may be used to change the payoff matrix.[5] For instance, a more powerful row player might use tactical linkage to change, or credibly threaten to change, the payoff matrix in figure 9.2 to the one presented in figure 9.3.[6] A large importer (read the United States) might threaten to bar imports from an exporter (read Japan) if the latter failed to make basic changes in the structure of its domestic economy, such as the distribution system.

One of the two forms of coordination (right right) is now unambiguously superior for both players, even though both forms of coordina-

FIGURE 9.3
Battle of the Sexes with Tactical Linkage

	Mountains Left	Ocean Right
Mountains Left	1 2	0 0
Ocean Right	0 0	2 3

tion are Nash equilibria. The players can secure the right right outcome with a minimum level of coordination—for instance, by playing the game in an extended form in which either player has the
option of going first. Once this outcome is reached it is both Nash
and Pareto optimal; there is no incentive for either actor to change.

In contrast to situations involving distributional choices along the
Pareto frontier (such as the Battle of the Sexes payoff structure),
problems of collaboration, which are generated by dilemmas of common interests, are concerned with market failure.[7] They are characterized by Pareto suboptimal outcomes; at least one actor can gain
without compromising the utility of others. The locus classicus of
this set of problems is Prisoner's Dilemma.

A great deal of the cooperation and regime literature in international relations has been devoted to analyzing how actors can escape
from a situation in which there are incentives to cheat but mutual
cooperation is better than mutual defection.[8] The fundamental question has been: how can players move toward the Pareto-optimal
outcome of mutual cooperation?[9]

Several answers have emerged. Cooperation is more likely when
there is iteration, no defined number of plays, discount rates are low,
and the difference between the payoffs for cooperation and defection
are modest.[10] Most important for the international relations research
program growing out of the literature on market failure is the investigation of the way in which cooperation can be facilitated by institutions that reduce the temptation to lie, cheat, and dissimulate by
increasing the symmetry and amount of information, raising the cost
of illegitimate behavior, promoting convergent expectations, and fostering cross-issue-area linkages.[11] The central normative concern of
cooperation theory is to develop institutional mechanisms that inhibit cheating.[12]

Market-failure analyses, which have dominated the literature on
international regimes, pay little attention to power. Once the game is
defined, all actors are treated symmetrically with regard to their
capabilities. Both the row and the column player have the same
competence to play the game. No one is eliminated through brute
force as opposed to choosing a bad strategy. In this game, clubs are
never trump.[13] Everyone could be better off, if only market-failure
problems could be solved. Power, which can be understood as the
ability to determine who plays the game, or to define the rules, or to

change the values within the payoff matrix, does not matter as much as information and monitoring capabilities. When analysts working within the cooperation research program have discussed the larger question of the context within which the game is specified, they have pointed to the ways in which issue-linkage or limiting the number of players might facilitate cooperation rather than the distributional consequences of power.[14]

GLOBAL COMMUNICATIONS

For international communications, however, market-failure problems have been irrelevant. Monitoring and information were never central considerations. Power—not just interest—did matter. The question was not about moving to the Pareto frontier, but rather which point along the frontier would be chosen.

In the four issue-areas considered in this essay—radio and television broadcasting, remote sensing, allocation of the electromagnetic spectrum, and telecommunications (telephone and telegraph links, including communications satellites)—there are no examples of harmony. In two cases, radio broadcasting and remote sensing, there are no international regimes. There has been no agreement on principles and norms because more powerful states have been able to secure their first best outcome through unilateral action. The critical weakness of some states in these issue-areas was their inability to regulate access to their own territory; they could not effectively block all broadcasting signals or remote sensing probes.

In the other two issue-areas—allocation of the electromagnetic spectrum and telecommunications—there have been international regimes. Both initially posed pure coordination problems; actors wanted to avoid the mutually undesirable outcomes of radio interference and incompatible national communications systems. In recent years, however, distributional issues have become more consequential. Third World statesmen have worried that the electromagnetic spectrum would be completely allocated before the future needs of their countries were manifest. The regime has changed in response to these concerns because in this case Third World countries have power conferred by their ability to interfere with other states' broadcasts and by their membership in the International Telecommunication Union (ITU).[15]

In the area of telecommunications, technological change has altered the capabilities of actors and increased distributional conflicts. International regimes have changed in response to these changes in capabilities. More precisely, technological innovation gave some private actors, primarily domiciled in the United States, an incentive to press for a more competitive telecommunications regime both domestically and internationally. The direct and indirect economic bargaining power conferred by these new technologies gave the United States the leverage to secure changes in the extant regime, which had legitimated national monopolies either through direct pressure or by changing the international market incentives confronting other actors.[16]

Modifications of the regime have been initiated by public threats of defection or unilateral action. Cooperation theory—which has focused heavily on market failures arising from dilemmas of common interests and the need for regimes that provide information to facilitate monitoring and enforcement—is not relevant for global communications.[17]

[*Editor's Note:* In his original paper, Professor Krasner proceeds to discuss the cases of radio and television broadcasting, remote sensing, allocation of the electromagnetic spectrum, and telecommunications. He finds that "in those areas where power was asymmetrically distributed and there was no agreement on basic principles and norms—radio broadcasting and remote sensing—no regime was formed. In those areas where distributional issues could not be unilaterally resolved—allocation of the radio spectrum and telecommunications—regimes were created, although both principles and rules changed with alterations in national power capabilities."]

CONCLUSIONS

The literature on international regimes has focused on market failures. It has emphasized the possibility of mutual gains. When the logic of individual utility maximization leads to Pareto-suboptimal outcomes, appropriate institutional constructs can enhance well-being. Power, the conventional focus of the literature on international relations, is not necessarily inconsistent with this perspective. Robert Keohane has argued that what he calls the contractual approach is not a substitute for a power-oriented or interdependence position, but is rather a supplement to these "traditional modes of political analysis" (Keohane 1990b:22–23; see also Keohane 1984:21).

Research programs, however, have both a denotation and a connotation. While the denotation, or explicit logic, of a research program based on the investigation of market failure is not inconsistent with a power-oriented analysis, the connotation of this research program is that power can be ignored. The connotation of a research program suggests which questions are most important, what kind of evidence should be gathered, and, often tacitly, which issues should be ignored. In a penetrating analysis of the positive theory of institutions, Terry Moe argues that

> over the last decade, as the positive theory of political institutions has developed as an intellectual enterprise . . . [t]he theme that gets driven home again and again is that political institutions help mitigate collective action problems—and that this is why they exist and take the forms they do. While the positive theorists are well aware that politics is a game of winners and losers and that institutions are crucial means by which winners win and losers lose, this is not an equally important theme. All too often, it is not discussed at all. (Moe 1990:1–2)

The research program that emerges from an emphasis on market failure—one specific manifestation of the problem of social choice—suggests that the most important issue is how to reach the Pareto frontier. Prisoner's Dilemma is the exemplary payoff matrix, but other situations such as Stag Hunt or Chicken, all of which can result in Pareto-suboptimal outcomes, are also examined. Deadlock, the one other game that has been mentioned with any frequency in the cooperation-under-anarchy literature, is not extensively discussed because it is not analytically interesting. Battle of the Sexes is hardly noted at all as a possible payoff matrix (for an excellent discussion of various payoff matrices, see Oye 1985:12–18). Analysis involves investigating the kinds of institutional arrangements that can overcome the problem presented by a payoff structure in which the Pareto-optimal outcome is not a Nash equilibrium. For example, although Keohane explicitly argues in *After Hegemony* that both power and exchange determine outcome, the most heuristically compelling section of the book (chapter 6), examines the ways in which institutions can overcome problems of market failure by, for instance, increasing the symmetry and amount of information, making it easier to establish reputation across several issue-areas, and promoting convergent

expectations. It is this chapter that has influenced the research program on cooperation, not Keohane's recognition of the fact that
institutions are created within a power-driven context.

Power is ignored because the research program based on the
analysis of market failure does not provide either heuristic insights
or analytic techniques for investigating relative capabilities. Power
recedes into the background not only because scholars have studied
absolute rather than relative gains (see Grieco 1988a), but also because it is not evident how power is relevant for solving problems of
market failure. If the purpose of international regimes is to enhance
both the amount and the symmetry of information, so that states can
be more confident that they can prevent cheating, then the cognitive
ability to construct efficacious institutional arrangements is more important than national power capabilities. Cleverness can make everyone better off.

Conversely, a power-oriented research program is not logically
inconsistent with the analysis of market failure. But again, the connotation of such a research program pushes issues of Pareto suboptimality, cheating, and monitoring into the background. The most
important issue for a power-oriented analysis is the distribution of
capabilities and benefits. Charles Perrow, for instance, argues that
there is always a struggle within an institution because control of the
institution can bring a variety of rewards including security, power,
and survival.[18] For a power-oriented research program, power is
exercised not to facilitate cooperation but to secure a more favorable
distribution of benefits.[19] And analysis seeks to explain outcomes in
terms of interests and relative capabilities rather than in terms of
institutions designed to promote Pareto optimality.

The primary motivation for establishing international regimes for
international telecommunications has been to solve coordination
problems that have distributional consequences—not to address
problems of market failure. States wanted some set of rules for the
allocation of the electromagnetic spectrum and international telecommunications including satellites, because the failure to coordinate
policies on noninterference and on the compatibility of national networks would have left everyone worse off. But because the decisions
would be consequential for the distribution of rewards, conflict arose
over how such coordination problems should be resolved—that is,
where along the Pareto frontier they would end up. While all actors

were better off with some form of coordination rather than none, the form of coordination adopted would affect them differently.

The regimes that have been established for the allocation of the radio spectrum and international telecommunications have reflected the relative power of states and have changed as the distribution of power has changed. Regimes were not irrelevant; without at least shared rules all actors would have been worse off, but the choice of rules benefited some actors more than others. Power has been determined by three considerations: technology and market size, which have influenced the relative opportunity costs of change and therefore the ability to make credible threats; membership in universal international organizations, which has given states the presumptive right to influence policies that are affected by one nation–one vote decision-making procedures (see Krasner 1985); and control over territorial access provided by juridical sovereignty. For instance, INTELSAT became much less of an American preserve as the technological capabilities of other states improved. Third World states were able to secure some changes in the first come–first serve principle of allocating the electromagnetic spectrum because they had a presumptive right to membership in the ITU and because, once they had their own broadcasting facilities, they could interfere with the radio signals of others. The United States was able to secure some movement toward a more market-oriented regime for global telecommunications because some actors in other states feared that they would be put at a competitive disadvantage by unilateral American action; but U.S. leverage was limited by the fact that state authorities controlled access to their own national networks.[20]

In two cases—radio broadcasting and remote sensing—there has been no agreement with regard to the basic issue of whether sending states have to secure the prior consent of targets. States opposed to prior consent could secure a better distribution of rewards through unilateral action—that is, by broadcasting or sensing without the prior consent of target countries rather than by attempting to coordinate with those opposed to the free dissemination of information. Third World states secured some data from remote sensing because their approval for territorial access was needed to realize the commercial benefits of some information.

There has been no systematic classification of international regimes with regard to whether market failure, coordination, or distributional questions have been central. Are interactions among states better characterized by Prisoner's Dilemma, Stag Hunt, Deadlock, the Battle of the Sexes, or some other payoff matrix? The literature on cooperation has focused on payoff matrices in which cheating is a central problem because the Pareto-optimal outcome is not a Nash equilibrium. This research program is academically attractive because it allows political scientists to deploy a heuristically powerful array of analytic tools developed by economists, not to speak of the appeal of identifying with a discipline higher on the social science pecking order and better able to present itself as a true science—Nobel prize and all.[21]

How important is a market failure for the study of international relations? It is illusory to suppose that this issue will be resolved on the basis of empirical studies. The literature now contains enough examples to suggest that both market failure and power-oriented research programs can present plausible analyses, often about the same issue.

There are, however, three aspects of the international system that suggest that a power-oriented approach is, in many cases, more appropriate than analyses based on market failure. First, there are some issues in international politics, especially but not exclusively related to security, that are zero sum. What is at stake is the power —that is, the relative capacity—of actors. Power-oriented concerns may be directed either toward altering the behavior of others or toward preserving one's own autonomy. Market failure is never at issue here; one actor's gain is another's loss.[22]

Second, in international relations it is possible to eliminate some players through the use of force, or to compel an actor to accept an outcome that it would never agree to voluntarily.[23] This is an option that is not analytically tractable for a market-failure research program which assumes that actors are in a position to make voluntary choices. The Austro-Hungarian empire did not choose to dismantle itself after the First World War. Munich compelled Czechoslovakia to accept an outcome that left it absolutely worse off.

Third, even if states are interested in absolute rather than relative gains, the initial allocation of property rights will have distributional consequences, even if any particular specification of such rights can lead to a Pareto-optimal outcome.[24] Different choices will differentially privilege different actors.[25] Changing the rules for using the radio spectrum, or setting tariffs for INTELSAT, or lending IMF resources, or assigning landing rights for international airlines, or limiting whale catches would benefit some actors at the expense of others. The issue here is movement along the Pareto frontier, not how to reach the frontier. Power and interests, not monitoring capacity, determine outcomes.[26] These three characteristics—concern with relative power, the ability to eliminate actors, and the assignment of property rights—are at the core of much of the literature on international relations.

This is not to say that institutions or market-failure problems are irrelevant. First, as John Ruggie in particular has elegantly argued, the existence of the basic actors in the contemporary international system—national states—must be understood in a larger, historically grounded institutional context. The issue here, however, is not the temptation to cheat and the ability to monitor but rather understanding how the players in the game came to exist in the first place (Ruggie 1983a). Second, the free-rider problem that emerges when there is a very asymmetrical distribution of power will lead to the Pareto-suboptimal provision of collective goods. In these circumstances, however, the problem is not cheating and monitoring but rather the fact that the more powerful state (or small group of states) prefers to provide the collective good regardless of what the smaller states do, and the smaller states prefer to defect regardless of what the larger state does. A situation of Prisoner's Dilemma arises only if there are a larger number of smaller states, no one of which is unilaterally willing to provide collective goods. Third, past institutional choices do influence the contemporary interests and power of actors exactly because such choices privilege some players at the expense of others.

Nevertheless, for a very large class of global issues, indeed the classic agenda of the study of international politics—security, autonomy, and the distribution of valued resources—power needs to be given pride of place. These issues are not characterized by the fact that Pareto-optimal outcomes are not Nash equilibria. Neoliberal speculations about the positive consequences of greater information are fascinating (even if empirical demonstrations of such benefits are scarce). But they obscure considerations of relative power capabilities which draw attention to how the payoff matrix was structured in the first place, how the available options are constrained, who can play the game, and, ultimately, who wins and who loses.

NOTES

1. The essence of conventional realist thinking as exemplified in the work of Kenneth Waltz is that the quest for power, which is inherently a relative concept, inevitably places states in a zero-sum situation. See Waltz (1979) as well as Joseph Grieco (1988a).
2. As Snidal (1985a:931) puts it: "Sometimes coordination is presented simply as the problem of two or more actors matching policies where they are indifferent about where they match. . . . Here there is no disjuncture between individual and collective rationality and no problem of collective action. It requires not more than communication and common sense to achieve an outcome that is both individually and collectively optimal."
3. Similar kinds of reasoning about commitment have been used in the recent literature on strategic trade theory. One element of this analysis is that state intervention to promote a particular industry is desirable because it demonstrates a level of national commitment that could not be provided by the action of private firms. See, for instance, James A. Brander (1986:30).
4. Snidal (1985a:938) points out that the threat of exclusion can itself be an effective bargaining tool. By threatening to exclude, a more powerful state might secure the compliance of a weaker state.
5. Underlying power capabilities or size may determine the payoff matrix in the first place. See John A. C. Conybeare (1987:2).
6. Albert Hirschman (1980) in 1945 argued that the credibility of such a threat would be determined by the relative opportunity costs of change. Tactical linkage is discussed in Ernst Haas (1980).
7. The terms *coordination* and *collaboration* are taken from Stein (1983).
8. Rober Axelrod and Robert O. Keohane point to Pareto suboptimality in general as the defining problem for the cooperation literature, arguing that "what is important for our purposes is not to focus exclusively on Prisoner's Dilemma *per se*, but to emphasize the fundamental problem that it (along with Stag Hunt and Chicken) illustrates. In these games, myopic pursuit of self-interest can be disastrous. Yet both sides can potentially benefit from cooperation—if they can only achieve it" (Axelrod and Keohane 1985:231).
9. Charles Lipson, for instance, argues that "because the Prisoner's Dilemma highlights both the potential gains from cooperation and the temptations that prevent it, it has been taken as an elegant expression of the most profound *political* dilemmas, including that of the social contract. Indeed, Jon Elster once defined politics as 'the study of ways of transcending the Prisoner's Dilemma' " (Lipson 1984:3).

10. For an exceptionally intelligent and nuanced discussion of the impact of these factors on the prospects for cooperation in Prisoner's Dilemma and other games, see Kenneth Oye (1985).
11. The most important exposition of the functions of institutions can be found in Robert O. Keohane (1984, chap. 6).
12. The central importance that neoliberal institutionalism accords to the problem of cheating is elegantly elaborated in Joseph M. Grieco (1990, esp. chaps. 1 and 2).
13. Grieco (1990:38) points out that one of Axelrod's premises is that there is no way to eliminate a player or to avoid interactions.
14. Axelrod and Keohane (1985:253) summarize: "We have seen that governments have often tried to transform the structure within which they operate so as to make it possible for the countries involved to work together more productively."
15. This same analysis of the allocation of radio frequencies is offered by Stein (1983:131–32).
16. Here and later in this essay I draw heavily on the superlative analysis of Peter Cowhey (see Cowhey 1990).
17. This argument has been forcefully made by Stein (1983:130). Stein's analysis offers a much more differentiated perspective on the problem of cooperation than most of the other regime literature because of the distinction between dilemmas of common aversions and dilemmas of common interests. While the latter have gotten most of the attention, in part because of the fixation on Prisoner's Dilemma, the former may, in fact, be the more common area of concern.
18. Charles Perrow (1986:132). Perrow criticizes economic analyses, such as the principal agent literature, for ignoring the distribution of power (230, 257–58).
19. Contrast the discussion in Axelrod and Keohane (1985:249) about the way in which background conditions, such as issue-linkage, can be altered to facilitate cooperation with the analysis in this essay, in which power is used to alter background conditions (players, issue-linkage, payoff matrix) to change the distribution of benefits.
20. Such control is not foreordained even for telephone communications. While international links for both satellite and cable are now connected to national systems through a limited number of easily regulated gateways, Motorola has announced plans to develop a portable telephone system that could send and receive calls point-to-point anywhere on earth by bouncing signals off seventy-seven satellites (*New York Times*, June 26, 1990, p. 1).
21. Robert Jervis has also argued that one of the attractions of Prisoner's Dilemma is that it lends itself to interesting manipulations (1988:323).
22. See Jervis (1988:334) for a similar formulation. Grieco (1990) places particular emphasis on the desire of states to preserve their freedom of action.
23. I am indebted to Terry Moe for pointing out this line of argument.
24. Ronald Coase (1960). John Conybeare has applied Coase's logic to prob-

lems of international organization. See Conybeare (1980, esp. 322–23), where Conybeare recognizes, although does not elaborate, the income effects of the initial distribution of property rights.

25. For instance, Joseph Grieco's recent study of the nontariff barrier codes negotiated during the Tokyo Round suggests that conventional concerns about relative power are a more persuasive explanation of outcomes than neoliberal considerations involving cheating and information. Grieco argues that both absolute and relative gains must be included in the utility function of states (Grieco 1990:40–49).

26. Snidal (1985a:935) demonstrates that a more powerful state (understood as the actor that is less in need of coordination) will, in a bilateral bargaining situation, secure an outcome closer to its most desired point than its weaker antagonist.

10

DO RELATIVE GAINS MATTER? AMERICA'S RESPONSE TO JAPANESE INDUSTRIAL POLICY

Michael Mastanduno

For the United States, which future world is preferable: one in which the U.S. economy grows at 25 percent over the next decade, while the Japanese economy grows at 75 percent, or one in which the U.S. grows at only 10 percent, while that of Japan grows 10.3 percent? Robert Reich of Harvard's John F. Kennedy School posed that choice in 1990 in a series of meetings with graduate students, U.S. corporate executives, investment bankers, citizens of Massachusetts, senior State Department officials, and professional economists. A majority of every group, with one exception, expressed a preference for the latter outcome. The economists unanimously chose the former and (Reich reports) were surprised that other Americans would voluntarily forgo fifteen percentage points of economic growth just to hamper the progress of one of America's principal trade and financial partners (Reich 1990).

While Reich may have biased the results somewhat by projecting Japanese growth at three times the rate of that of the United States, the overall results of his informal survey are consistent with the findings of other recent samplings of American attitudes. A *Wall Street Journal*/NBC News poll taken in July 1990 found that an overwhelming majority (86 percent) of Americans would prefer a policy of slower growth in both Japan and the United States, over one in which both grew faster, if the latter meant allowing Japan to take the lead economically. A *New York Times* poll conducted at about the same time found Americans believing that Japan would be the number one economic power in the world in the next century, and, by a substantial margin, that Japanese economic power posed a greater threat to American security than did the military power of the Soviet Union.[1]

These surveys suggest, among other things, that a significant part of the American public is concerned about *relative* gains, or relative position, in the country's economic relationship with Japan. Americans are concerned that even if both countries prosper from their relationship, Japan may grow faster than the United States, acquire a greater share of world markets and financial assets, or dominate the United States in the development and application of advanced technology. Over the long run, such developments could pose a threat to America's economic welfare, political autonomy, and perhaps even to its military security. As Reich notes, such concerns are the dark side of the U.S.-Japanese relationship—infrequently discussed, yet ever-present in the thinking of Americans, and perhaps of Japanese as well.

This essay addresses how much the U.S. government shares these concerns, and the extent to which they are reflected in American economic policy toward Japan. Do "relative gains concerns"—concerns that economic interaction with Japan, while mutually beneficial, may benefit Japan more than the United States and thereby pose a threat to American national security, broadly defined—have a significant influence on official U.S. thinking and policy? If so, why, in what ways, and under which circumstances? Are such concerns spread uniformly, or are they concentrated within certain executive agencies? Do they reflect anxiety over economic welfare, political autonomy, or military security?

I seek to answer these questions by examining America's response during the late 1980s to Japanese industrial policy in three areas—aircraft, satellites, and high-definition television (HDTV). My overall finding is that relative gains concerns do matter significantly, but not unconditionally. A sensitivity to such concerns was strongly evident in the U.S. policy *process* in each of the three cases, and reflected primarily anxiety over U.S. economic welfare. Policy *outcomes*, however, varied. In one case—satellites—U.S. officials adopted a controversial policy initiative that reflected relative gains considerations fully and unambiguously. In a second case—aircraft—relative gains concerns compelled U.S. officials to undertake, at considerable diplomatic cost, a major policy change, involving the reconsideration of a defense production agreement with Japan. Once the United States reconsidered, however, relative gains concerns were not decisive in shaping its final policy. In the third case—HDTV—relative gains concerns were apparent yet affected U.S. policy only modestly, if at all.

My explanation for this pattern is lodged at the intersection of international and domestic levels of analysis. International structural changes—the relative decline of U.S. economic power, the concomitant rise of that of Japan, and the diminution of the Soviet military threat—account for the increasing sensitivity of the United States to relative gains considerations during the latter half of the 1980s. In the absence of such changes, it is inconceivable that relative gains concerns or the policies associated with them would have emerged as prominently as they did in the formulation of U.S. policy toward Japan. U.S. officials, however, were deeply divided over the utility and desirability of a relative gains strategy. Officials at the Commerce Department and to a lesser extent at the Office of the U.S. Trade Representative (USTR) were sympathetic; those at the State and Defense departments and at the Council of Economic Advisors (CEA) were largely skeptical. These preferences reflected primarily the institutional missions of their respective agencies. Given these divisions, a struggle over policy emerged in each of the three areas under investigation. The outcomes of those struggles, and thus the extent to which relative gains concerns were ultimately translated into policy, were shaped by domestic factors—in particular, ideology and the institutional setting within which the policy struggles took place.

The next section of this essay places the concern over relative gains in the context of American foreign policy and international relations theory. The following three sections examine, respectively, the FSX fighter aircraft controversy, the decision to identify Japanese satellite practices as a "Super 301" target under the 1988 trade act, and the dispute over whether to provide U.S. government support for HDTV. A concluding section summarizes the argument and explores its analytical and policy implications.

RELATIVE GAINS, REALISM, AND AMERICAN FOREIGN POLICY

The question of America's sensitivity to relative gains considerations is relevant to both American foreign policy and international relations theory. The policy significance stems from the fact that over the past several years, a debate has emerged within the United States over how to deal with the growing economic power of Japan, pitting "traditionalists" against "revisionists." Although it is not generally characterized as such, the fundamental cleavage between the two schools involves whether U.S. policymakers should think and act in terms of relative gains.

Traditionalists believe that to focus on the pursuit of relative gains is at best misguided, and at worst, potentially destructive to the U.S.-Japan relationship (see, e.g., Packard 1987–88; Romberg 1988; Brock 1989; Tresize 1989/90; Destler and Nacht 1990–91; Ito 1990). It is misguided because both the United States and Japan benefit a great deal in absolute terms from their economic interaction, and their growing interdependence assures that neither side can effectively exploit the economic relationship to take advantage of the other politically. As Raymond Vernon has recently argued, in economic terms each country "has a hand on the other's throat," and for either to threaten the other would be tantamount to threatening a nuclear first strike.[2] Relative gains calculations can be destructive, to the extent that they lead to or reinforce the twin evils of protectionism and nationalism. A U.S. protectionist strategy—designed, perhaps, to slow the economic growth or technological progress of Japan—would be damaging in and of itself, and also could lead to a trade and investment war, which would leave both sides even worse off. Moreover, by casting the relationship in terms of a competition for relative gains, U.S. officials would risk inciting nationalist fervor, as America's "Japan bashers" and Japan's "American bashers" reinforced each other's worst tendencies.[3] Such an "orgy of mutual bashing," inspired, according to traditionalists, perhaps inadvertently by government officials who are still captives of antiquated notions of "national sovereignty" and "national interest," would create profound political conflict, and would jeopardize the close security ties that have developed between the United States and Japan in the postwar era (as quoted in Ito 1990:137, 146).

Revisionists, while not unconcerned with the above risks, never-theless tend to be more sympathetic to, if not openly supportive of, an American policy toward Japan inspired by a sensitivity to relative economic gains.[4] Revisionists are disturbed by patterns in U.S.-Japa-nese economic interaction which, they believe, if allowed to persist are likely to work over time to the detriment of America's national interests. America's growing financial dependence on Japan is one such trend, which has the potential to reduce the future real income of the United States and grant Japan a source of leverage over U.S. behavior. Even more disturbing is America's relative decline techno-logically, as Japanese firms outcompete their U.S. counterparts not only in traditional industries of the past but in the high-growth, technology-intensive activities of the present and future, such as semiconductors, fine ceramics, and robotics. Revisionists see little chance that such trends will be reversed, as long as the United States remains wedded to traditional policies that subordinate economic to political and security concerns, and treat Japan as a liberal capitalist state cast in the same mold as the United States. Such thinking and policies fail to grasp that Japan has institutionalized a distinctive version of capitalism, and that its technological and commercial suc-cess is driven by a government-business partnership that places growth, market share, and producer interests above the concerns of efficiency and consumer welfare. While Japan is clearly not an en-emy, its trade policies tend to be adversarial. The United States, according to revisionists, while not necessarily emulating Japan, needs to adjust itself ideologically and institutionally; it must, in the words of Chalmers Johnson, "recognize that Japan has replaced the USSR as America's most important foreign policy problem" and "adopt policies to get the United States back into consumer electronics and other industries of the future" (1989:26).

Thus, while traditionalists tend to believe that the risks of pur-suing a relative gains strategy outweigh any potential benefits, revisionists are more fearful of the risks of *not* pursuing such a strat-egy, of a complacent United States that fails to recognize and react to an economic challenge. Given their shared concern with what the United States *should* do, proponents of each should be inte-rested in an analysis that seeks to understand what the U.S. gov-ernment *can* do. Under what circumstances is it likely to be re-sponsive to relative gains concerns, and, since some are potentially more harmful than others, what policy instruments is it likely to employ?

The question of America's response has theoretical relevance as well. One of the key insights of the realist approach to international relations is that nation-states are consistently sensitive to considerations of relative gain and advantage.[5] As Robert Gilpin has observed: "Nation-states are engaged in a never-ending struggle to improve or preserve their *relative* power positions" (1975:35; emphasis added). Relative position matters because nation-states exist in anarchy, without a higher governing authority. Anarchy breeds fear and distrust, leading nation-states to worry, at the extreme, that they will be conquered or destroyed by their more powerful counterparts. Even if nation-states do not fear for their physical survival, they worry that a decrease in their power capabilities relative to those of other nation-states will compromise their political autonomy, expose them to the influence attempts of others, or lessen their ability to prevail in political disputes with allies and adversaries.

Realists thus expect the behavior of nation-states to reflect a sensitivity to changes in their relative position and capabilities. For example, realists anticipate that nation-states will *react* to shifts in relative military or economic power that disadvantage them, either by mobilizing resources internally or by devising some other means to lessen the impact or offset the consequences of such shifts.[6] At the extreme, states may opt for war; Thucydides suggests as much in his classical realist account by arguing that what made the Peloponnesian War inevitable was the "growth of Athenian power and the fear it caused in Sparta" (1954:49).

It follows that, for realists, the willingness of a nation-state to engage in cooperative ventures with others will be affected not only by whether and how much it believes it will gain in absolute terms but also by its perception and assessment of which states will gain more in relative terms. This is not to suggest that a nation-state in pursuit of relative gains will eschew cooperation altogether, or that it will refuse to participate if *any* gains are enjoyed by its partner. It is to suggest that while absolute gains seekers are more interested in the creation of joint benefits than in their distribution, relative gains seekers are more concerned with distribution, even at the expense of creation. More precisely, a nation-state in pursuit of relative gains will seek to avoid or restructure relationships or cooperative ventures

in order to reduce or eliminate gaps in benefits that favor its partners.[7] It would be prepared to accept less benefits in absolute terms,
if by so doing it could narrow a gap in benefits that favored its
partners. On the other hand, such a state would be willing to increase cooperation and mutual benefits, as long as the resulting
distribution of benefits did not widen the gap to its disadvantage.

In general, the extent to which state behavior exhibits a concern
for relative gains will vary, depending upon whether interaction
involves allies or adversaries, and economic or military relationships
(see Lipson 1984:12–18). Such concerns are likely to be most prominent in the military interactions (e.g., arms races and arms control)
of potential adversaries, who possess the capabilities—and perhaps
the motives—to destroy or otherwise physically harm each other.
Since economic power underpins political and military influence,
even economic relations among potential adversaries are likely to be
influenced strongly by relative gains considerations, as evidenced by
America's forty-year effort to use export controls to weaken Soviet
military, and at times economic, capabilities (Mastanduno 1992).

On the other hand, relative gains calculations can be expected to
be less important in economic relations among long-standing military
allies. Since such states pose far less of a security threat to each other,
they can afford to be less concerned by shifts in relative economic
capabilities. This inclination to downplay relative gains considerations is likely to be reinforced by the fact that alliance members share
an interest in enhancing their collective economic capabilities in absolute terms, in order to counter commonly perceived external security threats more effectively.

Nevertheless, realists would have to expect that, even in economic
relations among allies, relative gains concerns will not be completely
absent.[8] First, in an anarchical environment, the possibility of armed
conflict never disappears entirely. The prudent nation-state must
calculate that today's ally may be the adversary of tomorrow—or the
next decade—and thus is likely to be wary of patterns of economic
interaction or cooperative ventures that disproportionately benefit its
allies. Second, even if the chance of armed conflict remains remote,
states worry about the consequences of economic interaction for their
political autonomy. Asymmetrical interdependence may lead to political vulnerability, providing opportunities for other states—even
friendly ones—to constrain a nation-state's political choices or exer-

cise leverage over its behavior (Keohane and Nye 1977). Third, states may be concerned about the consequences for their national economic welfare, to the extent that mutually beneficial interaction puts their firms at a competitive disadvantage, leads to a shrinkage of their industrial base, or results in the movement of high value-added activity away from their territory. For any or all of these reasons, realists must expect states to pursue relative gains and, if necessary, forgo some of the benefits of cooperation or economic exchange in the short run, in order to assure security, broadly defined, over the long run.

In economic relations among allies, hegemonic or dominant states can be expected to be *least* sensitive to relative gains considerations. Such states possess a preponderance of economic advantages, including large size and exceptional productivity, and may be endowed with substantial financial assets and natural resources as well (Krasner 1976:317–43; Lake 1988). These advantages afford hegemonic states the luxury of being more complacent about their relative economic position than nonhegemonic states, which may aspire to hegemonic status or at least fear slipping further behind.

The general pattern of postwar American foreign economic policy toward Western Europe and Japan appears to bear out this logic. The United States found itself locked in a struggle for military and geopolitical influence with the Soviet Union and, particularly in the early postwar years, far ahead of its allies in terms of economic capabilities. Consequently, U.S. officials shaped America's economic relationships with Western Europe and Japan to support broader geopolitical objectives. The United States pursued absolute gains through the reduction of tariff barriers, and at the same time adopted policies (e.g., support for European integration, and tolerance for Japanese protectionism and restrictions on foreign direct investment) that discriminated asymmetrically against the United States (Gilpin 1975; Krasner 1982:29–48). Rather than pursuing relative gains itself, the United States facilitated the ability of its allies to strengthen their economic capabilities relative to those of the United States.

Realism would lead one to expect, however, that as structural conditions changed—that is, as America's relative economic power declined, and as the Soviet military threat diminished—U.S. policy in economic relations with its allies would come to reflect a greater sensitivity to relative gains. As its relative economic power declines, a hegemonic state will feel that it is less able to afford, and thus will be less likely to tolerate, "free riding" by its allies that works to its relative economic disadvantage. Furthermore, as commonly perceived military threats diminish, the hegemonic state will be less inclined, in economic disputes with its allies, to subordinate its national economic interests to the pursuit of political harmony or solidarity within the alliance. In short, the transformation of international economic and security structures should inspire a dominant state to act more as an "ordinary country" and strive for relative economic advantage in relations with its allies.

This essay may be viewed as a preliminary effort to examine the hypothesis that, as relative economic power declines and external security threats diminish, a hegemonic state is likely to pursue relative gains more forcefully in economic relations with its allies. While some scholars rightly emphasize that U.S. power remains considerable in absolute terms, it is equally clear that in relative terms U.S. economic power has declined significantly over the course of the postwar era.[9] By the latter half of the 1980s the United States still possessed the world's largest economy, but no longer enjoyed the unambiguous technological or financial superiority that had characterized its position in the two decades following the second World War (Gilpin 1987). Moreover, Japan emerged as the principal economic challenger to the United States. Japanese firms equaled and then surpassed their American counterparts in traditional industries such as automobiles and steel, and in high-technology areas such as semiconductors and automated machine tools (Ferguson 1989; Prestowitz 1990). The massive surpluses Japan accumulated in trade with the United States during the 1980s translated into increased financial power, as the United States came to rely upon Japanese investments to finance part of its persistent trade and budget deficits.

By the end of the 1980s, these shifts in relative economic power were accompanied by the now familiar changes in the international security environment—the end of the Cold War and the collapse of Soviet power in Central Europe. These changes, coupled with the profound political and economic crises confronting the Soviets domestically, rendered it unlikely that the Soviet Union would continue to be perceived unambiguously as a significant threat to Western security.

The three areas chosen for investigation—aircraft, satellites, and

HDTV—involve U.S.-Japanese competition in the development and commercialization of advanced technology. A realist might plausibly expect the United States to be sensitive to relative gains in these areas, since success in advanced technology is generally taken to be a critical asset in the pursuit of both economic welfare and military security. Moreover, each of the three areas was targeted in recent years by the Japanese government as a priority for technological and commercial success. That the Japanese government has sought to enhance the capabilities of Japanese firms in each of these areas should have provided an additional impetus for the United States to react in accordance with the logic of relative gains.

If realism is a useful guide to state behavior, then we would expect to find evidence of relative gains concerns in the U.S. policy process and in policy outcomes. The specific *policies* associated with relative gains concerns will vary, depending on the particular concern that is motivating policymakers. For example, if policymakers fear that mutually beneficial economic interaction will lead to a dangerous increase in their partner's military capabilities, they might be inclined to adopt export controls on militarily significant trade, as did the United States and its Western allies vis-à-vis the Soviet Union during the Cold War (Mastanduno 1992). If the concern is that economic interaction will provide another state with a significant source of political leverage, policymakers might seek to diversify either their sources of supply or their markets.[10] Finally, if the concern is that economic interaction will endanger a country's competitive position economically, we should expect officials to contemplate and adopt measures associated with strategic trade policy, such as the targeting or promotion of "strategic" industries, or the disruption of efforts by other governments to lend their industries a competitive advantage.[11]

[*Editor's Note:* In his original paper, Professor Mastanduno proceeds to discuss three cases: (1) the 1989 controversy over joint U.S.-Japanese development of the 'FSX' fighter aircraft; (2) U.S. use of trade sanctions to discourage Japanese efforts to protect industries developing commercial satellites; and (3) the failure of the U.S. to actually promote development of high-definition television in 1989. Although these case studies are omitted here, his conclusions follow.]

CONCLUSIONS

I hypothesized that as relative economic power declines and external security threats diminish, a hegemonic state is likely to pursue relative gains more forcefully in economic relations with its allies. States are "inherently inclined to strive for relative advantage against like entities on the international scene, even if only by means other than force" (Luttwak 1990:19). The failure to uncover evidence of such behavior would raise questions regarding the applicability of realist thought to foreign economic policy and international economic relations.

The cases examined provide strong though not unconditional support for the hypothesis. Prior to the 1980s the United States proved less sensitive to relative gains concerns, and in fact accepted or even encouraged patterns of interaction that worked to the relative economic advantage of Japan. In aircraft, the United States engaged in a series of coproduction arrangements that contributed to the development of Japan's nascent civilian industry. In satellites, the United States was obliged by treaty to enhance the technological capabilities of Japanese firms. In television, the United States tolerated the protection and cartelization of Japan's domestic market, and responded ineffectually to predatory pricing by Japanese firms in the American market.

By the latter half of the 1980s, however, clear signs of relative gains–seeking behavior appeared in the U.S. policy process. The immediate concern was not military security, but economic well-being. Some U.S. officials feared that certain patterns of economic interaction with Japan, even though mutually beneficial in absolute terms, would bring relatively greater economic benefits to Japan and over time work to the detriment of America's competitive position in the development and application of advanced technology. In response to this concern, a series of "strategic" policies emerged for consideration, including technology restrictions in aircraft, the disruption of Japan's home market sanctuary in satellites, and the promotion of American firms in the competition to develop HDTV.

Variation existed, however, in the extent to which policies associated with relative gains–seeking behavior were adopted. Such policies were adopted fully in satellites, and substantially but not fully in aircraft. They were not adopted in HDTV. Thus, while the impact of changes in international economic and security structures was felt in U.S. policy, it was not felt completely; something was lost in the translation from international system to policy outcome. It is necessary to move from the international to the domestic level of analysis in order to account for that variation.[12]

Relative gains concerns were forced to compete for attention in the U.S. policy process with others, such as the maintenance of sound political relations and defense ties with Japan, the short-term economic interests of particular American firms, and the preservation of a commitment to free trade and minimal intervention in the domestic economy. Moreover, the cases demonstrate that the U.S. policy process was fragmented, as agencies within the executive emphasized different concerns based on their particular institutional missions. The State Department's primary concern, evidenced most strongly in the FSX and Super 301 debates, was the maintenance of harmonious political relations with Japan. The Defense Department proved anxious to preserve and foster military cooperation with a close ally; within the DOD, DARPA's (Defense Advanced Research Projects Agency) behavior in the HDTV case reflected concern over the long-term viability of the U.S. defense industrial base. The Commerce Department proved most receptive to relative gains concerns, in light of its interest in the preservation and nurturing of the competitive position of U.S. manufacturing firms. The office of the USTR was primarily concerned with market access and the expansion of trade, yet also with the competitiveness of U.S. firms. The CEA's principal emphasis was on macroeconomic stability and the minimization of government's role in the economy.

Given these interagency preferences and divisions, one should not expect international structural forces to have translated easily or automatically into policy outcomes. In each case proponents of a relative gains strategy were forced to struggle with officials or agencies reflecting competing concerns. Three factors help explain why relative gains concerns, evident in the policy process across the three cases, were not consistently reflected in policy outcomes.

The first is ideology—in particular, the beliefs of executive officials regarding the appropriate role of government in the economy. Despite recent challenges, minimal government intervention domestically and the pursuit of free trade internationally remained dominant. Executive branch officials at that time believed that it was appropriate for the U.S. government to subsidize or promote military production, but not production in the civilian sector. Policies sensitive to relative gains considerations must now either overcome, or be rendered compatible with, these dominant beliefs.

In HDTV, for example, the burden of proof rested with proponents of a relative gains strategy, who had to demonstrate the overwhelming importance of their cause in order to justify a deviation from the U.S. government's traditional distaste for civilian industrial policy. Once CEA and the Office of Management and Budget (OMB) were able to recast the issue—from how to promote American industry in international competition to the proper role of the government in the economy—Commerce's battle for a relative gains approach to HDTV was lost.[13] In contrast, in the satellite case relative gains proponents held the ideological high ground. They could justify their preferred policy not only in terms of the relative benefits that would accrue to the United States but also as a contribution to free trade, through the removal of blatant and discriminatory barriers to market access. Consequently, Commerce and USTR were strongly united, and the State Department and the CEA were willing to acquiesce, once the fundamental issue of whether to employ Super 301 against Japan had been resolved.

Second, the institutional setting mattered. The ability to translate relative gains concerns into policy was influenced by the institutional arrangements that structured political interaction in each of the cases. As John Ikenberry has noted, "State structures are important in setting the framework that facilitates or inhibits access to political resources and the policy-making apparatus, including the role and influence of government officials themselves" (Ikenberry 1988:221). At issue in the FSX case was a defense Memorandum of Understanding (MOU), negotiated in accordance with standard procedures by DOD and State. The fact that economic agencies were excluded from those negotiations influenced both the content of the MOU and the extent to which it could subsequently be altered. Indeed part of the struggle over FSX involved an attempt by Commerce to restructure the relevant institutional arrangements and obtain a voice in the negotiation of future MOUs. The satellite case was recognized as a trade issue, which placed lead responsibility for formulating and implementing U.S. policy in the hands of USTR. The burden of proof fell on traditionalists and noninterventionists to show why the United

States should refrain from pursuing the elimination of trade barriers with all the means at its disposal. Finally, proponents of a relative gains policy in HDTV were forced to wander through the executive, with no place like the Ministry of International Trade and Industry (MITI) to call home. Commerce, the self-appointed guardian of U.S. competitiveness, lacked the tradition of intervention and the associated industrial policy instruments needed to overcome ideologically driven opposition. DARPA enjoyed both, but was constrained by its narrowly defined mission—the right to intervene and subsidize U.S. firms for direct military, but not broad industrial, purposes. DARPA was reminded of this fact when it sought, however tentatively, to expand its domain (a similar point is made by Inman and Burton 1990:126).

Third, the ability of relative gains proponents in the executive to achieve their preferred outcomes was significantly influenced by the extent to which they could mobilize (or were mobilized by) members of Congress. In the satellite case, significant pressure from Congress to employ Super 301 paved the way for the executive branch's strategy of industrial policy preemption. In the FSX case, there was overwhelming support in Congress for a reconsideration of the initial deal, but far less support for abandoning it altogether. With HDTV, a vocal minority in Congress pushed for industrial policy, but could not command the support of a broad coalition.[14]

Interested American firms appear not to have exerted a decisive influence over the extent to which the United States pursued policies consistent with relative gains concerns. The Bush administration pursued a relative gains strategy against the better judgment of U.S. satellite makers, and failed to pursue one in HDTV despite being urged to do so by the American Electronics Association. American firms were divided over the wisdom of the FSX deal; the decision to renegotiate it was supported by the AEA, but opposed by the prime contractor, General Dynamics, and by the Aerospace Industries Association. Although the interests and strategies of private firms were not examined in detail, the cases appear to provide little direct support for a society-centered, as opposed to a state- or system-centered, explanation of American foreign economic policy (Ikenberry, Lake, and Mastanduno 1988:1–14).

The evidence does suggest the need to be attentive to both international and domestic structures—and the relationship between the two—in constructing explanations of relative gains–seeking behavior. Domestic structural factors—ideology and institutions—shaped and constrained the extent to which relative gains concerns, generated by international structural changes, were translated into policy. Over time, however, it is possible that domestic structural arrangements themselves will be transformed, thereby rendering more likely the consistent pursuit of relative gains concerns. For example, the relative decline of U.S. economic power and the concomitant rise of Japan has helped to produce a serious challenge, within government and the private sector, to the ideological consensus in favor of free trade that has guided U.S. policy throughout the postwar era (Destler 1986; Milner and Yoffie 1989:239–72; Lawrence and Schultze 1990). Institutional arrangements may change as well. The effort by DARPA to broaden its domain to include civilian industrial policy, and that by Commerce to gain a role in defense coproduction agreements, represent examples of attempted institutional adjustment in the face of international structural change. Reports that the CIA and the National Security Agency, in response to the decline of the Soviet threat, are seeking to reorient their intelligence-gathering activities in anticipation of an economic cold war may reflect similar calculations.[15] The point is not to predict the future, but to suggest that domestic structures, like their international counterparts, are not immutable.

This essay began by noting the policy conflict in the United States between traditionalists and revisionists. For each, the results of this study bring good news and bad news. Revisionists may take comfort in the fact that the U.S. policy process has clearly developed a sensitivity to relative gains concerns in U.S. economic relations with Japan, but may regret that ideological and political factors continue to constrain the United States from exploring a full range of policy options pursuant to those concerns. Traditionalists will be relieved by the latter point, particularly when the excluded options include the rupturing of security agreements and the crafting of economic balance-of-power strategies directed against Japan. On the other hand, they must remain wary of the possibility that changes in international economic and security structures will continue to tempt the United States to find a "geo-economic" substitute for the receding geopolitical competition that has defined American policy in the postwar era (Luttwak 1990:19).

NOTES

1. Urban C. Lehner and Alan Murray, "Will the U.S. Find the Resolve to Meet the Japanese Challenge?" *Wall Street Journal,* July 2, 1990, p.A1; "American Express Worry on Japan, as Feelings Seem to Soften," and Michael Oreskes, *New York Times,* July 10, 1990, p.A11. The latter reported that by a margin of 58 percent to 26 percent, Americans viewed the economic power of Japan as a greater threat to American security than the military power of the Soviet Union.

2. Raymond Vernon (1989). Vernon refers, presumably, to a situation of mutual assured destruction in which strike and retaliation would devastate both.

3. American revisionists are frequently accused of "Japan-bashing" by their critics. The most celebrated example of Japanese "America-bashing" is Akio Morita and Shintaro Ishihara (1989), an unofficial English translation of which circulated widely in Washington during 1989 and 1990.

4. Leading revisionist thinkers and some of their works include Chalmers Johnson (1987); James Fallows (1989); Charles Ferguson (1989); Karel Van Wolferen (1989); and Clyde Prestowitz, Jr. (1990).

5. See Kenneth Waltz (1979); Robert Jervis (1988:334–36); and esp. Joseph Grieco (1990). A thoughtful conceptual critique of the realist position is Duncan Snidal (1989).

6. An attempt, grounded in realism, to predict how states with different domestic structures and international capabilities will react to shifts in internal and external power positions is Michael Mastanduno, David A. Lake, and G. John Ikenberry (1989:457–74).

7. Realists expect nation-states to avoid gaps that favor their partners, but not necessarily to maximize gaps in their own favor. Nation-states are not "gap maximizers." They are, in Joseph Grieco's terms, "defensive positionalists." See Grieco (1990:44–45), and Kenneth Waltz (1986).

8. Jervis (1988:335); Grieco (1990, chap. 7). Grieco finds that the extent to which members of the European Community were willing to support nontariff barrier code proposals during the Tokyo Round of multilateral trade negotiations was influenced significantly by their assessment of whether or not the United States would reap greater economic benefits in relative terms if such codes were implemented.

9. Those who stress America's enduring capabilities in absolute terms include Susan Strange (1987:551–74) and Joseph S. Nye, Jr. (1990). Those who emphasize relative decline include Krasner (1982); Robert Gilpin (1987); and Paul Kennedy (1987).

10. This concern is addressed in the specific context of the defense industry by Theodore H. Moran (1990:57–99). The classic account, first published in 1945, is Albert Hirschman (1980).

11. In general, strategic industries or activities are those that generate higher-than-normal economic returns, or that generate externalities or "spillovers" that benefit other parts of the national economy. See Paul R.

Krugman (1986) and J. David Richardson (1990). The pursuit of strategic trade policy is not necessarily incompatible with that of free trade, as illustrated by the satellite case (as detailed in the original version of this essay).

12. A theoretically informed effort to link international systems and foreign economic policies is Lake (1988).

13. Commerce received only lukewarm support from the Office of the U.S. Trade Representative, whose top officials were skeptical of industrial policy. USTR Carla Hills responded to EC proposals for cooperation against Japan in HDTV by emphasizing a related market access concern —the EC's proposed restrictions on the import of foreign television programming.

14. Proposed legislation calling for an active executive role in HDTV is found in U.S. Congress, House, Committee on Science, Space, and Technology, *High Definition Television,* hearings, 101st Cong., 1st Sess., March 22, 1989, pp. 330–47.

15. See, for example, Michael Wines, "Security Agency Debates New Role: Economic Spying," *New York Times,* June 18, 1990, p.A1.

IV REFLECTIONS ON THE DEBATE

11

INSTITUTIONAL THEORY AND THE REALIST CHALLENGE AFTER THE COLD WAR

Robert O. Keohane

At any given time, our ideas about international relations reflect conventional understandings of the subject: that is, how people in the past have thought about it, based on their observations, their understandings of causality, and their normative preoccupations. However, our views sometimes change. We make our own observations, and we may have different normative concerns or causal presuppositions from those of earlier thinkers. Changes in our views are typically prompted by inconsistencies between conventional understandings of world politics and what we observe going on around us, or by dissatisfaction with the normative implications of the actions we observe. Anomaly and dissatisfaction are friends to thought; complacency its enemy.

Yet changes in mood may lead to shallow and ephemeral shifts in thinking about international affairs. It is all too easy for those who lack understanding of history or political structure to see a "new world in the making" that exists only in their own imaginations. Hence arguments about the alleged novelty of contemporary world politics are always subjected to criticism from within the profession of social scientists studying world politics. Writers such as those represented in this volume participate in a sort of double dialectic: between conventional understanding and contemporary practice; between claims of novelty and analytical criticisms testing those claims.

From a distance, we can observe this double dialectic as it operated between 1914 and 1939. World War I naturally led thoughtful observers to challenge the complacency of conventional balance-of-power thinking, which regarded state sovereignty as inviolable and trusted in coalitional politics to produce moderation and stability, although not necessarily peace. The realization that war had become incomparably more destructive than previously led to schemes to prevent it, of which collective security as articulated by Woodrow Wilson was the most prominent. In reaction both to its utopian elements and the rise of Nazism in the 1930s, this liberal construction was criticized, most devastatingly by E. H. Carr in *The Twenty Years' Crisis* (1939), which, as Stanley Hoffmann (1977) observes, laid the modern foundations of "realism" as an approach to international relations.

Realism as espoused by Carr was by no means a simple antithesis to utopian thinking about international affairs. The theme of *The Twenty Years' Crisis* was that political interests, bargaining, and the threat of force underlay all international processes and institutions: as Carr said about international law, "It cannot be understood independently of the political foundation on which it rests and the political interests which it serves" (Carr 1939:179). But Carr, unlike some of his modern successors, did not stop with the analysis of power. He sought, above all, ways of achieving peaceful change, which would require, he thought, "some way of basing its operation not on power alone, but on that uneasy compromise between power and morality which is the foundation of all political life" (220).

As Hoffmann has pointed out, the professional study of international relations since World War II has been largely "an American social science" (Hoffmann 1977).[1] After World War II, realism became dominant in American thinking about international relations, yet America remained a liberal society. Hence realism's triumph was precarious; even some of its proponents were uneasy about the normative implications of its emphasis on power, as Hans J. Morgenthau (1948) acknowledged when he titled his most influential book, *Politics Among Nations: The Struggle for Power and Peace*. Much of Morgenthau's textbook is concerned with strategies to achieve moderation and peace even in the presence of anarchy. Indeed it is not difficult to find in this book passages that view a highly institutionalized world society as a desirable, indeed ultimately attainable, end.[2]

During the 1970s, realism was systematized in structural form by

Kenneth N. Waltz (1979), as this volume's predecessor shows (Keohane 1986b). In this neorealist formulation, the distribution of power is viewed as more strongly determining outcomes than in classical realism, and less attention is paid to processes of peaceful change or to international institutions. More precise than classical realism, neorealism was also more narrowly drawn, and more easily challenged. Yet its scientific ambitions gave it wide appeal, and when I refer below to "realism," I will be referring to this contemporary version of it.

Serious challenges to realism only arose when anomalies appeared between its presuppositions and patterns of action in the world. The anomalies that were noticed in the United States were, not surprisingly, those that liberals could easily recognize, including the increasing salience of economic interdependence and the apparent tendency of democracies to behave differently in foreign policy than authoritarian states. Commercial liberalism and republican liberalism—the beliefs that economic interdependence contributes to peace and that democracies are more peaceful, at least in some relationships, than nondemocracies—have long been important strains in liberal thinking (Keohane 1990a). So has what Joseph Nye calls "sociological liberalism," which in Nye's words, "asserts the transformative effect of transnational contacts and coalitions on national attitudes and definitions of interests" (1988:246).

My focus in this essay, however, is on an institutionalist argument that borrows elements from both liberalism and realism. Consistently with realism—and accounting for the fact that it is frequently denoted as "neorealist"—institutionalist theory assumes that states are the principal actors in world politics and that they behave on the basis of their conceptions of their own self-interests. Relative capabilities—realism's "distribution of power"—remain important, and states must rely on themselves to assure themselves gains from cooperation. However, institutionalist theory also emphasizes the role of international institutions in changing conceptions of self-interest. Thus it draws on liberal thinking about the formation of interests. Institutionalist thinking has focused its critical fire on realism rather than on harmony-oriented versions of liberalism, since the latter have been discredited in Anglo-American international relations theory for half a century. In the context of the intellectual debates of the 1970s and 1980s, therefore, it was appropriate to give it the label of "neoliberal" (Grieco 1988a; Nye 1988). But it is crucial to remember that it borrows as much from realism as from liberalism: it cannot be encapsulated as simply a "liberal" theory opposed at all points to realism. Indeed it is almost as misleading to refer to it as liberal as to give it the tag of neorealism.[3]

At any rate, in the 1970s critics of realist orthodoxy pointed not only to rising levels of interdependence but to persistent increases in the number and significance of international regimes, sets of rules designed to govern behavior within issue areas (Keohane and Nye 1977). Soon the discussion of international regimes, and how they should be explained, expanded to constitute an academic cottage industry (Krasner 1983a). Much of the contemporary debate centers on the validity of the institutionalist claim that international regimes, and institutions more broadly, have become significant in world politics. Realist authors have criticized this argument, holding that "international institutions are unable to mitigate anarchy's constraining effects on inter-state cooperation" (Grieco 1988a:486). Realists attempt to reinforce this argument by advancing the counterclaim, put forward most systematically by Joseph Grieco, that states care much more about relative than about absolute gains (Grieco 1990:40). In the first section of this essay, I will offer some brief reflections on this debate. Brevity is easy to achieve, since the 1991 paper by Milner (reprinted in this volume) discusses the concept of "anarchy" in a sophisticated way, and convincing analyses of the "relative gains debate" are provided in the essays by Powell and Snidal (also included here).

The dialectic between academic understanding and changes in the world has not come to an end. Quite to the contrary, the end of the Cold War where it started, in Europe, has once again challenged our presuppositions. The second part of this essay therefore seeks to examine how the debate over the significance of international institutions is illuminated by these events—which neither realists nor institutionalists anticipated. Western Europe provides a good arena for a comparative evaluation of realist and institutionalist approaches, since Western Europe was highly institutionalized in 1989. If strict realists are right, these institutions should not make much difference. With the reunification of Germany, Europe should be propelled, in John Mearsheimer's words, "back to the future"— doomed to repeat the struggles under anarchy that were such a fearsome feature of the first half of the century (Mearsheimer 1990a). If the theories of institutionalists have any validity, by contrast, the rich tapestry of institutions should both constrain states, through the operation of rules, and provide them with opportunities to cooperate, thus enabling them to pursue their own interests without posing the threats to other states that are so characteristic of realist anarchy. I will argue that preliminary evidence supports the institutionalist interpretation, and I will offer my own forecast of the future of the European Community, which differs sharply from that of Professor Mearsheimer.

Fortunately, debates in the field of international relations are not doomed to sterile repetition of competing claims. In his response to my criticisms and those of others, Joseph Grieco has interestingly amplified and commented on his earlier arguments, in a way that helps us, in my view, to move toward a more satisfactory synthesis of perspectives. During the next few years we should, I think, not retread these "realist vs. institutionalist" debates, but rather explore the extent, strength, and content of international institutions, examining *how*, not merely whether, they make a difference. In the third part of this essay, I address Grieco's response and issues of theoretical synthesis and research directions.

INSTITUTIONAL THEORY AND THE ISSUE OF RELATIVE GAINS

Rational institutionalist theory begins with the assumption, shared with realism, that states, the principal actors in world politics, are rational egoists. Contrary to realists, institutionalists argue that discord does not necessarily result from rational egoism:

> If the egoists monitor each other's behavior and if enough of them are willing to cooperate on condition that others cooperate as well, they may be able to adjust their behavior to reduce discord. They may even create and maintain principles, norms, rules and procedures—institutions referred to in this book as regimes. . . . Properly designed institutions can help egoists to cooperate even in the absence of a hegemonic power. (Keohane 1984:83–84)

Institutionalists do not elevate international regimes to mythical positions of authority over states: on the contrary, such regimes are established by states to achieve their purposes. Facing dilemmas of coordination and collaboration under conditions of interdependence, governments demand international institutions to enable them to achieve their interests through limited collective action (Keohane 1982; Stein 1982a).[4] These institutions serve state objectives not principally by enforcing rules (except when they coordinate rule-enforcement by the strong against the weak, as in the International Monetary Fund—IMF), but by facilitating the making and keeping of agreements through the provision of information and reductions in transactions costs. Even if such costs remain substantial, states will create and use such institutions as long as the institutions enable states to achieve valued objectives unattainable through unilateral or bilateral means. Cooperation will never be perfect and is intimately associated with discord. Nevertheless, those institutions that succeed in facilitating mutually beneficial cooperation will become valued for the opportunities they provide to states, they will therefore acquire a certain degree of permanence, and their rules will constrain the exercise of power by governments. Governments will still seek to attain their ends, including increasing their shares of the gains from cooperation, through the use of political influence. However, the exercise of influence will depend not merely on their material capabilities but also on the relationship between their ends and means, on the one hand, and the rules and practices of the international institution, on the other.

The Conditionality of Relative Gains

The analytics underlying the institutionalist approach adopt the conventional assumption of economics that actors, including states, care only about their own utility. They have no *intrinsic* interest in the welfare of others. However, in *After Hegemony* I explicitly recognized that interests may be interdependent. After discussing a variety of such situations, I noted the problem of what Grieco later referred to as "relative gains":

> Under conditions of severe competition, which is characteristic of power conflicts and particularly of arms races . . . gains for one side are seen as losses for the other. . . . By the argument I make here, negative evaluations of others' welfare gains should make international regimes harder to institute. (Keohane 1984:123n9)

Thus institutionalism recognizes the possibility that states' interests in relative gains will make cooperation more difficult. Such a recognition does not involve institutional theory in a contradiction, since the theory is explicitly *conditional*. As indicated at the very beginning of *After Hegemony*, "The theory that I develop takes the existence of mutual interests as given and examines the conditions under which they will lead to cooperation" (Keohane 1984:6).

In contrast, in his well-known article in *International Organization* in 1988, Joseph Grieco seemed to put forward an unconditional argument. He claimed that the fact of international anarchy means that *"the fundamental goal of states in any relationship is to prevent others from achieving advances in their relative capabilities"* (Grieco 1988a:498; italics in original). Reacting to the dangers of anarchy, states are "defensive positionalists," which "seek to prevent increases in others' capabilities" and which are therefore cautious about engaging in international cooperation (499). Cooperation, according to Grieco, is less significant than institutionalists believe.[5]

What I seek to show in the next few pages is that when the conditionality of Grieco's claims is recognized, his critique of institutionalist theory is greatly weakened. The contention that international anarchy dictates concern for relative rather than absolute gains is not sustainable. Relative gains may be important motivating forces for states and firms, but only when gains in one period alter power relations in another, and when there is some likelihood that subsequent advantages in power may be used against oneself. Since the theoretical validity of the claim that relative gains matter more than absolute gains is conditional, empirical analysis should accompany a priori argument, and Grieco's (1988a:495) claim of the "failure of the new liberal institutionalism" is exaggerated. I will begin this critical analysis with an analytic discussion, seeking to establish the criteria that a relative gains interpretation must meet; then I will briefly discuss the failure of Grieco's empirical argument in *Cooperation Among Nations* to meet those criteria.

In an essay reprinted in this volume, Robert Powell shows that a key variable is whether "the constraints defining the system create opportunities for one state to turn relative gains to its advantage and to the disadvantage of other states" (Powell 1991a:1315). Where these opportunities exist, relative gains may indeed be important, cooperation inhibited, and realist pessimism justified.[6] Powell's paper thus helps to delimit the scope of both realist and institutionalist arguments, by specifying more precisely the criteria under which concerns about relative gains could be important. Only if Powell's criteria are met does the claim that failure to cooperate is explained by concern about relative gains acquire a priori plausibility.

States evaluate intentions as well as capabilities. Even if asymmetrical gains from cooperation would increase the power of some states, those governments expecting smaller gains than those accruing to their partners (in Grieco's language, "absolute gains but relative losses") will not only ask whether these shifts in capabilities could be used against them, but how likely this is to happen. If such shifts in capability seem very unlikely to be used adversely, concern for relative gains in these relationships may be of minor significance. Thus the fact that asymmetrical gains have implications for a given set of future power relationships constitutes a necessary but not sufficient condition for states to worry more about relative than absolute gains.

As Duncan Snidal shows, even when states are motivated by the desire for relative gains, it is important not to overstate its impact. Concern for relative gains does not necessarily translate even in two-actor situations into intractable conflict. It is particularly important not to generalize casually from the effects of concern for relative gains in Prisoner's Dilemma (PD) to their effects in other games. "PD results significantly overstate the deleterious impact of relative gains on cooperation in other absolute gains situations" (Snidal 1991b:712; see also Hiscox and Franzese 1991).

Even more significantly, the concept of relative gains becomes fundamentally ambiguous as the number of actors becomes greater than two. Relative gains for state B in a dyadic relationship with state A may *help* state A in a contest with state C, if A and B are allies or B and C are adversaries. Which "relationship" counts? Is the fundamental goal of A to prevent B from achieving advances in its bilateral relationship, to prevent C from making gains in the A-C relationship, or to attain some unspecified position in the larger three-party game? Since the systemic nature of world politics guarantees that states are in many different relationships simultaneously, Grieco's statement, quoted above, that "the fundamental goal of states in any relationship is to prevent others from achieving advances in their relative capabilities" is difficult to interpret. Certainly it would provide no guide to policymakers facing choices in multiple, linked relationships.

As the number of actors increases, the impact of relative gains motivations on cooperation declines (Snidal 1991a:396). Furthermore, when relative gains are important in such situations, the result may well be what Snidal calls "defensive cooperation": the formation of "cooperative clusters" (such as international organizations or alliances) to achieve relative gains collectively versus others (Snidal 1991a:399–401). With many actors involved, concern for relative gains may promote rather than inhibit certain types of institutionalized cooperation.

The general point to be drawn from this discussion is simple. Any claims made about the impact of relative gains are highly conditional: they do not follow logically from the absence of common government, or "international anarchy." Where a system of more than two actors is involved, such claims are fundamentally ambiguous in the absence of specification of which relationships "count" for the purpose of relative gains calculations. As a result, the theoretical significance of relative gains is to qualify institutionalist theory rather than to demolish it.

Like Snidal and Powell, institutionalists have rejected the view that institutionalism and neorealism are diametrically opposed theories, and have focused instead on the conditions under which one or the other approach is valid. Institutionalism accepts the assumptions of realism about state motivation and lack of common enforcement power in world politics, but argues that *where common interests exist*, realism is too pessimistic about the prospects for cooperation and the role of institutions:

> The neoliberal institutionalist perspective . . . is relevant to an international system only if the actors have some mutual interests; that is, they must potentially gain from their cooperation. In the absence of mutual interests, the neoliberal perspective on international cooperation would be as irrelevant as a neoclassical theory of international trade in a world without potential gains from trade. (Keohane 1989:2–3)

Thus we need to be careful about where the predictions of institutionalism and realism converge, and where they diverge.

For situations with little mutual interest—in which international relations would approximate a series of zero-sum games—neoliberal theory's predictions would considerably overlap with those of neorealism. Under these conditions, states will be reluctant to cooperate with each other and will choose less durable rather than more durable arrangements. Linkages, furthermore, may well impede cooperation. The divergence between the predictions of the two theories will become apparent only when opportunities for joint gains through cooperation are substantial. Under these conditions, according to neoliberal theory, states' obsessions with relative gains will diminish. They will join quite durable institutions, with explicit rules and organizations; and issue linkage will often, though not always, facilitate agreement. (Keohane 1989:18n20)

In a recent study of patterns of cooperation on economic sanctions, Lisa L. Martin has provided an example of how realist and institutionalist theories can be combined. She argues that some cooperation on economic sanctions has been "coercive," with powerful states seeking to induce other states to cooperate on sanctions, even when the latter have no independent interest in doing so. On issues such as the European Community's sanctions against Argentina in the 1982 Falklands war, the coercive bargaining that took place was realist in character, but the institutional framework within which it took place was highly significant to the outcome, as predicted by institutionalist theory. Institutionalist theory by no means predicts harmony; Martin shows that theorists should pay more attention to asymmetrical games in which issue-linkage is a rational strategy (Martin 1992c:147; Sebenius 1992).

It is important to remember the conditionality of institutionalist theory: institutionalism by no means predicts universal cooperation. In his essay reprinted in this volume, Stephen Krasner (1991) interprets his finding that powerful states blocked the creation of regimes for radio and television broadcasting and remote sensing as evidence that institutional theory misleadingly distracts our attention from the realities of power. But institutionalists never argued that in the absence of potential mutual gains, international regimes would form. If powerful actors will gain higher levels of utility by blocking the enactment of international rules, we expect them to do so. Thus Krasner's findings are entirely consistent with institutionalist theory.

Conditions for Significant Concern About Relative Gains

By 1992 Professor Grieco had accepted the conditionality of his argument about relative gains (Grieco, chapter 12), so that this point is no longer in dispute. It appears to me that three specific questions now divide us. I argue, as elaborated above, that the concept of relative gains becomes ambiguous with more than two actors. Second, Professor Grieco holds that relative gains concerns (his "*k*") are always positive—that is, they inhibit cooperation—and often large: "The coefficient for a state's sensitivity to gaps in payoffs—*k*—can be expected to vary but always to be greater than zero" (Grieco chapter 12:323). This argument echoes his earlier claim that "gaps in payoffs favoring partners will always detract from a state's utility to some degree" (Grieco 1990:47) My view, by contrast, is that this coefficient can be positive, negative, or zero. It can be negative, contrary to Grieco's statement, in the case of stable alliances, where one ally seeks to reinforce the other's strength. Early in the Cold War, for instance, the United States deliberately built up the economic capabilities of its allies in Europe and East Asia, while striving hard to limit the technological competence of the Soviet Union and China. Indeed it seems to me that Professor Grieco has in effect conceded this point, since he approvingly quotes his book (Grieco 1990) as stating that "to the degree that there is a common enemy posing a clear and present danger, a state may actually welcome increases in an ally's capabilities" (Grieco, chapter 12:323). Clearly, if *k* can be negative or positive, it could also be zero insofar as negative and positive elements canceled one another out (or where concern about relative gains was negligible).

Our third disagreement concerns the empirical evaluation of situations where we observe tough bargaining, and wonder whether it might be accounted for by concern about relative gains. This problem of empirical evaluation is made even more difficult by the fact that two parties that are indifferent to one another's welfare will behave, at the margin, *as if* they care about relative gains. An actor seeking to maximize net benefits to itself, without regard to its partner's welfare, will seek both to achieve joint gains and to obtain as large a share of those gains as possible. Its strategies will link these two goals: for example, promises to agree on an exchange that provides joint gains are likely to be contingent on a specification of the division of those gains. Once it is clear what type of agreement will maximize the joint gains to be reaped by the parties, the effect of one party maximizing its own net benefits will be the same as if it were seeking to minimize the gains of its partners. To put this point another way, states making a mutually advantageous bargain can be viewed as both moving up to the contract curve, and moving along it to a single point. The first, outward movement is beneficial to both sides; but any movement along the contract curve benefits one party at the expense of the other. Thus it is incorrect to infer from the roughness of "life on the Pareto frontier" (Krasner 1991) that "relative gains" are significant motivations for states. Struggles for distributional advantage could account for tough bargaining along the contract curve, as they do in ordinary market situations such as the sale of a house from one person to a stranger.[7]

In his empirical attempts to refute institutionalist theory, Grieco (1990) does not convincingly address this ambiguity. He interprets EC-U.S. negotiations about standards (184) and technical barriers to trade (192, 196) as showing concern by the EC for relative gains. However, this is merely an *interpretation*. What Grieco actually reports with respect to standards (185–86) is that the EC sought to avoid rules that focused so strongly on the practices of central governments that the United States, with its federal system and heavy reliance on private contractors, would be less strictly regulated than its European partners. Such rules would not only have given the United States relative gains, but would have reduced the material benefits to the EC countries of an agreement. So we return to the fundamental ambiguity that bargaining for a larger share of overall benefits, and for relative gains, may be indistinguishable. Grieco interprets the evidence as supporting the relative gains hypothesis, but he fails to refute the alternative hypothesis that the EC pressed for more favorable agreements in order to maximize its members' own utility. Since both hypotheses predict *the same behavior*, his evidence is insufficient to establish one over the other.

Grieco also argues that the concern of Australia, Canada, and Argentina for relative gains led them to block an antidumping agreement that would have "generated absolute gains for all but more gains for the United States and the EC than for others" (1990:214). How, the reader asks, do we know that these three countries were not simply seeking a better deal for themselves? The European Monetary System (EMS) is said to reflect "relative gains concerns of weaker participants" through differential treatment of weaker partners and side-payments (222). Once again, it can be asked why the weaker states' demands did not merely reflect their desire to maximize their utility.[8]

Since alternative theories can predict the same behavior, it may be difficult to test interpretations based on tough bargaining for absolute gains against those positing concern for relative gains. Yet at least a preliminary test is provided by the analytical conditions essential for relative gains logic to apply, as discussed above. *For relative gains, rather than simply the desire to maximize utility, to account for tough negotiations, there must be some plausible way by which one's partner could use advantages gained from the international agreement to hurt oneself in a future period, and a significant prospective motivation for it to do so.* Only if the advocate of a relative gains interpretation can show that these conditions are met, is it plausible to entertain his hypothesis.

These conditions *are* sometimes met—as they were in U.S.-Soviet relations during the Cold War, or are in general between military adversaries. It would be foolish to deny that relative gains are sometimes important in world politics. But the proposition has to be viewed as *conditional*, and empirical investigation has to respect the conditions specified by a priori analysis.

Michael Mastanduno's discussion of America's response to Japanese industrial policy makes an important contribution to empirical research by exploring the international and domestic conditions that fostered or inhibited concern for relative gains. Mastanduno's discussion of the U.S. use of Section 301 to retaliate against Japanese barriers to the purchase of foreign communications satellites (his clearest example of relative gains making a difference) meets Powell's criterion: "U.S. firms were not only shut out of a market they could easily have dominated, but their competitors could use their protected home base as a 'sanctuary,' and from it launch an export drive" (Mastanduno 1991:98–99). Furthermore, if Japanese firms had succeeded in gaining market dominance, they would have had incentives to exploit those advantages to further weaken their American rivals. Mastanduno also seems to draw the right generalization. In situations such as these, he emphasizes, "relative gains concerns do matter significantly, but not unconditionally" (1991:74).

Grieco's evidence for relative gains motivations, however, is less compelling. It is theoretically plausible that the EC might, in the negotiations on standards and technical barriers to trade, have been motivated by concern for relative gains, since the EC acts as a single unit in trade (so the game was a two-party game) and oligopolistic competition might have been affected by decisions made.[9] However, it seems implausible that three usually competing small countries (Argentina, Australia, Canada) would really have turned down a bargain that would maximize their expected utility because it strengthened the EC and the U.S.—two much more powerful entities that would in any case have the power to coerce these small states in the future. What motivation would these weak, divided countries have for renouncing gains in their utility for the sake of avoiding "relative losses" with respect to trading partners with whose power they could never compete? Likewise, why should we believe that the smaller members of the EMS worried about relative gains toward a much more powerful Germany in the late 1970s but not at Maastricht in 1991?

Responding to these criticisms in chapter 12, Professor Grieco agrees that "states that fear that a partner might use force against them will be highly concerned about gaps in gains advantaging that partner." But he adds two other conditions: "uncertainties about one's partners and the efficacy of force, and fears about the non-military consequences of gaps in gains" (Grieco, chapter 12:313). His uncertainty category refers to uncertainty about other states' future actions: their hostility may increase, or the governments of these states may believe, even perhaps irrationally, that they could use force effectively. His fear category refers to concern that one will become dependent on the partner, as the partner grows relatively stronger. "An advantaged partner, states may worry, could use increased influence arising from its enjoyment of relative gains to force them to accept progressively less favorable terms" (Grieco, chapter 12:315).

Concern about dependence as a motivation for seeking relative gains is clearly included in the first part of my formulation above: rational fear of dependence would reflect the existence of "some plausible way by which one's partner could use advantages gained from international agreement to hurt oneself in a future period." Professor Grieco's discussion of uncertainty, however, seems to reflect confusion about the rational expected-utility formulation to which he, as a realist, is committed.

In a standard expected-utility formulation, states will not let mere *possibilities* determine their behavior. If so, they would behave like paranoids, to their great cost. On the contrary, in considering whether to worry about relative gains they will estimate not only the consequences of adverse action by their partners but the *probability* of such behavior. Risk-averse states will be cautious in the face of uncertainty, but mere uncertainty, which is characteristic of international affairs in general, will not by itself mandate significant concern for relative gains. There must appear to be some significant probability of harmful action for such concern to be rational.

Perhaps one could believe that generalized uncertainty and fear in world politics are so high, and so resistant to institutional means of reduction, that governments will treat possibilities as probabilities. Such governments would worry even about relative gains by partners that are much weaker than themselves, that have friendly governments, and to whom they are linked in cooperative institutions. But by eschewing opportunities for mutually beneficial exchange, these governments would be forgoing substantial benefits, and their leaders could be expected to suffer at the hands of members of their societies who seek those benefits. Where there is competition among elites—either democratically or otherwise—the argument that paranoia is essential to a sensible foreign policy seems unlikely to prevail indefinitely. And at the systemic level of analysis, if states were "defensive positionalists," as Professor Grieco argues, the "tendency of states to undertake their cooperation through *institutionalized* arrangements" (Grieco, chapter 12:335) would be particularly difficult to explain.

Joseph Grieco has made a significant contribution by focusing attention on the issue of relative gains, a subject that has been underemphasized, especially by liberal or neoliberal commentators on the world economy. Oligopolistic competition, whether among states or firms, may include concern for relative gains, albeit usually as part of an attempt to maximize long-term absolute gains. But to establish the significance of relative gains empirically requires careful analysis. Whether relative gains are important is not a matter of dogma, but is conditional on the opportunity and incentive to use them against others. Empirically, the point is that tough negotiations, or even their breakdown, by no means provide evidence for relative-gain motivations. To make a plausible case for such motivations, the analyst must show that the state or states resisting cooperation could have reasonably expected to be disadvantaged, in a future period, by the gains made in this current period by its potential partners.

REALIST AND INSTITUTIONALIST FORECASTS
AFTER THE COLD WAR

During the Cold War, it was difficult to evaluate the relative merits of institutionalist and realist theories of cooperation, because both approaches seemed broadly consistent with observation. Institutionalists such as myself pointed to the increasing visibility and specificity of international institutions such as the IMF and World Bank, GATT, NATO, and the European Community as evidence for a functional theory of international regimes: when attaining their interests required systematic and durable cooperation, governments were able to establish such institutions on the basis of mutual self-interest. Institutions helped them to overcome collective action problems by providing information and reducing the costs of transactions (Keohane 1984, chap. 6). Hegemony was not essential to the maintenance of regimes based on mutual interest, although American hegemony had been an important factor in establishing many of them in the first place. And although military force played an indirect role in U.S. relations with its closest allies, "changes in relations of military power have not been the major factors affecting patterns of cooperation and discord among the advanced industrialized countries since the end of World War II" (Keohane 1984:40–41).

Realists, on the other hand, emphasized that the strongest international regimes were constructed in a bipolar world in the shadow of U.S. hegemony, and most of them were led at least initially by the United States. Some versions of these arguments are compatible with institutionalist views. Joanne Gowa, for instance, argues on both theoretical and historical grounds that "the security externalities of agreements to open borders to trade imply that these agreements are more likely to occur within than between military alliances" (Gowa 1989:1253). That is, the security externalities of trade are positive for allies, negative for adversaries; the utility of trade regimes will therefore be enhanced for the former, diminished for the latter. Agreement with this proposition does not entail a belief that "relative gains are more important than absolute gains"; only an awareness of enduring realities of competitive security politics.

Gowa's argument suggests that as military alliances become less important, the security externalities that have reinforced liberal trade regimes will become less significant as well, and the regimes themselves may suffer. Institutionalist theories are ambiguous on the future of liberal economic regimes, since in the absence of a specification of interests (which will depend in part on domestic politics), institutionalist predictions about cooperation are indeterminate. That is, institutional theory takes states' conceptions of their interests as exogenous: unexplained within the terms of the theory. Unlike naive versions of commercial or republican liberalism, institutionalist theory does not infer a utility function for states simply from their material economic interests or the alleged values common to democracies. The key question with respect to global economic regimes such as GATT, therefore, is whether their principal members will regard their continuation or strengthening (whether in liberal or illiberal directions) as in their interests. Institutional theory makes no prediction about these interests, and therefore has no well-defined view on their evolution. Nor does realism predict interest. This weakness of systemic theory, of both types, denies us a clear test of their relative predictive power.[10]

Other patterns of change, however, may help to illuminate the value of the theories. Institutionalist theory has claimed to account for the increase in the number of international organizations from about one hundred in 1945 to over six hundred by 1980 by referring to increasing levels of economic and ecological interdependence, which are alleged to create demand for both rules and organizations (Keohane 1990b:740–48). Insofar as realism offers an account of this phenomenon, it is seen as a result of bipolarity and American hegemony. Hence realist theory should expect a decline in the number of international institutions after the Cold War, as the world returns to more traditional patterns of multipolar competition under anarchy. Institutionalism, by contrast, sees increased economic and ecological interdependence as secular trends, and therefore expects that as long as technological change prompts increased economic interdependence, and as long as threats to the global environment grow in severity, we will observe a continuing increase in the number and complexity of international institutions, and in the scope of their regulation. It is important to point out, however, that these institutions will not necessarily be liberal: it is quite possible for strong illiberal institutions, such as the Multifiber Arrangements for textiles, to be devised (Aggarwal 1985). The rate of growth in their numbers and in the scope of their action may also slow down; but if institutionalist theory is correct, they should not suffer a sharp decline.

Institutionalism also expects existing organizations to adapt quite easily to new purposes, within limits set by basic interests. Existing organizations should adopt new tasks more easily than new organizations can be created; incremental institutional change should prevail over both continual improvisation and radical institutional innovation. As I said in 1984, "It would count against my theory if most agreements made among governments were constructed not within the framework of international regimes, but on an ad hoc basis" (Keohane 1984:219).

So far, in Europe, most but not all evidence is consistent with institutionalist expectations. On issues of trade and the environment, the European Community is playing the predominant role, moving into new geographical or functional areas, as institutionalists would expect (Levy 1993; Nicolaides 1993). With respect to debt management and public international finance, however, the European Bank for Reconstruction and Development (EBRD) is an apparent anomaly for institutionalists, since the IMF and World Bank already operate in this area (Haggard and Moravcsik 1993). Institutionalist theory would have led us to expect that the IMF and World Bank, perhaps in conjunction with the European Community's European Investment Bank, would dominate this issue area, expanding to East Europe and crowding out newcomers. Realist theory, with its emphasis on distinct national interests, is better suited to understanding why the West European countries, led by France, wanted to establish the EBRD. Looking toward the future, institutionalist forecasts are ambiguous. On the one hand, institutionalist theory attributes considerable staying power to organizations such as the EBRD, once established; on the other hand, the IMF and World Bank are much stronger entities with better-entrenched networks.

If institutionalists are disturbingly vague in their forecasts on economic questions, realists are also annoyingly ambiguous in their preferred domain, that of security. Kenneth Waltz said at the 1990 American Political Science Association convention that "NATOs days are not numbered, but its years are." His sophisticated realist view acknowledged that institutions often persist beyond the conditions of their creation, but led him to believe that structural change would undermine NATO. However, another realist could point out that one of the unstated purposes of NATO has always been to inhibit independent action by Germany, and that this interest of Germany's NATO partners has only been enhanced by the end of the Cold War. Institutionalists would expect NATO to use its organizational resources to persist, by changing its tasks. And indeed NATO is shifting from the mission of deterring a Soviet threat to a variety of different political and lower-level military tasks, including co-opting East European governments in a NATO Cooperation Council, just as the March of Dimes, when polio was conquered in the United States, turned its attention to birth defects. So far, so good, for institutionalists. But institutionalists cannot tell us precisely "how sticky" organizations are in the face of changes in interests. Will NATO persist indefinitely, or should we only amend Waltz's comment to indicate that "its years are numbered on more than the fingers of one hand?" Once again, weak theory leads to ambiguous prediction.[11]

The most doctrinaire version of realism (which Charles Lipson at the 1992 meeting of the American Political Science Association referred to as "hyper-realism") generates more definite predictions. But its visions are disturbingly and often implausibly apocalyptic. John Mearsheimer has argued that bipolarity, an equal military balance, and nuclear weapons kept the peace in Europe during the Cold War, and that the reunification of Germany and the likely removal of the American guarantee—of both external protection and interalliance peace—will lead to intensified political rivalry and perhaps even military conflict among major European powers. "The root cause of the problem," he claims, "is the anarchic nature of the international system," which means that "all other states are potential threats" and "relative power, not absolute levels of power, matters most to states" (Mearsheimer 1990a:12).

One reason for being skeptical of such realist pessimism is that "anarchy," a constant for realists, cannot explain variation in patterns of conflict and cooperation among states. Although anarchy in the sense of lack of common government has been a constant throughout the history of the interstate system, cooperation among states has varied substantially. The proliferation of international institutions during the Cold War, and most notably the history of the European Community, show that anarchy does not necessarily prevent cooperation. Mearsheimer's argument really rests not on broad generalizations about anarchy but on more specific worries about hypernationalism in Eastern Europe and the effects of multipolarity (resulting both from the end of the Cold War and the decline of American dominance over Europe and Japan).[12]

In the absence of stabilizing institutions, multipolarity and hypernationalism are indeed dangerous. States will expect conflict and seek to protect themselves through self-help, as discussed by generations of realist writers. Where effective means of power are at stake, and a small number of highly competitive states is involved, they will seek relative gains. Alliances will form, providing a context in which nationalistic conflicts can set off large-scale war. The scenario is familiar: it is the story of 1914.

The underlying framework of analysis leading to this conclusion is shared by both realists and rational institutionalists such as myself: state action is based on rational calculation, meaning that leaders seek to maximize *subjective* expected utility. Calculations of expected utility incorporate both estimates of others' capabilities and their likely intentions; hence the decisions of leaders depend on their expectations about other states' likely actions. But focusing on expectations brings us back to institutions. International institutions exist largely because they facilitate self-interested cooperation by reducing uncertainty, thus stabilizing expectations. It follows that the expectations of states will depend in part on the nature and strength of international institutions. Hence a valid analysis of rational state policy in an area such as Europe, which is institutionally dense, must take international institutions into account.

The continued salience of international institutions after the end of the Cold War is quite evident from an examination of state strategies. All five major powers used international institutions in their strategies of adaptation to the structural changes of 1989–91. Germany sought to reassure its partners by its attachment to NATO as well as to the EC; the Soviet Union tried to use the Conference on Security and Cooperation in Europe (CSCE) to cover its military withdrawal from Eastern Europe, and to join Western economic organizations in order to integrate itself with the capitalist world economy. The United States, which had developed a highly successful strategy of working through international institutions in Europe, sought not to diminish but to reinforce those organizations and rules, NATO in particular. France used the EC to try to help control the process of German reunification, which it feared; even Britain, with its dislike of supranationalism, resorted to international institutions —in this case NATO—to counter attempts by Germany and France to strengthen EC security arrangements (Keohane, et al., 1993).

The propensity of states to use existing international institutions, at least in the short run, hardly refutes sophisticated realist arguments, although it does suggest that claims, such as Grieco's cited earlier, that "international institutions are unable to mitigate anarchy's constraining effects on inter-state cooperation" are misleading (Grieco 1988a:486). Indeed Grieco's own analysis of the European Community, and particularly European Monetary Union, in chapter 12 refutes his earlier argument: in his later interpretation, smaller European states sought institutionalized cooperation in order to reduce Germany's ability to pursue autonomous policies that could hurt them. The absence of supranational enforcement, overcoming anarchy, does not imply the insignificance of international institutions.

As Mearsheimer suggests, the European Community provides fairly clear grounds for a comparative test between strong realist contentions, based on anarchy and relative gains, and institutionalist arguments. Mearsheimer argues that the European Community will be weakened by the end of the Cold War. In his words, "the Cold War provided a hothouse environment in which the EC could flourish. If the Cold War ends and the stable order it produced collapses, the EC is likely to grow weaker, not stronger with time" (Mearsheimer 1990b:199).

My view is just the opposite, since my version of institutionalist theory embeds it selectively in a larger framework of neoliberal thought. As commercial liberalism or interdependence theory emphasizes, the EC has provided substantial economic and political gains for its members. Its members are all resolutely democratic, in their social as well as their political institutions: republican liberalism stresses the significance of this fact. As "sociological liberalism" (Nye 1988:246) would emphasize, extensive transnational ties and coalitions criss-cross the Continent. Finally, the institutions of the EC are firmly entrenched, and it continues to perform crucial functions. Thus there is a "synergy" among these four aspects of liberalism, which are arguably mutually reinforcing.[13]

Within the European Community, commitment to its institutions is an essential condition for Germany to be able to pursue its interests and to exercise the influence that its economic strength and political coherence create, without unduly alarming its partners. Those of its partners that follow coherent domestic policies and realistic foreign policies may be able to use the institutional constraints of the EC to exercise some influence over policies, such as monetary policy, that would otherwise (given the level of economic interdependence in Europe) be determined unilaterally by Germany.[14] Externally, the EC reinforces Europe's power vis-à-vis the United States, on the one hand, and the now-fragmented states to the East on the other. Europe has become a magnet for peripheral states. Those that are ready, such as Austria and Sweden, seek to join the EC; others, such as the Czech Republic, Hungary, and Poland, attempt to adapt their laws and practices in anticipation of future membership (Keohane, et al., 1992). If the former Soviet Union becomes a conflict-ridden zone of hypernationalism (which in the absence of institutions based on common interests would not be surprising to an institutionalist), the EC will, in my view, have even stronger motivations to stick together.

The Maastricht agreement, negotiated in December 1991, was a patchwork of provisions that satisfied no one. Its provisions for monetary union implied a transition period in which exchange rates would be fixed in the Community but capital would move freely across borders and national governments and central banks would retain control over monetary as well as fiscal policy. In December 1992, after a series of currency crises, the President of the Bundesbank labeled this "exchange rate mechanism" as "a powerful incentive for speculation" (*Financial Times*, December 2, 1992, p. 1). Britain's opting-out of the Social Charter created anomalies in the Treaty, as well as contributing to the parliamentary controversy over ratification. Debates on the treaty have revealed both the gulf between elite and popular views in Europe and the widespread resistance to centralization at the European level. The controversy over ratification of Maastricht, exemplified in 1992 by the close Danish "No" vote and the almost equally close French "Yes," seems to make it unlikely that the most ambitious aspirations of advocates of European union will be met. It should also remind us both that elected officials in Europe still depend for their tenure on national electorates, not technocrats in Brussels, and that Europe's progress toward greater unity has never been either smooth or linear.

Increasing the size of the European Community is likely to take precedence over increasing the authority of EC institutions; the EC will continue to be run by states in a system of pooled sovereignty, not by a Commission of international civil servants or by a supranational government responsible to the European Parliament; authority will not be concentrated in Brussels. Discord among members of the European Community will persist and is even likely to intensify as the EC engages in more important activities (such as monetary policy) and controls greater resources. But discord and cooperation go together in bargaining relationships: cooperation is political, and closer in many ways to discord than to harmony (Keohane 1984:51–55). Since common interests are likely to persist, and the institutions of the European Community are well-entrenched, institutionalist theory implies at a minimum that the EC will remain a durable and important entity, at least as long as continued cooperation will help governments to attain their economic and political interests. Even taking prospects of tough bargaining into account, I am willing to predict that the EC will be larger and have greater impact on its members' policies in the year 2000 than it was when the Berlin Wall came down in November 1989 (Keohane and Hoffmann 1991).[15]

UNDERSTANDING INTERNATIONAL INSTITUTIONS

Joseph Grieco and I seem now to agree on more points than may have been evident to either of us, or to others, at the outset of our debate over "relative gains" (Grieco 1988a; Keohane 1989, chap. 1). Both of us believe that social scientists have only begun to develop theories that would account adequately for the impact of international institutions on world politics (Keohane 1990b). We both see the "renaissance" of the European Community as an anomaly for realism, which requires new thinking about institutions and state policy. Thus the "double dialectic" of understanding and practice, and of claim and counterclaim, seems to be leading to a certain convergence of our general perspectives.

We also agree more than might be expected about the empirical analysis of *After Hegemony*. In that volume, I never claimed, as Professor Grieco implies (in chapter 12), to offer proof for my theory. In my broad theoretical argument, I emphasized less than Professor Grieco does that "cheating inhibits cooperation,"[16] stressing instead the broader point that international institutions facilitate cooperation through the provision of information and reduction of transactions costs. I sought in my empirical analysis of the trade, monetary, and oil issue areas between 1945 and 1981 to criticize the theory of hegemonic stability and provide some evidence for the plausibility of my own view; but I was not attempting a definitive test of theory but rather what Harry Eckstein (1975:108–109) refers to as a "plausibility probe," conducting "loose and inconclusive, but suggestive tests," in an attempt to discover "whether potential validity may reasonably be considered great enough to warrant the pains and costs of testing." I tried to make it clear (Keohane 1984:217–18) that my analysis did not constitute proof of my thesis: "These examples [of financial cooperation] do not, of course, prove the validity of my point. . . . No decisive test of the independent value of the conceptions of cooperation and regimes put forward in chapters 4–7 is possible at this time. . . . The implications of my functional theory of international regimes are not tested in this volume." Furthermore, I observed in *After Hegemony* that the persistence of American predominance meant that (as Grieco emphasizes), the patterns of cooperation that I observed were overdetermined (Keohane 1984:217–18).

If I did not err in *After Hegemony* by making false claims of having proved my theory, I did make a major mistake by underemphasizing distributive issues and the complexities they create for international cooperation. Joseph Grieco has made an important contribution by focusing on this point. Seeking to demonstrate the plausibility of nonhegemonic cooperation, I underemphasized distributional struggles over the terms of cooperation, the variety of types and degrees of cooperation that are possible, and the importance of sequence and commitment strategies in affecting both the likelihood and type of cooperation actually to materialize (Sebenius 1992). I explicitly recognized that cooperation involves discord, but I did not sufficiently explore the implications of that insight.[17] Showing that states use international institutions to achieve their objectives—and that these institutions often perform functions of information-provision, monitoring, and reduction of transactions costs—is relatively easy (Keohane 1984; Oye 1986: Zacher 1987; Kapstein 1989; Martin 1992a). But functional explanations are incomplete, since many different sets of rules and organizations could enable states to achieve joint gains. "The weakness of such functional reasoning is that, in most interesting issues in international relations (and in the social sciences more generally) there are many stable paths to cooperation that cannot readily be differentiated in terms of their consequences for aggregate welfare" (Garrett and Weingast 1993:2). To understand these paths, we have to understand strategies, sequences, commitments, and how perceptions and expectations of actors are formed.

For his part, Grieco has in his recent work emphasized the conditionality of concerns about relative gains, which had been obscured by statements such as the one quoted earlier in this paper, that "the fundamental goal of states in any relationship is to prevent others from achieving advances in their relative capabilities" (Grieco 1988a:498). Accepting the conditionality of concerns about relative gains undermines his former claims about the "failure" of neoliberal theories of institutions for overlooking such a fundamental aspect of world politics. The whole argument about relative gains appears more as a useful qualification to institutionalist theory than as a refutation of it.

Both Grieco and I seek to formulate a theory of international institutions. What I have done is to synthesize elements of realism and liberalism in an attempt to create the basis for such a theory, whose core is a concern with how institutions affect incentives facing self-interested states. Grieco says that "realism needs to develop a theory of international institutions" (Grieco, 1992c:38). But why limit the theory to the boundaries of realism? I think that we should be breaking down artificial barriers between academicians' doctrines rather than creating camps of "realists" and "liberals," each with their own dogma, to fight meaninglessly on a darkling plain. *We students of international affairs* need a better theory of institutions. Joseph Grieco seems partly to accept this inclusive formulation, when he says that institutionalist theories may help to explain states' fears about cheating. Furthermore, while professing not to disagree with Professor Mearsheimer, he views the EC's "renaissance" in the 1980s as genuine and seeks to explain it within realist theory (Grieco 1992c:32). Indeed he proposes a "binding" thesis, to account for efforts at European Monetary Union, that seems entirely consistent with institutionalist arguments.

This thesis stresses the opportunities provided to weaker states in the EC for "voice." It would seem to make sense to add, consistent with Grieco's earlier emphasis on uncertainty as a source of concern for relative gains, that EMU could reduce France and Italy's uncertainty about future German monetary policy (which would be constrained by the European Central Bank). In chapter 12, Grieco denies this point: "The problem for France and Italy in the EMS has not been, as Keohane imagines, that they are uncertain about German behavior." It is unclear to me why Professor Grieco wishes to define "the problem" so narrowly. Of course, France and Italy believe with good reason that an independent German central bank will behave adversely to them, and they want a voice in its policy; but the degree to which Germany will behave adversely is indeed uncertain, and this uncertainty poses another problem for its partners. Could France and Italy have predicted Kohl's decision not to raise taxes to pay for reunification, which created the conditions for the crisis of September 1992? An explanation of French and Italian support for the EMS that included both their desire for voice and their desire to reduce uncertainty would seem more plausible than one stressing only the former motivation.[18] Such an account would be consistent with neoliberal institutionalism by emphasizing how international institutions affect the incentives facing self-interested states.

Finally, both Professor Grieco and I agree that even such a synthesized theory at the systemic level will be inadequate. Although often unfairly maligned on this point, Kenneth Waltz has also made it clear that systemic theory cannot provide a complete explanation of state action.[19] In *After Hegemony* I emphasized at the outset (1984:15, 26) that no system-level theory could be complete. Without a theory of interests, which requires analysis of domestic politics, no theory of international relations can be fully adequate. Systemic theory is worthwhile, but it can only take us part of the way; and we should be careful to avoid retreating behind it: a major task, as Grieco stresses in his paper, is to link domestic politics with international relations in a theoretically meaningful and analytically rigorous way.

Our weak current theories do not take us very far in understanding the behavior of the United States and European powers at the end of the Cold War. Their reliance on international institutions suggests that these institutions are indeed significant for state policy. But the fact that international institutions are used by states to pursue their interests does not demonstrate how significant they will be when interests change. Realists and institutionalists agree that without a basis either of hegemonic dominance or common interests, international institutions cannot long survive. The disappearance of the Warsaw Treaty Organization or the Council of Mutual Economic Assistance, after the transformation of politics and values in Eastern Europe, should surprise no one. However, institutionalists argue that organizational inertia, considerations of reputation, and connections to domestic politics mean that institutions often persist even when the conditions for their creation have disappeared, and that institutions exert impacts on state policy when policies are not dictated by clear interests. One of their most important effects, which has not been emphasized here, is to affect domestic politics within states (nonmembers as well as members) in such a way as to change conceptions of interest, and therefore governments' policies. As Nye says about neofunctional theories, "they emphasized the political process of learning and of redefining national interests, as encouraged by institutional frameworks and regimes" (Nye 1988:239).[20]

We need more evidence on these effects of institutions. I suggest that to gather such information, more research will have to be undertaken at the level of the state, rather than the international system as a whole. We will have to examine more closely how domestic politics are linked to international institutions. One promising approach is to focus on what Axelrod and I, in chapter 4 above, refer to as "multi-level games" (see also Putnam 1988). Another is to follow the lead of regional integration theorists and to look at institutional change, trying to understand the extent to which past decisions affect future ones, through transnational as well as interstate linkages (Keohane and Hoffmann 1991; Moravcsik 1991). It could also be worthwhile to focus on the degree of state compliance with agreed-upon rules when such compliance is contested—that is, when opposition to compliance is manifest in domestic politics. Preliminary work that I have done on this subject with respect to American foreign policy indicates that commitments are sometimes violated—the rules of international institutions are by no means sacrosanct—but that even when inconvenient, they are sometimes maintained.

Insofar as international institutions have significant effects, understanding their content is important. The coalitions that establish international institutions have purposes, which they expect their rules and organizations to promote. Multilateralism may create a presumption in favor of the norm that principles of conduct must be generalized to all members of the institution, imparting greater consistency to behavior and favoring weaker states (Ruggie 1992). Particular institutions embody distinctive variants of this norm, such as the principles of nondiscrimination and reciprocity in the GATT. Generalized principles of conduct, however, can be less symmetrical: they may provide, as in the IMF, that all *debtors* must adopt disciplined fiscal policies to be eligible for international aid—a principle that has notably not been applied to the United States during the last decade. On the other hand, the European Community now seems gradually to be institutionalizing the principle of aid to poorer members as part of the process of creating a Single Market and Monetary Union: thus resource transfers occur that would not take place in the absence of European Community institutions. International institutions vary in their content—variation that we have hardly begun to explore or explain. One working hypothesis, consistent with realism, is that such variation is accounted for by the specific possessive interests— in wealth, protection from disruption of customary ways of life, or environmental quality—of states. States use their capabilities to secure these rather self-evident goals. In an alternative view, however, the ideas held by policymakers, publics, or "epistemic communities" (Haas 1992) exert a decisive effect on how these interests are defined.

The institutionalist research program encompasses a number of puzzles, including why the number of international regimes has grown, what effects they have on state policies, and how the content of their rules and norms affects value-laden outcomes (Keohane 1990b). Perhaps in the next few years, analysts who are willing to synthesize elements of realism, liberalism, and arguments about domestic politics will be able better to explain variations in the content and strength of international regimes.

CONCLUSIONS

The double dialectic of international relations theory continues to operate. In its latest cycle, institutionalists have attempted to explain the unprecedented institutionalization of aspects of world politics since 1945, and realists have subjected their claims to critical scrutiny. Perhaps this volume will contribute to wider agreement on a new synthesis of these views. Since rationalistic approaches to international institutions build on realism by trying to specify conditions under which institutions will be significant, such a synthesis would not be a contradiction in terms. And since both modern realists such as Joseph Grieco and Kenneth Waltz, and institutionalists such as myself and Duncan Snidal, believe that theories should be systematically tested with evidence, there is some prospect that increased scholarly consensus might emerge from further empirical work.

The end of the Cold War has overtaken the academic debate between institutionalists and realists, thus adding a dialectic between theory and practice to that between academicians. This change in world politics is fortunate for social scientists seeking to evaluate the quality of different interpretations, since realism and institutionalism have different implications. Strict realism should lead one to expect a decline in the number and significance of international institutions; institutionalists such as myself expect no such decline. Institutionalists expect existing international institutions to adapt and to persist more easily than new institutions, formed by states on the basis of changing interests, can be created. Realists make no such prediction. Most dramatically, some realists such as John Mearsheimer forecast a collapse or at least weakening of the European Community, due to the demise of bipolarity. However, I expect the European Community to become larger and more significant, although the reaction to Maastricht in 1992 shows that the EC may again take a step backward before it moves forward. Joseph Grieco's discussion of the European Community's "renaissance" in chapter 12 suggests that he agrees more with me than with Mearsheimer. We should welcome such disagreement within "camps" since it demonstrates that thought remains alive.

When we use our weak theories to offer predictions about the future, we must be humble, since during the last several years we have failed to anticipate major changes in world politics. Mearsheimer has made an important contribution by clearly offering his own forecasts and challenging others to do likewise. As he says, "We will then wait and see whose analysis proves most correct" (Mearsheimer 1990b:199). Those of us who make forecasts may well be embarrassed by the results, but we can hope, at least, that our imperfect efforts will not only provide amusement for our colleagues and students but also help some of them to do better.

NOTES

1. An upsurge of recent analytical work on international politics in Germany would make Hoffmann's statement much more problematical if made today. It is somewhat unfortunate that the selections in this volume do nothing to counter the prevailing insularity.
2. "The ultimate ideal of international life—that is, to transcend itself in a supranational society—must await its realization from the techniques of persuasion, negotiation, and pressure, which are traditional instruments of diplomacy" (Morgenthau 1948:548).
3. The hope that I expressed in *After Hegemony* (1984:12) was in vain, but I repeat it here: "I hope that readers will be careful not to seize on words and phrases out of context as clues to pigeonholing my argument. Is it 'liberal' because I discuss cooperation, or 'mercantilist' because I emphasize the role of power and the impact of hegemony? Am I a 'radical' because I take Marxian concepts seriously, or a 'conservative' because I talk about order? The simplemindedness of such inferences should be obvious." In view of the links between institutionalist thinking and both liberalism and realism, I now prefer the simple appellation "institutionalist" to "neoliberal institutionalist" or "liberal institutionalist." A recent paper by Andrew Moravcsik (1991) on liberalism is at pains to differentiate liberal international relations theory quite sharply from institutional theory, on the grounds that institutional theory (like realism) takes states' preferences as given. Dr. Otto Keck of the Free University of Berlin has suggested the appelation of "rational institutionalism," which avoids the unfortunate connotation of "liberal" and the ambiguity of "neoliberal."
4. *Collaboration* refers to games such as Prisoner's Dilemma (PD) in which equilibrium outcomes are suboptimal, *coordination* to games such as Battle of the Sexes in which multiple equilibria exist, with one preferred by each player. Lisa Martin adds the category of "suasion" situations, which have equilibrium outcomes leaving one player dissatisfied (see Martin 1992b).
5. In his response to my argument in my paper for the 1992 meeting of the American Political Science Association, Grieco agreed that the significance of relative gains is conditional, and pointed to passages in his article in the *Journal of Politics* (Grieco 1988b) and in his book (Grieco 1990) that treat relative gains as a variable. As discussed below in the third part of the present essay, I welcome his explicit emphasis on conditionality, although I note that other careful readers have also viewed some of his arguments as essentially unconditional. For example, Helen Milner, to whose review essay Grieco has referred favorably, writes that

"concern for relative gains should be a variable, but Grieco tends to employ it as a constant" (1992:485).

6. Powell also shows that the model of iterated PD, on which Axelrod and I have relied in formulating and illustrating institutionalist theory, is inadequate, since it assumes that no such opportunities exist.

7. If tough bargaining does not prove the validity of concerns about relative gains, neither does occasional cooperation prove the validity of institutionalist insights. Where balanced relative achievement of gains can be attained, realists expect cooperation to take place; but realists hold that it will be more constrained, and less durable, than institutionalists expect (Grieco 1988a:501–503). Merely to find instances of cooperation does not, therefore, refute realism any more than to find conflict refutes institutionalism. Empirical evaluation of these approaches is more difficult.

8. In his paper for the 1992 American Science Association meeting (Grieco 1992c), Grieco seems to me to concede this point. He does not explain the support of Germany for the Economic and Monetary Union (EMU) —any more than he accounts for *U.S.* agreement to provisions in the Tokyo Round codes that allegedly gave relative gains to the EC. His interpretation of the support of weaker EC members for EMU is that they seek to ensure voice opportunities for themselves and to "ameliorate their domination by stronger partners" (Grieco, chapter 12:331). But "amelioration" seems to have more to do with reducing the uncertainty resulting from German autonomy in a situation of interdependence, than with reducing German relative gains.

9. Theoretical plausibility does not establish empirical correctness. As I have tried to show, Grieco does not demonstrate that his interpretation, plausible though it may be, is superior to the alternative distributive-gains interpretation, which is at least as plausible on a priori grounds.

10. In an illuminating paper on liberalism, Andrew Moravcsik argues that liberalism's most important contribution to international relations theory is to develop arguments about how states' foreign policy preferences are shaped by the character of domestic society and politics. He makes a claim, on these grounds, for the importance of liberalism to the theory of international relations and its superiority, in some respects, over both realist and institutionalist theory. See Moravcsik 1992.

11. For an interesting attempt to specify realist and institutionalist predictions about the future of NATO, see Hellmann and Wolf 1992.

12. Jack Snyder (1990) and Stephen Van Evera (1990–91) also come to different conclusions than Mearsheimer, although both Snyder and Van Evera adopt the assumption of anarchy.

13. I am particularly indebted for this point, and the phraseology, to Joseph S. Nye, Jr.

14. It is instructive that during the European currency crisis of September 1992, and particularly during the week following the French referendum on the Maastricht treaty, the Bundesbank apparently intervened heavily on behalf of the French franc. The contrast between the Bundesbank's

support for the franc—even at the risk of significantly increasing Germany's money supply, and its pressure for quick devaluations of the Italian lira and British pound—indicates that it remains true that "Franco-German relations, based on a series of mutually beneficial bargains, have always been at the core of the politics of the European Community" (Keohane and Hoffmann 1991:17). German support for the franc also suggests that the Franco-German axis has "cash value." Of course, all international assistance is limited and conditional; it is easy to imagine situations in which German support for France would not be forthcoming because it was too costly from the German standpoint. Institutions can furnish levers for influence, but they do not provide unconditional props.

15. I am unwilling to make the same forecast about NATO because it is not clear that both the United States and Europe will regard NATO as continuing to be in their interests. NATO is less closely linked to the domestic political economies of its members than is the EC; Europe could provide for its own defense if it chose to do so; the United States has decreasing interests in providing a costly security guarantee, although there remain good reasons for it to be linked militarily to Europe at a lower level of expense. The general point is that institutionalist theory does not mindlessly predict the continuation of all international institutions. Interests in cooperation must persist.

16. The word "cheating" does not appear in my index, suggesting that although coping with cheating was indeed part of my argument, it was not by any means its exclusive focus, nor in my view the central one.

17. Milner (1992:486) declares that "the lack of interest in the nature of the cooperative solution shown by Axelrod and the *Cooperation Under Anarchy* [Oye 1986] volume is an important oversight." This point applies to *After Hegemony* as well.

18. These motivations surely do not exhaust those of the French and Italian governments, both of which sought to use their public commitments to EMU to increase the credibility of their own macroeconomic policies. As the divergent fates of the franc and the lira in the crisis of September 1992 showed, however, verbally committing one's government to an international institution does not guarantee a successful currency defense. France both had restrictive policies and a strong link with Germany; Italy neither had the requisite economic policies nor a similar political bond.

19. "A theory of international politics bears on the foreign policies of nations while claiming to explain only certain aspects of them. It can tell us what international conditions national policies have to cope with. To think that a theory of international politics can in itself say how the coping is likely to be done is the opposite of the reductionist error" (Waltz 1979:71).

20. The experience of the postwar Federal Republic of Germany shows dramatically how international institutions may help to shape conceptions of self-interest and identity. See Anderson and Goodman 1993.

12

UNDERSTANDING THE PROBLEM OF INTERNATIONAL COOPERATION: THE LIMITS OF NEOLIBERAL INSTITUTIONALISM AND THE FUTURE OF REALIST THEORY

Joseph M. Grieco

In recent years there has been a vigorous debate about the problem of international cooperation. This debate has involved *modern realist theory*, as articulated by such scholars as Robert Gilpin (1975, 1981, 1987), Kenneth Waltz (1979, 1986), and Stephen Krasner (1991), and what I initially called neoliberal theory (Grieco 1987), and later called *neoliberal institutionalism* (Grieco 1988a, 1988b, 1990)—that is, the work of such scholars as Robert Keohane (1983, 1984), Arthur Stein (1983), Charles Lipson (1984), Robert Axelrod (1984), and Axelrod and Keohane (1985).[1] I have participated in this debate, and have been asked to comment on it.

My remarks are presented in three sections. In the first I assess the extent to which neoliberal institutionalism meets one of its main theoretical goals—to challenge realism—and I restate my view that in this respect neoliberalism has been unsuccessful. I also evaluate neoliberal theory as a basis for interpreting the empirical record of cooperation in the postwar period; here too I find several problems

I wish to thank David Baldwin, Peter Feaver, Robert Jervis, John Mearsheimer, Robert Powell, Mark Zacher, and Stephen Walt for their helpful comments on earlier drafts of this essay.

with the approach. In the second section I turn to some of the criticisms that have been made of my own contribution to the debate between realism and neoliberal institutionalist theory. Finally, in the third section I offer some reflections about the future of realism and the question of international cooperation. I suggest that the renaissance of the European Community severely challenges realist theory. Yet I also suggest that it is possible to distill from realist theory an argument about international institutions that is based on core realist assumptions and that is able to help us understand the EC's revitalization.

THE LIMITATIONS OF NEOLIBERAL INSTITUTIONALISM

Scholars in the realist tradition have long recognized that cooperation is an important feature of world politics, and they have sought to identify the conditions necessary for it. For example, they have studied the security dilemma and its effects on cooperation (Jervis 1978; Van Evera 1985), hegemonic leadership and international economic cooperation (Gilpin 1972, 1975, 1987; Krasner 1976, 1985, 1991), power balancing and military alliances (Morgenthau 1958:169–75; Aron 1966:128–36; Waltz 1979:125–27; Walt 1987, 1988; G. Snyder 1990), linkages between military alliances and economic cooperation (Gilpin 1972, 1975; Gowa 1989), and the effects of systemic change on the prospects for European cooperation (Mearsheimer 1990). In general, realists have argued that cooperation is possible under anarchy, but that it is harder to achieve, more difficult to maintain, and more dependent on state power than is appreciated by the institutionalist tradition.

Neoliberal institutionalism seeks to challenge this realist assessment of the possibilities for international cooperation and the role of international institutions in promoting such cooperation. For example, Robert Keohane argues (1984:84) that "By reexamining Realism in the light of rational-choice theory and with sensitivity to the significance of international institutions, we can become aware of its weaknesses as well as its strengths." By doing so, he suggests, "We can strip away some of the aura of verisimilitude that surrounds Realism and reconsider the logical and empirical foundations of its claims to our intellectual allegiance."

Earlier institutionalists tried to challenge realism by questioning its core assumptions—the centrality of the state and the salience of international anarchy—but they were unsuccessful. The new liberals are at once more cautious and more daring. They claim to accept realism's view that anarchy inhibits cooperation, but they argue that institutions can alleviate the inhibitory effects of anarchy on the willingness of states to work together when they share common interests. Anarchy, they suggest, impedes cooperation because it creates cheating problems. They suggest further that institutions increase interactions among states, and thereby make it easier for them to pursue TIT-for-TAT strategies of conditional cooperation. International institutions, in other words, make cheating less profitable and cooperation more attractive. Hence, neoliberals argue, cooperation is less difficult to achieve, and institutions are more important in promoting it, than is recognized by realist theory.

The neoliberal institutionalist argument appears to be able to incorporate key realist premises about states *and* to undercut major realist arguments about international institutions. Yet there is a fundamental flaw with the neoliberal challenge to realism. As I have suggested in recent years, notwithstanding their claims to accept realist premises, neoliberals actually misconstrue core elements of realist theory. Neoliberals argue that they accept the salience of anarchy, which they say means that, because of the absence of effective international government, states fear being cheated by others. Yet realists argue that anarchy means that states fear not just being cheated but also being dominated or even destroyed by others. As a result, while neoliberals see states as "rational egoists" interested in their own utility, realists view states as what I have called "defensive positionalists" interested in achieving and maintaining relative capabilities sufficient to remain secure and independent in the self-help context of international anarchy.[2] In turn, while neoliberals focus on the problem of cheating for cooperation, realists argue that an equally big problem is the fear on the part of some states that others might achieve disproportionate gains and thereby become more domineering friends or even potentially more powerful adversaries. Realists therefore argue that states must solve *both* the cheating and the relative gains problem in order to achieve cooperation. Hence, while neoliberals are right in stressing the problem of cheating, by doing so they do not show that realism's arguments about the difficulties associated with cooperation among nations are wrong, for there still remains the problem of relative gains. They have, in short, achieved only a partial understanding of realist theory, and thus only a partial engagement with its arguments about the problem of cooperation.

In addition, if one looks at the most extensive attempt by neoliberalism to substantiate its claims through empirical analysis, namely, Keohane's *After Hegemony*, then additional serious concerns arise about this approach. In brief, Keohane reviews postwar cooperation among the advanced democracies in trade, money, and oil; he finds that U.S. leadership initiated cooperation in these areas; he observes that cooperation came to vary across the three domains during the 1970s as U.S. power waned but still more or less held up; and he suggests that international regimes—embodied in such organizations as the General Agreement on Tariffs and Trade (GATT), the International Monetary Fund (IMF), and the International Energy Agency (IEA)—facilitated this continuing cooperation. Keohane concludes that "More cooperation has persisted than the theory of hegemonic stability would have predicted" (1984:215), and argues that while U.S. power helps explains cooperation during this period, "We can only understand the often puzzling mixture of cooperation and discord that we observe today if we recognize the continuing impact of international regimes on the ability of countries with shared interests to cooperate" (216).

There are, however, at least five problems with the analysis in *After Hegemony*. First, the basic empirical argument of the book prevents Keohane from undertaking an effective competitive test of his ideas about institutions and realist arguments about the problem of international cooperation. As noted above, Keohane's argument is that economic cooperation among the advanced industrialized countries decreased to some degree during the 1970s as U.S. relative power waned, but not to the extent that may have been predicted by realists and others who had developed the hegemonic leadership thesis in the mid-1970s. This characterization of relations among the advanced countries during the 1970s is crucial for Keohane, for it creates the opportunity for him to make his main argument—namely, that cooperation among these countries continued in part because of continuing U.S. hegemonic leadership *and* because of the role and significance of international economic regimes.

The flaw in Keohane's line of inquiry is that his description of the world political economy during the 1970s in *After Hegemony*—reduced advanced-country economic cooperation but overall a high level of collaboration—is actually very close to the analysis and expectations put forward by the realists in the middle of that decade. For example, noting that a mercantilist perspective might yield the prediction that the erosion of U.S. power would result in a fragmentation of the world economy into regional blocs, and while acknowledging that there were risks that the world economy might so fragment, Robert Gilpin suggested in 1975 that "mercantilists either ignore or ascribe too little significance to certain primary facts." He explained that "the scale, diversity, and dynamics of the American economy will continue to place the United States at the center of the international economic system," and that "the universal desire for access to the huge American market, the inherent technological dynamism of the American economy, and America's additional strength in both agriculture and resources—which Europe and Japan do not have—provide a cement *which could be sufficient to hold the world economy together* and to keep the United States at its center" (Gilpin 1975:253; emphasis added). Similarly, reviewing trends in trade protection from the 1820s to the late-1960s, Stephen Krasner suggested in 1976 that "the present situation is ambiguous" and that "on balance, there has been movement toward greater protectionism since the end of the Kennedy Round, *but it is not decisive*" (Krasner 1976:326; emphasis added). In addition, Krasner at that time did not predict a collapse of the international economy in the face of declining U.S. power, but instead suggested that domestic-level factors would cause the United State to continue to sponsor an open world economy; that is, "having taken the critical decisions that created an open system after 1945, the American Government is unlikely to change its policy until it confronts some external event that it cannot control, such as a world-wide deflation, drought in the great plains, or the malicious use of petrodollars" (1976:343).

Hence, realists in the 1970s argued that the international economy was experiencing turbulence in the face of declining U.S. power. However, they suggested that the United States would continue to work for, and help maintain, a basically open world economy characterized by a high degree of cooperation among the advanced countries. This, as noted above, is the description of the world economy offered by Keohane in *After Hegemony*. Given that both the realists in the mid-1970s and Keohane in the early 1980s put forward the same empirical characterization of the world, it is difficult to see how Keohane can claim that the fact that cooperation among the advanced states did continue confounds realist expectations and supports institutionalist claims.

The second major problem with Keohane's empirical analysis concerns his use of case-study methodology. As Harry Eckstein (1975:118–20) and Arthur Stinchcombe (1968:19–20) have taught us, the most powerful way to test a theory is to determine if the propositions derived from it hold in circumstances in which they are highly unlikely to do so, and in which comparable but divergent propositions from competing theories very much ought to be validated. An important feature of Michael Mastanduno's essay (1991; reprinted in this volume), for example, is that it shows that relative gains concerns motivated the U.S. government not in negotiations with the Soviet Union on security matters, but rather in talks with Japan on the joint production of aircraft and satellites. Similarly, a key feature of Stephen Krasner's essay on global communications (1991; also reprinted in this volume) is that it too shows that distributional conflicts can occur not just when states have opposed interests, but when they share strong common interests. Finally, I sought to evaluate competing neoliberal claims about the importance of regimes, and realist arguments about the relative gains problem, through examination of a "hard" case for that approach, namely, U.S.-EC diplomacy regarding the GATT and nontariff barriers (NTBs) to trade (Grieco 1990).

If Keohane, in seeking to understand the effects of institutions on posthegemonic cooperation, had followed what might be called the golden rule of theory testing—be hard on your own approach and be easy on alternatives—he would have searched for cases of cooperation in which states shared substantial *but not overwhelming interests,* and in which there were factors at play that, according to competing theories, should have brought about a *breakdown* in that cooperation. Instead Keohane focused on the mixed but overall high level of cooperation that obtained among the advanced industrialized democracies during that period. As noted above, realist theory, with its idea of hegemonic leadership, expected such cooperation. In addition, in light of the continuing challenge during the 1970s of the then-USSR, realism's arguments about state balancing would fortify its view that if *any* countries had an interest in working together during that period, it was the advanced democratic states. Similarly, and emphasizing completely different factors from those stressed by real-ist theory, neofunctional integration theory and interdependence theory teach us that, if *any* countries in the world should have coop-erated during the 1970s because they had overwhelmingly high mu-tualities of interest, it was the advanced democratic societies.[3] Fi-nally, the literature on domestic structures and foreign policy also yields the expectation that, if *any* countries in the world should have been oriented to cooperation with each other during that decade because of the character of their national political institutions, it was the advanced democratic nations.[4] The observed outcome of strained but, overall, high cooperation among the advanced states during the 1970s is, in other words, acutely overdetermined by conditions that are emphasized by both complementary and competing theories of international relations. By focusing on an instance of cooperation that was in fact so highly overdetermined, Keohane elected to test his theory about the role of institutions in promoting cooperation not with a difficult case but with the easiest possible, and therefore his empirical findings *at best* provide only weak support for his theory.

Third, there are serious problems with Keohane's use of case materials. It will be recalled that Keohane's analytical argument is that cheating inhibits cooperation among states, but that institutions can reduce it and thereby facilitate collaboration. The expected causal sequence, then, is variance in cooperation in different issue areas; preceded by and correlated with variance in cheating problems across the areas; preceded in turn and explained ultimately by variance in institutionalization in those areas. Yet Keohane does not provide us with clear empirical indicators in *After Hegemony* of such vital con-cepts as level of cooperation, severity of cheating, or degree of insti-tutionalization. Moreover, he provides only impressionistic evidence about the character of cooperation during the 1970s in trade, money, and oil. In addition, it is not clear why trade and money, where there were clearly formed regimes, should be compared to oil, in which there never was a regime among the advanced states. In the end, Keohane offers what must be called a personal assessment that co-operation diminished the most in oil, "followed by money and trade" (1984:194). No evidence about cheating is provided in regard to money or trade during the 1970s, and Keohane only asserts that Prisoner's Dilemma captures the behavior of the advanced countries during the energy crisis of 1973–74 (223). Finally, while noting that U.S. power accounts for most of the continued cooperation we see in the monetary area, Keohane goes on to say that the *existence* of the IMF is itself evidence that it too must have played a role in facilitating that cooperation; in his words, "The maintenance of international monetary institutions in the tumultuous years since the Nixon shock of 1971 suggests that governments indeed value international regimes" (209). However, without showing that cheating was a problem in money, or that the IMF reduced such cheating, it is difficult to accept this claim.

Fourth, Keohane has especially severe problems with what is supposed to be his *best* case: the IEA and the start of the Iran-Iraq war in 1980. He acknowledges that many factors helped prevent an oil crisis at that time, including "high levels of stocks, general weakness in demand, and the willingness of Saudi Arabia to increase production" (235). Yet he goes on to suggest that "this is not the whole story. In 1980 the IEA energy regime seems to have mattered; in several ways, it helped to prevent another disaster of uncoordinated responses to a problem of collective action" (235). However, it is not clear what the IEA actually did to help manage the crisis. It did not create or enforce rules, as institutionalism might expect; Keohane reports that in fact the IEA secretariat avoided rules for fear of *deterring* cooperation (235–36). Instead it consulted with companies and "reassuring public statements were made" (236). Keohane, in the end, is able only to make the very weak claim that "although it is *impossible to specify how much difference* the IEA made in the 1980 crisis, it seems clear that it *'leaned in the right direction'* " (236; emphasis added).

Fifth, and finally, Keohane makes his argument difficult to assess empirically, at least for the foreseeable future. Acknowledging that cooperation during the 1970s was largely due to American power, he says that "no decisive test of the independent value of the conceptions of cooperation and regimes put forward in chapters 4–7 is possible at this time, since we are only just entering the post-hegemonic era in the world political economy" (218). He says this is desirable since his claims can be treated as predictions to be tested in the future. Yet Keohane is asking too much of his readers: on the one hand, he wants us to agree that his arguments about institutions are supported by the events of the 1970s; and, on the other, he also wants us not to draw these claims into question by reference to events during that decade on the grounds that the latter is too early

to test his theory. Moreover, saying that the end of American hegemony is a prerequisite to knowing whether institutions matter makes
it very difficult to know when we will be able to evaluate Keohane's
ideas, for such analysts as Bruce Russett (1985), Samuel Huntington
(1988–89) and Joseph Nye (1990) have shown that American relative
power stabilized at a high level by the early to mid-1970s.

Keohane has two responses to these criticisms. First, he argues
that he was not trying to show that regimes mattered in the 1970s
because they ameliorated cheating problems. Instead he suggests
that he was making the "broader point" that institutions facilitated
cooperation because they provided information and reduced transaction costs among partners (Chapter 11:292). One problem with this
argument is that even if we were to agree that Keohane is not
interested in *After Hegemony* in the problem of cheating but rather the
problem of uncertainty and transaction costs, this would not put his
empirical analysis in a better light: he does not provide empirical
indicators for either uncertainty or transaction costs; he does not
show that they varied in any systematic way across trade, money,
and oil; he does not show that variance in them correlates with
variance in cooperation in the three domains; and he does not show
how variance in institutionalization may be associated with any such
variance in uncertainty or transaction costs.

A second problem with Keohane's response is that uncertainty
and transaction costs in international relationships, *according to Keohane himself*, result from and are symptoms of the basic problem of
interest to neoliberal institutionalists—namely, the possibility of
cheating by states in the context of international anarchy. For example, in his discussion of transaction costs, Keohane notes that if a
state behaves in ways contrary to provisions of the GATT, it is not
just taking an isolated action but is engaging in a violation "with
serious implications for a large number of other issues." Viewing the
likely result (the state is deterred from attempting the particular
violation because of fear of widespread retaliation) from the perspective of game theory or market-failure theory yields the same insight,
according to Keohane: "incentives to *violate* regime principles are
reduced," and therefore "international regimes reduce transaction
costs of legitimate bargains and increase them for *illegitimate* ones"
(1984:90; emphasis added). Similar connections exist in Keohane's
analysis between uncertainty and cheating. He notes that in situa-

tions of interest to him—those in which there are collective action problems and which are captured by Prisoner's Dilemma—"actors have to worry *about being deceived and double-crossed,* just as the buyer of a used car has to guard against purchasing a 'lemon' " (93; emphasis added). He also suggests that "asymmetrical information" might inhibit otherwise mutually beneficial agreements because "awareness that others have greater knowledge than oneself, and are therefore capable of manipulating a relationship *or even engaging* [*in*] *successful deception and double-cross,* is a barrier to making agreements" (93; emphasis added). He also argues that "this problem of asymmetrical information *only appears when dishonest behavior is possible*" (93; emphasis added). Finally, Keohane summarizes his discussion of uncertainty and transaction costs with this point: "*In general, regimes make it more sensible to cooperate by lowering the likelihood of being double-crossed*" (97; emphasis added). In short, while Keohane talks about uncertainty and transaction costs in *After Hegemony,* he does so because *from his viewpoint* they are symptoms of the more fundamental problem of cheating.

Keohane's second response (chapter 11:291–92) is that "I never claimed, as Professor Grieco implies in chapter 12, to offer proof for my [Keohane's] theory." He says that "I sought in my empirical analysis of the trade, monetary, and [oil] issue areas between 1945 and 1981 to criticize the theory of hegemonic stability and provide some evidence for the plausibility of my own view; but I was not attempting a definitive test but rather what Harry Eckstein (1975:108–109) refers to as a 'plausibility probe,' conducting 'loose and inconclusive, but suggestive tests,' in an attempt to discover 'whether potential validity may reasonably be considered great enough to warrant the pains and costs of testing' " (chapter 11:292).

It is surprising to learn that Keohane had such modest objectives in *After Hegemony.* I cannot find in the book a statement alerting the reader to the point that its empirical analysis is an Ecksteinian plausibility probe. At the same time, passages of the book suggest that Keohane believed that his empirical analysis had important implications for our understanding of world politics. For example, in a preview of his analysis of trade, money, and oil in chapter 9 of the book, he says that "as the theory developed in Part II would have anticipated, international regimes have tended to persist longer than they would have if the theory of hegemonic stability were correct"

(1984:135–36). He then says that "chapter 10 shows that the newest major international economic regime linking the advanced industrialized countries—the International Energy Agency—performs in a way that is consistent with the argument of Part II, although within a framework established by the structure of world power" (136).

Moreover, even if one grants that Keohane *was* undertaking a plausibility probe in *After Hegemony* in the manner discussed by Eckstein, it is clear that he did not do so with great success. Eckstein notes that he decided to test his theory of social structure and government performance through analysis of the case of Norway partly for "extraneous" reasons, but "the main reason for selecting it, however, was that Norway seemed somehow critical for the theory to be tested, in the sense that the theory could hardly be expected to hold widely if it did not fit closely there" (1975:111–12). Here (though he does not mention it in his essay for this volume) Keohane could say that just as Norway was critical to Eckstein in the sense that it was the easiest case for his theory, and therefore if not useful there was probably not worth pursuing further, so too the case of relations among the advanced democracies constituted the easiest case for him and thus provided a basis for deciding whether his theory was worth pursuing further.

Yet Eckstein makes it clear that, in addition to being an easy case, the Norway case was desirable as a test for his theory because it allowed him to control what from the viewpoint of his approach were perturbing variables. Eckstein reports that "the theory related social (i.e., nongovernmental) structure to governmental performance, but selected from all facets of such structure one special aspect that intrinsically could remain unchanged while all or most others changed, or, conversely, could change while others remained constant" (1975:112). Eckstein found that governmental stability and performance remained high in Norway, while overall social structures changed substantially and the particular aspect of social structure of interest to him—"social solidarity" or a "sense of community" (Eckstein 1966)—remained highly constant in that country. This suggested to him that it was the constancy of a sense of community that explained the continuity in high performance of the Norwegian polity. This ability to control for extraneous variables in the Norway case—that is, changes in overall social structures—also allowed Eckstein to suggest that "confidence that the theory might withstand concerted comparative study was greatly increased" (1975: 112).

Eckstein teaches us that, in selecting cases that will serve as a plausibility probe of a given theory, we should make every effort to control what for that theory are extraneous variables. I would add that special care should be taken to control for variables that are highlighted by competing theories. It is in this respect that Keohane's research design is fundamentally flawed. As noted above, a key goal of Keohane is to criticize realism. Yet, as also noted above, *both* the factor emphasized in realism (U.S. power) *and* the factor of interest to him (international institutions) yield the same expectation of continued cooperation among the advanced countries in trade, money, and oil during the 1970s. Thus precisely what Eckstein accomplishes with his selection of Norway as the basis for a plausibility probe— control for potentially perturbing variables—is exactly what Keohane fails to do by focusing on advanced-country relations.

While I have misgivings about *After Hegemony*, I would also emphasize that Professor Keohane and other neoliberal institutionalists have made at least four important contributions to the study of world politics. First, they have shown how the anarchical structure of the international system creates the problem of cheating for international cooperation. Second, they have focused our attention on the capacity of international institutions to help states manage that problem and its symptoms. Third, by challenging realist theory, they have caused students who work in that tradition to focus more carefully on problems for cooperation that are generated by international anarchy but are not emphasized by the institutionalists—for example, the relative gains problem. Finally, by drawing attention to international institutions, the neoliberals have encouraged students in the realist tradition, and others, to think more carefully about how their own preferred approach views the role and significance of institutions in the international system.

RESPONSES TO THE REALIST CRITIQUE OF NEOLIBERAL INSTITUTIONALISM

A useful contribution to the debate between realism and neoliberalism is the paper by Robert Powell (1991a; reprinted in this volume). He shows that gaps in gains from cooperation detract from a state's utility, and may cause it to choose not to cooperate, *if* it fears that the advantaged partner could use the additional capabilities produced by the gap in gains to be a greater military threat. This finding supports the basic realist argument about the relative gains problem for cooperation. However, as I discuss elsewhere (Grieco 1993), Powell and realists differ on the causes of state concerns about relative gains, and this leads Powell and realists to have different expectations about the incidence of the relative gains problem for cooperation.

States in Powell's model are concerned about relative gains because of fears for their security. Powell emphasizes that a formalization of realism's understanding of state concerns about relative gains must depict this "specter of war," and he criticizes the use by neo-liberal institutionalists of repeated games because the latter do not depict the possibility that force may be used by the players (1991a:1309–11). He emphasizes that his model is designed to address this problem: "States will now have the explicit option of using force if that seems to them to be in their best interest. More importantly, the model has been explicitly designed so that relative gains and losses matter because they affect a state's ability to use force successfully to further its interests" (1311). Powell then determines with his model that "if the use of force is at issue because the cost of fighting is sufficiently low, cooperation collapses in the model. This is in keeping with the expectations of structural realism." On the other hand, "if the use of force is no longer at issue, cooperation again becomes feasible. This is more in accord with neoliberal institutionalism" (1311; also see p. 1314).

Realists would agree with Powell that states that fear that a partner might use force against them will be highly concerned about gaps in gains advantaging that partner. Yet realists would argue that there are at least two other sources of state concerns about relative gains: uncertainties about one's partners and the efficacy of force, and fears about the nonmilitary consequences of gaps in gains. These two factors, they would suggest, cause the relative gains problem to come into operation more frequently than might be expected on the basis of Powell's model.

Realists, I have suggested, "find that defensive state positionalism and the relative gains problem for cooperation essentially reflect the persistence of uncertainty in international relations" (1990:45). States, realists emphasize, cannot be certain how states that are friendly in the present will choose to act in the future: as Robert Jervis suggests (1978:168), "Minds can be changed, new leaders can come to power, values can shift, new opportunities and dangers can arise." This leads states to be concerned about relative gains. Waltz, for example, in arguing that states worry that an advantaged partner may become a threat, points out that "the impediments to collaboration may not lie in the character and the immediate intention of either party. Instead, the condition of insecurity—*at the least, the uncertainty of each about the other's future intentions and actions*—works against their cooperation" (1979:105; emphasis added). Hence, even if a state is confident that a partner will not use gaps in gains against it in the present or in the *foreseeable* future, it may still worry about such gaps because it cannot be certain that new leaders or a new regime in the more distant future might yield a partner more willing and motivated to so employ gaps in a manner harmful to it.

In addition, states may experience uncertainties about the efficacy of force. In Powell's model the "technology of warfare" determines the "cost of fighting" (1312–14). The latter determines the efficacy of force and thus underpins state concerns about relative gains. Powell makes no explicit assumption about the capacity of states to assess the "technology of warfare" or the "cost of fighting." It would seem to be a reasonable inference, however, that, within the framework of the model, states have a capacity to make such assessments, for only if they did so could they estimate whether force is or is not "at issue," and thus could judge whether they should or should not care about relative gains. Yet realists would suggest that states may not be confident about the accuracy of such assessments; that if states determine that war is irrational, they cannot be sure that their partners share this view; that even if they believe at present that force is irrational, they cannot be certain that this will be true in the future; and, finally, that if they believe that force will remain inefficacious in the future, they cannot be sure that their partners will hold this same view at that future time. Moreover, in light of the possible consequences of being wrong about the efficacy of force—enslavement or even extinction—states are likely to approach these matters as highly risk-averse actors. They may by consequence choose to err on the side of caution and assume that there is at least some chance that force could be at issue at some point in the future.

In sum, realists would argue that states cannot be sure about the future costs and efficacy of war, and they cannot be certain about the future interests and goals of their partners. As a result, while accepting Powell's view that state concerns about gaps in gains are rooted in their interest in security, realists would expect states to react to the uncertainties inherent in world politics with great risk aversion and thus to experience relative gains concerns more frequently and with a wider range of partners than might be expected on the basis of his model.

In addition, international anarchy may lead states to be concerned about gaps in gains from cooperation not just because they seek security and survival, but also because they value their independence. Anarchical environments are self-help arenas, and by consequence agents in such environments seek to retain some minimum capacity to protect their interests. This need for self-help sufficiency leads states to value autonomy and independence: "In an anarchic realm, the units are functionally similar and tend to remain so. Like units work to maintain a measure of independence and may even strive for autarchy" (Waltz 1979:104). On the basis of this insight, Waltz argues that states tend to be wary about cooperation out of a fear of becoming dependent on their partners (106–107).

This interest in independence, in my view, could also make states sensitive to gaps in gains from cooperation. An advantaged partner, states may worry, could use increased influence arising from its enjoyment of relative gains to force them to accept progressively less favorable terms in the joint arrangement in which the gap originated, and in arrangements in other domains as well. In addition, through a cumulative process of converting gaps in gains into better deals, the advantaged partner might also become powerful enough to restrict the capacity of the disadvantaged partners for independent choice and action in the domain in which cooperation is occurring and in others to which that domain is related.

Michael Mastanduno, in his essay reprinted in this volume, has demonstrated that concerns about relative gains and cumulative shifts in national capabilities were a significant factor in U.S. policy on collaboration with Japan on the FSX jet fighter and commercial space satellites. (He also shows that elements of the U.S. government had similar concerns in the case of high-definition television, but that these concerns did not affect U.S. policy.) Mastanduno shows that the United States sought in the first case and to some extent the second to redress what it thought were divisions of gains disproportionately favoring Japan, and emphasizes that "the immediate concern was not military security, but economic well-being. Some U.S. officials feared that certain patterns of economic interaction with Japan, even though mutually beneficial in absolute terms, would bring relatively greater economic benefits to Japan *and over time work to the detriment of America's competitive position in the development and application of advanced technology*" (Mastanduno 1991:109; emphasis added). Similarly, I suggest in *Cooperation Among Nations* that the EC feared during the 1980s that the United States would gain the most from an aggressive implementation of the Tokyo Round codes on government procurement and technical standards; that the Europeans viewed these two issue areas as having a major impact on their capacity to retain an independent technology base; and that this concern about relative gains in strategically important areas led the EC to limit its commitment to the two codes (Grieco 1990:182–209). Thus while Powell's model would lead us to expect states to be attuned primarily to the risks that gaps in gains might entail for their military security, realist theory would lead us to expect states to focus on these risks *and* the risks that such gaps may pose for their relative bargaining power and independence.

In sum, Powell's model supports the core realist view that there is a strong link between anarchy, security, and the relative gains problem for cooperation. However, aspects of his model diverge from realist views about the range of sources of state concerns about relative gains, and, in particular, Powell and realists disagree as to whether states may have concerns about relative gains that are not immediately connected to their military security. These divergences lead to different expectations about the prevalence of the relative gains problem for cooperation. At least in regard to the question of the scope of security-based state concerns about relative gains, the differences in expectations about the incidence of the relative gains problem are due to dissimilarities in the level of uncertainty that states are assumed to experience, and the associated amount of risk states are assumed to be willing to accept, as they evaluate opportunities to cooperate. A juxtaposition of Powell's model and realist theory thus highlights the importance of risk and uncertainty as factors influencing state concerns about gaps in gains, and by consequence the incidence and severity of the relative gains problem for cooperation. Further investigation of these issues is likely to produce extremely interesting results. Thus Powell's essay helps identify important research issues, while providing additional analytical support for the realist position.

Duncan Snidal, in his essay (1991b; reprinted in this volume), argues that realism is wrong to emphasize the relative gains problem for cooperation. He characterizes realist thinking about this problem in these terms: "States are seen to seek relative gains and the inference is drawn that this inhibits cooperation" (703).[5] He notes that "I do not address the plausibility of relative gains–seeking as a description of international behavior, I accept it as an assumption." Snidal does so in order to refute its implications: "By accepting the assumption of relative gains maximization, I show that it does not have the general inhibiting effect on international cooperation widely ascribed to it" (703). Using what he takes to be the realist assumption about state preferences for relative gains, Snidal presents models of two-state and large-*n* interactions. He claims that the former provides partial support for his understanding of realist thinking about relative gains and cooperation.[6] On the basis of the latter, however, which is obviously more relevant for world politics, Snidal argues that relative gains calculations do not inhibit cooperation to the degree realism suggests. Thus, "the relative gains argument cannot provide a decisive response to the institutionalist claim that decentralized cooperation is possible under anarchy" (719).

Elsewhere I identify several problems with Snidal's analysis (Grieco 1993). Here I will focus on the main deficiency—namely, that Snidal simply defines the problem of relative gains out of existence by assumption. He does this in two ways. First, he assumes in his large-*n* model that states *by definition* receive equal gains from cooperation. Second, he asserts that, if cooperation does generate gaps in gains, these gaps *by definition* are narrowed to the satisfaction of the disadvantaged partner.

Snidal bases his large-*n* model on the assumption that states by definition receive equal gains from cooperation and thus by definition do not experience changes in their relative position because of collaboration. Snidal says that he assumes in his large-*n* model that if two states cooperate, each will enjoy "constant returns." This means that the "gains from cooperation are proportional to the size of the involved states *and are shared equally between them"* (1991b:715; emphasis added). As a result, Snidal says, "In *absolute* terms, states have the same interest in cooperation regardless of their respective sizes" (715; emphasis in original). Most important, with the assumption of constant returns, "In terms of *relative* position (as measured by absolute gaps between states), cooperation does not lead to relative gains" (715; emphasis in original). Snidal goes on to specify that, for the two referent states in his large-*n* model, state *i* and state *k*, "Since *i* and *k* gain equally from cooperation, *neither achieves any relative gain over the other through joint cooperation"* (717; emphasis added).

Snidal emphasizes that the constant-returns assumption is "key" to his model (715), and that "the conclusion concerning the equality of the gains is most important in the general argument" (715). Why? What would happen if we relaxed this "key" and "most important" assumption and allowed states to receive asymmetric gains from cooperation? Snidal provides the answer in a footnote: "Unequal gains diminish the incentives of one side to cooperate (and increase the incentives of the other side) for both absolute *and relative gains* reasons" (725n29; emphasis added). In other words, if we drop the constant-returns premise and assume that states receive asymmetric gains, we find that such asymmetries can induce relative gains concerns in the disadvantaged states and thereby impair cooperation. The opposite is of course also true: if states by assumption receive symmetric payoffs if they cooperate, then by definition the whole question of gaps in gains from cooperation is simply irrelevant to them. Thus, because he uses the constant-returns assumption, Snidal's model can only yield the "finding" that gaps in mutual gains do not affect the propensity of states to cooperate.

Moreover, and most important in light of Snidal's claims, while the constant-returns assumption may be a "key" aspect of his model, it is also the Achilles' heel for any engagement by him of realist theory. Kenneth Waltz's well-known statement of the realist understanding of the relative gains problem—which Snidal himself cites as the basis for his understanding of the realist perspective on this matter—makes its clear that for realists the emergence of the problem is predicated upon the prospect of gains that are *unequal* ◁ lead to a *change in relative position* among partners. That is, *"* faced with the possibility of cooperating for mutual gain, st⟋ feel insecure must ask how the gain will be divided. The⟋

pelled to ask not 'Will both of us gain' but 'Who will gain more?' If an expected gain is to be divided, say, in the ratio of two to one, *one state may use its disproportionate gain to implement a policy to damage or destroy the other.* Even the prospect of large absolute gains for both parties does not elicit their cooperation *so long as each fears how the other will use its increased capabilities"* (Waltz 1979:105, emphasis added; cited in Snidal 1991b:703 without emphasis). Similarly, I have suggested that defensive state positionalism "generates a relative gains problem for cooperation" in the sense that "a state will decline to join, will leave, or will sharply limit its commitment to a cooperative arrangement *if it believes that gaps in otherwise mutually positive gains favor partners"* (1990:10; emphasis added).

What Snidal has done, then, is to exclude *by definition* the exact situation realists posit as triggering the relative gains problem for cooperation—one partner does better than another and enjoys an advance in relative position over the latter. Indeed the situation analyzed in his model—states receive symmetric mutual-cooperation payoffs, and there is no change in relative position because of cooperation—is exactly the one in which realists would not expect the relative gains problem to come into operation. Grounded as it is on the assumption of constant returns from cooperation, Snidal's large-*n* model simply avoids the realist argument about the relative gains problem for cooperation.

Snidal avoids the relative gains problem in another way, by assuming that gaps in gains, if they do emerge, will be immediately and automatically adjusted. After acknowledging that relative gains problems may limit "the range of viable cooperative arrangements because states will not accept deals that provide disproportionately greater benefits to others," Snidal asserts that this is a "less important" problem. In his view, this is because "if distribution is the primary relative gains problem, states can alter the terms of the cooperative arrangement or offer side-payments until the distribution of gains is sufficiently proportionate" (703).[7] So, for Snidal, if relative gains problems do arise, reforms or side-payments are *by definition* forthcoming and effective in resolving them.

In my work I argue that, in the face of relative gains concerns of disadvantaged states, advantaged partners may agree to recraft agreements or to provide side-payments. I also emphasize that international institutions can promote cooperation precisely because they often help facilitate these deals regarding side-payments and the terms of agreements (1990:222–26, 230–31, 233–34). The defect in Snidal's treatment of this important matter is his failure to offer any basis for the assertion that these *potential* solutions to relative gains problems are typically undertaken and, if attempted, are reliably able to ameliorate such problems. In fact, the available scholarship suggests that (1) reforms and side-payments are sometimes provided but sometimes are not; (2) such efforts sometimes resolve relative gains but sometimes do not; and (3) in situations in which satisfactory adjustments are not made, the relative gains problem can hamper or cripple interstate cooperative arrangements (see Grieco 1990:47–48, 220–26, and 230–31; Krasner 1991; Mastanduno 1991; and Tucker 1991).

Moreover, saying that relative gains problems do not inhibit cooperation because states *can* in principle ameliorate them through reforms or side-payments is equivalent to saying that cheating problems do not inhibit cooperation because states *can* in principle resolve them by establishing verification and sanctioning arrangements. Both assertions are of course true in the abstract. Yet international relations is an important field of study in large measure because we know that solutions to relative gains and cheating problems sometimes are available and sometimes are not, and we want to know why. We know also that solutions to these two types of problems sometimes work and sometimes do not, and again we want to understand why. Finally, we know that the availability and efficacy of such solutions can affect the patterns of cooperation and conflict that we see in the international system, and we want to investigate and understand those patterns and their consequences for world politics. For Snidal, relative gains issues are either defined as nonexistent by assumption, or they are defined from the outset as easily settled and therefore uninteresting. In the real world, however, they are frequently problematic and sometimes vitally important.

In sum, Snidal is asking us to accept, on the basis of his large-*n* model, the following line of analysis: *by assumption*, states receive equal gains from cooperation, or readily redress imbalances in gains if they arise; thus, states effectively never experience gaps in gains if they cooperate; by consequence, state concerns about gaps in gains arising from joint action do not occur; and, therefore, state concerns about relative gains do not inhibit cooperation, and realism is wrong to emphasize the relative gains problem for cooperation. Yet in the real world states can and sometimes do receive unequal gains; states are sometimes concerned about such gaps in gains; and these concerns can sometimes impair cooperation. Finally, and again despite his claims, Snidal's employment of the inappropriate assumption that states receive constant returns from cooperation, and his reliance on the implausible premise that relative gains are resolved as a matter of course, cause him to fail with his model to engage, let alone challenge, realist theory and its understanding of the relative gains problem for cooperation.

In his essay for this volume, Professor Keohane offers three criticisms of my work. First, citing a footnote in *After Hegemony* (1984:123), he argues that, contrary to my claims, he recognizes the problem of relative gains for cooperation (chapter 11:274). Indeed, in this footnote and in another (1984:54) which I cite in my work (1990:47n51), Keohane does say that there are circumstances in which the gains of some states are viewed as losses by others, and that this can make cooperation difficult if not impossible.

Yet these two footnotes illustrate the differences, and not the similarities, between Keohane's ideas and those of the realists about the range of circumstances producing, and thus the salience of, the relative gains problem for cooperation. For Keohane, such situations need to be almost or actually zero-sum in character. For example, his footnote at page 123 indicates that relative gains matter for states "under conditions of severe competition, which is characteristic of power conflicts and particularly of arms races." Similarly, his footnote at page 54 says that relative gains matter when states pursue "positional goods" such as "status." In contrast, realists argue that states lose utility to some degree as a result of gaps in gains not just in security matters, but in other areas as well, and that states are sensitive about gaps in gains not just when there is severe competition among them, but when there is the prospect of gains for all and the partners are close friends. That is, the relative gains problem can occur, according to realists, not just in zero-sum situations, as Keohane acknowledges, but in increasing-sum situations as well. Notwithstanding Keohane's claims, *After Hegemony* misses by far the range of circumstances in which, according to realism, disadvantaged states experience losses in utility as a result of asymmetries in otherwise mutually positive gains.[8]

Other writers, it should be noted, have observed that neoliberal-ism ignores the issue of relative gains. For example, Stephen Kras-ner, in discussing the analysis of regime formation in *After Hegemony*, observes that "power is ignored because the research program based on the analysis of market failure does not provide either heuristic insights or analytic techniques for investigating relative capabilities. Power recedes into the background not only because scholars have studied absolute rather than relative gains, but also because it is not evident how power is relevant for solving problems of market failure" (1991:362). In the same vein, Joanne Gowa has shown (1986:175–79) that Axelrod's analysis of the possibility of conditional cooperation is based on a definition of egoism in which actors care only about their own gains. More generally, Powell virtually begins his essay in this volume with the point that "Neoliberal institutionalism assumes that states focus primarily on their individual absolute gains and are indifferent to the gains of others" (1991a:1303). And finally, neoli-beral institutionalists themselves have stressed that their approach assumes that states focus on absolute as opposed to relative gains. For example, Arthur Stein emphasizes that even highly self-inter-ested actors like states can have "things in common," and thus can cooperate, and he goes on to say that "this is very much a liberal, not mercantilist, view of self-interest; it suggests that actors focus on their own returns and compare different outcomes with an eye to maximizing their own gains" (1983:134). Yet this view of states causes neoliberalism to fail to understand how and why states worry about gaps in otherwise mutually positive gains favoring partners, and this causes it to fail to appreciate the incidence or severity of the relative gains problem for cooperation.

Keohane's second criticism is that while I understate his aware-ness of the relative gains problem for cooperation, I overstate the salience of this problem in international affairs. He charges that I "put forward an unconditional argument" (chapter 11:275) because I say that states always seek to prevent advances by others in their relative capabilities. Drawing from Powell's essay, he says that only if states believe that advantaged partners might use gaps in gains against them will they care about such asymmetries, and he cites the building up by the United States of its allies in Western Europe and Asia at the outset of the Cold War as proof that states may not care about, and may in fact promote, advances by partners in their relative capabilities.

I do not make the kind of unconditional argument depicted by Keohane. For example, after presenting in *Cooperation Among Nations* a model of state concerns about relative gains, I say, in regard to the decision of referent state A to cooperate with referent state B, that "*Whether* state A finds that the game is Amended Prisoner's Dilemma, where cooperation is difficult but possible, *or* Amended Deadlock, where cooperation is impossible, *depends on* state A's sensitivity to gaps in gains and on the difference in R and P payoffs achieved by itself and state B" (1990:43; emphasis added). Moreover, in my essay in *Journal of Politics* I clearly specify that the term representing state sensitivity to gaps in gains—k—can be viewed as a variable, and indeed I offer numerical illustrations of how variation in k can make cooperation more or less attractive to a state (1988b:614–17). I also say in that essay that "*depending* upon its sensitivity coefficient, state A may be *more or less* likely to choose to cooperate" (614; emphasis added). Further, I say in *Cooperation Among Nations* that "it should be emphasized that, from a realist viewpoint, the coefficient for a state's sensitivity to gaps in payoffs—k—can be expected to vary but always to be greater than zero" (1990:45). Here I am stressing that states always care about relative gains *to some degree*, but I am also clearly indicating that these concerns can vary.

In fact, in *Cooperation Among Nations* I discuss six different sources of variance in state sensitivity to gaps in gains. I begin by suggesting that "In general, k is likely to increase as a state transits from relationships in what Karl Deutsch terms a 'pluralistic security community' to those approximating a state of war." I then say that "the level of k, for example, will be lower if a state's partner is a long-term ally rather than a longtime adversary." Hence, experience with and the character of the partner can affect k. I also suggest that "to the degree that there is a common enemy posing a clear and present danger, a state may actually welcome increases in an ally's capabilities." The presence or not of external challengers is, then, a second factor affecting k. (I then note that a state may worry about relative gains even in regard to allies, but I do so in conditional terms: "*as that common threat becomes less severe*, a state's tolerance for gaps in gains favoring allies will probably decrease" [1990:46; emphasis added].) I then go on to specify four other sources of variance in k: the domain in which cooperation occurs (k should be lower in economic than in security affairs), a state's power trajectory (k will be lower for a state in ascendancy than for one in decline), the convertibility of gaps into influence and the fungibility of this influence across domains (k is likely to go down as convertibility and/or fungibility decreases), and the current power status of the state (very small and very big states are likely to have lower k's than middle-sized states). Finally, I argue that the sheer size of the gaps in mutual gains affects the level of state concerns about relative gains (1990:43–44), and I provide stylized illustrations of this in the *JOP* essay (1988b:615–16).

In my work I suggest that states worry about gaps in gains from cooperation to some degree with virtually all partners and in virtually all domains. But I also argue that the severity of the relative gains problem depends on the degree of state sensitivity to gaps in gains from cooperation and the size of the such gaps. Moreover, I specify k as a variable, identify six sources of variance in k, analyze the effects of such variance on cooperation, and discuss the impact on cooperation of differences in the size of gaps in gains. Hence, I do not understand Keohane's claim that I have ever made an unconditional argument about the relative gains problem for cooperation.

Finally, Keohane faults my empirical analysis. In *Cooperation Among Nations* I argue that variance during the 1980s in the effectiveness of the six codes on nontariff barriers to trade established during the Tokyo Round resulted largely from variance in U.S.-EC cooperation, which, I argue further, stemmed from variance in EC concerns about the distribution of gains generated by each agreement. In those codes in which the EC was satisfied with its gains (for example, the customs valuation accord), it cooperated fully with the United States and the code was a success; in the case in which it thought it would only lose and the United States would be the big gainer (the subsidies accord), it resisted the U.S. vigorously and the code was effectively a failure. Most important for my analysis, in the codes in which the EC achieved positive gains but feared that the United States might achieve even larger gains—namely, the government procurement and technical barriers agreements—the EC resisted the U.S. in some measure and the codes achieved only mixed success.

In support of my finding regarding the technical barriers and government procurement codes, I show that a maximalist interpretation of the two codes favored by the United States would have yielded it disproportionate gains. Informed by interviews with U.S., EC, national European, and GATT officials, I also report EC concerns about relative gains recorded in the minutes of code committee meetings. Third, in much the same way that Mastanduno demonstrates that the United States was concerned about satellites and fighter aircraft, I show that the EC states viewed government procurement and technical standards to be strategic issue areas in the sense that developments in them would affect the capacity of the EC countries to retain an autonomous industrial base able to compete with and remain independent of the United States and Japan. Fourth, I link EC concerns about relative gains in the two codes to differences in institutional arrangements in Europe and America in the issue areas covered by the agreements. Finally, I report a case in which the EC rejected U.S. and Nordic approaches to the extension of the technical barriers code to a new area (mutual recognition of product tests and testing facilities), and advocated its own approach. I show that the U.S.-Nordic approach and the EC alternative would have yielded the Economic Community roughly equal absolute gains, taking into account the magnitude of potential benefits and the probability that these benefits would in fact be achieved, and I therefore suggest that, from the viewpoint of expected utility, the EC did not appear to propose its alternative approach in order to increase its absolute gains. At the same time, I show that the EC thought that the U.S-Nordic approaches would favor America disproportionately. I also show that the EC believed with good reason that their approach would lead to greater symmetry in gains between its member countries and the United States (1990:182–86, 194–96).

Keohane's critique of this analysis is in two parts. First, he argues that U.S.-EC disagreements in the technical barriers code may have resulted not from EC concerns about relative gains—although he agrees that this is "theoretically plausible"—but because of EC efforts to maximize absolute benefits, and he asserts that I do not address this alternative explanation satisfactorily (chapter 11:281). As noted above, in fact, I specifically address this alternative explanation in the case of negotiations to extend the standards code to testing practices, and find that the importance of the case rests on its capacity to permit rejection of the absolute-gains maximization thesis at the same time that it validates the gaps-in-gains minimization perspective (1990; see esp. pp. 194–96).

Second, Keohane argues that, in order to say that a state is motivated by relative gains concerns, *"there must be some plausible way by which one's partner could use advantages gained from [the] international agreement to hurt oneself in a future period, and a significant prospective motivation for it to do so"* (chapter 11:281; emphasis in original). He says that Mastanduno meets this standard in regard to U.S.-Japanese relations, and that it could be found of U.S.-Soviet relations during the Cold War. But, he suggests, the evidence I present on this matter "is less compelling." He accepts the "theoretical" plausibility of my interpretation of the EC and the technical barriers code—but notes that I do not make the case empirically—and goes on to say that "it seems implausible that three usually competing countries (Argentina, Australia, Canada) would really have turned down a bargain that would maximize their expected utility because it strengthened the EC and the U.S.—two much more powerful entities that would in any case have the power to coerce these small states in the future." He also asks "why should we believe that the smaller members of the EMS worried about relative gains toward [a] much more powerful Germany in the late 1970s but not at Maastricht in 1991?" (chapter 11:282).

As I note above, my findings about the EC and the government procurement and technical barriers codes actually run parallel to Mastanduno's findings about the United States and satellites and fighter aircraft: in both cases, national concerns about the strategic economic importance of issue areas led to relative gains concerns in collaborative arrangements in those issue areas. Hence, Keohane's critique comes down not to an engagement with the core of my empirical analysis–that is, U.S.-EC relations in the Tokyo Round. Nor does it even try to address my use of the U.S.-EC materials in chapter 6 of *Cooperation Among Nations* to disprove the efficacy of a neoliberal institutionalist interpretation of the NTB code experience. Instead his critique centers on two secondary cases—negotiations on an aspect of the antidumping code in which the United States and the EC cooperated, and the negotiations among the EC countries leading to the formation in 1978 of the European Monetary System (EMS).

While neither case was a major focus of analysis in my book, both support my basic argument. I did not discuss the current EC effort to move from EMS to EMU at all in *Cooperation Among Nations,* but I am now working on that subject and discuss it, as well as the establishment of the EMS, in the next section. The other case involved "basic-price mechanisms" through which national authorities can initiate antidumping investigations if importers bring a good into the country priced below a preset level. The signatories to the antidumping code realized when the code came into effect in 1981 that these systems would hurt the code, but could be allowed by one possible interpretation of Article 8:4 of the agreement. The United States and the EC made several proposals to close this loophole, but, since both had basic-price mechanisms in effect for steel, these proposals would have permitted their continuation. Argentina, Canada, and Australia turned them down, arguing that they could not accept an agreement in which all would gain—but the United States and the EC would gain more. In the end the signatories accepted a joint statement providing no effective protection against basic-price mechanisms (1990:209–14).

Keohane says this behavior cannot reflect relative gains thinking on the part of Argentina, Canada, and Australia because they could not reasonably believe that whatever relative gains effects an agreement on Article 8:4 might have generated would have changed what for them is already a hopeless balance of power. As noted above, in my work I have said that very small countries are likely to be less sensitive to gaps in gains than middle-sized countries because they begin from such a weak power position (1990:46). It is also true that the United States can "hurt" these countries. Yet as Keohane himself has demonstrated with Joseph Nye (1977), this does not mean that Canada and Australia do not negotiate with the United States on a variety of issues in regard to which relative influence matters. As a result, what is important for these smaller countries in facing Article 8:4-type negotiations is the principle of not conceding terms that provide relative advantage to a stronger partner, for doing so would exacerbate imbalances in influence in that domain and it might lead to demands for such terms in other domains as well. Contrary to Keohane's claims, the Article 8:4 case supports the realist interpretation of the relative gains problem for cooperation.

While I am not convinced by Keohane's critique of *Cooperation Among Nations,* I believe that there are numerous grounds for effective and productive criticism of that book, as Helen Milner demonstrates in her review (1992) of it together with Peter Haas's *Saving the Mediterranean*.[9] For example, while I mention, as possible influences on state sensitivities to gaps in gains, the convertibility of such gaps into increments of additional influence and the fungibility of this additional influence across issues (1990:46), Milner is correct in suggesting that I did not pay enough attention to these factors (1992:487). Additional work should be done on this topic, and might begin with David Baldwin's discussions (1979, 1980) of the concepts of power fungibility and the scope and domain of power in international affairs, and Stephen Van Evera's discussion (1984:80–82, 180–87, 339–47) of the cumulativity of power resources in world politics. Moreover, based on my conversations with friends in comparative politics, I now know all too well that, in my haste to test neoliberal institutionalism against realism and to integrate domestic institutional factors into the latter, I failed to examine an alternative to both of the systemic approaches—namely, domestic structuralism as presented by such scholars as Peter Katzenstein (1978, 1985) and Peter Gourevitch (1986). Finally, although I refer in my previous work to an interest in independence and a preference not to be vulnerable to pressure from others as contributing to state sensitivity about relative gains, I should have emphasized this point more clearly and more forcefully. I try to redress this shortcoming in my discussion above of Powell's essay and the sources of state concerns about relative gains.

REALISM AND THE STUDY OF COOPERATION AFTER THE COLD WAR

Neoliberal institutionalism is inadequate as a critique of realism and as a basis for analysis of real-world international cooperation. Of course, realism too has serious problems (see Grieco 1992a). Moreover, as I have suggested in earlier works, whatever we think of neoliberal institutionalism, we have not seen the end of the debate between realism and the institutionalist tradition. Instead, scholars in two other branches of institutionalism—the embedded liberalism argument as presented by John Ruggie (1982) and Friedrich Kratochwil (1984), as well as their work together (1986), and the epistemic communities approach developed by Ernst Haas (1990) and Peter

Haas (1990)—strongly challenge realist arguments about states, anarchy, and cooperation, and they are now coming forward with a substantial literature suggesting that their arguments are empirically plausible (Haas 1992).

In addition, there is the challenge to realist theory presented by the renaissance of the European Community.[10] Modern realists have been skeptical of the EC.[11] For example, Waltz has argued that European cooperation has been largely the result of bipolarity (1979:70–71). This yields a pessimistic prognosis for the future of the EC: if U.S.-Soviet competition has been necessary for European integration, and if that competition has now ended, then we should see the Europeans becoming less able to cooperate. This in fact is the argument pursued by John Mearsheimer in his ground-breaking essay on the future of Europe (1990:46–48).

Yet at least since the mid-1980s, there has been more, not less, EC cooperation. This increased EC cooperation covers trade (the Single Market Program), EC decision-making (the Single European Act, or SEA), high-technology (ESPRIT and the Technology Framework Programme), and, most important, economic and monetary affairs (the effort to attain Economic and Monetary Union, or EMU). The EC's renaissance thus brings into conflict a key realist assumption—that states are instrumentally rational in selecting policies—and its proposition that international institutions are of little importance to states. It also casts doubt on another crucial assumption of realism, namely, that anarchy shapes the substantive rationality of states. Europe continues to be characterized by interstate anarchy, and bipolarity appears to be waning. Yet while there remains in force the factor that, according to realist theory, inhibits cooperation and incapacitates international institutions, and while there is an abatement of the particular structural circumstances that are thought by realism to be needed for European cooperation, the Europeans are intensifying their cooperation and are doing so precisely through institutions.

Realists might respond by arguing that the EC's reform efforts are likely to fail—witness the Danish rejection in 1992 of the Maastricht accord, the very close positive vote on the accord in France, and the partial collapse of the EMS—or meet with only limited success. By developing a realist-informed argument that ends with this expectation *if certain conditions come to pass,* such as the withdrawal by the United States from Europe, Mearsheimer has made an important contribution to the study of post–Cold War international politics. However, even if the reform efforts of the EC countries ultimately fail or fall short, there is still the stubborn fact that the EC countries *are now trying* to build stronger regional institutions. It is this fact that I believe realists need to address, notwithstanding my appreciation of the view that systemic forces could ultimately undermine the European Community. Thus Keohane misinterprets my work as a challenge to Mearsheimer (chapter 11:297). In fact, Mearsheimer and I are focusing on different issues and different time periods: I am trying to understand the *current* efforts by the EC members to strengthen the institutions of the European Community, and he is suggesting that, in the *future,* the EC may experience severe and potentially crippling strains.

Another response available to realists at present to the EC's renaissance is that they can in fact explain the latter with their concept of *balancing* (Waltz 1979:124–27; and Walt 1987, 1988). Realists might argue that, as their theory expects, the European nations are joining together under the auspices of the EC in order to counter the rising challenge of Japan, and in this respect they could cite the work of authors linking closer European cooperation to fears of Japan (Sandholtz and Zysman 1989:103–106; Garrett 1992:538–39). However, by itself the balancing argument has a key drawback. That is, just as Japan is becoming more powerful in the world economy, Germany is becoming more powerful in Europe. As David Cameron (1992:67) suggests, "The new unified Germany is indisputably the most important economic actor in the Community." Hence, French support for a stronger EC as a means of balancing against Japan entails what from realism's own viewpoint would appear to be a serious empirical anomaly—namely, apparent French and Italian bandwagoning toward an increasingly hegemonic Germany.

Moreover, realism's problems are highlighted by the fact that alternative explanations account for aspects of the EC's revitalization. For example, in support of domestic-level arguments, the EC's recent successes are surely the result in part of the convergence in thinking among European political elites about the need to facilitate heightened market-competition in Europe (Hoffmann 1989; Sandholtz and Zysman 1989; Moravcsik 1991; Cameron 1992). Institutionalist arguments can also be helpful. For example, EMU will include rules limiting national deficits and ECB lending to national central banks

(Ungerer et al. 1990:48). This emphasis on rules against opportunism would be easily expected by neoliberal institutionalism.[12]

Yet the EC's renaissance also presents anomalies for these approaches. For example, domesticists might argue that EMU reflects a growing consensus among European elites about the benefits of financial liberalization; yet there is then the question of why the EC members are pursuing a centralized form of EMU *as opposed to more market-oriented alternatives,* namely, Britain's competing-currencies proposal in 1989 and its "hard-ECU" proposal in 1990. Similarly, neoliberal institutionalists can explain the EMU's safeguards against opportunism, but not the interests of the EC states motivating them to want to move toward it. Neofunctional integration theory might explain these interests with its concept of *spillover:* the EC states want EMU because they have become dissatisfied with the performance of EMS in the light of the financial aspects of the Single Market Program (for example, an EC directive on capital liberalization in 1988 and one on banking in 1989). Yet the timing of events is not in accord with the spillover thesis. That is, the move toward EMU has occurred *with, and not after,* financial liberalization: EMU was clearly specified as a goal in the SEA in 1986, and the key committee on EMU (chaired by EC Commission President Jacques Delors) was formed in 1988 and presented its EMU blueprint in 1989. Moreover, there do not appear to be *technical* grounds for dissatisfaction with EMS, for it has promoted price stability and (until late 1992) exchange-rate stability among its members.

I have tried to address these puzzles regarding EMU, and more generally to respond to the crisis posed for realism by the EC's renaissance (Grieco 1991, 1992b). My realist-informed argument begins with the point that, for weaker partners, the rules of a collaborative arrangement will provide them with more or fewer opportunities for having effective "voice opportunities" (Hirschman 1970) in the process of deciding how cooperation will proceed with the arrangement and thus how they will be treated by their stronger partners.[13] This yields what I call the binding thesis: *if states share a common interest and undertake negotiations on rules constituting a collaborative arrangement, then the weaker but still influential partners will seek to ensure that the rules so constructed will provide for effective voice opportunities for them and will thereby prevent or at least ameliorate their domination by stronger partners.*

This binding thesis may help explain the movement from EMS to EMU. The former was established in 1978, and in response to the breakdown of the "snake" common-margins agreement. The EMS was designed to promote EC monetary coordination, and to reduce German domination of European monetary affairs. For example, it included a "divergence indicator" designed to ensure that both deficit and surplus countries would be obliged to take actions to support EMS exchange-rate stability (Ludlow 1982). Returning then to Keohane's critique of *Cooperation Among Nations*, it was precisely because many EC countries were concerned about German monetary power in the 1970s that they first established but then abandoned the "snake," and then set up the EMS with features that would address the relative gains concerns of countries such as France that had led to the collapse of the snake.

Yet as Francesco Giavazzi and Alberto Giovannini argue (1989:195), "Although 'symmetry' was the word most frequently pronounced at the Bremen and Brussels summits where the EMS was created, and notwithstanding rules designed with the explicit purpose of 'sharing the burden of adjustment,' the system has worked effectively as a DM-zone." As a recent IMF study of the operation of the EMS during the 1980s delicately puts the matter, from the viewpoint of France and Italy, "the hegemonic role of German economic policy was contrary to the community character of the EMS" (Ungerer et al. 1990:10). Hence, the problem for France and Italy in the EMS has not been, as Keohane imagines, that they are uncertain about German behavior (chapter 11:294). Instead, France and Italy and other EMS countries have come to learn with *very* great certainty that the Bundesbank will raise interest rates in the face of a rise in inflation in Germany, and that the Bundesbank will do so even at the cost of less growth and employment in Germany *and* the other EMS countries.

To address the problem of unequal power in the EMS, France and Italy have pressed hardest for EMU *of a particular sort*. The result was the 1991 Maastricht accord. It specifies January 1994 as the starting point for Stage II of the EMU process, during which the members will seek economic convergence and establish a nascent central bank, the European Monetary Institute. It also indicates that as early as January 1997, and no later that January 1999, qualified EC countries will move toward the third and final stage of EMU. In Stage III the members will lock their exchange rates irrevocably. They will also transfer responsibility for their monetary policy to a European System of Central Banks (ESCB). Its operational arm will be the successor to the EMI, the European Central Bank (ECB). The ECB's key decision-making body will be a Governing Council, whose members will be the governors of the member-states' national central banks and the six members of the ECB Executive Board (who will be appointed by the European Council). The ECB's decisions will be taken on the basis of majority voting. The ECB will manage the members' unified external exchange rate and foreign exchange reserves, and it will be responsible for issuance of the European Currency Union (ECU), which will become a genuine currency. Finally, there will be strict rules limiting the size of national public deficits and the means by which they can be financed, and there will be sanctions that can be applied against members that run "excessive deficits" (European Community 1991; Bank of England 1992:64–68).

Responsibility for EC monetary policy will be invested in a centralized European institution; its governing body will be composed in part of heads of national central banks, and its other members will be selected by the EC governments meeting as the European Council; and, most important, that body's decisions will be taken by majority vote. Despite provisions requiring ECB council members to be independent and forbidding them from taking instructions from national authorities (European Community 1991:203–204), these Stage III elements of EMU will ensure greater symmetry in voice opportunities for, and therefore power among, the EC members in the monetary domain. Indeed, in response to charges by French conservatives that Maastricht would lead to French subservience to the Bundesbank, then-Prime Minister Pierre Bérégovoy, according to the *Financial Times* (May 13, 1992, p. 13), "reminded his compatriots that the Maastricht path represents a path in which France, far from losing independence, can regain a degree of control over monetary affairs at present largely ceded to the Bundesbank."

Viewing EMU as a binding mechanism helps unravel some of puzzles regarding EMU that are not fully resolved by other approaches. For example, as noted above, the European Community's movement from EMS to EMU is a puzzle for functionalist theories, for the EMS has been rather successful and, until the September 1992 currency crisis triggered by the French referendum on Maastricht, it had readily accommodated new EC efforts at financial liberalization. Here the binding thesis may help, for it accounts for the interest of France and Italy to move the European Community away from EMS and toward its vision of EMU. That is, while the EMS has been an arrangement that is efficacious from a strictly technical economic viewpoint, it has also been a system that is emphatically dominated by Germany.

In addition, the binding thesis may be helpful in resolving the problem posed by EMU for the domesticists—namely, explaining why Britain failed to garner support for its market-oriented proposals for monetary integration. According to its competing-currencies proposal, each EC member would retain its own currency (and therefore its central bank), but each would accept the others' currencies as legal tender, and through a Darwinian struggle in the market some currencies (if not one) would come to be more preferred by individuals and firms than others. This proposal would have allowed closer market integration and continued formal national monetary independence. However, because the DM would have been the currency the most likely to be highly preferred by Europeans, the competing-currencies approach would not have reduced, and it might actually have increased, German domination of European monetary affairs. The same would have been true for the hard-ECU approach. It would entail the fixing of the value of the ECU in terms of EC currencies, an EC commitment that it would never be devalued (hence it would be "hard"), and an agreement that each national central bank would exchange these "hard-ECUs" (to be issued by a European Monetary Fund) for their respective currencies. Eventually, "hard-ECUs" would circulate as a parallel currency. This approach would have facilitated EC integration without requiring a European central bank. However, keeping responsibility for monetary policy with the national central banks would have meant continued German control over European monetary policy for the foreseeable future (Dowd 1991:221–22), an outcome unacceptable to France and Italy.

In sum, the binding thesis appears to help resolve important puzzles about the EMU case: political dissatisfaction with EMS in spite of its technical efficacy and stability; the decision to move from it toward EMU; the selection of a centralized form of EMU; and the rejection of alternative forms that were more market-oriented.[14] It may then provide a basis for realism to contribute to our understanding of the EC's renaissance.

CONCLUSIONS

At least five conclusions emerge from the above discussion. First, neoliberal institutionalism does not meet one of its major theoretical goals—namely, to challenge realism—and it does not provide a particularly firm basis for the empirical analysis of international relations. Second, if we want to achieve progress in the study of international relations, we need to be ruthlessly difficult on our theories as we design empirical tests for them. Third, if we want to show that a theory is defective because its assumptions can be employed in ways yielding results contrary to those the theory currently offers, then we should use assumptions that correspond to those actually contained in the theory, and we should surely not employ assumptions precisely the opposite of those specified in it.

Fourth, realism has provided a number of arguments about international cooperation—for example, the literature on hegemonic leadership and the scholarship on balancing and alliances—but to date it has not offered an explanation for the tendency of states to undertake their cooperation through *institutionalized* arrangements. Realism, then, needs to develop a theory of international institutions. The binding thesis may help us move toward this goal, for it may be able to explain some of the key interests of such middle-sized states as France and Italy as they elect to cooperate with, but seek to avoid domination by, a stronger partner such as Germany. At the same time, institutionalist theories help explain other state concerns (that is, fears about cheating), and thus can help account for other characteristics and functions of international institutions. This yields my fifth and final conclusion: while realism and liberal institutionalism surely compete on many dimensions, and while realism will doubtless remain the superior approach so long as there is no centralized world authority, both approaches can help us in our quest to understand the politics of cooperation among nations.

NOTES

1. When I delivered my Duke working paper (Grieco 1987) on realism and what I had been calling "neoliberal theory" to a seminar at Harvard in

October 1987, Joseph Nye wisely suggested that I add the qualifier "institutionalism," to distinguish the branch of liberalism of interest to me from others that do not focus on international institutions. I thereafter employed the label *neoliberal institutionalism*.

2. My argument that realist theory views states as "defensive positionalists," in contrast to the neoliberal institutionalist characterization of states as "rational egoists," resulted from an extremely helpful telephone conversation with Robert Jervis in 1987.

3. See the work by Ernst Haas (1968), Edward Morse (1970), Richard Cooper (1972), and Keohane with Joseph S. Nye (1977).

4. On this see Katzenstein (1985), Gourevitch (1986), and, more generally, Doyle (1983).

5. Snidal thinks that realists argue that the relative gains problem results from states seeking to *maximize* gaps in gains *to their own advantage*. Yet as can be observed of Waltz's 1979 statement of the problem reprinted in the body of this essay, it is a defensively positional concern that partners might do better, and not an offensively oriented interest in doing better oneself, that drives the relative gains problem for cooperation. Snidal makes the same error in his essay in *International Studies Quarterly* (1991a).

6. Snidal assumes in his two-country model that "the game is symmetric. . . . This means that two states are equally well situated to benefit or hurt one another and fashion their cooperative arrangement to provide equal absolute gains" (1991b:705). This assumption of equal gains, as is discussed in the text in regard to the large-n model, is the opposite of that specified in realist theory as generating the relative gains problem. Therefore one cannot, in contrast to Snidal's claims, find support for realism in his two-state model.

7. Snidal observes that I have argued against a perfect symmetry assumption "because it entails equal payoffs from mutual cooperation." He then says that "I have argued that this can be easily achieved by adjusting the terms of cooperation and is not central to the relative gains argument" (1991b:723n8). As I suggest in the text, realists would not accept so easily or so uncritically this assertion that symmetry in payoffs "can be readily achieved," and therefore they would say that it is exactly the question of unequal gains that is "central to the relative gains argument."

8. Keohane contends at the beginning of chapter 11 (274–75) in this volume that he recognized in *After Hegemony* what I came to call the relative gains problem for cooperation, but acknowledges toward the end of the essay (292) that he had not appreciated this problem sufficiently in that book.

9. While I find Milner's review to be very useful and insightful, I nevertheless disagree with two of her main criticisms. First, she argues that "Concern for relative gains should be a variable, but Grieco tends to employ it as a constant" (1992:485). I discuss this criticism above in regard to Keohane; I would only add that in the conclusion of the book I ask "can we identify variations in the sensitivity of states to gaps in gains

across different cooperative arrangements, and can any such observed differences be related to the fungibility or convertibility of gains generated by the endeavors?" (1990:230).

Milner's second criticism is that "Grieco tends to overlook domestic variables," that I raise and dismiss such factors in the introduction to the book, but that my case studies "slip" them back into the analysis (1992:490–91). I focus on systemic concerns in *Cooperation Among Nations*. Yet at the outset of the book I say in regard to EC relative gains problems in the technical barriers and government procurement that "accounting for those relative-gains concerns on the part of the EC, as chapter 7 demonstrates, requires an analysis of the differences between European and American institutions and policies in the issue-areas covered by the two agreements, and European perceptions of the likely impact of those institutional differences on the distribution of gains generated by the two accords"; and I say further that "this study argues that it is sometimes fruitful *and even necessary* to combine systemic and unit-level explanations of state preferences" (1990:25; emphasis added). Attention to domestic factors is a significant part of *Cooperation Among Nations,* and their incorporation into a realist framework is an explicit theme of the project.

10. I discuss the problems for realism posed by the EC's renaissance more fully in Grieco (1991).

11. In this respect they agree with more classical writers such as Raymond Aron (1966:744–49) and Stanley Hoffmann (1968).

12. Although I believe that neoliberal institutionalist theory can help us understand the EC's revitalization, Professor Keohane's discussion of the European Community in his essay for this volume seems to me to be unpromising. On the one hand, he argues (285) that no systemic theory —whether it is drawn from the realist or liberal institutionalist tradition —has an explanation for the interests of the "principal members" (that is, the advanced democracies) in such global liberal international economic regimes as the GATT, and thus cannot help us make predictions about the future of such regimes; but, on the other hand, he argues (291) that institutionalist theory can serve as the basis for precisely the prediction that there will be increased cooperation in the EC. (Of course, Keohane is utterly incorrect in asserting that realism does not provide a theory of state interests.) In addition, in arguing that it is not possible to make predictions based on institutionalist theories about the future of global regimes that include the advanced democracies as its principal members, Keohane refers (285) to commercial and republican forms of liberal theory as being "naive"; yet he bases (289) his own optimistic predictions about the EC in large measure on commercial and republican forms of liberal theory. Finally, it is unclear how Keohane can argue (293) that his version of international "theory" constitutes a synthesis of realist and institutionalist arguments while at the same time claiming (289) that the EC provides a useful context for a "comparative" (i.e., competitive) testing of the two approaches.

13. In developing this argument, I have drawn upon Hans Morgenthau's thinking about the EC (1958:497–99), Stephen Krasner's analysis of developing countries and international economic regimes (1985), Paul Schroeder's historical analysis of military alliances (1976), and studies by Michael Hogan (1987) and John Gillingham (1991) of the roots of European regionalism.

14. The binding thesis addresses the question of why *weaker* countries may seek institutionalization of cooperative ties with *stronger* partners. Keohane raises the important question of why would Germany accept such an arrangement if its partners are seeking to constrain its power (chapter 11:299n8). As I discuss elsewhere (1991), a large part of the explanation must be located in German domestic political and economic institutions, for since 1945 they have resulted in a country highly interested in export-led growth based on cooperative ties in Europe and with America (Gourevitch 1986; Katzenstein 1992). From a realist viewpoint, Germany may accept binding for at least three additional reasons. First, Germany may believe that the strengthening of EC institutions may reduce its influence in some measure, but that it will not be to the extent that it cannot defend its important interests in Europe. Second, Germany may believe that it cannot match Japan's growing economic power on its own, and therefore it is willing to accept limitations on its influence in Europe as the price for developing a more effective balancing coalition against Japan. Third, Germany may be concerned that its major European partners might turn inward if a stronger European Community is not established, and such protectionism in Europe would make it even harder for it to compete with Japan in the international economy. Germany, in other words, needs its European partners, and in such circumstances it may accept binding in the monetary issue area, for example, so long as it can be assured of its core interest in price stability.

BIBLIOGRAPHY

Adam, John A. 1990. "Competing in a Global Economy." *IEEE Spectrum* (April): 20–24.

Aggarwal, Vinod. 1983. "The Unravelling of the Multi-Fiber Arrangement, 1981: An Examination of Regime Change." *International Organization* 37 (Autumn): 617–46.

────── 1985. *Liberal Protection: The International Politics of Organized Textile Trade.* Berkeley: University of California Press.

Akerlof, George A. 1980. "A Theory of Social Custom, of Which Unemployment May Be One Consequence." *Quarterly Journal of Economics* 94 (June): 749–75.

Alger, Chadwick. 1963. "Comparison of Intranational and International Politics." *APSR* 62 (June): 406–19.

Alker, Hayward R. 1977. "A Methodology for Design Research on Interdependence Alternatives." *International Organization* 31 (Winter): 31

────── 1986. "The Presumption of Anarchy in International Politics." Unpublished manuscript.

Allison, Graham T. 1971. *Essence of Decision: Explaining the Cuban Missile Crisis.* Boston: Little, Brown.

Anderson, Jeffrey and John B. Goodman. 1992. "Mars or Minerva: A United Germany in a Post–Cold War Europe." In Keohane, Nye, and Hoffmann 1993:23–62.

Andrews, Bruce. 1978. "Surplus Security and National Security: State Policy as Domestic Social Action." Unpublished mimeograph. Washington, D.C.: International Studies Association Convention.

Aron, Raymond. 1966. *Peace and War: A Theory of Peace and War.* Translated by Richard Howard and Annette Baker Fox. Garden City, N.Y.: Doubleday.

Aronson, Jonathan David and Peter F. Cowhey. 1988. *When Countries Talk: International Trade in Telecommunications Services.* Cambridge, Mass.: Ballinger.

Art, Robert and Robert Jervis. 1986. *International Politics.* 2d ed. Boston: Little, Brown.

Ashley, Richard. 1984. "The Poverty of Neorealism." *International Organization* 38 (Spring): 225–86.

────── 1986. "The Poverty of Neorealism." In Keohane 1986b.

Axelrod, Robert. 1967. "Conflict of Interest: An Axiomatic Approach." *Journal of Conflict Resolution* 11 (March): 87–99.

—— 1970. *Conflict of Interest: A Theory of Divergent Goals with Applications to Politics*. Chicago: Markham.

—— 1979. "The Rational Timing of Surprise." *World Politics* 31 (January): 228–46.

—— 1981. "The Emergence of Cooperation Among Egoists." *American Political Science Review* 75 (June): 306–18.

—— 1984. *The Evolution of Cooperation*. New York: Basic Books.

Axelrod, Robert and Robert O. Keohane. 1985. "Achieving Cooperation Under Anarchy: Strategies and Institutions." *World Politics* 38 (October): 226–54.

—— 1986. "Achieving Cooperation Under Anarchy." In Oye 1986.

Axelrod, Robert and William D. Hamilton. 1981. "The Evolution of Cooperation." *Science* 211 (March 27): 1390–96.

Axline, W. Andrew. 1977. "Underdevelopment, Dependence, and Integration: The Politics of Regionalism in the Third World." *International Organization* 31 (Winter): 83–105.

Badger, Daniel and Robert Belgrave. 1982. *Oil Supply and Price: What Went Right in 1980?* Paris: Atlantic Institute for International Affairs.

Balassa, Bela and Carola Balassa. 1984. "Industrial Protection in the Developed Countries." *World Economy* 7 (June): 179–86.

Baldwin, David A. 1971. "Money and Power." *Journal of Politics* (August) 33: 578–614.

—— 1978. "Power and Social Exchange." *American Political Science Review* (December) 72: 1229–42.

—— 1979. "Power Analysis and World Politics: New Trends Versus Old Tendencies." *World Politics* 31 (January): 161–94.

—— 1980. "Interdependence and Power: A Conceptual Analysis." *International Organization* 34 (Autumn): 471–506.

—— 1985. *Economic Statecraft*. Princeton: Princeton University Press.

—— 1989. *Paradoxes of Power*. New York: Basil Blackwell.

—— 1990. "Politics, Exchange, and Cooperation." In Bernd Marin, ed., *Generalized Political Exchange*, vol. 1. New York: Westview.

Bank of England. 1992. "The Maastricht Agreement of Economic and Monetary Union." *Bank of England Quarterly Bulletin* 32 (February): 64–68.

Barry, Brian. 1981. "Do Countries Have Moral Obligations? The Case of World Poverty." In Sterlin McMurrin, ed., *The Tanner Lectures on Human Values*, vol. 2. Salt Lake City: University of Utah Press.

Benoit, Jean-Pierre and Vijay Krishna. 1985. "Finitely Repeated Games." *Econometrica* 53: 905–22.

Betts, Richard. 1987. *Nuclear Blackmail and Nuclear Balance*. Washington, D,C.: Brookings Institution.

Bilder, Richard B. 1963. "The International Coffee Agreement: A Case History in Negotiating." *Law and Contemporary Problems* (Spring) 28: 328–91.

Blatherwick, David E. S. 1987. *The International Politics of Telecommunications.* Research Series. Berkeley: Institute for International Studies.

Blau, Peter M. 1964. *Exchange and Power in Social Life.* New York: John Wiley.

Blechman, Barry M. and Stephen S. Kaplan. 1978. *Force Without War: U.S. Armed Forces as a Political Instrument.* Washington, D.C.: Brookings Institution.

Boulding, Kenneth E. 1963. "Towards a Pure Theory of Threat Systems." *American Economic Review* (May) 53: 424–34.

——— 1978. *Ecodynamics: A New Theory of Scocial Evolution.* London: Sage.

——— 1989. *Three Faces of Power.* London: Sage.

Brams, Steven J. 1975. *Game Theory and Politics.* New York: Free Press.

Brander, James A. 1986. "Rationales for Strategic Trade and Industrial Policy." In Krugman 1986.

Breslauer, George W. 1983. "Why Détente Failed: An Interpretation." In Alexander L. George et al. *Managing U.S.-Soviet Rivalry: Problems of Crisis Prevention.* Boulder, Colo.: Westview.

Brock, David. 1989. "The Theory and Practice of Japan-Bashing." *The National Interest* 17 (Fall): 17–28.

Bull, Hedley. 1977. *The Anarchical Society.* New York: Columbia University Press.

Bumpus, Bernard and Barbara Skelt. 1985. "Seventy Years of International Broadcasting." *Communication and Society.* Paris: UNESCO.

Burns, Tom and Walter Buckley. 1974. "The Prisoners' Dilemma Game as a System of Social Domination." *Journal of Peace Research* 11: 221–28.

Cameron, David R. 1992. "The 1992 Initiative: Causes and Consequences." In Alberta M. Sbragia, ed., *Euro-Politics: Institutions and Policymaking in the "New" European Community,* pp. 23–74. Washington, D.C.: Brookings Institution.

Carr, E. H. 1939 (2d ed. 1946; reissued 1964). *The Twenty Years Crisis, 1919–1939: An Introduction to the Study of International Relations.* London: Macmillan; New York: St. Martin's.

Carroll, Thomas M., David H. Ciscil, and Roger K. Chisholm. 1979. "The Market as a Commons: An Unconventional View of Property Rights." *Journal of Economic Issues* 13 (June): 605–27.

Claude, Inis L. 1956. *Swords into Plowshares.* New York: Random House.

——— 1962. *Power and International Relations.* New York: Random House.

——— 1981. "Comment on Political Realism Revisited." *International Studies Quarterly* 25 (June): 198–200.

Clausewitz, Carl von. 1976 [1833]. *On War.* Edited and translated by Michael Howard and Peter Paret. Princeton: Princeton University Press.

Cline, William. 1982. " 'Reciprocity': A New Approach to World Trade Policy?" Policy Analyses in International Economics, no. 2 (September). Washington, D.C.: Institute for International Economics.

Coase, Ronald. 1960. "The Problem of Social Cost." *Journal of Law and Economics* 3: 1–44.

Codding, George A. and Anthony M. Rutkowski. 1982. *The International Telecommunication Union in a Changing World*. Dedham, Mass.: Artech House.

Coffey, Peter. 1984. *The European Monetary System: Past, Present, and Future*. Dordrecht, the Netherlands, and Boston: Martinus Nijhoff.

Cohen, Benjamin J. 1979. "Europe's Money, America's Problems." *Foreign Policy* 35 (Summer): 31–47.

——— 1990. "The Political Economy of International Trade." *International Organization* 44: 261–81.

Colino, Richard R. 1986. "Global Politics and INTELSAT: The Conduct of Foreign Relations in an Electronically Wired World." *Telecommunications Policy* 10 (September).

Conybeare, John A. C. 1980. "International Organization and the Theory of Property Rights." *International Organization* 34 (Summer): 307–34.

——— 1985. "Trade Wars: A Comparative Study of Anglo-Hanse, Franco-Italian, and Hawley-Smoot Conflicts." *World Politics* (October): 147–72.

——— 1987. *Trade Wars: The Theory and Practice of International Commercial Rivalry*. New York: Columbia University Press.

Cook, Thomas I. and Moos, Malcolm. 1953. "The American Idea of National Interest." *American Political Science Review* 47 (March): 28–44.

Cooper, Richard N. 1972. "Economic Interdependence and Foreign Policies in the 1970s." *World Politics* 24 (January): 158–81.

——— 1975. "Prolegomena to the Choice of an International Monetary System." *International Organization* 29 (Winter): 63–97.

Cowhey, Peter. 1990. "The International Telecommunications Regime: The Political Roots of International Regimes for High Technology." *International Organization* 44.

Crawford, Beverly and Stefanie Lenway. 1985. "Decision Modes and International Regime Change: Western Collaboration on East-West Trade." *World Politics* 37 (April): 375–402.

Curzon, Gerard. 1965. *Multinational Commercial Diplomacy*. London: Michael Joseph.

Dahl, Robert. 1968. "Power." In *International Encyclopedia of the Social Sciences*. New York: Free Press.

——— 1984. *Modern Political Analysis*. 4th ed. Englewood Cliffs, N.J.: Prentice-Hall.

Dahl, Robert and Charles Lindblom. 1953. *Politics, Economics, and Welfare*. New York: Harper and Row.

Defense Science Board Task Force. 1976. *An Analysis of Export Control of U.S. Technology: A DOD Perspective*. Washington, D.C.: Office of the Director for Defense Research and Engineering (February 4).

Destler, I. M. 1986. *American Trade Politics: System Under Stress*. Washington, D.C.: Institute for International Economics.

Destler, I. M. and Michael Nacht. 1990–91. "Beyond Mutual Recrimination: Building a Solid U.S.-Japan Relationship in the 1990s." *International Security* 15 (Winter), no. 3: 92–119.

Deutsch, Karl W. 1988. *The Analysis of International Relations.* 3d ed. Englewood-Cliffs, N.J.: Prentice-Hall.

Deutsch, Karl et al. 1957. *Political Community and the North Atlantic Area.* Princeton: Princeton University Press.

Dictionary of Political Science. 1964. Edited by Joseph Dunner. Totona, N.J.: Littlefield, Adams.

Dowd, Kevin. 1991. "Evaluating the Hard ECU." *World Economy* 14 (June): 215–25.

Downs, George W. and David M. Rocke. 1990. "Arms Races and Cooperation." In Downs and Rocke, *Tacit Bargaining, Arms Races, and Arms Control.* Ann Arbor: University of Michigan Press.

Downs, George W., David M. Rocke, and Randolph M. Siveron. 1985. "Arms Races and Cooperation." *World Politics* 205–35, 323–53.

Doyle, Michael. 1983. "Kant, Liberal Legacies, and Foreign Affairs. Parts 1 and 2." *Philosophy and Public Affairs* 12: 205–35, 323–53.

——— 1986. "Liberalism and World Politics." *American Political Science Review* 80 (December): 1151–69.

Dunn, Frederick. 1948. "Research Note: The Scope of International Relations." *World Politics* 1 (October).

Dunn, John, ed. 1990. *The Economic Limits to Modern Politics.* Cambridge: Cambridge University Press.

Easton, David. 1965. *The Political System.* New York: Knopf.

Eckstein, Harry. 1966. *Division and Cohesion in Democracy: A Study of Norway.* Princeton: Princeton University Press.

——— 1973. "Authority Patterns: A Structural Basis for Political Inquiry." *American Political Science Review* 67 (December): 1142–61.

——— 1975. "Case Study and Theory in Political Science." In Fred I. Greenstein and Nelson W. Polsby, eds., *Strategies of Inquiry,* vol. 7 of *The Handbook of Political Science.* Reading, Mass.: Addison-Wesley.

Elster, Jon. 1976. "Some Conceptual Problems in Political Theory." In Brian Barry, ed., *Power and Political Theory: Some European Perspectives.* London: John Wiley.

——— 1978. *Logic and Society: Contradictions and Possible Worlds.* New York: John Wiley.

Elster, Jon. 1979. *Ulysses and the Sirens: Studies in Rationality and Irrationality.* Cambridge: Cambridge University Press; Paris: Editions de la maison des sciences de l'homme.

Ennis, Peter. 1989. "Inside the Pentagon-Commerce Turf War." *Tokyo Business Today* (October).

Evans, John W. 1971. *The Kennedy Round in American Trade Policy: The Twilight of GATT?* Cambridge: Harvard University Press.

Fagan, Richard I. 1970. *Central American Economic Integration: The Politics of Unequal Benefits.* Berkeley: Institute of International Studies.

Fallows, James. 1989. "Containing Japan." *Atlantic Monthly* (May): 40–54.

Farnsworth, Clyde. 1989. "Move Made in Congress on Japan Deal." *New York Times,* May 11.

Farrell, Joseph and Eric Maskin. 1989. "Renegotiation in Repeated Games." *Games and Economic Behavior* 1: 327–60.

Feldman, Mildred. 1975. *The Role of the United States in the International Tele-communication Union and Pre-ITU Conferences.* Baton Rouge, La.: Mildred L. Bos Feldman.

Ferguson, Charles. 1989. "America's High-Tech Decline." *Foreign Policy* 74: 123–44.

Finlayson, Jock A. and Mark W. Zacher. "The GATT and the Regulation of Trade Barriers: Regime Dynamics and Functions." In Krasner 1983a.

Fisher, Bart S. 1972. *The International Coffee Agreement: A Study in Coffee Diplomacy.* New York: Praeger.

Fox, William T. R. 1949. "Interwar International Relations Research: The American Experience." *World Politics* 2: 67–79.

——— 1968. *The American Study of International Relations.* Columbia: University of South Carolina Press.

——— 1989. "A Middle Western Isolationist Internationalist's Journey Toward Relevance." In Joseph Kruzel and James N. Rosenau, eds., *Journeys Through World Politics: Auotobiographical Reflections of Thirty-Four Academic Travelers.* Lexington, Mass.: Lexington Books.

Friedman, David. 1977. "A Theory of the Size and Shape of Nations." *Journal of Political Economy* 85: 59–77.

Fuller, Lon L. 1978. "Law and Human Interaction." In Harry M. Johnson, ed., *Social System and Legal Process: Theory, Comparative Perspectives and Special Studies.* San Francisco: Jossey-Bass.

Fudenberg, Drew and Eric Maskin. 1986. "The Folk Theorem in Repeated Games with Discounting or with Incomplete Information." *Econometrica* 54: 533–54.

Gaddis, John L. 1983–84. "The Rise, Fall and Future of Détente." *Foreign Affairs* 62 (Winter): 354–77.

Galenson, Walter. 1981. *The International Labor Organization: An American View.* Madison: University of Wisconsin Press.

Garrett, Geoffrey. 1993. "International Cooperation and Institutional Choice: The European Community's Internal Market." In Judith Goldstein and Robert O. Keohane, eds. *International Organization* 46 (Spring): 533–60.

Garrett, Geoffrey and Barry Weingast. 1992 "Ideas, Interests and Institutions: Constructing the EC's Internal Market." Unpublished paper for a project, led by Judith Goldstein, on ideas and foreign policy. *Ideas and Foreign Policy: Beliefs, Institutions and Political Change.* Ithaca: Cornell University Press, forthcoming.

Gellner, Ernest. 1958. "How to Live in Anarchy." *The Listener* (April 3): 579–83.

George, Alexander L. and Juliette L. George. 1964. *Woodrow Wilson and Colonel House: A Personality Study.* New York: Dover.

George, Alexander L. and Richard Smoke. 1974. *Deterrence in American Foreign Policy: Theory and Practice.* New York: Columbia University Press.

Giavazzi, Francesco and Alberto Giovannini. 1989. *Limiting Exchange-Rate Flexibility: The European Monetary System.* Cambridge: MIT Press.

Gilbert, Felix. 1951. "The 'New Diplomacy' of the Eighteenth Century." *World Politics* 4 (October): 1–38.

——— 1961. *To the Farewell Address: Ideas in Early American Foreign Policy.* Princeton: Princeton University Press.

Gillingham, John. 1991. *Coal, Steel, and the Rebirth of Europe, 1945–1955.* Cambridge: Cambridge University Press.

Gilpin, Robert. 1972. "The Politics of Transnational Economic Relations." In Robert O. Keohane and Joseph S. Nye, Jr., eds., *Transnational Relations and World Politics*, 48–69. Cambridge: Harvard University Press.

——— 1975. *U.S. Power and the Multinational Corporation: The Political Economy of Foreign Direct Investment.* New York: Basic Books.

——— 1981. *War and Change in World Politics.* Cambridge: University Press.

——— 1986. "The Richness of the Tradition of Political Realism." In Keohane 1986b.

——— 1987. *The Political Economy of International Relations.* Princeton: Princeton University Press.

Goodin, Robert E. 1976. *The Politics of Rational Man.* London: John Wiley.

Gorove, Stephen. 1985. "International Direct Television Broadcasting by Satellite: 'Prior Consent' Revisited." *Columbia Journal of Transnational Law* 24, no. 8.

Gourevitch, Peter A. 1977. "International Trade, Domestic Coalitions, and Liberty: The Crisis of 1873–1876." *Journal of Interdisciplinary History* 8 (Autumn): 281–313.

——— 1986. *Politics in Hard Times: Comparative Responses to International Economic Crises.* Ithaca: Cornell University Press.

Gowa, Joanne. 1986. "Anarchy, Egoism, and Third Images: The Evolution of Cooperation and International Relations." *International Organization* 40 (Winter): 167–86.

——— 1989. "Bipolarity, Multipolarity and Free Trade." *American Political Science Review* 83 (December): 1245–56.

Grieco, Joseph M. 1984. *Between Dependency and Autonomy: India's Experience with the International Computer Industry.* Berkeley: University of California Press.

——— 1987. "States, Anarchy, and Cooperation: A Realist Critique of Neoliberal Theory." Duke University Program in International Political Economy. Working Paper no. 10 (January).

——— 1988a. "Anarchy and the Limits of Cooperation: A Realist Critique of the Newest Liberal Institutionalism." *International Organization* 42 (August): 485–507.

——— 1988b. "Realist Theory and the Problem of International Cooperation: Analysis with an Amended Prisoner's Dilemma Model." *Journal of Politics* 50 (August): 600–24.

——— 1990. *Cooperation Among Nations: Europe, America, and Non-Tariff Barriers to Trade.* Ithaca: Cornell University Press.

——— 1991. "The Renaissance of the European Community and the Crisis of Realist International Theory." Duke University Program in Political Economy. Working Paper no. 151 (October).

——— 1992a. "Realist Theory and the Study of International Relations." Presented to the Peter B. Lewis lecture series on "New Thinking in International Relations Theory." Princeton University (April).

——— 1992b. "State Binding and International Rule Trajectories: The Politics of European Economic and Monetary Union." Duke University Program in Political Economy. Working Paper no. 170 (August).

——— 1992c. "Understanding the Problem of International Cooperation: The Limits of Neoliberal Institutionalism, and the Future of Realist Theory." Paper presented at the annual meeting of the American Political Science Association, Chicago, September 3–6.

——— 1993. "Realist Theory and the Relative Gains Problem for International Cooperation: Development in the Debate and Prospects for Future Research." Forthcoming in *American Political Science Review*.

Gross, Leo. 1979. "Some International Law Aspects of the Freedom of Information and the Right to Communicate." In Kaarle Nordenstreng and Herbert I. Schiller, eds. *National Sovereignty and International Communication*. Norwood, N.J.: Ablex.

Haas, Ernst B. 1958. *The Uniting of Europe: Political, Economic, and Social Forces, 1950–1957*. Stanford, Calif.: Stanford University Press.

——— 1964. *Beyond the Nation-State: Functionalism and International Organization*. Stanford, Calif.: Stanford University Press.

——— 1968. "Technology, Pluralism, and the New Europe." In Joseph S. Nye, Jr., ed., *International Regionalism*. Boston: Little, Brown.

——— 1975. "Is There a Hole in the Hole? Knowledge, Technology, Interdependence, and the Construction of International Regimes." *International Organization* 29 (Summer): 827–76.

——— 1980. "Why Collaborate: Issue-Linkage and International Regimes." *World Politics* 32 (April): 357–405.

——— 1983. "Words Can Hurt You; Or, Who Said What to Whom About Regimes." In Krasner 1983a.

——— 1990. *When Knowledge Is Power*. Berkeley: University of California Press.

Haas, Ernst B., Mary Pat Williams, and Don Babai. 1977. *Scientists and World Order: The Uses of Technical Information in International Organizations*. Berkeley: University of California Press.

Haas, Peter M. 1990. *Saving the Mediterranean: The Politics of International Environmental Cooperation*. New York: Columbia University Press.

——— ed. 1992. "Knowledge, Power and International Policy Coordination." *International Organization* 46 (Winter).

Haggard, Stephan and Andrew Moravcsik. 1993. "The Policitical Economy of Financial Assistance to Eastern Europe, 1989–1991." In Keohane, Nye, and Hoffmann 1993:246–85.

Hardin, Garrett. 1968. "The Tragedy of the Commons." *Science* 162 (December 13): 1243–48.

Hardin, Russell. 1971. "Collective Action as an Agreeable n-Prisoners' Dilemma." *Behavioral Science* 16 (September): 472–81.

—— 1982. *Collective Action*. Baltimore: Johns Hopkins University Press, for Resources for the Future.

—— 1983. "Unilateral Versus Mutual Disarmament." *Philosophy and Public Affairs* 12: 236–54.

Hart, Jeffrey A. and Laura D'Andrea Tyson. 1989. "Responding to the Challenge of HDTV." *California Management Review* 26 (Summer).

Hartz, Louis. 1955. *The Liberal Tradition in America*. New York: Harcourt, Brace and World.

Haskel, Barbara. 1976. *The Scandinavian Option: Opportunities and Opportunity Costs in Postwar Scandinavian Foreign Policies*. Oslo: Universitetsforlaget.

Hazelwood, Arthur. 1979. "The End of the East African Community." *Journal of Common Market Studies* 18 (September).

Heckscher, Eli F. 1955. *Mercantilism*. Rev. ed. 2 vols. Translated by Mendel Shapiro. New York: Macmillan.

Hellmann, Gunther and Reinhard Wolf. 1992. "Neorealism, Neoliberal Institutionalism, and the Future of NATO." *Security Studies*, Forthcoming.

Herz, John H. 1950. "Idealist Internationalism and the Security Dilemma." *World Politics* 1 (January) 157–80.

—— 1981. "Political Realism Revisited." *International Studies Quarterly* 25 (June): 182–203.

Heymann, Philip B. 1973. "The Problem of Coordination: Bargaining and Rules." *Harvard Law Review* 86 (March): 797–877.

Hinsley, F. H. 1963. *Power and the Pursuit of Peace*. London: Cambridge University Press.

Hirsch, Fred. 1978. "The Ideological Underlay of Inflation." In John Goldthorpe and Fred Hirsch, eds., *The Political Economy of Inflation*. London: Martin Robertson.

Hirschman, Albert O. 1970. *Exit, Voice, and Loyalty: Responses to Declines in Firms, Organizations, and States*. Cambridge: Harvard University Press.

—— 1980 [1945]. *National Power and the Structure of Foreign Trade*. 2d ed. Berkeley: University of California Press.

Hirshleifer, J. 1977. "Economics from a Biological Viewpoint." *Journal of Law and Economics* 20 (April): 1–52.

—— 1978. "Competition, Cooperation, and Conflict in Economics and Biology." *American Economic Review* 68 (May): 238–43.

Hiscox, Michael J. and Robert J. Franzese, Jr. 1991. "International Cooperation and the Problem of 'Relative Gains.' " Unpublished manuscript (Cambridge: Department of Government, Harvard University, December).

Hobbes, Thomas. 1958 [1651]. *Leviathan*. Indianapolis: Bobbs-Merrill.

Hoffmann, Stanley. 1965. *The State of War: Essays in the Theory and Practice of International Politics*. New York: Praeger.

—— 1968. "Obstinante or Obsolete." In Joseph S. Nye, Jr., ed., *International Regionalism*, 177–230. Boston: Little, Brown.

—— 1970. "International Organization and the International System." *International Organization* 24 (Summer): 389–413.

———— 1973a. "Choices." *Foreign Policy* 12: 3–42.

———— 1973b. "International Organization and the International System." In Leland M. Goodrich and David A. Kay, eds., *International Organization: Politics and Process*. Madison: University of Wisconsin Press.

———— 1977. "An American Social Science: International Relations." *Daedalus* (Summer): 41–59. Reprinted in Hoffmann 1987: 3–24.

———— 1984. "Détente." In Joseph S. Nye, ed., *The Making of America's Soviet Policy*. New Haven: Yale University Press for the Council on Foreign Relations.

———— 1987. *Janus and Minerva: Essays in the Theory and Practice of International Politics*. Boulder, Colo.: Westview.

———— 1989. "The European Community and 1992." *Foreign Affairs* 68 (Fall): 27–47.

Hogan, Michael. 1987. *The Marshall Plan: America, Britain, and the Reconstruction of Western Europe*. Cambridge: Cambridge University Press.

Holsti, Ole R. 1970. *Crisis Escalation War*. Montreal: McGill University Press.

Howard, Nigel. 1971. *Paradoxes of Rationality: Theory of Metagames and Political Behavior*. Cambridge: MIT Press.

Hudec, Robert. 1975. *The GATT Legal System and World Trade Diplomacy*. New York: Praeger.

Huntington, Samuel P. 1988–89. "The U.S.—Decline or Renewal?" *Foreign Affairs* 67 (Winter): 76–96.

Ikenberry, G. John. 1988. "Conclusion: An Institutional Approach to American Foreign Economic Policy." In G. John Ikenberry, David A. Lake, and Michael Mastanduno, eds., *The State and American Foreign Economic Policy*. Ithaca: Cornell University Press.

Ikenberry, G. John, David A. Lake, and Michael Mastanduno. 1988. "Introduction: Approaches to Explaining American Foreign Economic Policy." In Ikenberry, Lake, and Mastanduno, eds., *The State and American Foreign Economic Policy*. Ithaca: Cornell University Press.

Inman, B. R. and Daniel F. Burton, Jr. 1990. "Technology and Competitiveness: The New Policy Frontier." *Foreign Affairs* 69 (Spring), no. 2.

International Encyclopedia of the Social Sciences. 1968. New York: Free Press.

Ito, Kan. 1990. "Trans-Pacific Anger." *Foreign Policy* 78 (Spring): 131–52.

Jackson, John H. 1978. "The Crumbling Institutions of the Liberal Trade System." *Journal of World Trade Law* 12 (March–April): 93–106.

Jacobson, Harold K. 1984. *Networks of Interdependence: International Organizations and the Global Political System*. 2d ed. New York: Knopf.

Janis, Irving J. 1980. *Groupthink*. 2d ed. Boston: Houghton Mifflin.

Jentleson, Bruce W. 1986. *Pipeline Politics: The Complex Political Economy of East-West Energy Trade*. Ithaca: Cornell University Press.

Jervis, Robert. 1970. *The Logic of Images in International Relations*. Princeton: Princeton University Press.

———— 1976. *Perception and Misperception in International Politics*. Princeton: Princeton University Press.

————— 1978. "Cooperation Under the Security Dilemma." *World Politics* 30 (January): 167–214.

————— 1982. "Security Regimes." *International Organization* 36 (Spring): 357–78.

————— 1985. "From Balance to Concert: A Study of Internationl Security Cooperation." *World Politics* 38 (October): 58–79.

————— 1988. "Realism, Game Theory, and Cooperation." *World Politics* 40 (April): 317–49.

Johnson, Chalmers. 1987. "How to Think about Economic Competition from Japan." In Kenneth Pyle, ed., *The Trade Crisis: How Will Japan Respond?* Seattle: Society for Japanese Studies.

————— 1989. "Their Behavior, Our Policy." *The National Interest* 17 (Fall).

Johnson, Harry. 1953. "Optimal Tariffs and Retaliation." *Review of Economic Studies* 21: 142–53.

Jones, Stephen B. 1954. "The Power Inventory and National Strategy." *World Politics* 6 (July) 421–52.

Kahler, Miles. 1985. "European Protectionism in Theory and Practice." *World Politics* 37 (July): 475–502.

————— ed. 1986. *The Politics of International Debt.* Ithaca: Cornell University Press.

Kaplan, Morton A. 1957. *System and Process in International Politics.* New York: John Wiley.

Kaplan, Stephen S. 1981. *Diplomacy of Power: Soviet Armed Forces as a Political Instrument.* Washington, D.C.: Brookings Institution.

Kapstein, Ethan. 1989. "International Coordination of Banking Regulations." *International Organization* 43 (Spring): 323–47.

Katzenstein, Peter J. 1985. *Small States in World Markets: Industrial Policy in Europe.* Ithaca: Cornell University Press.

————— ed. 1978. *Between Power and Plenty: Foreign Economic Policies of Advanced Industrialized States.* Madison: University of Wisconsin Press.

————— ed. 1992. "The Taming of Power." In Meredith Woo-Cumings and Michael Loriaux, eds., *The Past as Prelude: History in the Making of a New World Order.* Boulder, Colo.: Westview.

Kavenaugh, Andrea. 1986. "Star WARCs and the New System: An Analysis of U.S. International Satellite Policy Formation." *Telecommunications Policy* (June).

Kennedy, Paul. 1987. *The Rise and Fall of the Great Powers: Economic Change and Military Conflict from 1500 to 2000.* New York: Random House.

Keohane, Robert O. 1971. "The Big Influence of Small Allies." *Foreign Policy* 2 (Spring): 161–82.

————— 1982. "The Demand for International Regimes." *International Organization* 36 (Spring): 325–56. Reprinted in Krasner 1983a.

————— 1983. "The Demand for Regimes." In Krasner 1983a.

————— 1984. *After Hegemony: Cooperation and Discord in the World Political Economy.* Princeton: Princeton University Press.

—— 1986a. "Realism, Neorealism and the Study of World Politics." In Keohane 1986b: 1–26.

—— ed. 1986b. *Neorealism and Its Critics*. New York: Columbia University Press.

—— 1986c. "Reciprocity in International Relations." *International Organization* 40 (Winter).

—— 1989. *International Institutions and State Power*. Boulder, Colo.: Westview.

—— 1990a. "International Liberalism Reconsidered." In Dunn 1990: 165–94.

—— 1990b. "Multilateralism: An Agenda for Research." *International Journal* 45 (Fall): 731–64.

—— 1992. "Institutionalist Theory and the Realist Challenge After the Cold War." Paper presented at the annual meeting of the American Political Science Association, Chicago, September 3–6.

Keohane, Robert O. and Joseph S. Nye, Jr. 1972. "Introduction" and "Conclusion." In Keohane and Nye, eds. *Transnational Relations and World Politics*. Cambridge: Harvard University Press.

—— 1977. *Power and Interdependence: World Politics in Transition*. 2d ed., 1989. Boston: Little, Brown.

—— 1987. "Power and Interdependence Revisited." *International Organization* 41: 723–53.

Keohane, Robert O., Joseph S. Nye, and Stanley Hoffman, eds., 1993. "Strategies of Adaptation: International Politics and Institutions in Europe After the Cold War." *After the Cold War: Institutions and State Strategies in Europe, 1989–1991*. Cambridge Harvard University Press.

Keohane, Robert O. and Stanley Hoffmann. 1991. "Institutional Change in Europe in the 1980's." In Keohane and Hoffmann, eds., *The New European Community: Decisionmaking and Institutional Change*, 1–40. Boulder, Colo.: Westview.

Kindleberger, Charles P. 1973. *The World in Depression, 1929–39*. Berkeley: University of California Press.

Kock, Karin. 1969. *International Trade Policy and the GATT 1947–1967*. Stockholm: Almqvist and Wiksell.

Krasner, Stephen D. 1976. "State Power and the Structure of International Trade." *World Politics* 28 (April), no. 3: 317–45.

—— 1978. *Defending the National Interest: Raw Materials Investments and U.S. Foreign Policy*. Princeton: Princeton University Press.

—— 1982. "American Policy and Global Economic Stability." In William P. Avery and David P. Rapkin, eds., *America in a Changing World Political Economy*. New York: Longman.

——, ed. 1983a. *International Regimes*. Ithaca: Cornell University Press.

—— 1983b. "Regimes and the Limits of Realism." In Krasner 1983a.

—— 1985. *Structural Conflict: The Third World Against Global Liberalism*. Berkeley: University of California Press.

—— 1987. *Asymmetries in Japanese-American Trade: The Case for Specific Rec-*

iprocity. Policy Papers in International Affairs, no. 32. Berkeley: University of California Press for the Institute of International Studies.

———— 1991. "Global Communications and National Power: Life on the Pareto Frontier." *World Politics* 43 (April): 336–66.

Kratochwil, Friedrich. 1984. "The Force of Prescriptions." *International Organization* 38 (Autumn): 685–708.

Kratochwil, Friedrich and John Gerard Ruggie. 1986. "International Organization: The State of the Art on the Art of the State." *International Organization* 40 (Autumn): 753–75.

Kreps, David, Paul Milgrom, John Roberts, and Robert Wilson. 1982. "Rational Cooperation in a Finitely Repeated Prisoner's Dilemma." *Journal of Economic Theory* 27: 245–52.

Krugman, Paul, ed. 1986. *Strategic Trade Policy and the New International Economics.* Cambridge: MIT Press.

Kurth, James R. 1980. "The Creation and Destruction of International Regimes: The Impact of the World Market." Paper delivered at the annual meeting of the American Political Science Association, Washington, D.C., August.

Lakatos, Imre. 1970. "Falsification and the Methodology of Scientific Research Programs." In Lakatos and Musgrave, eds., *Criticism and the Growth of Knowledge.* London: Cambridge University Press.

Lake, David. 1984. "Beneath the Commerce of Nations: A Theory of International Economic Structures." *International Studies Quarterly* 28: 143–70.

———— 1988. *Power, Protection, and Free Trade: International Sources of U.S. Commercial Strategy, 1887–1939.* Ithaca: Cornell University Press.

Larson, Deborah Welsh. 1988. "The Psychology of Reciprocity in International Relations." *Negotiation Journal* 4: 281–301.

Lawrence, Robert Z. and Charles L. Schultze, eds. 1990. *An American Trade Strategy: Options for the 1990s.* Washington, D.C.: Brookings Institution.

Levy, Marc A. 1993. "East-West Environmental Politics After 1989: The Case of Air Pollution." In Keohane, Nye, and Hoffmann 1993:310–41.

Lewis, David K. 1969. *Convention: A Philosophical Study.* Cambridge: Harvard University Press.

Lewis, George Cornewall. 1970 [1832]. *Remarks on the Use and Abuse of Some Political Terms.* Facsimile of 1832 text. Columbia: University of Missouri Press.

Lieber, Robert J. 1983. *The Oil Decade: Conflict and Cooperation in the West.* New York: Praeger.

Lipson, Charles. 1982. "The Transformation of Trade: The Sources and Effects of Regime Change." *International Organization* 36 (Spring). Reprinted in Krasner 1983a.

———— 1983. "The Transformation of Trade: The Sources and Effects of Regime Change." In Krasner 1983a.

———— 1984. "International Cooperation in Economic and Security Affairs." *World Politics* 37 (October): 1–23.

—— 1985. "Banker's Dilemmas: Private Cooperation in Rescheduling Sovereign Debts." *World Politics* 38 (October): 200–25.

Little, Richard. 1984. "Power and Interdependence: A Realist Critique." In R. B. Barry Jones and Peter Willetts, eds., *Interdependence on Trial*. London: F. Pinter.

Luce, R. Duncan and Howard Raiffa. 1957. *Games and Decisions: Introduction and Critical Survey*. New York: John Wiley.

Ludlow, Peter. 1982. *The Making of the European Monetary System*. London: Butterworth.

Luther, Sara Fletcher. 1988. *The United States and the Direct Broadcast Satellite: The Politics of International Broadcasting in Space*. New York: Oxford University Press.

Luttwak, Edward N. 1990. "From Geopolitics to Geo-Economics." *The National Interest* 20 (Summer): 17–24.

Markham, Jesse W. 1968. "Oligopoly." In *International Encyclopedia of the Social Sciences*, vol. 11. New York: Macmillan.

Marks, David. 1983. "Broadcasting Across the Wall: The Free Flow of Information Between East and West Germany." *Journal of Communication* 33 (Winter).

Martin, John L. 1958. *International Propaganda: Its Legal and Diplomatic Control*. Minneapolis: University of Minnesota Press.

Martin, Lisa L. 1992a. "Institutions and Cooperation: Sanctions During the Falklands Island Conflict." *International Security* 16 (Spring): 25–50.

—— 1992b. "Interests, Power and Multilateralism." *International Organization* 46 (Fall).

—— 1992c. *Coercive Cooperation: Explaining Multilateral Economic Sanctions*. Princeton: Princeton University Press.

Mastanduno, Michael. 1991. "Do Relative Gains Matter? America's Response to Japanese Industrial Policy." *International Security* 16 (Summer): 73–113.

—— 1992. *Economic Containment: CoCom and the Politics of East-West Trade*. Ithaca: Cornell University Press.

Mastanduno, Michael, David A. Lake, and G. John Ikenberry. 1989. "Toward a Realist Theory of State Action." *International Studies Quarterly* 33 (December), no. 4: 457–74.

Masters, Roger. 1964. "World Politics as a Primitive Political System." *World Politics* 16 (July).

McClintock, Charles Graham. 1972. "Game Behavior and Social Motivation in Interpersonal Settings." In McClintock, ed., *Experimental Social Psychology*. New York: Holt, Rinehart and Winston.

McDougall, Walter A. 1985. "Space-Age Europe: Gaullism, Euro-Gaullism, and the American Dilemma." *Technology and Culture* 26 (April): 179–203.

McGinnis, Michael. 1986. "Issue-Linkage and the Evolution of International Cooperation." *Journal of Conflict Resolution* 30 (March):141–70.

Mearsheimer, John. 1990a. "Back to the Future: Instability in Europe After the Cold War." *International Security* 15 (Summer): 5–56.

────── 1990b. "Correspondence: Back to the Future, Part II." *International Security* 15 (Fall): 194–99.

────── 1991. "Back to the Future: Instability in Europe After the Cold War." In Sean Lynn-Jones, ed., *The Cold War and After: Prospects for Peace*, 141–92. Cambridge: MIT Press.

Midgaard, Knut. 1976. "Co-operative Negotiations and Bargaining: Some Notes on Power and Powerlessness." In Brian Barry, ed., *Power and Political Theory: Some European Perspectives*. London: John Wiley.

Milner, Helen. 1991. "The Assumption of Anarchy in International Relations Theory." *Review of International Studies* 17 (January): 67–85.

────── 1992. "International Theories of Cooperation Among Nations: Strengths and Weaknesses." *World Politics* 44 (April): 466–96.

Milner, Helen and David Yoffie. 1989. "Between Free Trade and Protectionism: Strategic Trade Policy and a Theory of Corporate Trade Demands." *International Organization* 43 (Spring): 239–72.

Mitrany, David. [1943] 1966. *A Working Peace System*. Chicago: Quadrangle Press.

Modelski, George. 1978. "The Long Cycle of Global Politics and the Nation-State." *Comparative Studies in Society and History* 20 (April): 214–35.

Moe, Terry M. 1990. "Political Institutions: The Neglected Side of the Story." Paper prepared for the Yale Law School, *Journal of Law, Economics, and Organization* Conference on the Organization of Political Institutions, April 27–28.

Moran, Theodore H. 1990. "The Globalization of America's Defense Industries: Managing the Threat of Foreign Dependence." *International Security* 15 (Summer), no. 1: 57–99.

Moravcsik, Andrew. 1991. "Negotiating the Single European Act: National Interests and Conventional Statecraft in the European Community." *International Organization* 45 (Winter): 19–56. Reprinted in Robert O. Keohane and Stanley Hoffmann, eds. *The New European Community: Decisionmaking and Institutional Change*, 41–84. Boulder, Colo.: Westview.

────── 1992. "Liberalism and International Relations Theory." Working Paper no. 92 (October 6). Center for International Affairs, Harvard University.

Morgenthau, Hans J. 1946. *Scientific Man vs. Power Politics*. Chicago: University of Chicago Press.

────── 1948 (rev. 1958, 1967, 1973, 1978, and 1985). *Politics Among Nations: The Struggle for Power and Peace*. New York: Knopf.

────── 1952. "Another 'Great Debate': The National Interest of the United States." *American Political Science Review* 46 (December): 961–88.

Morita, Akio and Shintaro Ishihara. 1989. *The Japan That Can Say No: The New U.S.-Japan Relations Card*. Kobunsha: Kappa-Holmes.

Morrow, James. 1990. "Modelling International Regimes." Paper presented at the annual meeting of the American Political Science Association, San Francisco.

Morse, Edward S. 1970. "The Transformation of Foreign Policies: Modernization, Interdependence and Externalization." *World Politics* 22 (April): 371–92.

Moss, Laurence S. 1980. "Optimal Jurisdictions and the Economic Theory of the State: Or, Anarchy and One-World Government Are Only Corner Solutions." *Public Choice* 35: 17–26.

Murty, B. S. 1968. *Propaganda and World Public Order: The Legal Regulation of the Ideological Instrument of Coercion.* New Haven: Yale University Press.

Mytelka, Lynn Krieger. 1973. "The Salience of Gains in Third-World Integrative Systems." *World Politics* 25 (January): 236–46.

—— 1979. *Regional Development in a Global Economy: The Multinational Corporation, Technology, and Andean Integration.* New Haven: Yale University Press.

Naderi, F. Michael. 1988. *Overview of the Communications Satellite Industry in Japan and Europe.* Washington, D.C.: National Aeronautics and Space Administration (NASA) Headquarters (April 30).

Nagel, Jack H. 1975. *The Descriptive Analysis of Power.* New Haven: Yale University Press.

Nicholson, Michael. 1972. *Oligopoly and Conflict: A Dynamic Approach.* Liverpool: Liverpool University Press.

Nicolaides, Kalypso. 1993. "East European Trade in the Aftermath of 1989: Did International Institutions Matter?" In Keohane, Nye, and Hoffmann 1993: 196–245.

Niebuhr, Reinhold. 1944. *The Children of Light and the Children of Darkness.* New York: Scribner's.

Nisbet, Richard and Lee Ross. 1980. *Human Inference: Strategies and Shortcomings of Social Judgment.* Englewood Cliffs, N.J.: Prentice-Hall.

Noam, Eli and Gerard Pogerel, eds. Forthcoming. *Asymmetric Deregulation: The Dynamics of Telecommunications Policies in Europe and the United States.* Norwood, N.J.: Ablex.

North, Robert C. 1977. "Toward a Framework for the Analysis of Scarcity and Conflict." *International Studies Quarterly* 21 (December): 569–91.

Nye, Joseph S. Jr. 1971. "Comparing Common Markets: A Revised Neo-Functional Model." In Leon N. Lindberg and Stuart A. Schiengold, eds., *Regional Integration: Theory and Research.* Cambridge: Harvard University Press.

—— 1988. "Neorealism and Neoliberalism." *World Politics* 40 (January): 235–51.

—— 1990. *Bound to Lead: The Changing Nature of American Power.* New York: Basic Books.

Olson, Mancur. 1965. *The Logic of Collective Action.* Cambridge: Harvard University Press.

Olson, Mancur and Richard Zeckhauser. 1966. "An Economic Theory of Alliance." *Review of Economics and Statistics* 48 (August): 266–79.

Organski, A. F. K. 1968. *World Politics.* 2d ed. New York: Knopf.

Osgood, Robert E. and Robert W. Tucker. 1967. *Force, Order, and Justice.* Baltimore: Johns Hopkins University Press.

Oye, Kenneth. 1979. "The Domain of Choice." In Kenneth Oye, Donald Rothchild, and Robert Lieber, eds., *Eagle Entangled: U.S. Foreign Policy in a Complex World.* New York: Longman.

———— 1985. "Explaining Cooperation Under Anarchy: Hypotheses and Strategies." *World Politics* 38: 1–24.

———— ed. 1986. *Cooperation Under Anarchy.* Princeton: Princeton University Press.

Packard, George R. 1987–88. "The Coming U.S.-Japan Crisis." *Foreign Affairs* 66 (Winter), no. 2: 348–67.

Pannenberg, Charles O. 1979. *A New International Health Order: An Inquiry into the International Relations of World Health and Medical Care.* Germantown, Md.: Sijthoff and Noordhoff.

Parsons, Talcott. 1963. "On the Concept of Political Power." *Proceedings of the American Philosophical Society* 107: 232–62.

Pelkmans, Jacques. 1979. "Economic Cooperation Among Western Countries." In Robert J. Gordon and Jacques Pelkmans, eds., *Challenges to Interdependent Economies: The Industrial West in the Coming Decade.* New York: McGraw-Hill.

———— 1987. "The New Approach to Technical Harmonization and Standardization." In Peter Robson and Jacques Pelkmans, eds., *Making the Common Market Work,* a special issue of *Journal of Common Market Studies* 25 (March): 249–69.

Pelton, Joseph N. 1974. *Global Communications Satellite Policy: Intelsat, Politics and Functionalism.* Mount Airy, Md.: Lomond Books.

Perrow, Charles. 1986. *Complex Organizations: A Critical Essay.* 3d ed. New York, Random House.

Powell, Robert. 1990. "Conflict and Cooperation in Anarchy" (unpublished typescript. University of California, Berkeley).

———— 1991a. "The Problem of Absolute and Relative Gains in International Relations Theory." *American Political Science Review* 85 (December): 1303–20.

———— 1991b. "In the Pursuit of Power and Plenty" (unpublished typescript, University of California, Berkeley).

Prestowitz, Clyde, Jr. 1990. *Trading Places: How We Are Giving Our Future to Japan And How To Reclaim It.* Rev. ed. New York: Basic Books.

Pruitt, Dean G. and Melvin J. Kimmel. 1977. "Twenty Years of Experimental Gaming: Critique, Synthesis, and Suggestions for the Future." *Annual Review of Psychology* 28: 163–92.

Puchala, Donald J. 1975. "Domestic Politics and Regional Harmonization in the European Communities." *World Politics* 27 (July): 496–520.

Puchala, Donald J. and Raymond F. Hopkins. 1983. "International Regimes: Lessons from Inductive Analysis." In Krasner 1983a.

Putnam, Robert D. 1988. "Diplomacy and Domestic Politics: The Logic of Two-Level Games." *International Organization* 42 (Summer): 427–61.

Quester, George. 1990. *The International Politics of Television*. Lexington, Mass.: Lexington Books.

Rapoport, Anatol. 1960. *Fights, Games and Debates*. Ann Arbor: University of Michigan Press.

Rapoport, Anatol and Albert M. Chammah (with the collaboration of Carol J. Orwant). 1965. *Prisoner's Dilemma: A Study in Conflict and Cooperation*. Ann Arbor: University of Michigan Press.

Rapoport, Anatol and Melvin J. Guyer. 1966. "A Taxonomy of 2 X 2 Games." *General Systems* 2: 203–14.

Rapoport, Anatol, Melvin J. Guyer, and David G. Gordon. 1976. *The 2 X 2 Game*. Ann Arbor: University of Michigan Press.

Rasmusen, Eric. 1989. *Games and Information*. Oxford: Basil Blackwell.

Rawls, John. 1971. *A Theory of Justice*. Cambridge: Harvard University Press.

Reich, Robert. 1990. "Do We Want U.S. to Be Rich Or Japan Poor?" *Wall Street Journal*, June 18.

Richardson, J. David. 1990. "The Political Economy of Strategic Trade Policy." *International Organization* 44 (Winter), no. 1: 107–35.

Richardson, Lewis F. 1960. *Arms and Insecurity: A Mathematical Study of the Causes and Origins of War*. Edited by Nicolas Rachevksy and Ernesto Trucco. Pittsburgh and Chicago: Boxwood Press and Quadrangle Books.

Riker, William H. 1962. *The Theory of Political Coalitions*. New Haven: Yale University Press.

Romberg, Alan. 1988. "U.S.-Japan Relations: A Partnership in Search of Definition." *Critical Issues 1988–1*. New York: Council on Foreign Relations.

Rosecrance, Richard. 1981. "International Theory Revisited." *International Organization* 35: 691–713.

——— 1986. *The Rise of the Trading State*. New York: Basic Books.

Rosenau, James. 1963. "Calculated Control as a Unifying Concept in the Study of International Politics and Foreign Policy." Princeton: Center for International Studies, Princeton University.

Rousseau, J. J. 1917. *A Lasting Peace through the Federation of Europe*. Translated by C. E. Vaughan. London: Constable.

Ruggie, John Gerard. 1972. "Collective Goods and Future International Collaborations." *American Political Science Review* 66 (September): 874–93.

——— 1975. "International Responses to Technology: Concepts and Trends." *International Organization* 29 (Summer): 557–83.

——— 1982. "International Regimes, Transactions and Change: Embedded Liberalism in the Postwar Economic Order." *International Organization* 36 (Spring): 379–416. Reprinted in Krasner 1983a.

——— 1983a. "Continuity and Transformation in the World Polity: Toward a Neorealist Synthesis." *World Politics* 35 (January).

——— 1983b. "International Regimes, Transactions, and Change embedded Liberalism in the Postwar Economic Order. In Krasner 1983a.

——— 1992. "Multilateralism: The Anatomy of an Institution." *International Organization* 46 (Fall).

Russell, Frank M. 1936. *Theories of International Relations.* New York: Appleton-Century.

Russell, Robert W. 1973. "Transgovernmental Interaction in the International Monetary System, 1960–1972." *International Organization* 27 (Autumn): 431–64.

Russett, Bruce M. 1963. *Community and Contention.* Cambridge: MIT Press.

———— 1983. *The Prisoners of Insecurity.* San Francisco: W. H. Freeman.

———— 1985. "The Mysterious Case of Vanishing Hegemony; or, Is Mark Twain Really Dead?" *International Organization* 39 (Spring): 20–32.

Russett, Bruce M. and John D. Sullivan. 1971. "Collective Goods and International Organization." *International Organization* 25 (Autumn): 845–65.

Samuels, Richard and Benjamin Whipple. 1989. "Defense Production and Industrial Development: The Case of Japanese Aircraft." In Chalmers Johnson, Laura D'Andrea Tyson, and John Zysman, eds., *Politics and Productivity: The Real Story of Why Japan Works.* Cambridge, Mass.: Ballinger.

Sandholtz, Wayne and John Zysman. 1989. "1992: Recasting the European Bargain." *World Politics* 42 (October): 95–128.

Sandler, Todd M. and Jon T. Cauley. 1977. "The Design of Supranational Structures: An Economic Perspective." *International Studies Quarterly* 21 (June): 251–76.

Sandler, Todd M., William Loehr, and Jon T. Cauley. 1978. "The Political Economy of Public Goods and International Cooperation." Monograph Series in World Affairs, no. 15.

Schelling, Thomas C. 1960. *The Strategy of Conflict.* Cambridge: Harvard University Press.

———— 1966. *Arms and Influence.* New Haven: Yale University Press.

———— 1978a. "Economics or the Art of Self-Management." *American Economic Review* 68 (May), no. 9: 290–94.

———— 1978b. "Hockey Helmets, Daylight Savings, and Other Binary Choices." In Schelling 1978c.

———— 1978c. *Micromotives and Macrobehavior.* New York: W. W. Norton.

———— 1984. "Confidence in Crisis." *International Security* 8 (Spring).

Scherer, F. M. 1970. *Industrial Market Structure and Economic Performance.* Chicago: Rand McNally.

Schilling, Warner R. 1956. "The Clarification of Ends: Or, Which Interest Is the National?" *World Politics* 8 (July): 566–78.

Schick, Frederic. 1977. "Some Notes on Thinking Ahead." *Social Research* 44 (Winter): 786–800.

Schroeder, Paul W. 1976. "Alliances, 1815–1945: Weapons of Power and Tools of Management." In Klaus Knorr, ed., *Historical Dimensions of National Security Policy.* Lawrence: University of Kansas Press.

Scoville, Herbert, Jr. 1981. *MX: Prescription for Disaster.* Cambridge: MIT Press.

Sebenius, James K. 1992. "Challenging Conventional Explanations of International Cooperation: Negotiation Analysis and the Case of Epistemic Communities." *International Organization* 46: 323–66.

Shubik, Martin. 1970. "Game Theory, Behavior, and the Paradox of the Prisoner's Dilemma: Three Solutions." *Journal of Conflict Resolution* 14 (June).

—— 1971. "Games of Status." *Behavioral Science* 16 (March): 117–29.

—— 1975. *Games for Society, Business and War: Towards a Theory of Gaming.* New York: Elsevier.

Simon, Herbert. 1982. *The Sciences of the Artificial.* 2d ed. Cambridge: MIT Press.

Smale, Steve. 1980. "The Prisoner's Dilemma and Dynamical Systems Associated to Non-Cooperative Games." *Econometrica* 48 (November): 1617–34.

Small, M. and J. D. Singer. 1979. *Explaining War.* Beverly Hills: Sage.

Smith, Bruce L. 1986. "A New Technology Gap in Europe?" *SAIS Review* 6 (Winter–Spring): 219–36.

Snidal, Duncan. 1979. "Public Goods, Property Rights, and Political Organizations." *International Studies Quarterly* 23 (December): 532–66.

—— 1985a. "Coordination Versus Prisoners' Dilemma: Implications for International Cooperation and Regimes." *American Political Science Review* 79: 923–42.

—— 1985b. "The Limits of Hegemonic Stability Theory." *International Organization* 39: 579–614.

—— 1989. "Relative Gains Don't Prevent International Cooperation" (unpublished manuscript).

—— 1991a. "International Cooperation Among Relative Gains Maximizers." *International Studies Quarterly* 35: 387–402.

—— 1991b. "Relative Gains and the Pattern of International Cooperation." *American Political Science Review* 85 (September): 701–26.

Snyder, Glenn H. 1990. "Alliance Theory: A Neorealist First Cut." *Journal of International Affairs* 103–23.

Snyder, Glenn H. and Paul Diesing. 1977. *Conflict Among Nations.* Princeton: Princeton University Press.

Snyder, Jack. 1990. "Avoiding Anarchy in the New Europe." *International Security* 14 (Spring): 5–41.

Soroos, Marvin. 1986. *Beyond Sovereignty; The Challenge of Global Policy.* Columbia: University of South Carolina Press.

Spiro, Herbert. 1966. *World Politics: The Global System.* Homewood, Ill.: Dorsey Press.

Sprout, Harold and Margaret Sprout, eds. 1945. *Foundations of National Power.* Princeton: Princeton University Press.

—— 1965. *The Ecological Perspective on Human Affairs: With Special Reference to International Politics.* Princeton: Princeton University Press.

—— 1971. *Toward a Politics of the Planet Earth.* New York: Van Nostrand.

Stegemann, Klaus. 1989. "Policy Rivalry Among Industrial States." *International Organization* 43: 73–100.

Stein, Arthur A. 1981. "The Hegemon's Dilemma: Great Britain, the United States, and the International Economic Order." Paper presented at the annual meeting of the American Political Science Association, New York, September 4.

———— 1982a. "Coordination and Collaboration Regimes in an Anarchic World." *International Organization* 36 (Spring): 299–324.

———— 1982b. "When Misperception Matters." *World Politics* 35 (June): 438–62.

———— 1983. "Coordination and Collaboration: Regimes in an Anarchic World." In Krasner 1983a.

———— 1984. "The Hegemon's Dilemma." *International Organization* 38: 355–86.

Steinbruner, John D. 1974. *The Cybernetic Theory of Decision.* Princeton: Princeton University Press.

Stern, Robert, ed. 1987. *United States Trade Policies in a Changing World Economy.* Cambridge: MIT Press.

Stinchcombe, Arthur L. 1968. *Constructing Social Theories.* New York: Harcourt, Brace.

Strange, Susan. 1976. "International Monetary Relations of the Western World, 1959–1971." In Andrew Schonfield, ed., *International Economic Relations of the Western World, 1959–1971,* vol. 2. Oxford: Oxford University Press for the Royal Institute of International Affairs.

———— 1987. "The Persistent Myth of Lost Hegemony." *International Organization* 41 (Autumn), no. 1: 551–74.

Tatsuno, Sheridan M. 1990. *Created in Japan: From Imitators to World-Class Innovators.* New York: Ballinger.

Taylor, Michael. 1976. *Anarchy and Cooperation.* London: John Wiley.

———— 1987. *The Possibility of Cooperation.* Cambridge: Cambridge University Press.

Taylor, Paul. 1983. *The Limits of European Integration.* New York: Columbia University Press.

Telser, Lester G. 1972. *Competition, Collusion, and Game Theory.* Chicago: Aldine-Atherton.

———— 1980. "A Theory of Self-Enforcing Agreements." *Journal of Business* 53 (January): 27–44.

Thiel, Henri. 1971. *Principles of Econometrics.* New York: John Wiley.

Thucydides. 1954. *The Peloponnesian Wars.* Translated by Rex Warner. New York: Penguin.

Tinbergen, Jan. 1978. "Alternative Forms of International Co-operation: Comparing Their Efficiency." *International Social Science Journal* 30.

Tollison, Robert E. and Thomas D. Willett. 1979. "An Economic Theory of Mutually Advantageous Issue Linkage in International Negotiations." *International Organization* 33 (Fall): 425–49.

Tresize, Philip. 1989–90. "Japan, the Enemy?" *Brookings Review* (Winter): 3–13.

Treverton, Gregory F. 1978. *The "Dollar Drain" and American Forces in Germany: Managing the Political Economics of Atlantic Alliance.* Athens: Ohio University Press.

Tsoukalis, Loukas. 1977. *The Politics and Economics of European Monetary Integration.* London: Allen and Unwin.

Tucker, Jonathan B. 1991. "Partners and Rivals: A Model of International Collaboration in Advanced Technology." *International Organization* 45 (Winter): 83–120.

Tucker, Robert W. 1977. *The Inequality of Nations.* New York: Basic Books.

Turner, Victor. 1969. "Liminality and Communitas." In *The Ritual Process: Structure and Anti-Structure.* Ithaca: Cornell University Press.

Tversky, Amos and Daniel Kahneman. 1974. "Judgment Under Uncertainty: Heuristics and Biases." *Science* 185 (September): 1125–31.

Ungerer, Horst et al. 1990. *The European Monetary System: Developments and Perspectives.* IMF Occasional Paper no. 73. Washington, D.C.: International Monetary Fund.

Vaitsos, Constantine V. 1978. "Crisis in Regional Economic Cooperation (Integration) Among Developing Countries: A Survey." *World Development* 6 (June): 747–50.

Van Evera, Stephen W. 1984. "Causes of War." Ph.D. diss., University of California at Berkeley.

——— 1985. "Why Cooperation Failed in 1914." *World Politics* 38 (October): 80–117.

——— 1990–91. "Primed for Peace: Europe After the Cold War." *International Security* 15 (Winter): 7–57.

Vernon, Raymond. 1989. "On Glass Houses and Japan-Bashing." *New York Times*, June 21.

Viner, Jacob. 1937. *Studies in the Theory of International Trade.* New York: Harper and Brothers.

——— 1948. "Power Versus Plenty As Objectives of Foreign Policy in the Seventeenth and Eighteenth Centuries." *World Politics* 1: 1–29.

Wagner, R. Harrison. 1983. "The Theory of Games and the Problem of International Cooperation." *American Political Science Review* 77 (June): 330–46.

Wallerstein, Immanuel. 1974. *The Modern World System*, vol. 1. New York: Academic Press.

——— 1979. "The Rise and Future Demise of the World Capitalist System." In Wallerstein, *The Capitalist World System.* Cambridge: Cambridge University Press.

Walt, Stephen. 1987. *The Origin of Alliances.* Ithaca: Cornell University Press.

——— 1988. "Testing Theories of Alliance Formation: The Case of Southwest Asia." *International Organization* 42 (Spring): 275–316.

Waltz, Kenneth N. 1959. *Man, the State, and War: A Theoretical Analysis.* New York: Columbia University Press.

——— 1975. "Theory of International Relations." In Fred Greenstein and

Nelson Polsby, eds., *The Handbook of Political Science*. Reading, Mass.: Addison-Wesley.

—— 1979. *Theory of International Politics*. Reading, Mass.: Addison-Wesley.

—— 1986. "Reflections on *Theory of International Politics*: A Response to My Critics." In Keohane 1986b.

—— 1990. "Realist Thought and Neorealist Theory." *Journal of International Affairs* 44 (Spring–Summer): 21–37.

Weber, Max. 1978. *Economy and Society*, vol. 1. Edited by Guenther Roth and Claus Wittich. Berkeley: University of California Press.

Whitman, Marina V. N. 1977. "Coordination and Management of the International Economy: A Search for Organizing Principles." In William Fellner, ed., *Contemporary Economic Problems*. Washington, D.C.: American Enterprise Institute for Public Policy Research.

Wight, Martin. 1978 [1946]. *Power Politics*. Harmondsworth, N.Y.: Holmes and Meier.

Wiklund, Claes. 1970. "The Zig-Zag Course of the Nordek Negotiations." *Scandinavian Political Studies* 5.

Winham, Gilbert. 1980. "Robert Strauss, the MTN, and the Control of Faction." *Journal of World Trade Law* 14 (September–October).

—— 1986. *International Trade and the Tokyo Round Negotiation*. Princeton: Princeton University Press.

Wolferen, Karel van. 1989. *The Enigma of Japanese Power*. New York: Knopf.

Wolfers, Arnold. 1949. "Statesmanship and Moral Choice." *World Politics* 1 (January): 175–95.

—— 1962. *Discord and Collaboration*. Baltimore: Johns Hopkins University Press.

Wolfers, Arnold and Laurence W. Martin, eds. 1956. *The Anglo-American Tradition in Foreign Affairs*. New Haven: Yale University Press.

Woolcock, Stephen. 1982. *Western Policies on East-West Trade*. Chatham House Papers no. 15. London: Routledge and Kegan Paul for the Royal Institute of International Affairs.

Wright, Quincy. 1952. "Realism and Idealism in International Politics." *World Politics* 5 (October): 116–28.

Yamamura, Kozo and Jan Vandenberg. 1986. "Japan's Rapid-Growth Policy on Trial: The Television Case." In Kozo Yamamura and Gary Saxonhouse, eds., *Law and Trade Issues of the Japanese Economy*. Seattle: University of Washington Press.

Yoffie, David B. 1983. *Power and Protectionism: Strategies of the Newly Industrializing Countries*. New York: Columbia University Press.

Young, Oran. 1979. *Compliance and Public Authority: A Theory with International Applications*. Baltimore: John Hopkins University Press.

—— 1980. "International Regimes: Problems of Concept Formation." *World Politics* 32 (April): 331–56.

—— 1982. "Regime Dynamics: The Rise and Fall of International Regimes." *International Organization* 36 (Spring): 277–98. Reprinted in Krasner 1983a.

——— 1986. "International Regimes: Toward a New Theory of Institutions." *World Politics* 39 (October).

Yudkin, Joel S. and Michael Black. 1990. "Targeting National Needs: A New Direction for Science and Technology Policy." *World Policy Journal* 7 (Spring), no. 2: 251–88.

Zacher, Mark. 1987. "Toward a Theory of International Regimes: Explorations into the Basis of Mutual Interests." *Journal of International Affairs* 44: 1–19.

Zacher, Mark W. and Richard A. Matthew. 1992. "Liberal International Theory: Common Threads, Divergent Strands." Paper presented at the annual meeting of the American Political Science Association, Chicago, September 3–6.

Zartman, I. William. 1977. "Negotiations as a Joint Decision-making Process." *Journal of Conflict Resolution* 21 (December): 620–23.

Zis, George. 1984. "The European Monetary System, 1979–84: An Assessment." *Journal of Common Market Studies* 23 (September).

Zysman, John. 1977. *Political Strategies for Industrial Order: State, Market, and Industry in France.* Berkeley: University of California Press.

——— 1983. *Governments, Markets, and Growth: Financial Systems and the Politics of Industrial Change.* Ithaca: Cornell University Press.

INDEX

Absolute gains, states' concerns for, 22, 203n6, 206n29, 245, 272; and cooperation, 204n18, 229n2; among democratic states, 131-132; evidence of, 279-281, 283; games of, 176-177, 182-183, 185-186, 204n17; and interdependence, *see* Interdependence; long term, 6; and the use of military force, 210, 224; and Neoliberal institutionalism, 5-6, 117-118, 132, 137n14, 170, 208, 213, 227-229n1, 322; and the Prisoner's Dilemma, 171, 181-183; and Realism, 117, 127; and regimes, 233-234; versus relative gains, 5-6, 173-174, 178-179, 202n1, 204n11; short term, 6; and uncertainty, 202n3; and U.S. policy, 256

Aerospace Industries Association, 262

Adaptation lags, 59n45

After Hegemony (Keohane), 115n6, 145, 241-242, 274-275, 291-292, 294, 298n2, 300n17, 304-312, 321-322, 336n8

Africa, 120

Aggarwal, Vinod, 112, 133, 286

Airbus Industrie, 121, 133

Aircraft: U.S. policy on, 251, 259, 261-262, 315

Akerlof, George A., 52

Alger, Chadwick, 162

Alker, Hayward R., 46, 144

Alliances, 12, 71, 101, 103, 277; burden sharing in, 197; and cooperation, 284-285, 302; and international order, 60; and the provision of public goods, 205n22; and states' concerns for relative gains, 129, 131-133, 255, 279, 323-324

Allison, Graham T., 59n43

Altruism, 9; negative, 138n21

American Electronics Association, 262

American Political Science Association, 286-287, 298n5-299n8

Anarchy, 4-5, 11, 13, 29-30, 34, 45, 53, 60, 62, 65, 72, 74, 80-81n1, 83n22, 113, 138n18, 143, 153, 225; as central concept in international politics, 143-145, 167; consequences of, 14-15; and cooperation, 117, 145, 170, 211, 216-217, 221, 226-229, 287-288, 303; definitions of, 4, 14, 85-86, 145-153; and the distribution of power, 156; and economic issues, 86; exaggerated importance of, 4-5; versus hierarchy, 156, 168n10; and international institutions, 303; and interdependence, 163, 168n2; and military force, 153; nature of, 4-5, 14-15; and Neoliberal institutionalism, 13, 121, 123, 126, 130, 132, 211, 226-227, 303; and Neorealism, 4-5, 13-14, 143, 211-212, 226-227; and positivism, 144; and the Prisoner's Dilemma, 171, 183; and Realism, 14, 116, 118-119, 126-127, 130, 132, 146, 170, 172, 303-304; and states' concerns for relative gains, 254, 275, 277, 287, 315; and security issues, 86; and international society, 146; and international structure, 144-145; and state behavior, 118-119; and state formation, 37; and state interests, 7; and war, 126-127

Andean Pact, 199

Anderson, Jeffrey, 300n20

Andrews, Bruce, 83n27

Anglo-French naval arms race (1852), 101

Anglo-Hanse trade wars, 95

Argentina, 93, 278, 280, 282, 326-327

Ariane, 121

Arms control, 42, 46, 75, 83n26, 91, 94, 99-101, 103, 111-112, 255

Arms races, 30, 42, 46, 71, 89, 101, 107-108, 120, 139n23, 255, 274, 321

Aron, Raymond, 119, 127, 135n1, 138n17, 217-218, 302, 337n11

Art, Robert, 144

ASEAN, 199

Ashley, Richard, 135n1, 144

Asia, 120; and U.S. policy, 279

Assurance (game), 33fig2.2, 175, 177, 180-183, 186, 203n9, 204n16, 205n21, 206n25

Athens, 254

Great Britain, 77-78, 88, 95-96, 99, 101-102, 104, 110, 139*n*30; and the EMU, 334
Great Depression, the, 112
Great powers, 48, 151, 155
Grieco, Joseph M., 4-8, 13, 23, 120, 139*n*26, 168*n*14, 172, 175, 177, 200, 202*n*1, 203*n*8, 204*n*12, 204*n*15, 207*n*34, 229*n*1-3, 229*n*7, 232*n*26, 242, 246*n*1, 247*n*12-13, 248*n*22, 248*n*25, 264*n*5, 264*n*7-8, 272-273, 275, 278-280, 301, 306, 313, 316-317, 320, 328, 331, 336*n*1, 336*n*9; Keohane's response to, 282-283, 289-297, 298*n*5, 299*n*8-9
Grotian world views, 13. *See also* Liberalism
Guyer, Melvin J., 56*n*23, 176

Haas, Ernst B., 12, 58*n*35, 114*n*3, 119-120, 135*n*3, 136*n*7, 140*n*32, 246*n*6, 296, 328, 336*n*3
Haas, Peter M., 328-329
Haggard, Stephen, 286
Hamilton, William D., 82*n*11
Hanseatic League, 95, 102, 110
Hardin, Garrett, 57*n*25
Hardin, Russell, 55*n*14, 62, 82*n*12, 176
Harmony, 235, 239; versus cooperation, 85; game of, 175, 177, 180-181, 183, 186, 204*n*13, 205*n*19-20; and interdependence, 163-164
Harz, Louis, 81
Haskel, Barbara, 139*n*30, 140*n*30, 140*n*33
Heckscher, Eli F., 25*n*4
Hegemonic stability theory, 23, 48, 292, 304, 310-311
Hegemony, 78, 89, 124; and provision of collective goods, 84*n*37; and cooperation, 76-80, 207*n*33, 302; decline of, 79, 136*n*10, 172, 197-198, 251; economic, 55; and regimes, 284; and states' concerns for relative gains, 198, 256-257, 259; and war, 218
Hellmann, Gunther, 299*n*11
Herz, John H., 12, 24
Heymann, Philip B., 57*n*26
Hierarchy: versus anarchy, 156, 168*n*10; and domestic society, 154-155
High Definition Television (HDTV), U.S. policy for, 250-251, 258-262, 265*n*13, 315
Hills, Carla, 265*n*13
Hinsley, F.H., 12
Hirsch, Fred, 98

Hirschman, Albert O., 164, 246*n*6, 264*n*10, 331
Hirshleifer, J., 53*n*2
Hiscox, Michael J., 276
Hobbes, Thomas, 11, 81
Hobbesian world view, 55*n*13, 60, 146, 148-149, 171. *See also* Realism; Neorealism
Hoffmann, Stanley, 99-100, 105, 119, 229*n*1, 270, 291, 295, 298*n*1, 300*n*14, 330, 337*n*11
Hogan, Michael, 338*n*13
Holsti, Ole R., 136*n*6
Hopkins, Raymond F., 53*n*1, 140*n*32
Howard, Nigel, 81*n*6
Hudec, Robert, 77
Hungary, 290
Huntington, Samuel, 309
Hyper-realism, 287

ICBMs, 83*n*28, 107
Idealism, versus Realism, 12, 24
Ideology, and state policies, 260-261
Ikenberry, G. John, 261-262, 264*n*6
India, 68
Information, and interdependence, 165
Inman, B.R., 262
Institutions, domestic, 63, 158, 160, 162, 295-296; and government, 151-152
Institutions, international, 3, 8, 11, 30, 85, 87, 146, 158, 160, 162; and anarchy, 303; impact on cheating, 303, 309-310, 312; cooperation in, *see* Cooperation, international; definition of, 112; and East-West disputes, 136*n*9; and iteration, 124; and knowledge, 140*n*32; legitimacy of, 152; limits of, 121; maintenance of, 51; and market failure, 242; and Neoliberal institutionalism, 117, 120, 121-124, 126, 137*n*12, 271-273, 285, 287, 294-295, 297, 302; and Neorealism, 271-272, 285, 289, 294-295, 297; and norms, 140*n*32; and North-South disputes, 136*n*9; obsolescence of, 112; positive theory of, 241; and Realism, 116, 119, 123, 329-330, 335; versus regimes, 46; continued salience of, 288-289; and the shadow of the future, 94; theories of, 293; and transaction costs, 309-310; and uncertainty, 309-310; and war, 12. *See also* Regimes, international
Integration: European, 5; problems of, 136*n*10; regional, 12, 139*n*30; and concerns for relative gains, 139*n*30; theories of, 136*n*4

Positivism: and anarchy, 144; and Neorealism, 144

Powell, Robert, 6-7, 9, 23-24n1, 174, 229n6, 272, 275-276, 299n6, 312-314, 322; Grieco's response to, 312-317

Power, 3, 5, 7, 11, 13, 48, 109, 129, 147, 152, 158-160, 162, 208; analysis of, 15-22; and coordination, *see* Coordination; definitions of, 15-16; in domestic politics, 158-162; elements of, 17-18; fungibility of, 20-22, 155, 324, 328; and interdependence, 164; compared to money, 21; and Neoliberal institutionalism, 15; and international organizations, 243; and Realism, 15, 175, 270, 302; and regimes, 110; 233-234, 242-246; and states' concerns for relative gains, 242; as a research program, 242, 244-246; and technology, 243; and zero-sum models, 18-19. *See also* Capabilities

Predominance model, 59n39

Prestowitz, Clyde, Jr. 257, 264n4

Prisoner's Dilemma, 35-36fig2.4, 42, 47-49, 55n10-11, 55n13, 55n15, 56n23, 57n25, 59n43, 61-76, 81n3, 81n5, 82n8, 82n14, 87-95, 103-105, 122, 130, 145, 150, 165, 180-183, 201, 203n6, 205n19-20, 206n25, 211, 231n17, 238, 241, 244-245, 246n8-10, 247n17, 247n21-22, 298n4, 299n6, 307, 310; and states' concerns for absolute gains, *see* Absolute gains; amended, 323; and anarchy, 171, 183; and cooperation, *see* Cooperation; definition of, 114n1; and institutions, 63; iterated, *see* Iteration; limits of, 218-220; and the utility of military force, 218; and Neoliberal institutionalism, *see* Neoliberal institutionalism; and Neorealism, 214; use by political scientists, 35-36; and Realism, 5, 61; and states' concerns for relative gains, 171, 175-177, 183-187, 204n10, 204n13-16, 205n21, 218-219, 276; solutions for, 63

Propaganda, 24

Property rights, 31, 53n2, 59n46, 245, 248n24

Protectionism, 305; U.S. policy, 252. *See also* Trade, strategic

Prussia, 130

Pruitt, Dean G., 56n23

Przeworski, Adam, 82n19

Public goods, 67, 150; and alliances, 205n22; and cooperation, 197; and security issues, 198; theories of, 115n6. *See also* Collective goods

Puchala, Donald J., 53n1, 136n10, 140n32

Putnam, Robert, 295

Raiffa, Howard, 140n33

Rapoport, Anatol, 22, 56n23, 66, 137n15, 176

Rasmusen, Eric, 231n19

Rationality: collective, 61; definition of, 125; parametric, 67, 82n15, 84n36; strategic, 65, 82n15

Rawls, John, 56n22

Realism: and absolute gains, *see* Absolute gains; and anarchy, *see* Anarchy; and the balance of power, 10; central tenets, 8, 116, 118-119, 132, 246n1; and change, 270; classical, 3, 7, 11; connotations of, 9-10; and cooperation, *see* Cooperation, international; critics of, 9; and economic issues, 259; emergence as dominant paradigm, 12; and the European Community, *see* European Community; and hegemonic decline, 136n10; versus Idealism, 12, 24; and institutions, *see* Institutions, international; and interdependence, 80; and mercantilism, 11; and the utility of military force, *see* Military force; modern foundations, 270; modern version, 301; versus Neoliberal institutionalism, 116-136, 137n13, 140n32, 202n1; versus Neorealism, 135n1, 229n5, 270-271; and NATO, 299n11; and power, *see* Power; and regimes, 53, 284; and security issues, 131; and states' concerns for relative gains, 118, 127-133, 170-173, 183, 187, 196-197, 201, 254, 256, 258, 264n7, 303-304, 313-319; and state-centrism, 13; and state interests, 118-119, 127-128, 132; and Structural realism, 144; and war, 138n17; versus world systems analysis, 136n5. *See also* Neorealism

Realist liberalism, 24

Realization lags, 59n45

Recessions, economic, 79-80

Reciprocity, 22, 33, 65, 75, 78, 87, 92, 94, 96, 109, 114n4, 122, 124, 296; in multilevel games, 103-107; and regimes, 110; synchronic, 81n6; and TIT-for-TAT, 64-65

Reductionism, 167

Regimes, domestic, 31, 37

Regimes, international, 3-4, 7-8, 31-35, 48, 60-61, 89, 94, 136n11; and absolute gains, *see* Absolute gains; assurance, 54n8; change of, 50-52, 233; and the provision of collective goods, 37; and

icy, *see* High Definition Television; and relations with Japan, *see* Japan; and NATO, *see* NATO; and concerns for relative gains, *see* Relative gains; and satellite policy, *see* Satellites; and global telecommunication, *see* Telecommunications, global; and relations with the Soviet Union, *see* Soviet Union; and the Vietnam War, 19
USTR, *see* Office of the U.S. Trade Representative
Utopianism, 10

Vaistos, Constantine V., 140n30
Van Evera, Stephen W., 89, 91, 107-109, 299n12, 302, 328
Variable-sum game, 74
Veil of ignorance, 56n22
Vernon, Raymond, 252, 264n2
Vietnam War, 19
Viner, Jacob, 25n4, 229n1
Voluntary export restraints (VERs), 34

Wagner, R. Harrison, 82n8-9
Wallerstein, Immanuel, 136n5
Wall Street Journal, 68, 82n17, 249n10, 264n1
Walt, Stephen, 302, 330
Waltz, Kenneth N., 5-6, 13, 80-81, 118-119, 126-127, 135n1, 138n18-19, 138n21-22, 144, 147, 159-160, 166-168n8-11, 169n16, 264n5, 297; views on anarchy, 148-150, 152, 155-156, 168n13, 301-302; views on balancing behavior, 330; views on bipolar systems, 199-200; views on cooperation, 329; views on domestic politics, 153-154; views on earlier variants of Realism, 3; views on foreign policy, 300n19; views on interdependence, 168n13, 169n15; views on international structure, 221, 225-226, 228; views on markets, 209; views on the utility of military force, 158, 218; views on the future of NATO, 286-287; views on Neorealism, 211, 229n5, 246n1, 271; views on political structure, 211; views on power, 15-16, 25n7; views on states' concerns for relative gains, 172-174, 204n11, 208, 219, 229n1, 229n7, 264n7, 314-315, 318-319, 336n5; views on state capabilities, 17, 21-22; views on states as functionally alike, 156-157, 161; views on state sovereignty, 30; views on systemic theory, 294
War, 20, 147, 221; and anarchy, 126-127;

and cooperation, *see* Cooperation, international; power resources for, 17-18; and states concerns for relative gains, *see* Relative gains; and technology, *see* Technology
Wars of the Roses, 102
Warsaw Treaty Organization, 295
Washington Naval Treaty (1922), 99
Weapons systems, 83n25; defensive, 49, 74, 107; offensive, 49, 59n43, 75, 83n23, 107; testing, 70
Weber, Max, 51-52, 148, 150, 152, 158, 168n5
Weingast, Barry, 293
Welfare state, 98, 119-120
Western Europe, 43, 48, 68, 72, 77, 79, 84n33-34, 89-90, 92, 106-107, 121, 136n7, 151, 198, 272, 286, 288. *See also* European Community
Whitman, Marina, 57n26
Wight, Martin, 148, 168n3
Wiklund, Claes, 140n33
Willett, Thomas D., 99
Williams, Mary Pat, 140n32
Wilson, Woodrow, 12, 136n4, 270
Winham, Gilbert, 101, 121
Wolf, Reinhard, 299n11
Wolferen, Karel Van, 264n4
Wolfers, Arnold, 12, 135n4, 229n1
Woolcock, Stephen, 136n10
World Administrative Radio Conference, 58n32
World Bank, 77, 284, 286
World Health Organization, 50
World Systems Analysis: versus Liberal institutionalism, 136n5; versus Realism, 136n5
World War I, 89-91, 100, 107, 111, 270, 288
World War II, 102, 105, 158
Wright, Quincy, 12

Yalu River, 102
Yoffie, David B., 112, 263
Yom Kippur War, 120-121
Young Oran, 53n1, 58n35, 112, 138n19, 138n21

Zacher, Mark W., 25n3, 121, 292
Zartman, William I., 58n35
Zeckhauser, Richard, 55n16, 197, 205n22
Zero-sum model, 11, 18-20, 58n38, 146, 171, 173-174, 177, 180, 183, 194, 201, 235, 244, 246n1, 277-278, 321
Zis, George, 140n33
Zysman, John, 120, 330